The

Grand Ole Opry

HISTORY OF COUNTRY MUSIC

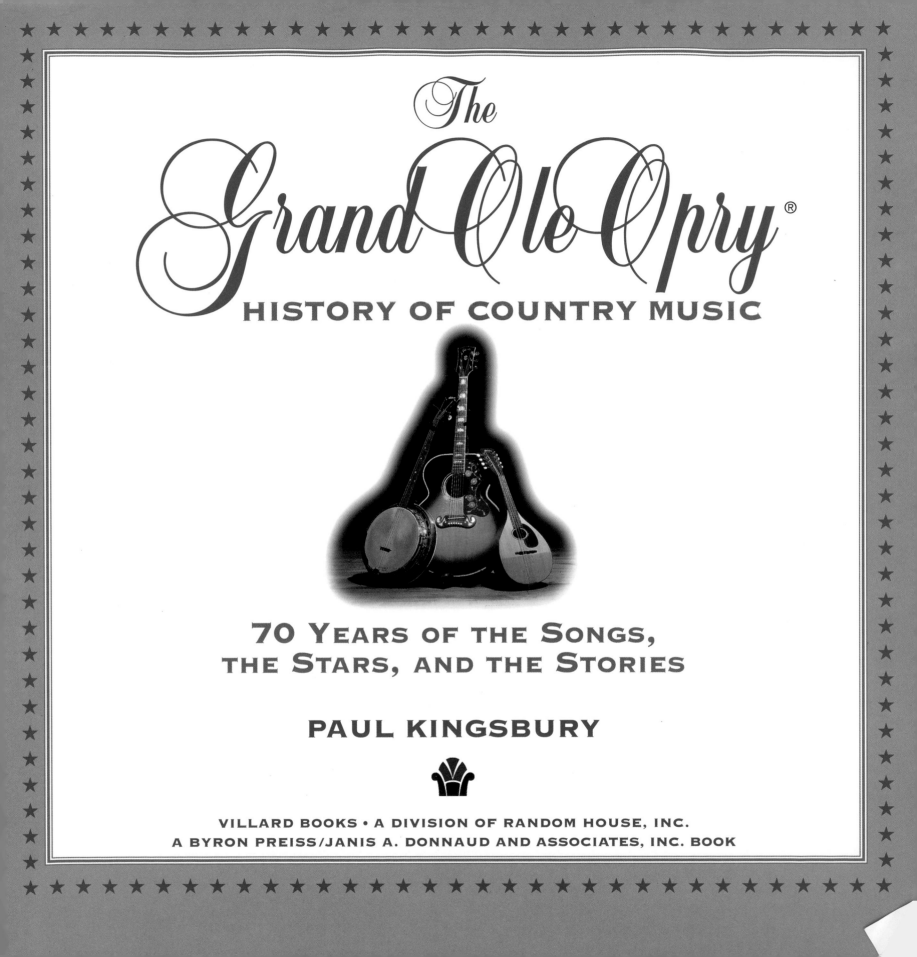

The Grand Ole Opry®

HISTORY OF COUNTRY MUSIC

70 YEARS OF THE SONGS, THE STARS, AND THE STORIES

PAUL KINGSBURY

VILLARD BOOKS • A DIVISION OF RANDOM HOUSE, INC.
A BYRON PREISS/JANIS A. DONNAUD AND ASSOCIATES, INC. BOOK

To June, a cowboy's sweetheart for sure

Contents

Acknowledgments

Although it's true as a rule that books don't get written by committee, they rarely appear in print without lots of help. Thanks to Janis Donnaud, Laura Schoeffel, Lynn Rosen, and Kathy Huck for shepherding this book so skillfully and sensitively from conception through production; to Hal Durham, Jerry Strobel, and Bob Whittaker of the Grand Ole Opry for generously sharing their time and insights; to Steve Thomas for getting a tenderfoot author started on the right foot; to Bill Ivey and Kyle Young of the Country Music Foundation for their support; and, most of all, to the singers, songwriters, and pickers for making music so much a part of our lives that listening isn't enough—we want to read and write about what we've heard.

Foreword
by Dolly Parton

Country music means a lot to me. It's been my roots and my livelihood. I grew up with it in the mountains of east Tennessee, and it's taken me around the world. Country music has enabled me to experience things I only dreamed of back in our two-room hillside cabin, and it's taught me a lot about myself along the way. I can't imagine a more satisfying way for me to earn a living than to write and sing country songs. And I don't think there's a more loyal or supportive audience than country fans.

I wanted to be a part of country music as far back as I can remember. My mother used to sing old folk songs to my brothers and sisters and me, and I quickly followed her example. Even before I had an instrument I was making up my own tunes. By the age of ten, I was singing songs at a Knoxville television station—before we had a TV at home!

It was just natural that I would set my sights on the Grand Ole Opry in Nashville. It was—and still is, in my opinion—country music's greatest stage. Luckily for me it was only a four-hour drive from the Smokies to Nashville. Fame was so close I could almost touch it.

The first time I went to the Opry, I was eleven years old. I was in awe. The sparkling costumes. The bright lights. The hushed audience. And the music. The music was always wonderful. From the moment I first sat in the Opry audience at the old Ryman Auditorium, I was determined that I was going to be on that stage someday. And that I was going to be one of the chosen few who get invited to join the cast of the Grand Ole Opry.

Well, wishes can come true. My friends Carl and Pearl Butler arranged for me to make a guest appearance on the Opry when I was only thirteen. And ten years later, after I had made many duet appearances with Porter Wagoner, the Opry invited me to be a permanent cast member. It's a memory I'll always treasure.

There's a lot of history in the Grand Ole Opry, and I'm proud to say that I've been a part of it. The Opry is more than just a nice place to spend a Friday or Saturday night. It's the reason that Nashville became "Music City, U.S.A." All the music business that has grown up in Nashville—the record companies, the music publishers, the tour booking companies—got started because the Grand Ole Opry was already in town. For seventy years now the Opry's been going strong. With all the love country fans and artists have for the Opry, I imagine it will be around for a long time to come.

This book tells how the Opry came to be and how it grew to be the great institution it is today—America's longest-running radio show. Along the way, this book also explains the Opry's role in the wider world of country music, because country music is America's music, after all, and it doesn't all come from the Grand Ole Opry and Nashville. You'll find a lot of great behind-the-scenes stories in these pages—what Hank Williams was like, how Minnie Pearl got her name, why Garth Brooks gave up on Nashville the first time he came to town, why Faron Young kissed Willie Nelson on the lips at Tootsie's Orchid Lounge (no, they weren't dating!). I've been in country music a few years now, and I even learned a few things from reading this book. Now that's saying something.

The publishers of this book asked me to say a few words about what country music is. Now that's a tough one. It's been so many things through the years—fiddle tunes and cowboy songs and Hank Williams moanin' the blues and Bill Monroe singing his high lonesome bluegrass music and Billy Ray Cyrus getting us all to do the Achy Breaky Dance and on and on and on. There's a whole world in country music once you look into it, just as there is in any art form that people give their heart and soul to. The more you listen, the more you want to know.

But if I had to try to sum up country music in one succinct definition, I would turn to my friend Tom T. Hall. Tom T. is as literate a country artist as I know. He's written several books, and many hit songs, and he knows how to put things just right with a few choice words. He said (and I quote): "Country music is a basic American music played by rural people on stringed instruments for their own enjoyment. Country music is lead-free, has no cholesterol, is salt-free, needs no refrigeration, will not stain your clothes, is not harmful to pets or wildlife, will not shrink, fits in your shirt pocket, and can be enjoyed while operating heavy machinery. Have some."

Amen to that. Now you can read this book for the rest of the story!

The Grand Ole Opry

HISTORY OF COUNTRY MUSIC

The house lights dim, the curtain goes up, and another Grand Ole Opry is under way for the 4,400 fans in the Opry House and thousands more listening on radio across the country.

A Night at the Opry

Any Friday or Saturday night you can hear live country music from half past six to midnight. It's the oldest radio show in America, and it's known as the Grand Ole Opry. Its history extends back almost as far as the first country music recordings. It began one magical Saturday night with a solitary fiddler reeling out his old hoedown tunes and jigs in a cozy little radio studio in downtown Nashville, Tennessee. Before the fiddler put down his bow, the station was deluged with telephone calls and telegrams clamoring for more down-home entertainment. Within weeks, the program grew into quite a bustling show, brimming with local country music talent. Within a few years it became truly a national showcase. It still is. And you're invited.

A visit to the Grand Ole Opry is different from a concert or a TV taping. There's a lot of milling around onstage with people coming and going, sometimes right in the middle of a song. In the wings, folks are catching up on gossip while old cronies play practical jokes on each other as various musicians are tuning up. Just a few feet away, another act is onstage and on the air. That's the way it's always been. It's understood that people not involved in the song at that moment can roam around the stage and do whatever they need to do. Because it's a radio show. Just like the old days. That sense of informality, of spontaneity, is central to the Opry.

Despite its appearance of sheer chaos, the Opry is a smooth-running machine. Performers amble up to hit their marks right on the dot of the appointed hour. Stagehands change microphones quickly and unobtrusively. Musicians in the ten-member Opry staff band swap places as necessary and will even run down the hallway to write out and photocopy a last-minute song arrangement. The audience is never the wiser. Stage manager Tim Thompson keeps his eye on the clock and pages performers backstage who should fail to be in the wings five minutes before their moment.

Occasionally mistakes happen. "One night Lester Flatt was onstage and I was waiting for my spot," said Jean Shepard, an Opry cast member since 1955. "I was sitting in the greenroom, talking with Del Wood and they called me onstage. Well, I didn't hear it, and Lester just went on and did another song. Then they called me out again, and I *still* didn't hear it and they did another song. When I finally got out there, I had missed my spot! They say you're not really a member of the Grand Ole Opry until you miss a spot, so I guess I officially made it."

Jean Shepard, the Opry's senior female singer, has been with the show since 1955. Even so, she says, she didn't really feel that she had become properly initiated until the first time she missed her cue to appear for her appointed spot on the show.

Then there is the now legendary story of the curtain that wouldn't go up back in 1982. The late Roy Acuff had taken the stage with his band, the Smoky Mountain Boys. They got their cue to start playing, and the heavy red curtain, which separates the performers from the audience between half-hour segments, didn't rise. It wouldn't budge. But the Opry *is* a radio show. So Acuff and the Smoky Mountain Boys played on for the listeners at home, as technicians scrambled to lift the curtain. Cast members and dancers even got into the act, grunting and pushing and lifting, so the studio audience could at least see *something*. "Everyone handled it with good grace," Shepard said. "The radio audience was never aware of any problem. We all had a good laugh about it later."

Backstage the Grand Ole Opry is even more informal. There are seventy-one Opry cast members. On a typical night backstage, it seems as if they're all wandering around in the labyrinthine hallways, popping in and out of dressing rooms, or hanging out in the large greenroom where they can watch television (sports shows are very popular) and drink coffee or punch until their stage call. Usually, twenty to twenty-five acts appear on the Opry each night. Some of them bring their own bands, and they all invite close friends, family, or business associates. That's why it can get a bit crowded backstage—a little like high

The greenroom backstage: an oasis of calm at the bustling Opry and a place to chat, grab refreshments, and sneak peaks at TV sports events.

school between classes, especially since the hallways are lined with lockers from which performers pull clothes and instruments. There's Pete Kirby, pulling a pair of old blue overalls from one locker. Better known as "Bashful Brother Oswald," he played dobro with Roy Acuff at the Opry from 1939 until Acuff's death in 1992. "Oz," who joined the Opry cast in January 1995, still dresses in his hillbilly duds, ready to light up the crowd with his smooth playing or with his braying laugh.

His old boss, though, is dearly missed. The Opry cast's senior member, Roy Acuff joined the show back in 1938 well before there was a music industry in Nashville, when the Opry offered mostly old-time fiddling and hoedown bands. Acuff was a fiddler and he led a string band. But he was also a showman, balancing his fiddle and bow on his chin or whirling a yo-yo this way and that. Even more than his flair for spectacle, what distinguished Roy Acuff from the rest of the cast and ultimately made him the Opry's grandest star was his ability to deliver sincerity in song. "I'm a seller and not a singer," the gruff-voiced Acuff told *Newsweek* for a 1952 cover story. "I'm strictly a seller. There's something about me. I'm able to reach the people."

Until his death in November 1992, Acuff routinely held court backstage. The other thirteen dressing rooms in the backstage hallways had

Since the passing of Roy Acuff in 1992, former Smoky Mountain Boys Pete Kirby (better known as "Bashful Brother Oswald") and Charlie Collins (right) have continued as a regular Opry attraction.

Roy Acuff in the spotlight: a singer brimming with sincerity and a showman in the grand ole style.

a small sign saying: PERFORMERS ONLY PLEASE. (The dressing rooms are assigned for the evening's show, and their doors are often shut as performers get ready.) Dressing Room 1, the closest to the stage, was different. Its sign read: ROY ACUFF and its door was always open. There Acuff would visit with musicians and fans, taking time out for all who stopped by. When it was his turn to take the Opry stage, Acuff would stride purposefully down the hallway, through the wings, and onto the stage to gales of applause. He'd usually offer his old classics, the train epic "The Wabash Cannonball" and the religious allegory "The Great Speckled Bird." Sometimes in his later years he sang slightly off key, but

Acuff's dressing room door was always open to fans and, of course, friends like Minnie Pearl, and cowboy star Gene Autry and his wife, Ina Mae.

In the golden days of radio when Roy Acuff rose to prominence, the Grand Ole Opry was a kingmaker. It made stars of nearly every performer who graced its stage. Roy Acuff. Ernest Tubb. Hank Williams. Minnie Pearl. Eddy Arnold. Patsy Cline. The list of Opry stars over the past seventy years includes well over 200 famous names and voices. Today the Opry's role is different. Now it serves as a keeper of tradition, a vital link to our common bedrock past in this cyberspace age of video screens, sound bites, and virtual reality.

Yet the show remains surprisingly alive and vital for such a venerable institution. "I probably get forty requests a week," said Opry manager Bob Whittaker, "from new artists wanting to guest appear on the Grand Ole Opry. I could pull out a drawer, and you're just gonna see tons of tapes that unfortunately I can't even find time to listen to."

What still makes the Grand Ole Opry such a magnet for talent? Its hallowed reputation has something to do with it, but the Opry isn't resting on its laurels. "I labor over the format of the show," said Whittaker, who begins lining up acts for the show

he still whirled his fiddle bow around his head and gave a pretty good imitation of a train whistle for "Cannonball." Then he'd toddle off backstage and entertain some more.

Today Dressing Room 1 is much as Acuff left it. It's still sparsely furnished with a small table and a few chairs. Like the other Opry dressing rooms, it has a dressing table and mirror running the length of the wall opposite the door. What catches the eye, though, are the photographs and mementos papering the walls: a movie poster from the 1940 film *Grand Ole Opry* in which he starred; a faded publicity photograph of Acuff and his Smoky Mountain Boys, ca. 1938; autographed pictures of him with Presidents Reagan and Nixon, with Roy Rogers, Dolly Parton, and Johnny Cash; his favorite sign reading NOTHING'S GONNA HAPPEN TODAY THAT ME AND THE LORD CAN'T HANDLE. Dressing Room 1 today is usually reserved for the younger guest acts on the Opry. "That's the way we think he would have wanted it," said Grand Ole Opry president Hal Durham. "It gives them something to think about, to see his dressing room as he left it."

weeks, sometimes months, in advance. He asks each cast member to commit to twelve appearances a year. That's an easier commitment for the older acts who are no longer touring as widely as the young chart toppers, so Whittaker leaves three or four slots open right up until the Thursday before a show just in case a busy young star like Garth Brooks or Reba McEntire should have an opening in his or her schedule.

As a result, on any given weekend, the Opry can offer an unusually representative cross-section of country music talent. "There are generally four members of the Country Music Hall of Fame who are here most Friday and

Saturday nights—Bill Monroe, Jimmy Dickens, Hank Snow, and Grandpa Jones," said Whittaker, "and I can't think of another venue anywhere in the country that can boast of four Hall of Famers appearing in . . . anything. Then on top of that, you can usually count on eight or ten true legends of the industry. . . . Then you've got up-and-coming new acts breaking into the business. . . . Finally, on many nights you'll have a Vince Gill, a Garth Brooks, an Alison Krauss. So you have four categories that make up a typical showbill on the Grand Ole Opry. It's the greatest entertainment bargain in the country."

Grandpa Jones, who first joined the cast in 1946, has been one of the Opry's great links to old-time music.

★ ★ ★

On a Saturday night in the fall of 1994, just the sort of show Bob Whittaker described takes place. People are milling around as the big red curtain rises and tall, dark, imperially slim Jim Ed Brown steps onstage precisely at 6:30. He treats the crowd to a faithful rendition of "The Three Bells" (the 1959 million seller he recorded with his two sisters) before slipping backstage to chat with guests.

Sure enough, Grandpa Jones is on hand, looking just as he did on "Hee Haw" with his trademark getup of plaid workshirt, suspenders, gray striped old-timey pants, and brown slouch hat. As he takes the stage, the house lights seem to be blinking. But it's just camera flashes going off as fans stream toward the stage to get a good photo while "Everybody's Favorite Grandpa" performs the classic "Dark as a Dungeon," written by his old friend Merle Travis. Just a couple of weeks shy of his eighty-first birthday, Jones seems full of life and still quick with a joke. Later that evening, he loses track of time and yells to the wings, "How long we got till?"

"Ten-fifteen," comes the reply.

"Oh? I better get a-goin', then," he says with a chuckle. "Your mind slips, you know." He pauses as the crowd titters. "That ain't all, I'll tell you that!" A roar of

Acuff and Ricky Skaggs light into a tune backstage.

laughter wells up from the audience. A bemused Jones takes it all in, adding offhandedly, "I b'lieve I'll just stand here a minute."

When Jones closes the first half hour of the evening and the curtain comes down, Little Jimmy Dickens, all four foot ten inches of him, steps up to greet him. Old friends, they shake hands warmly and clap each other on the back. Dickens looks splendid in his fire engine-red suit studded with rhinestones and accented with a gaudy, spreadwinged bird on the back (in honor of his 1965 No. 1 hit, "May the Bird of Paradise Fly up Your Nose"), all set off grandly with white boots, white shirt, and white tengallon hat. As the curtain again rises, he launches into his trademark hit, "I'm Little but I'm Loud." When Dickens walks over to chat with announcer Kyle Cantrell between numbers, only his hat appears above Cantrell's podium.

As Dickens winds up his number, a tall thin figure in a powder blue western suit nervously tunes his big arch-top guitar and quietly picks out little bits of music. It's the "Jolly Green Giant," Jack Greene, formerly one of Ernest Tubb's Texas Troubadours. In 1965 he stepped out from behind his drum kit to start his own career. A year later he had a No. 1 hit and the Country Music Association Song of the Year with "There Goes My Everything."

With a last-minute adjustment of his ten-gallon hat, Little Jimmy Dickens readies himself for a big Opry crowd.

That's the song he favors the crowd with this night.

Down the hall backstage an open dressing room has a small crowd of people gathered around with cameras and souvenir programs. Inside, Ricky Skaggs and Vince Gill are intently rehearsing, both voices raised in impossibly high harmony, both working their guitars hard and fast, on a traditional bluegrass gospel song popularized by the Carter Family in the 1930s, "Working on a Building."

When Ricky Skaggs pops out, people ask about the condition of his teenage son, Andrew, recovering in Vanderbilt Hospital from a recent automobile accident. "He's doing a lot better, thank you," says Skaggs as he heads for his dressing room. At 7:23 P.M. Skaggs is back out in black suit and buttoned-up white shirt, with his Martin guitar strapped on. Awed onlookers part before him as he ducks into the rehearsal room, where the imposing figure of Bill Monroe, the acknowledged Father of Bluegrass, dressed impeccably in black suit and white Stetson, holds court. Vince Gill drops in behind him. Folks press in close with programs and souvenir

Bill Monroe picks a little bluegrass with one of his greatest admirers, Ricky Skaggs.

booklets, hoping for an autograph. Gill, the reigning CMA Entertainer and Male Vocalist of the Year, graciously obliges the two or three fans brave enough to step forward for a photo or a signature. Inside, Ricky Skaggs and Bill Monroe begin harmonizing on Monroe's classic bluegrass tune "I'm Going Back to Old Kentucky." Vince Gill slips back in to join them on a reprise rehearsal of "Working on a Building." The best entertainment bargain in the country? Those privileged to be standing in the Opry's crowded backstage hallway surely feel that it's more than that.

At precisely 7:29 P.M. the wings stage right are jampacked with musicians and onlookers. As the curtain rises, Bill Monroe, who seemed frail and unsteady when he took the arm of a young musician to reach the wings, looks noticeably stronger as he gathers himself and strides out into the spotlights to join Ricky Skaggs. One of the pillars of the Opry, a member of the cast since 1939, Monroe likes to remind people that he's been late to the Opry only three times—once because of a flat tire as he was leaving his nearby farm, another time when his stretch limousine caught fire a hundred miles outside of Nashville, and when his bus nearly got washed off the road in eastern Kentucky. Tonight he's right on time as usual.

After a little folksy banter, Skaggs, Monroe, and Monroe's four-piece Blue Grass Boys

Opry member Vince Gill brings a touch of bluegrass to his smooth country sound.

band plunge into the double-time tempos of "I'm Goin' Back to Old Kentucky," first recorded in 1946 when Lester Flatt and Earl Scruggs were still in Monroe's band. Tonight Skaggs takes Flatt's part as lead singer while Monroe contributes falsetto harmony on the choruses and then rips out a blazing mandolin solo that would put many younger pickers to shame. As if that weren't enough, when the fiddler takes a solo, Monroe skips into the old buck-and-wing dance he used to do on Chicago's National Barn Dance radio show in the 1930s. Following the bluegrass tour de force, it's Vince Gill's turn. He obliges the crowd with an acoustic version of his funky hit, "What the Cowgirls Do." Backstage, a couple of grandmotherly women are tapping their toes and remarking on how handsome and good-natured Vince Gill is. They are completely oblivious to the presence of Gill's wife, singer Janis Gill of Sweethearts of the Rodeo, who is sitting on a small bench right in front of them. When Gill finishes his second number, with harmony courtesy of rising bluegrass star Alison Krauss, Ricky Skaggs leads the applause saying, "Mr. Monroe says that's powerful good singing right there. And Mr. Monroe knows good singing." As he walks smiling over to the wings, turning over the stage to Krauss, the seemingly perennial CMA Male Vocalist of the Year calls back

In 1993 rising star Alison Krauss became the Opry's youngest cast member (then twenty-one)—and the first bluegrass act added to the show's roster since 1964.

building, I'm a workin' on a building," sing Monroe and company, "for my Lord, for my Lord." With the Blue Grass Boys digging in behind Monroe's mandolin and the high-flying voices, the old hymn sounds earthy and rarefied at the same time.

After this all-star bluegrass spectacular ends, the TV lights go out and the throng backstage thins considerably. Still, at eight o'clock the night has just begun, and there are plenty of high moments left. The Melvin Sloan Dancers are striking in their red-and-white gingham shirts and dresses, their impossibly stiff torsos balanced against their crazily swinging legs. The crowd loves the throwback to the square dancers the Opry has always featured. Then there's Porter Wagoner, resplendent in his turquoise western suit accented with wagon wheels. He offers the crowd a song he

calls "a big hit for me in 1965—I hope you remember it." It's "The Green Green Grass of Home," and you can tell by the warmth of the applause they do.

Meanwhile Hank Snow is waiting stage left, looking composed yet intensely focused. Even at age eighty, after nearly forty-five years on the Grand Ole Opry, he still carefully rehearses his Rainbow Ranch Boys band backstage before the show. Known for his sartorial elegance, even in a field famous for glittering stage wear, Hank Snow has outdone himself tonight. He's wearing a white western suit with layer upon layer of appliqués of sequins, rhinestones, black-and-scarlet embroidered flowers, and tassels.

As Hank Snow readies his band for their segment, a group of young, long-haired musicians drifts into the wings. It's the new L.A. country band Boy Howdy, making their first

to Krauss, laughing, "Alison, you were great! How was I?"

Onstage, Bill Monroe introduces Alison Krauss ("a wonderful singer and a fine fiddle player") for a quiet, thoughtful number that allows her fluttery soprano free rein. Immediately afterward, the stage fills as Gill, Monroe, and Skaggs join her for a rousing rendition of that old Carter Family chestnut "Working on a Building," with the Father of Bluegrass taking the lead vocal in his piercing high tenor. "It's a holy ghost building, it's a holy ghost

Opry veteran Porter Wagoner (center) gives the boys from Boy Howdy a few pointers in his dressing room on the night of their first appearance on the show.

appearance at the Opry. "He's totally cool," one of them says, elbowing a band member and leaning his head toward Hank Snow, host of the segment.

Onstage, Boy Howdy seamlessly re-create the smooth harmonies and rock-sharp guitar licks of their big hits "She'd Give Anything" and "They Don't Make 'Em Like That Anymore." Standing at the announcer's podium, Snow responds unconsciously to the beat of the music, drumming his fingers and tapping his boot, his face impassive. Afterward, Hank graciously waves up the applause, although there's really no need. Boy Howdy was note-perfect and the crowd loves them.

Snow's numbers display his own brand of attention to detail as he offers a couple of old classics, "From a Jack to a King" and "Beggar to a King," chosen with an obvious theme in mind but a reason known only to Snow himself. The little nasal quaver is still there in his distinctive voice, and he still can flat-pick a mean guitar with the best of them. The curtain rings down on the stage at nine, signaling the end of the Opry's first show. Outside in the evening chill, another crowd has lined up, anxious to take seats in the Opry House for the second show.

On the way out after the first show, you pass Little Jimmy Dickens returning from the parking lot. He probably went out to get a late dinner, as many of the acts do, maybe across the street at the Nashville Palace, where Randy Travis used to fry up hamburgers and catfish, and take an occasional break from the kitchen to sing a song. Little Jimmy Dickens is heading back for the second show and his spot before a whole new crowd at 10:15 P.M. He's still wearing that red suit and that white hat, and he looks like the tallest four-foot-ten you've ever seen.

"Thanks for the great show, Mr. Dickens," you say at the door.

Hank Snow, resplendent as ever in his usual rhinestones, is still "movin' on," in the words of his first big hit from 1950.

"Well, thank you," he responds with a wink and a smile. "And you come back real soon."

The remarkable thing here is that you and Little Jimmy Dickens have never met before. He simply recognizes a fan when he sees one, and in recognizing a fan, a friend. Now that's country.

The Crook Brothers Band: Herman Crook and Lewis Crook (on top), Blythe Poteet, Kirk McGee, and Bill Etter (below), ca. 1933.

The Hills Are Alive

ROOTS AND BRANCHES

Country. The term fits the music like a well-worn boot fits a cowboy. It's a handy, thoroughly apt description for this quintessentially American music. *Country.* In one word it suggests who makes the music and who listens to it. It evokes a picture of life far from the hurly-burly of the big city. It summons up our common rural past. It's a term rich with meaning, and so far it's stuck to the music for forty-odd years. Yet before *Billboard* magazine named its record charts "Country & Western" in June 1949, hardly anyone called the music "country." Performers and fans alike referred to it as "folk music" or "hillbilly." Before that it had a number of quainter names, such as "old-time tunes," "old familiar tunes," and "hill-country tunes," because even in its infancy the music sounded old-fashioned and traditional.

The naming of country music is part of the story this book aims to tell: how an earthy strain of American music met American business and how we are all richer for it. Country music and the Grand Ole Opry, its greatest showcase, have enjoyed a lively, tightly intertwined history replete with happy accidents and shrewd commercial judgments. Much of country's charm derives from its abiding respect for tradition and its reverence for the old-fashioned way of doing things. Across its many styles—bluegrass, honky-tonk, western swing, rockabilly, old-time—country music survives more as a traditional approach to song (through lyrical themes, vocal styles, and familiar instrumentation) than as a static sound. Eck Robertson's fiddling on "Sallie

Gooden" in 1922 doesn't sound much like Garth Brooks doing "Friends in Low Places" at all, but there's a line of tradition that connects them. That indelible connection is what this history of the Grand Ole Opry and country music is all about: how country's past gives meaning to its present, and how country's current stars revere and keep faith with the past.

★ ★ ★

The dazzling variety found in the cast of the Grand Ole Opry—or on your local country radio station—is hardly a recent development in the music. From the very beginning, the music we now call country came from a number of sources.

We can trace country's deepest roots to the ancient airs and tunes of the British Isles, whose immigrants dominated the colonization of North America. Country music standards like "Knoxville Girl," "Barbara Allen," and "Who's Going to Shoe Your Pretty Little Feet" have survived into the twentieth century still bearing great similarities to their original English versions. English folk songs and fiddle tunes, though, are just part of the fabric of modern country music. The notion that country music is the direct product of pure rural folk music, carried across the Atlantic by British settlers and carefully handed down intact and unsullied through generations in the Appalachians, is a pretty but outright fiction. On the contrary, country music is more like a patchwork quilt, its pieces borrowed from beautiful scraps of American music.

Almost as soon as British colonists set foot in the New World, they began altering the old English songs to fit their new surroundings. (Thus, the British "Wexford Girl" eventually became our "Knoxville Girl," though the song's tale of murder remains much the same.) The settlers also began making up their own songs to describe their New World experiences. Frequently they accompanied themselves on the violin or fiddle (what you call it depends on how you're playing it). The fiddle quickly became the favorite instrument of America's pioneers because it was portable, easy to tune, and musically versatile, capable of handily accompanying a jig or a lullaby. Before long, America's British colonists came into contact with immigrants and music from other nations—Spain, France, Germany—and absorbed those influences. Africans, brought to the Americas as slaves, carried their exuberant, rhythmic music with them, along with new instruments like the banjo. All of it went into the melting pot.

Until the 1800s, the music heard in America was, for the most part, *folk music*, performed for free and strictly for personal amusement, reflecting the values of the community. It was almost never written down in the standard European musical notation that preserved Bach and Beethoven. (Until the twentieth century, no one considered the tunes themselves any more valuable than, say, nursery rhymes.) Folk songs simply reflected the spirit of a community, helping to pass the time while working in the fields or to mark an important event, such as a wedding.

Country music, as we know it, began to coalesce in the nineteenth century. Music was then a cherished pastime for many rural Americans, but it could be shared in only two ways: through sheet music and face to face. While sheet music circulated classical music and music-hall songs of the big city, it was in face-to-face contacts that country music took shape. These musical meetings took many forms. In parlors and on front porches, gray-haired elders taught bright-eyed youngsters the folk songs of yesteryear. In small-town squares and theaters, troupes of blackface minstrel entertainers sang brand-new songs by Stephen Foster and others, which often sounded remarkably like old folk songs from the hills and the cotton fields. In square dances and fiddle contests, folks cut loose with the most exuberant music they knew; the purpose was celebration, but learning something new —a song, a lick—was always a by-product for the musicians. In churches, entire communities shared old English hymns and spread the gospel farther afield with new songbooks.

Instead of remaining distinct, these different kinds of music mixed with one another as folks moved through their daily rituals of work, worship, and relaxation. From traveling entertainers to townsfolk, friends to neighbors, parents to children, scraps of ancient British airs, hymns, plantation spirituals and blues, vaudeville songs, and later, jazz and ragtime tunes passed back and forth and mingled. Most musicians in rural areas played by ear. As a result, the music became casually arranged and rearranged like so much small-town gossip. Thus, a published popular song from 1860 that started out "I'll twine mid the ringlets of my raven black hair" could be transformed into "I'll twine with my mingles and waving black hair"—the charmingly garbled first lines of the Carter Family's famous "Wildwood Flower." Was it a folk song? Most assuredly not, since someone had written it back in 1860 for pay. But when the Carter Family recorded it in 1928, it seemed to speak so evocatively of life in the Blue Ridge Mountains that it might as well have been a folk song. This was the music that would become known as country: a mongrel of mixed European and African ancestry, brought up on a varied diet of professional and amateur influences, and completely ignored by moneyed interests right up into the 1920s.

Two technological developments, though, brewing since the end of the nineteenth century, utterly transformed the nature of entertainment. They were the phonograph and the radio, and in the 1920s they provided the catalyst to transform rural music into commercial country music in all its various forms and styles.

★ OLD FAMILIAR TUNES MADE NEW

The 1920s brought sweeping change to American life. The United States had just emerged from the "war to end all wars." Buoyed primarily by war production, the nation's wealth had increased tremendously. At the dawn of this reckless decade, some 8.9 million automobiles were plying the nation's roads at what seemed breakneck speeds of around twenty miles an hour. By 1920, more than half the nation's population of 117 million lived in towns of 2,500 or more. Women entered the workforce in earnest, and 1920 saw the passage of the Nineteenth Amendment to the Constitution, finally giving women the hard-earned right to vote. Young "flappers" cut their hair in boyish bobs to demonstrate their newfound independence, while young men shaved for a clean, sophisticated look. In war-ravaged Germany, moviegoers thrilled to the dark impressionism of *The Cabinet of Dr. Caligari,* while American audiences laughed till they cried over the tragicomic antics of Charlie Chaplin and little Jackie Coogan in *The Kid.* In 1920 twenty-five-year-old George Herman Ruth was sold to the New York Yankees by the Boston Red Sox for $125,000; that summer the "Babe" would turn the hit-and-run game upside down with a record fifty-four home runs.

In the autumn of that year, the Westinghouse Corporation, in an effort to sell radio receivers, opened station WDKA in Pittsburgh. In its first major broadcast on November 2, it transmitted the news that Warren G. Harding had won the presidential election over James M. Cox. Modernity was beckoning.

Not everyone was comfortable with the new wonders of the twentieth century. Faced with such wrenching changes, many Americans recoiled. Even captains of industry felt a keen nostalgia for days gone by. Certain that the new jazz sounds were damaging to America's morals, technocrat Henry Ford sponsored fiddle contests through his car dealerships, hoping the familiar strains of the pioneer instrument would slow the wheels of progress—progress which he himself had set into high gear. Like Henry Ford, many Americans longed for the good old days.

Paradoxically, the new phonograph technology offered a way to revisit the past, especially through sentimental, familiar old songs. Phonographs (at an average cost of $25) had made their way into some 7 million American parlors by 1920. For the most

part, though, the records were made in the big city and catered to big-city tastes. New York record moguls simply had no idea that folks down on the farm would pay good money to hear their own kind of music.

The first country music recording sessions had to wait until the summer of 1922, and even then they came about not through a shrewd move by a record company but by the sheer audacity of a couple of hoedown fiddlers. After performing at a Confederate veterans convention in Richmond, Virginia, thirty-four-year-old Eck Robertson and seventyish Henry Gilliland traveled by train to New York City in hopes of recording for the Victor Talking

Standard bearer: Eck Robertson, country music's first recording artist, ca. 1922.

Stacks of Wax

Prior to World War II, country music recording often took place far away from the major music centers of New York, Chicago, and Los Angeles. The business of making hillbilly records was still so new that it was often more productive to beat the bushes for rural talent rather than expect it to walk through the door in Manhattan. Thus, A & R (artist and repertoire) pioneers like Ralph Peer (Okeh, Victor), Art Satherley (Columbia), and Frank Walker (Victor) made many of their greatest country recordings through what were known as field recording sessions. During most of these sessions, a variety of acts would be recorded over several days—hillbilly bands, blues singers, gospel quartets. When the now-famous bluesman Robert Johnson recorded in Dallas in 1937, for example, he was preceded and followed by a number of hillbilly acts, including Al Dexter, Roy Newman, and the Light Crust Doughboys.

In a typical session of the era, the field recording team would come to town and rent the entire floor of a warehouse or hotel. They needed that much space because the equipment, though portable, was still quite bulky. The gear typically consisted of microphones connected to a simple tone-control panel that in turn was connected to the disc-cutting turntable. Usually the turntable was driven by a system of weights and pulleys suspended from a six-foot tower. It worked much like a grandfather clock and ensured a constant rate of speed in the event of a power failure. Out in the studio area, which might be a hotel bedroom or the corner of a warehouse, performers got their cue to record by a sort of traffic light. In this case, the green light meant STOP and red meant RECORD.

Since magnetic tape wasn't available until after World War II (it was a German wartime invention), these recordings were made on thick wax master discs. Refrigerated until needed, a blank disc was first scraped with a razor to make the recording surface smooth. Then it was placed in a warming cabinet to bring the wax to the desired consistency (a lightbulb usually did the trick). During the recording session, the disc rotated on a turntable as a diamond or sapphire stylus cut recording grooves into the surface. Bad cuts could be reshaved and used again, much as modern magnetic tape can be erased. But this could be done only so many times. "When you made a few mistakes on that wax you couldn't use it anymore; it was too thin," recalled Alton Delmore of the Delmore

Henry Whitter scrimped and saved to make his first train trip from Virginia to New York for a recording session in early 1923. Two years later, the former mill worker was able to buy a Ford Model T with his royalties.

Machine Company. Though they showed up unannounced, the fiddlers amazingly got an opportunity to record ten fiddle tunes over the next two days, June 30 and July 1, 1922. From those groundbreaking (though completely unheralded) sessions, the Victor Company eventually selected one fiddle duet ("Arkansaw Traveler") and one solo tune ("Sallie Gooden") to release to the public. But because no one at Victor had any idea whether the old-timey instrumentals would sell, the company didn't even release that first country record until March of the following year.

Back in his native Texas, Eck Robertson was nevertheless primed and ready when his 78-rpm platter finally appeared at his local record dealer. Now that he had a record, he wanted to advertise it. He knew that Fort Worth's radio station, WBAP, was open to airing such music. When Eck Robertson got his turn at the WBAP mike on March 29, 1923, he didn't play just any old fiddle tunes; he played the two numbers on his brand-new record, becoming the first country musician to plug his recording on the air.

In retrospect, it's easy to see Eck Robertson's first recording as a milestone. No one else had bothered to record genuine old-time Southern music and offer it for sale. No one had thought of it. Yet at the time no one, least of all the Victor Company, took much notice of Robertson's record as being something new and distinct. Victor didn't even give Robertson a chance to record again until seven years later, in October 1929, when once again the intrepid fiddler pushed for a new session.

What got the country music record industry started in earnest was withering competition from radio. In 1922 record sales hit the 100 million mark, a new high. By 1925, however, sales fell almost by half that total. In contrast, sales of radio sets, which had amounted to a little over half a million units for 1923, had topped 2 million by 1925. True, the large parlor sets were still pricey. But the relatively inexpensive Crosley "Pup" single-tube radios could be had for as little as $10, and battery-powered crystal radio sets (in which a "cat tail" crystal rubbed up against a cylinder of copper wire) were going for $1. In comparison, the latest records generally cost 75¢ apiece, sometimes as much as $1.25. At such prices, radio was bound to win the tug-of-war for the public's dollar in the short term.

Faced with a dwindling mainstream market, the record companies went looking for new niche-markets like jazz and blues. It was while trying to tap these markets that the Okeh Records label stumbled onto country music almost by accident. At the time, the company was more interested in the sales potential of records for black audiences. In 1920 Okeh had sold a million copies of Mamie Smith's "Crazy Blues." On a tip from their leading record distributor in the South, Atlanta furniture dealer Polk Brockman (phonographs were still considered furniture), Okeh's talent scout Ralph Peer took a newfangled portable recording unit to Atlanta in June 1923 to see what untapped black talent could be recorded. Peer and Brockman cut about thirty sides, recording mostly blues singers and jazz bands. But it was the lone country fiddler, feisty old Fiddlin' John Carson, who would change the course of history.

John Carson was the genuine article: a mountain-bred entertainer with a down-home style. Fifty-five years old, moon-faced, jug-eared, outspoken (though he stuttered), and tough as leather, John Carson had been entertaining people for nearly his entire life, first in northwest Georgia's mountainous Fannin County and later in and around Atlanta. He held jobs, by turns, as a jockey, a cotton-mill worker, and a building painter; but he considered fiddling and singing his life's work. The tunes he did were a mixture of old folk songs, reworkings of popular songs, and his own songs. His rough, unadorned style included a fondness for alcohol and for singing with a jawbreaker candy rolling around his tongue. Playing a 200-year-old fiddle his grandfather had brought from Ireland in a flour sack, Carson performed anywhere he

Brothers. "If they used it nowadays, some of the artists never would get on record because it would take too much wax. And the recording director watched that wax like it was gold. If you missed one, two, or three times, he would come in with a blank look on his face and tell you to rehearse some more before another take."

In that sense, all these recordings were "live"; there was no opportunity for "punch ins," or overdubs, to fix a musical mistake later. The performance had to be right on the money each time. A & R men were also careful always to get more than one good take, just in case something happened to a wax master subsequent to the session. After a session, the discs were packed in felt insulation for protection and sent to New York or Chicago for plating and pressing into 78-rpm records.

A & R men simply made the best of their surroundings. When recording in warehouses, Ralph Peer's standard operating procedure was to hang sheets of burlap, both as a sound damper and as a way to cordon off a recording area. To prevent potential distraction, he also hid the recording equipment behind the burlap, so that the performers could see only the microphone. For a session in Memphis at the Gayoso Hotel, Art Satherley once took the extraordinary measure of cutting a hole in the wall between the bathroom and the suite (he made arrangements with the hotel management first). Then he had the engineer use the toilet as a chair with the recording equipment set up in the bathtub.

With a practiced performer, a session could go exceptionally well. When Art Satherley recorded Roy Acuff during the "bathroom session," everything fell into place despite the awkward setting: "He recorded for me eight numbers in one hour and three-quarters. Bang, bang, bang, bang. One master at a time but three of everything to make sure we'd get it back to New York because of the heat." On other occasions, no matter how professional the performance, technical difficulties could stymie everyone. During a recording session at a warehouse in New Orleans in 1935, the Delmore Brothers had a devil of a time because of a busy nearby alley. "I don't know how many records we had to make over," recalled Alton Delmore. "We would have one just about completed, and then there would come a truck and ruin it."

Fiddlin' John Carson made his first record a year after Eck Robertson did, but it was Carson's that got the country business started.

Till death shall call my dog and me to find a
    better home
Than that little old log cabin in the lane.

Everyone knew the sentimental old song. But when Fiddlin' John Carson played and sang it, it became—make no mistake—a country song. And it connected. Only halfway through his program, telephones at the station began ringing. The home folks wanted more.

Word of Carson's success didn't reach beyond the range of WSB, and certainly not as far as the streets of New York and the offices of Okeh Records. It took Polk Brockman's hunch to get Fiddlin' John on record.

On Thursday, June 14, 1923, bending close to an acoustical horn in the middle of an empty warehouse on Atlanta's Nassau Street, Carson sang and fiddled his way through "The Little Old Log Cabin in the Lane" and a fiddle instrumental called "The Old Hen Cackled and the Rooster's Going to Crow." Ralph Peer didn't hear much in the performances, later remembering them as "horrible" and "pluperfect awful." Carson's untutored leathery voice creaked, and his fiddle wheezed as it doubled the simple, sing-song melodies. But Polk Brockman knew the local audience and ordered 500 copies of the record. In less than a month, Brockman's hunch was proved right. On Friday, July 13, 500 of Carson's records arrived by railway express in Atlanta. Brockman got them to the Elks Club convention, where he had arranged a fiddlers' contest. Carson, of course, was on hand to play and hawk his new record across the footlights. The entire shipment of records sold out that night. "I'll have to quit making moonshine and start making records," quipped Carson to a very pleased Polk Brockman, who immediately phoned Okeh, saying: "This is a riot! I've got to have 10,000 records here right now."

Back in New York, Ralph Peer was amazed. He had had so little faith in the Car-

could get an audience: at political rallies, on trolley cars, at fiddling contests (he won seven), and inevitably, on the radio.

Carson had established himself as a local fixture in Atlanta when he made his first appearance at the city's new radio station, WSB ("Welcome South, Brother"), located on the fifth floor of the Biltmore Hotel. *The Atlanta Journal* had opened the 100-watt station—the first in the South—on March 16, 1922. Six months later, on September 9, Carson made his first appearance, playing and singing "The Little Old Log Cabin in the Lane." Written by

Will S. Hays in 1871, it was a nostalgic minstrel song about the passing of the old country ways, calculated to tug at the heartstrings:

The footpath now is covered o'er that led us
    'round the hill
And the fences all are going to decay
And the creek is all dried up where we used to go
    to mill.
The time has turned its course another way.
But I ain't got long to stay here, and what little
    time I got
I'll try and be contented to remain

son record that he had ordered Brockman's initial shipment pressed without an Okeh catalog number. But Peer was too canny a businessman to let pride get in the way of making a buck, and he quickly reissued Carson's "horrible" record with a number (Okeh 4890) and sent hundreds of Carson discs down to Brockman in Atlanta within the week. By November, Peer had invited Carson up to New York to record a dozen more tunes. The grizzled fiddler gladly complied, though he immediately noted a big difference between the streets of Gotham and home: "I been here a whole week," he declared, "and I haven't seen a dad-blamed person I know!"

As Ralph Peer and Polk Brockman moved to capitalize on the untapped market for "old time tunes" (as the Okeh company labeled them in catalogs), other record companies made similar serendipitous discoveries. Columbia Records found the fiddle-guitar team of Gid Tanner and Riley Puckett in Georgia. Vocalion Records had singer-guitarist Blind George Reneau from the Tennessee hills. In time, nearly every large record label would give one of these old-time singers or fiddlers a try. Still, no one had a very solid sense of the size of the audience.

It was a Southern singer living in the city who turned the trickle of country music recording into a torrent. Born in Texas, Marion Try Slaughter went to New York in 1912 to sing opera. Changing his name to Vernon Dalhart (taken from the names of two Texas towns), he made a middling career as a tenor in musical theater productions and as a singer of minstrel songs on records. By 1924 he was

Fiddlin' John Carson (left) and Gid Tanner, longtime rivals at Georgia fiddle contests, went head to head in record stores when the Columbia label signed Tanner in March 1924.

forty-one years old, no longer a boyish leading man, and seemingly near the end of his singing career.

Dalhart caught wind of the rustic renditions of "old familiar tunes" coming from down South. One song in particular struck him as having possibilities for re-energizing his flagging career: "The Wreck on the Southern Old 97" [*sic*] a recounting of a 1903 train wreck near Danville, Virginia. After finding Henry Whitter's Okeh recording of the old song (which hit the market in January 1924), Dalhart copied down the song word for word and committed it to memory. In May of 1924 he finally persuaded the Edison company to record his version of it. When the record didn't sell to his satisfaction, Dalhart simply took his business to another company, Victor.

On August 13, 1924, he recorded the song again, this time backed with "The Prisoner's Song," an amalgamation of traditional sentimental lyrics pulled together by his cousin and set to music by a Victor musical director.

Released on Victor in October 1924, the record sold like hotcakes. Dalhart's plain readings of the songs—at once formal and rustic—propelled the bouncy railroad disaster song and the prisoner's poignant lament to unparalleled sales for rural music. By early 1925, the record had sold a million copies.

What could account for such massive popularity? The songs themselves must have spoken to listeners. Certainly, they told tales that were familiar and principled. In "The Prisoner's Song" a contrite prisoner wishes to be reunited with his innocent love; "The Wreck of the Old 97" (as Dalhart retitled it) offers a driving, thrilling account of a famous disaster, with a Victorian moral tacked on the end:

Now, ladies, you must take warning
From this time now and on.
Never speak hard words to your true,
*   loving husband.*
He may leave you and never return.

The delivery on both songs was exactly what the audience wanted. The instrumental backing was kept simple: just Dalhart's jaunty harmonica and a toe-tapping guitar on "The Wreck of the Old 97"; a lightly strummed guitar and a single plaintive violin on "The Prisoner's Song." Dalhart, meanwhile, communicated plainly and directly, as if he were

Light-opera singer Vernon Dalhart broke the hillbilly music business wide-open with his million-selling hit "The Wreck of the Old 97" / "The Prisoner's Song" in 1924.

telling news to a neighbor over the fence. He took pains to enunciate clearly (how could he abandon years of opera training?), but he also stamped each song with a noticeable Texas twang. Though Dalhart didn't sound half as rustic or colorful as Fiddlin' John Carson, his style was far more relaxed than, say, the brassy declamations of Al Jolson, then popular music's biggest star.

Victor Records quickly set about promoting Dalhart's new career. His next hit was made to order and squarely in the railroad-disaster mold. For two weeks in February 1925, a young spelunker named Floyd Collins lay trapped underground near Mammoth Cave, Kentucky. Thanks to the *Louisville Courier Journal*, word of Collins's plight spread across the nation. Hundreds of people flocked to the cave site—so many that the Kentucky state militia arrived to keep the peace. In the end it was all for naught. After an eighteen-day vigil, Floyd Collins died in the cave, on February 17, 1925.

The story didn't end there. The death of Floyd Collins sparked an idea for Polk Brockman, the enterprising Atlanta record dealer. For $25, he commissioned an original country song on the topic, and within two months he had Fiddlin' John Carson recording it (April 14, 1925). Somehow, the Okeh Company was not able to exploit this Carson record, but the canny Brockman did. He sold the song to A & R man Frank Walker, who passed it along to Dalhart. On September 9, 1925, with unobtrusive backing from guitar and violin, Dalhart recorded the story of "a lad we all know well," who "now lies sleeping in a lonely sandstone cave." Victor paired it with yet another fresh disaster item essayed by Dalhart—"The Wreck of the Shenandoah," concerning the recent crash of a U.S. Navy dirigible. Within a few months the record became Dalhart's second million seller.

Boosted by these hits, Dalhart would remain the best-selling artist in the new "old-time" genre right up through 1928. He was so much in demand that he recorded for all the major companies, under more than a hundred pseudonyms, often recording as many as three times a day. With his earnings, he bought a lavish two-story Tudor home in Mamaroneck, New York, complete with maid and underground garage. Eventually interest in his disaster songs and sentimental readings played out, and he lost a great deal of money in the 1929 stock market crash. At his death of a heart attack in 1948, Dalhart had been working as a night watchman and a vocal coach in Bridgeport, Connecticut. None of his students realized his earlier hillbilly stardom; in his homemade ads for his vocal coaching, Dalhart himself made no mention of it, preferring to extol the virtues of his work in opera, light opera, and oratorios. His last recording session was in 1936.

With the floodgates opened by Dalhart, the record companies began seeking out more rural-style musicians. Columbia Records established a "Familiar Tunes" series. Okeh had its "Old Time" series. Vocalion had begun to highlight "Special Records for Southern States" in its catalogs. Victor Records had its "Olde Time Fiddlin' Tunes." Together, the record labels began releasing about fifty such discs a month. As it turned out, 1925 was a watershed year for this new commercial form of music. A name that captured the many styles of this new musical market was found on January 15 of that year, when a string band quartet of young men drove up from around Galax, Virginia, to record for Okeh's Ralph Peer in New York. When Peer asked the group's leader, Al Hopkins, what the group called themselves, Hopkins replied offhandedly, "We're nothing but a bunch of hillbillies from North Carolina and Virginia. Call us anything." Chuckling, Peer dubbed them "The Hill Billies" and thereby coined a name for the music that would stick for the next thirty years.

By the year's end (December 15), Victor's newsletter *The Talking Machine World* felt the need to assess "What the Popularity of Hill-Billy Songs Means in Retail Profit Possibilities." The conclusion: "Probably we have had an overproduction of songs of the fox-trot order and in self-defense the public has revolted and turned to that which was a most radical change, the sob songs of several generations ago, brought up to date and made into a pathetic song on some current topical event or catastrophe." The anonymous writer of the newsletter summed up smugly by adding: "Psychologically, this can be answered, it being well known that when groups revolt they go to extremes." The revolt, it appeared, was on.

★ TURN YOUR RADIO ON!

Though interest in these old-time records was gathering steam, it was radio that was really taking off. As radio stations sprang up across the country (600 by June 1924), performers of this old-time music helped fill the programming gaps on many new stations, especially in the undesirable early morning and noon hours. Unlike a pop or classical orchestra, a hillbilly act didn't cost much to book. In fact, with amateur musicians so eager to show off their talent on the air for friends and neighbors, hillbilly talent often came free. In the case of Chicago's WLS, owned and operated by the "World's Largest Store," Sears, Roebuck, the station looked to old-time music from the very beginning, in large part because Sears catered to a very large audience of farmers. The store's rural customers were a natural audience for down-home music.

On April 19, 1924, exactly one week after going on the air, WLS inaugurated a program devoted to old-time, rural musical fare. "This program is to be sincere, friendly, and formal," announced station director Edgar Bill from the ballroom of Chicago's Sherman Hotel, "planned to remind you folks of the good fun and fellowship of the barn warmings, the

In 1925 the Okeh label advertised the Southern rural music of Fiddlin' John, Roba Stanley, and Ernest Stoneman as "Old Time Tunes." Today we call it country.

husking bees, and the square dances in our farm communities of yesteryear and even today." Kicking off that first down-home evening for the newly christened WLS Barn Dance was a local fiddle band and square-dance caller. By the end of the evening more than 250 telegrams had arrived—a clear indication of the show's standing with the audience. "Mother and I pulled up the carpet and danced for the first time in years," wrote one

man. "The Barn Dance brings happy memories of our youth," said another letter.

The WLS Barn Dance, like other radio barn dances that would spring up on stations across the South and Midwest over the next two decades, was simply a variety show, with an emphasis on old-time music and comedy. No one had a better intuitive grasp of the powerful allure of such programs than George D. Hay. From lessons he learned at WLS, he would go on to build the grandest barn dance of them all, the Grand Ole Opry. A Midwesterner born in Attica, Indiana, George Dewey Hay had joined Memphis's *Commercial Appeal* as a court reporter following military service in World War I. At the paper he soon gained a following for his popular column, "Howdy, Judge." The column raised his profile high enough that, when the *Commercial Appeal* established its own radio station, WMC, on January 21, 1923, Hay was soon prevailed upon to serve as late-night station announcer and radio editor for the paper. Taking advantage of Memphis's Mississippi River locale, Hay regularly introduced programs with toots from a steamboat whistle he dubbed "Hushpuckena," after a small town in northern Mississippi. And he gave himself a snappy moniker, the "Solemn Old Judge," which was not a reflection of his age or his temperament but was lifted from his *Commercial Appeal* byline: "G.D.H., Solemn Old Judge."

Within a year he had made a name for himself beyond Memphis and was invited as a guest announcer for WLS the week the station went on the air. That week, station director

Edgar Bill offered the twenty-eight-year-old Hay a job as a WLS announcer. Hay, not in any rush to leave Memphis and the South, decided to hold out for $75 a week, thinking he'd break the deal right there. WLS accepted and Hay was soon back in Chicago, where he had lived before the war.

Hay adapted quickly to his new surroundings. He traded in his steamboat whistle for a train whistle. He honed his on-air patter, peppering it with fanciful descriptions of the station as a train ("the WLS Unlimited") riding the rails ("the trackless paths of the air"). As that train's engineer, he punctuated broadcasts with blasts from his train whistle. That summer of 1924 he won a Gold Cup from *Radio Digest* (the *TV Guide* of its day) for being voted the nation's favorite announcer by 150,000 readers from across the country. A few years later Hay summed up his easy transition from newspapers to radio: "The announcer must have a nose for news. Radio is the world's newspaper and the announcers are its reporters." Now the hottest young announcer in radio, George D. Hay would soon play a major role in making country music and Nashville synonymous.

★ A Hot Time in the Old Town of Nashville

In the summer of 1925, American audiences howled with laughter at Hal Roach's first *Our Gang* shorts and shuddered at Lon Chaney's *Phantom of the Opera*. Young people flocked to the hottest new dance, the Charleston. In New York, publisher Harold Ross founded a smart new magazine, *The New Yorker,* intended to reflect the glittering world of the city's young sophisticates. In Spokane, Washington, a young Harry Crosby, soon to be known as Bing, was just beginning his musical career.

In Nashville, the executives of the thriving National Life & Accident Insurance Company were preparing to plunge into radio. In February 1924 the company had moved into a brand-new five-story building on the corner of Seventh and Union streets, just down the hill from the capitol. The impetus behind the company's move into radio had come from National Life vice president Edwin Craig, the thirty-two-year-old son of company board chairman C. A. Craig. Edwin Craig was fascinated by radio, but the firm's board of directors were initially skeptical about its usefulness. Eventually, though, he convinced them that radio could help sell insurance policies. What no one could have foreseen was that this farfetched notion for advertising insurance policies would lead directly to the Grand Ole Opry.

Once National Life committed to the station, however, it did so in style. Edwin Craig canvassed the country researching radio stations and hired noted experts to consult on his plans for the station. National Life lavished $50,000 on the project, as the company installed a state-of-the-art studio on the downtown building's top floor and twin radio towers two miles away at 15th Avenue South, near the Ward-Belmont girls' school.

With its ornate crystal chandelier, a grand piano, comfortable high-backed Victorian chairs, torchère lamps, Oriental rugs, and four large picture windows set off with luxurious crimson draperies made of fine velvet, that first studio (later dubbed Studio A) looked rather like an elegant but sparsely furnished Victorian parlor. Only the tall WSM microphones scattered about the twenty-one-by-twenty-four-foot room and the large, horizontal observation window near the hallway suggested the room's real purpose.

National Life's new station hit the airwaves for the first time on Monday, October 5, 1925. At 1,000 watts, it had the strongest signal in the South, next to the venerable WSB in Atlanta, and was more powerful than 85 percent of the stations in the country. That evening marked the station's gala opening ceremonies. Outside the station, hundreds of eager listeners gathered on Union Street, where two

Between 1925 and 1934, the Grand Ole Opry was broadcast from the fifth floor of the National Life Building in downtown Nashville.

In this late twenties shot, a pop band led by Vito Pellettieri (standing) holds court at the Hermitage Hotel. In 1934, Vito would become the Opry's stage manager, a job he would hold for forty years.

Western Electric bullhorn speakers had been rigged up, making the station's inaugural program audible a block away.

Just after seven o'clock, Edwin Craig stepped to the microphone to announce: "This is station WSM—"We Shield Millions"—owned and operated by the National Life & Accident Insurance Company, Nashville, Tennessee." (It was the custom in those days for radio station call letters to be assigned at random, but Edwin Craig insisted on having

the initials of the company's motto. National Life negotiated with the Department of Commerce to transfer the letters WSM from a Navy ship to the fledgling station, an order that Secretary of Commerce Herbert Hoover signed personally.)

A bustling metropolis of 130,000, Nashville considered itself "The Athens of the South." The to-do at WSM certainly reflected civic pride; the parade that followed Craig to the microphone that night included an invoca-

tion by Dr. George Stuart of the West End Methodist Church, the national anthem courtesy of the Al Menah Shrine band, a welcome from Chairman C. A. Craig, as well as congratulatory comments from Tennessee governor Austin Peay and Nashville mayor Hilary Howse. Afterward there was music galore. Joseph T. McPherson held forth with his operatic baritone; solo violinists and pianists played classical pieces; choruses from the city's two black colleges, Roger Williams and Fisk, har-

Pickin' and grinnin': Uncle Dave and son Dorris show off for fellow Opry performers (from left) Amos Binkley, Tom Andrews, Walter Liggett, Paul Warmack, Bert Hutcherson, unidentified, Charlie Arrington, and Dr. Humphrey Bate.

monized on spirituals, including "Swing Low, Sweet Chariot." Two dance bands provided music via remote feeds: From the Hermitage Hotel Ballroom, Beasley Smith's jazz orchestra "kept the ether all pepped up for more than half an hour," according to the *Nashville Banner*; and from the Andrew Jackson Hotel, Francis Craig's Columbia Recording Orchestra played sophisticated dance music from midnight until nearly 1 A.M. Finally, between 1 and 2 A.M., almost as an afterthought, Miss Bonnie Barnhardt, who had worked for At-

lanta's WSB as the station's program director for the past three years and who was serving as WSM's acting program director, offered what were described in the program as "Southern melodies." Ironically, given the station's future, that was as close to down-home, old-time music as the opening festivities got.

As had become customary for such an inaugural broadcast, celebrity announcers from other stations were on hand. Each took his turn on the air as well: Leo Fitzpatrick, known as "The Merry Old Chief" at his home

station of WDAF in Kansas City; Lambdin Kaye, the five-foot-four-inch "Little Colonel" from WSB, Atlanta; and from WLS George D. Hay, the "Solemn Old Judge" himself, who blew his old steamboat whistle. All the men were in their thirties and all were national celebrities, thanks to the power of radio. It was Hay, the *Radio Digest* Gold Cup winner, who got a job offer before he left Nashville.

Hay had done well in Chicago, but he missed the South, and the WSM job was definitely a promotion—from radio announcer at WLS to "radio director in charge of WSM," as one newspaper account put it. He accepted the job on Monday, November 2, exactly one month after the WSM inaugural broadcast, and arrived back in Nashville on November 9.

When Hay reported to WSM, the station had been offering a mix of live music, mostly light classical and pop acts, but the station was trying old-time music as well. Three weeks after WSM went on the air, a string band led by Dr. Humphrey Bate from nearby Castalian Springs made an appearance on Saturday night, October 24, 1925, playing from 10 to 11 P.M. For the next few weeks, Dr. Bate's string band appeared on WSM nearly every Saturday night.

WSM also tested the popularity of old-time music when the station broadcast the city's annual policemen's benefit show from the Ryman Auditorium on Thursday, November 5. In addition to Beasley Smith's jazz orchestra and a few other pop performers, the bill featured Dr. Bate's band as well as the banjo-playing songster Uncle Dave Macon and partner Fiddlin' Sid Harkreader. Reportedly, the show filled the house, and listeners at home could hear hundreds of feet stomping in time to tasty numbers like Dr. Bate's "How Many Biscuits Can You Eat" and Uncle Dave's "Bile Them Cabbage Down."

Hay sized up the situation at WSM quickly. Though he would continue to program Irish tenors, jazz bands, and classical string quartets, he was determined to broadcast the sort of music he'd experienced at the WLS Barn Dance. (Certainly Edwin Craig was not averse to it, having played mandolin as a schoolboy.) In the Tennessee hills, Hay thought, he would find down-to-earth, authentic old-time music makers, still playing the folk-songs of days gone by.

★ THE GRAND OLE OPRY IS BORN

Dr. Humphrey Bate's Saturday night visits seemed a start in the right direction. One Saturday night when Dr. Bate was otherwise engaged, Hay recruited a seventy-eight-year-old white-bearded fiddler for a broadcast. Hailing from a nearby hamlet, Uncle Jimmy Thompson had been eager to get on radio. As he colorfully put it, "I want to throw my music all over the American." And he did. At eight o'clock on that evening of November 28, 1925, Hay sat the spry old country gentleman down in one of the studio's easy chairs and showed his niece Eva Thompson Jones (whom the old fellow called "Sweetmeats") to the piano. She provided what little accompaniment her energetic uncle needed to reel out versions of "Tennessee Wagoner," "Grey Eagle," and "Give the Fiddler a Dram" on his favorite fiddle, "Old Betsy." Shortly after nine, concerned about the old man's stamina, Hay asked if Uncle Jimmy was getting tired after an hour's playing. "An hour?" he replied. "Fiddlesticks! A man can't get warmed up in an hour. This program's got to be longer." That evening, telephone calls and telegrams began pouring in, praising the delightful, toe-tapping fiddling of Uncle Jimmy Thompson. Legend has it that toward the end of the program building superintendent Percy Craig burst into Studio A, exclaiming that the station had received a call or telegram from every state in the union. In any case, it was manifestly clear to those in charge that Hay's hypothesis had tested positively. He could start his own barn dance at WSM. And that date marks the beginning of what would become the Grand Ole Opry.

A month later WSM made it official. Reports in Nashville's morning newspaper the *Tennessean* trumpeted in a story headlined "WSM to Feature Old Time Tunes": "Because of this recent revival in the popularity of the old familiar tunes, WSM has arranged to have an hour or two every Saturday night, starting Saturday, December 26. 'Uncle' Dave Macon, the oldest banjo picker in Dixie, and who comes from Readyville, Tenn., and 'Uncle' Jimmy Thompson of Martha, Tenn., will answer any requests for old time melodies. . . ."

Already the WSM Barn Dance—as it casually came to be known in 1926—was much more than a local show. Thanks to its strong broadcast signal, WSM could be heard miles away. The Barn Dance elevated Uncle Jimmy Thompson to stardom almost overnight. On January 2, 1926, a story appeared in a Boston paper in which Mellie Dunham, the 1925 national fiddling champion (crowned by Henry Ford, no less), challenged Uncle Jimmy to a fiddling duel. "Let him come to Tennessee," growled Uncle Jimmy, "and I'll lie with him

The men who started the Opry: announcer George D. Hay (with trademark steamboat whistle in arm) and seventy-eight-year-old Uncle Jimmy Thompson, ca. 1925.

George Wilkerson & His Fruit Jar Drinkers, ca. 1933: (from left) Wilkerson, Claude Lampley, Thomas Leffew, and Howard Ragsdale ready to take a nip from the fruit jar.

Of all the show's local acts, though, Uncle Dave Macon shined the brightest. In fact, Macon was the only member of the early Barn Dance cast who had established a following through records and touring. Fifty-five years old when he became a Barn Dance regular, he had been playing the banjo since the age of fourteen. But it had been strictly an amateur's pastime for him while he established himself as a farmer and family man. For almost twenty years, from 1901 to 1920, he ran the Macon Midway Mule and Wagon Transportation Company, hauling freight, vegetables, and liquor between Murfreesboro and Woodbury, a distance of nineteen miles. During his run, he'd often leave the mules on "automatic pilot," dropping the reins so he could entertain himself and passersby with tunes like "Go 'Long, Mule." Unfortunately, by 1920 the automobile effectively put him out of business, for the route that took him two days by wagon

like a bulldog." The contest never took place, but it's fascinating to note the rapidity of radio's power to make stars.

For his new WSM Barn Dance, Hay drew heavily on amateur acts from the surrounding area. His favorites were the string bands, the "hoedown bands," as he called them, who provided the "punctuation marks in our program which get us back down to earth the minute they plunk the first note." Determined to have the Barn Dance reflect rural life, Hay gave the bands colorful monikers, such as the Dixie Clodhoppers, the Fruit Jar Drinkers, and the Gully Jumpers. He encouraged them to play older songs that they may have learned from fathers and grandfathers, and discouraged them from playing the latest pop songs. He also had them dress up for publicity photos in overalls and beat-up old hats instead of their best Sunday-go-to-meeting clothes. To dress the part of the Solemn Old Judge, Hay himself wore a long-tailed frock coat, a black homburg, and a billowing black cravat.

Paul Warmack & His Gully Jumpers, ca. 1933: (from left) Bert Hutcherson, Roy Hardison, Charlie Arrington, and Warmack.

could be easily covered in a day by truck. Uncle Dave never did learn to drive a car. Come 1927, in a record called "Jordan Is a Hard Road to Travel," he'd sing: "I may be wrong but I think I'm right / The auto's ruined this country. / Let's go back to the horse and buggy, / And try to save some money!") Luckily he had his music to fall back on. Around 1923, discovered by a manager for the Loew's Theater circuit, Uncle Dave began touring vaudeville, making $100 a week.

His recording career began in July 1924, when, like Vernon Dalhart, he heard a recording of "The Wreck of the Old 97." He felt he could outdo the singer (Blind George Reneau) and soon convinced a local record distributor who hooked him up with the Aeolian Vocalion Record Company in New York. When WSM hit the airwaves a year later, Vocalion had already released more than twenty of his records. In truth, Uncle Dave didn't need the WSM Barn Dance—especially since WSM didn't pay its performers for the first few years. He was used to vaudeville rates and picked his spots on the Barn Dance carefully, preferring to spend his time in lucrative personal appearances. But he and George Hay became fast friends, and Uncle Dave continued to make sporadic appearances on the radio show until around 1930, when the Depression had cut into his recording and touring opportunities.

Uncle Dave Macon with son Dorris at the Opry. He was such an exuberant, boisterous performer that George Hay claimed he had difficulty keeping Uncle Dave consistently on mike.

Any time he appeared on the show, Uncle Dave was the undisputed star, living up to the sign on his banjo case that read: WORLD'S GREATEST BANJO PLAYER. Of course, that was just advertising. A couple of his WSM colleagues could probably play a banjo faster or sweeter. Many could hit truer, smoother notes when they sang, for Uncle Dave's nasal, mushmouthed twang was as homely as his face. What Uncle Dave offered that couldn't be equaled was all-around, down-home entertainment: jokes, stories, songs old and new, trick banjo-playing, all in one rambunctious, winking, smiling package. "It ain't what you

got, it's what you put out," Uncle Dave liked to say. "And boys, I can deliver."

With his gold-toothed smile, his white billy-goat beard, and his hat with a band around it saying OLD BUT REGULAR, Uncle Dave was the very picture of the mischievous old family uncle. He was such an exuberant, boisterous performer that George Hay claimed he had difficulty keeping Uncle Dave consistently on mike. No matter. Even if the folks at home couldn't see Uncle Dave—whirling the banjo before him like the hand of a clock, passing the banjo under his legs, stomping his feet, and plunking a tune all the while—the music and the feeling came across. (It didn't hurt when the equally colorful George Hay described Uncle Dave's banjo shenanigans by saying, "Now we'll show you how Uncle Dave handles a banjo like a monkey handles a peanut!") Audiences everywhere ate it up.

The lines between black and white music in the 1920s had not been firmly drawn by record companies and radio stations. Of course, radio doesn't transmit any color at all. In a 1928 Brunswick Records brochure, Uncle Dave Macon fondly recalled a letter he received from one admiring fan that underscores radio's color blindness:

Uncle Dave Makins:
We certainly did enjoy you over our

Radiator last night, and from the way you talk, laugh, and sing, you must be one of the most wonderful old Negroes in the South.

Uncle Dave summed up the situation accurately: "Now the good old sister just could not see me over the air." Which brings us to DeFord Bailey, the Barn Dance's (and country music's) first black star. Few people listening to the radio on Saturday nights in the 1920s and 1930s realized that the "Harmonica Wizard" on WSM was black. Even if they did, it wouldn't have mattered. As the letter to Uncle Dave suggests, old-time music had not yet been thoroughly segregated on record and radio (that wouldn't happen until well into the 1930s). In the beginning, rural folks of both races tuned in to shows like the WSM Barn Dance and appreciated a sprightly old tune, no matter who played it.

A four-foot-ten dynamo (he stood on a Coca-Cola crate to reach the mike), DeFord Bailey was without doubt one of the show's most popular performers almost from the beginning. It's part of Opry legend that DeFord so delighted George Hay during his audition that the Solemn Old Judge threw his steamboat whistle into the air at the end of DeFord's first number. Thus, at age twenty-six, DeFord Bailey became a bona fide radio star. In 1928, two years after he joined the show, he made

DeFord Bailey, the "Harmonica Wizard," was one of the early Opry's most popular performers.

twice as many appearances as any other act—forty-nine Saturdays out of fifty-two. Into the late 1930s, he was a big draw out on the road, even among largely white audiences.

Bailey could play banjo and guitar and sang sometimes as well, but harmonica pieces

were the meat and potatoes of his act. A blend of country and blues styles, his unique specialty was the way he mimicked the sounds of everyday life with his instrument. For instance, in "Fox Chase" he imitated fox howls, barking dogs, and the huntsman's call to the hounds. In "Pan American Blues" he not only depicted the clacking sound of the train on the tracks and the train whistle, he even uncannily reproduced the Doppler effect of the train's approach and departure. Both pieces remained audience favorites for years.

It was Bailey who inspired Judge Hay to give the show the name Grand Ole Opry. On a Wednesday night in early December 1927, Hay and a few of his Barn Dance regulars were standing by in the WSM studio just before ten o'clock, waiting for the end of a classical program originating from Chicago over the NBC network. Hay had assembled the musicians merely to fill in for half an hour, after which WSM would switch to a remote feed from a hotel where a pop dance band would take over. Always a good improviser, Hay somehow found his imagination tickled by the challenge of making a transition from the network's classical show to his down-home segment. So, after Bailey signed WSM on locally with "Pan American Blues," Hay followed by saying, "For the past hour we have been listening to the music taken largely from Grand Opera,

COUNTRY MILESTONES	NOVEMBER 2, 1920 — RADIO BROADCASTING BEGINS: WKDA IN PITTSBURGH CARRIES PRESIDENTIAL ELECTION RETURNS	MARCH 16, 1922 — WSB IN ATLANTA GOES ON THE AIR, THE FIRST STATION IN THE SOUTH	RECORDINGS FOR VICTOR COMPANY IN NEW YORK	JANUARY 4, 1923 — WBAP IN FORT WORTH AIRS FIRST RADIO BARN DANCE SHOW	MARCH 29, 1923 — ECK ROBERTSON PERFORMS BOTH SIDES OF HIS FIRST RECORD AT WBAP IN FORT WORTH
AUGUST 15, 1877 — THOMAS EDISON SUCCESSFULLY TESTS FIRST PHONOGRAPH		JUNE 30–JULY 1, 1922 — ECK ROBERTSON AND HENRY GILLILAND (FROM TEXAS AND OKLAHOMA) MAKE FIRST COUNTRY	SEPTEMBER 9, 1922 — FIDDLIN' JOHN CARSON MAKES HIS RADIO DEBUT AT WSB IN ATLANTA	MARCH 1923 — ECK ROBERTSON'S FIRST RECORD OFFERED FOR SALE IN VICTOR CATALOG	
1904 — THE FIRST DOUBLE-SIDED RECORDS ISSUED					

Dr. Humphrey Bate & His Possum Hunters in 1933, dressed according to Judge Hay's instructions: (from left) Walter Liggett, Oscar Stone, Dr. Bate, Oscar Albright, Buster Bate (age nineteen), and Staley Walton.

but from now on we will present the Grand Ole Opry!" The name stuck. The following Sunday, the morning paper was already referring to the show as the "Grand Old Op'ry."

Sparked by the performances of Bailey, Dr. Bate's Possum Hunters, Uncle Dave Macon, and about a dozen other regular acts, the Grand Ole Opry grew by leaps and bounds. Hay assembled a cast of talented local amateur acts, about fifteen in all. The initial one- to two-hour broadcast increased to four hours—eight to midnight—and on January 7, 1927, WSM increased its transmitting power to 5,000 watts, allowing the station to reach homes in half the country. That fall, fan mail poured in from thirty-two states to the tune of 200 letters a week. In the space of a few short years, radio had transformed a folksy variety program, populated with amateur musicians, into a national showcase for old-time, down-home music.

Between 1920 and 1927, as America struggled to hold fast to its traditions while riding the careering engine of progress, a remarkable thing had happened: Country music was born. Thanks to the powerful technologies of radio and recording, a group of related musical styles had been given a new identity and new-found commercial value. The old familiar tunes, played simply on rude fiddles and guitars, had a power no one seems to have suspected prior to the recordings of Fiddlin' John Carson and Vernon Dalhart. In Nashville, George D. Hay quickly realized that gathering together a number of such performers for a "barn dance" like the Grand Ole Opry had a way of charming city dweller and farmer alike.

Country music had found two surefire ways to reach its audience, but as we'll see, radio and recording didn't simply preserve country music like a dragonfly in amber. Instead, these two powerful mediums allowed for musical experimentation as never before. Pointing the way toward innovation in the old familiar tunes would be two acts as different as night and day—the Carter Family and Jimmie Rodgers. Each act, in its own way, would define the limits of the new musical genre and suggest myriad inspiring possibilities.

JUNE 14, 1923 — FIDDLIN' JOHN CARSON MAKES HIS FIRST RECORD FOR OKEH COMPANY IN ATLANTA

JULY 13, 1923 — FIDDLIN' JOHN CARSON'S RECORD IS RELEASED AT ATLANTA FIDDLERS' CONVENTION

JANUARY 1924 — OKEH RELEASES HENRY WHITTER'S "THE WRECK ON THE SOUTHERN OLD 97"

APRIL 12, 1924 — WLS IN CHICAGO GOES ON THE AIR

APRIL 19, 1924 — WLS AIRS ITS FIRST BARN DANCE PROGRAM

AUGUST 13, 1924 — VERNON DALHART RECORDS "THE WRECK OF THE OLD 97"/"THE PRISONER'S SONG" FOR VICTOR, COUNTRY MUSIC'S FIRST MILLION-SELLING RECORD

1925 — ACOUSTIC RECORDING HORNS ARE REPLACED BY MORE SENSITIVE ELECTRICAL MICROPHONES

SEPTEMBER 9, 1925 — VERNON DALHART RECORDS "THE DEATH OF FLOYD COLLINS," COUNTRY'S SECOND MILLION SELLER

The Carter Family at home in Poor Valley, Virginia, 1920s: Maybelle on guitar, Sara on autoharp, and Sara's husband, A. P.

From Blue Yodels to Cowboy Tunes

THE BRISTOL SESSIONS

In the summer of 1927 most Americans were abuzz with what seemed the news of the century: Charles Lindbergh had flown his *Spirit of St. Louis* nonstop from New York to Paris. Another historic event would be etched into the American consciousness as Babe Ruth smacked his record-breaking sixtieth home run in October of that year. Between those grand headlines, another less heralded, though no less momentous, development would take place far from the big cities, in the bustling Appalachian mountain town of Bristol: the first recordings of both the Carter Family and Jimmie Rodgers. The discovery of these two innovative acts and their unforgettable songs would decisively nudge the hillbilly business away from age-old folk songs and toward brand-new material done in the folk style.

Record scout Ralph Peer, who had left Okeh and subsequently joined the Victor Company, planned a trip south to hunt for more hill-country talent. Though Victor was still leading the industry with Vernon Dalhart's records, there weren't many other hillbilly singers hanging around the streets of New York. Peer's job, then, was to seek out new hillbilly and "race" artists (as black performers were then called, thanks to another coinage by Peer himself). Though he often recorded blacks and whites one after another in the same town during the same sessions, Peer believed, as everyone else in the record business did, that black and white record buyers represented two different markets; exceptions like DeFord Bailey just didn't figure into the equation.

Amazing as it sounds today, Nashville was not Peer's destination.

True, Nashville did have an upstart old-time music show on the radio, but in mid-1927 the Opry had only just begun broadcasting with enough power to reach any appreciable distance outside Tennessee. The show and the city had not yet acquired a reputation for down-home music. The words "Music City, U.S.A." wouldn't be coined for another couple of decades.

That summer, on the first leg of a trip south that would later see sessions in Charlotte and Savannah, Peer headed for Bristol, located on the border of Tennessee and Virginia. This was no rinky-dink experiment: The Victor Company had allocated $60,000 for the three-city recording tour, for several major hillbilly acts had already emerged from the Appalachian region, most prominently Henry Whitter, Blind George Reneau, the Hill Billies, and Ernest Stoneman. Of these, Peer himself had recorded all but Reneau while at Okeh. Bristol represented the northeast corner of Tennessee's Tri Cities area (Bristol–Kingsport–Johnson City), which with 32,000 people could collectively boast of being the largest population center in the Appalachians. As such, Bristol seemed an ideal spot for fishing for more of this sort of talent.

Before coming down from New York with his carload of recording equipment, Peer was careful to make appointments with a number of acts in the area. Some appointments would renew old acquaintances of his, such as Henry Whitter, whom Peer had first recorded at Okeh back in 1923. Peer had Whitter come over from Fries, about one hundred

◆ ◆ ◆ ◆ ◆ ◆ ◆ ◆ ◆ ◆ ◆ ◆ ◆ ◆ ◆

◻

OPRY SPOTLIGHT

1927—WSM INCREASES ITS POWER TO 5,000 WATTS AND JOINS THE BRAND-NEW NBC RADIO NETWORK

FEBRUARY 1, 1928—HARRY STONE JOINS OPRY AS STAFF ANNOUNCER

SEPTEMBER 28–OCTOBER 6, 1928— RALPH PEER RECORDS SEVERAL OPRY ACTS, INCLUDING DEFORD BAILEY AND THE CROOK BROTHERS. PEER NEVER RECORDS IN NASHVILLE AGAIN

1930—HARRY STONE REPLACES GEORGE D. HAY AS WSM PROGRAM DIRECTOR

1931—THE VAGABONDS, A HARMONY TRIO FROM CHICAGO, JOIN THE OPRY

OCTOBER 1932—WSM INCREASES POWER TO 50,000 WATTS ON A CLEAR-CHANNEL FREQUENCY

1933—THE DELMORE BROTHERS JOIN THE OPRY

FEBRUARY 1934—THE OPRY MOVES TO STUDIO C, WITH A 500-SEAT CAPACITY, IN THE NATIONAL LIFE BUILDING

OCTOBER 1934—THE OPRY MOVES TO THE HILLSBORO THEATER, SEATING 800

JUNE 12, 1936—DR. HUMPHREY BATE DIES OF A HEART ATTACK AT HOME. HE WAS SIXTY-ONE

JUNE 13, 1936—THE OPRY MOVES TO THE DIXIE TABERNACLE, SEATING 3,500

◻

miles to the east, to rerecord his popular "Fox Chase" for Victor. Because Peer had brought along brand-new electrical microphones recently developed by Western Electric, he had hopes of being able to sell the old harmonica favorite all over again.

Rerecording instrumentals was all well and good, but Peer had already determined that what he and Victor really needed were singers. With the new electronic microphones replacing the old acoustical horns, singers no longer had to shout. The technological breakthrough that in a couple of years would make Bing Crosby's crooning career possible would also profoundly affect the old-time music business.

Peer and his engineers converted a vacant hat warehouse on Bristol's State Street into a temporary recording studio. Over the next two weeks, from Monday, July 25, through Friday, August 5, Peer would record seventy-six performances by nineteen different acts. Two of those acts made impressive use of the new Western Electric microphones. A week after he commenced the sessions, on Monday evening, August 1, 1927, Peer set about recording "Mr. and Mrs. Carter from Maces Springs," as he had first identified them in his notes. An itinerant fruit tree salesman, A. P. Carter was a tall, raw-boned thirty-five; Sara Carter was the twenty-nine-year-old mother of three children. Though Peer probably didn't realize it, the Carters had spent most of the previous day making the twenty-five mile trip from Maces Springs to Bristol in a Model A Ford borrowed from A. P.'s brother Eck. Also "borrowed" from Eck Carter for the trip was his eighteen-year-old wife, Maybelle, then eight months pregnant. Eck wasn't very happy with his brother's fool idea of gallivanting across the country, dragging his wife off to make a phonograph record or two. But she provided the guitar and an important voice in the little family band, and they needed her. Plus, she was Sara's cousin.

The family trio didn't come uninvited; Peer had made arrangements with them a couple of months before on the recommendation of a Bristol record dealer. But he hadn't auditioned them until that August afternoon. What the sophisticated young record scout heard quickly beguiled him.

Peer could not help but note the distinctively bouncy rhythm in Maybelle's plucky guitar playing, but it was the homespun yearning in Sara's singing that truly won him over. Almost as deep and tough as a man's tenor, yet infinitesimally more tender, Sara Carter's voice spoke volumes about the life of the rural working woman. "As soon as I heard Sara's voice, that was it," Peer later recalled. "I knew that it was going to be wonderful." They recorded four numbers that first night, two takes on each. Sara sang lead and played autoharp, Maybelle propelled the group with the old Stella guitar that she nearly left at home, and she and A. P. both chimed in with harmony vocals here and there. Peer invited the Carters back the next morning for a nine o'clock session, but for some reason A. P. didn't even show up, leaving the women to carry on alone. It was fine with Peer, who had the Carter women record two more numbers. Afterward, the Carters were overjoyed to receive the $300 that Peer paid them ($50 per song). Not only was it more money than they ever expected to earn from music, it also allowed them to replace the tires they'd blown out on the trip up so they could make their way home that night. Little did they suspect what was next in store for them in the record business; they were more concerned about getting their corn crop planted.

Two days later, Thursday, August 4, Peer made his second great discovery in Bristol. He had actually auditioned the Jimmie Rodgers Entertainers the morning before, when they arrived from Asheville, North Carolina, a hundred miles to the south. That Wednesday

Jimmie Rodgers (wearing the specs) with his short-lived band, just a couple of months before he made his first recordings in August 1927.

worked with along the way. In 1924 he contracted tuberculosis. In that day and age it was a death sentence—3.5 million people died of the disease between 1920 and 1925. There was no cure. A less cocksure man would have wadded up his dreams and thrown them away. The indefatigable Rodgers simply used the disease as an excuse to give up railroad work and focus on music.

He headed up to the Appalachian resort town of Asheville, North Carolina, in January 1927, ostensibly to get some railroad work. When he was turned down by the local railroad office, Rodgers merrily continued on his way, grabbing music gigs where he could. Upon finding a string-band trio from Bristol called the Tenneva Ramblers, Rodgers quickly took over leadership of the group and dubbed them the Jimmie Rodgers Entertainers. After playing for a couple of months at resorts and over the brand-new radio station in Asheville, WWNC (until their show was dropped), the fearless leader persuaded the band to head back to Bristol to audition for Ralph Peer. It was at this point that the jury-rigged band fell apart; when the Entertainers didn't want to be known as Jimmie's band on record, Rodgers figured he could throw out a few versions of pop hits that he'd done on radio and put them over on record by sheer force of personality. Peer, however, wanted old-time music—or at least sentimental or rustic songs that could pass for old familiar tunes. Most of all, Peer wanted uncopyrighted material that he could copyright himself, for that was where he saw the money in this hillbilly business.

Jimmie Rodgers at his home in Kerrville, Texas, in 1930, with (from left) Mrs. Peer, Jimmie's daughter Anita, producer Ralph Peer, and Jimmie's wife Carrie.

night, however, the group quarreled over how they'd be credited on record, and the nominal leader left the group. So on Thursday they recorded separately. The three remaining Entertainers carried on as a trio, called the Tenneva Ramblers, and they did fine string-band music for Peer that morning. But it was jaunty Jimmie Rodgers, a month shy of his thirtieth birthday, who showed flashes of something a little different. Born in Mississippi, the son of a railroad man, he had worked the rails himself for a dozen years in his teens and early twenties. A dreamer and a showboat, he was never cut out for a regular job and he'd tried several, including truck driving, stoking furnaces, running a filling station, and working as a mechanic. Always gravitating to music, he joined medicine shows and minstrel shows at the drop of his straw boater hat, teaming up with this act and that, picking up a feel for the blues from black musicians he

Louisville, Kentucky, June 1931: (from left) Jimmie Rodgers, Maybelle Carter, A. P. Carter, and Sara Carter.

So Peer pushed Rodgers—as Peer did all his acts—for something old-sounding that was also new. Rodgers came up with two pieces Peer consented to record: "The Soldier's Sweetheart," a sentimental World War I–era ballad about the death of a soldier from the woman's point of view, and "Sleep, Baby, Sleep," an old vaudeville lullaby from the 1860s that had already been recorded a few times by others. Peer allowed Rodgers seven complete takes—more tries than he allowed any other act at Bristol—just to get the two songs right for record, in a session running from two to four-twenty in the afternoon. Peer may have been intrigued by the way Rodgers personalized "Sleep, Baby, Sleep" with a series of yodels that fit the song perfectly yet stood out as something special. Years later Peer would say, "I thought he had his own personal and peculiar style, and I thought his yodel alone might spell success." That afternoon Rodgers left the makeshift studio with $100 for his labors and an open-ended contract with Victor that gave the company the option on his next recording.

Ralph Peer finished up the sessions on Fri-day, August 5, and packed up the wax record masters for shipping up to New York, then set out for his next stop in Charlotte. Had the Carter Family and Jimmie Rodgers been like most old-time acts in those days, that would have been the end of it. Maybe there would be record releases, maybe there wouldn't. As much as Peer may have liked these two acts, he didn't rush to release their records. It wasn't until October 1927 that Victor got around to trying out Rodgers's two songs, and November when the Carter Family got a hearing with "The Poor Orphan Child"/"The Wandering Boy."

By late November Jimmie Rodgers got itchy to show Peer what else he could do. In what was becoming the grand hillbilly tradition, Rodgers went uninvited to New York to see Peer and get another opportunity to record. Peer agreed, took him to Victor's offices in Camden, New Jersey, and got four more sides from Jimmie Rodgers on November 30. "Sleep, Baby, Sleep" from the Bristol sessions netted Rodgers a disappointingly skimpy $27 in royalties, but Peer knew what Rodgers didn't—that the record had already sold about 6,000 copies, not bad for an unknown artist. The Camden sessions produced even better results. One of the selections, "Blue Yodel (T for Texas)," captured the public's fancy with its blues verses of adultery and revenge, topped off with Jimmie's inimitable blue yodels.

The record quickly sold over half a million copies. In less than a year, Rodgers would scale heights even he scarcely dreamed—headlining a vaudeville tour of the South on the Loew's circuit, broadcasting a weekly show from Washington, D.C., and making $2,000 a month from record royalties alone. Effortlessly, Jimmie Rodgers mixed hillbilly music with the blues, and the public loved him for it.

Ralph Peer didn't forget the Carter Family. He released two more of their records from the Bristol sessions at the end of 1927 and the early part of 1928. The Carters were selling, maybe not as spectacularly as the Blue Yodeler, but steadily. That spring, Peer invited the Carters up to Camden to make a dozen more records and sent tickets to pay the Family's way. As with Rodgers, the Camden session proved the charm. The songs they recorded there became revered classics: "Keep on the Sunny Side," "Little Darling Pal of Mine," "Will You Miss Me When I'm Gone," and the immortal "Wildwood Flower." That last song, sung beautifully by Sara, showcased Maybelle's dazzling blend of melody and rhythm on the guitar. Recorded May 10, 1928—Maybelle's nineteenth birthday— "Wildwood Flower" would soon sell over 100,000 copies, an impressive amount in the days when radio had cornered the music market. More important, "Wildwood Flower" would influence country guitar pickers for years to come as they labored to reproduce Maybelle's bouncy "Carter scratch," in which she plucked out the melody on the bass strings while chording a rhythm on the treble strings.

The Carters continued to record for Peer—in Camden, Louisville, Atlanta, Memphis, Charlotte—at a steady pace of one or two sessions a year through 1934. Later they recorded for the American Record Corporation, Decca, Okeh, and RCA's Bluebird subsidiary—all in all, 250 released sides. They never had a million seller, but during one two-year stretch in the late twenties they sold 700,000 copies of fourteen discs. They never got rich, either, though Maybelle did buy a new guitar and A. P. bought a Chevrolet. (In fact, the Depression hit Sara and A. P. so hard in late 1929 that A. P. briefly moved up to Detroit and factory work to try to earn some extra money for the family.) Amazingly, the Carter Family wasn't even quite a family after 1933 when Sara left A. P. Carter, divorcing him six years later. Nevertheless, they continued recording until 1941.

In contrast to Jimmie Rodgers, the Carters never became big stage successes. Rodgers toured vaudeville, playing big houses on the RKO circuit in Atlanta and Dallas. The

Ever jaunty, ever optimistic, Jimmie Rodgers gave the world the thumbs-up even as he slowly succumbed to tuberculosis.

In 1943, after the Carter Family disbanded, A. P. Carter opened this general store back home at the foot of Clinch Mountain. The store kept irregular hours because its absent-minded owner only went to work there when he felt like it.

Carters performed locally, at schoolhouses and courthouses, and never toured nationally. While Rodgers was making a movie in 1929 (albeit a fifteen-minute short filmed in Camden, not Hollywood), the Carters were nailing up their own posters. For two winters between 1938 and 1940, the Carters lived in Del Rio, Texas, working just across the border in Mexico for powerful "border blaster" stations like XERA and XEG. These stations broadcast at 100,000 watts or more, which was beyond what was allowed in the United States. At such power, the Carters' music (and that of other country music acts) was beamed across much of the United States and all the way up into Canada.

Even so, the Carters' impact came primarily through their remarkable recordings, and the old-time folk verses and melodies that A. P. collected and "worked up," as he described it. Though he went door to door—actually taking short trips around the Blue Ridge Mountains—looking for people who might have old folk songs to teach him, he didn't collect songs for the sake of preservation. Rather, he wrote the words down and memorized the melodies just so he could have material for the next Carter Family recording session. In many cases he added new words, new verses, and new melodies to existing folk songs. "Wildwood Flower," "Keep on the Sunny Side," "I'm Thinking Tonight of My Blue Eyes," "Jimmie Brown the Newsboy," "My Clinch Mountain Home," "My Dixie Darling," "You Are My Flower," "Worried Man Blues," "Wabash Cannonball," "Can the Circle Be Unbroken"—the titles constitute a veritable country music songbook.

For his part, Jimmie Rodgers also contributed great songs to the country canon—"In the Jailhouse Now," "Daddy and Home," "Waiting for a Train," "My Rough and Rowdy Ways," "Muleskinner Blues (Blue Yodel No. 8)," "Miss the Mississippi"—in a variety of styles. But more than anything he displayed personality on record. A skyrocket of talent during his brief, brilliant career, Jimmie Rodgers lit up the old-time music business like no one before him—touring with Will Rogers, recording alongside string bands, jug bands, Hawaiian musicians, pop orchestras, even jazzman Louis Armstrong. Though his recording career lasted only six years, he managed to record 110 titles—the equivalent today of two albums a year! Like the Carters, he created a body of country standards, but perhaps even more importantly he brought a genuine sense of style to old-time music. One testament to his influence: Gene Autry, Jimmie Davis, Hank Snow, and Ernest Tubb all broke into music as Jimmie Rodgers imitators. Long after his passing on May 26, 1933, when he finally succumbed to tuberculosis at age thirty-five, Jimmie Rodgers continued to exert a profound influence on country music.

★ TONIC FOR A DEPRESSION

Ironically, though they were the two most influential acts of the time, the Carter Family and Jimmie Rodgers rarely were heard on radio (with the exception of the Carters' X-station stint), and neither act ever performed on the two biggest radio showcases of old-time music, the Grand Ole Opry and the WLS Barn Dance. As a matter of fact, success on records in the 1920s and 1930s often didn't translate into radio appearances. In those days, most people considered radio and records completely distinct and separate musical outlets, with radio being the more desirable (and lucrative) showcase for a musician.

The sad truth was that records didn't pay a hillbilly musician very well: a $25 to $50 one-time recording fee, and maybe—*maybe*—a

The Opry cast at WSM's Studio B, ca. 1928. Front and center are (from left) announcer Harry Stone, station founder Edwin Craig, and announcer George D. Hay. Uncle Dave is in the next row (left) and DeFord Bailey is on the far right.

royalty of half a cent on each record sold. On a record that sold 10,000 copies (a good seller in those days), that would mean just another $50. In contrast, a job on the radio, even at $5 or $10 a week, quickly added up to much more, plus it offered the opportunity to advertise for show dates, which promised more money.

During the twenties, just listening to the radio or going to the movies, one might have assumed that everything in America was a laugh and a song. Movies talked, with Al Jolson breaking the silence dramatically in *The Jazz Singer* of 1927. Mickey Mouse danced to the old-time sounds of "Turkey in the Straw" in *Steamboat Willie*. The Marx Brothers ran wild in *The Cocoanuts*. A new comedy debuted on NBC radio August 19, 1929. Running Monday through Saturday, fifteen minutes every evening, "Amos 'n' Andy" quickly became the most popular show on radio.

But that was entertainment, voices coming through the air and images flickering on a screen. In reality, America was ripe for a fall. Though corporate dividends and stocks stood at an all-time high, working people hadn't been receiving their share of the pie through the Roaring Twenties. Deep in debt, their credit overextended, they couldn't afford to keep buying what the factories were turning out. When the go-go stock market fell off the precipice on Black Thursday, October 24, 1929—13 million stock shares sold in a single panic-stricken day—it sent shock waves throughout America. Fortunes accumulated over a lifetime vanished overnight. In 1930 and 1931 three thousand banks failed. One out of every four working Americans was jobless by 1933. Out on the Great Plains, long-term drought and freakish winds combined to carry precious topsoil away, turning America's breadbasket into a Dust Bowl. Farmers' livelihoods were literally gone with the wind.

The record industry, which had been reeling from the competition of radio's live performances, crashed. In 1927, the year the Carter Family and Jimmie Rodgers first recorded, the public bought 104 million records. In 1932 sales had plummeted to a paltry 6 million. Yet, though times were very hard, two out of every five homes had radios in 1932; that number would climb to four out of five by 1938. That year, a survey of American farm families would find that 70 percent had radios—9.4 million homes—and that on average people listened to radio five and a half hours a day. For the rest of the decade and into the forties, radio remained king, because if you could just get near a set, listening was free.

As the Depression took hold, National Life Insurance executives began to realize that the good-natured, freewheeling radio show Judge Hay had developed was a genuine appreciating asset. Thus, even as the nation tightened its belt during the Depression, the Grand Ole Opry and WSM grew. A new studio was built to accommodate the overflow crowds that were spilling out into the hallways and stairways of the National Life Building every Saturday night. The new Studio B seated an audience of about 200, separated from the performers by a glass wall. After years of giving free shows, performers finally got paid. It wasn't much at first—$5—but at the time it meant a great deal.

New announcers were hired to help Judge Hay. Thirty-year-old Harry Stone signed on as an assistant announcer-engineer February 1, 1928, with years of experience in radio already behind him. He had helped get Nashville's first station—100-watt WCBQ—on the air in May 1924, broadcasting from the basement of the local First Baptist Church and funded by the Baptist Sunday School Board.

WSM program director Harry Stone (center) rubs shoulders with Governor Gordon Browning (Stone's left) of Tennessee.

College-educated and skilled in musical arranging, the Vagabonds brought a new sophistication to the Opry stage in 1931.

But it wasn't preaching that stirred Stone; it was the limitless power of radio. He scheduled programs, he rounded up talent, he announced, eventually becoming manager of the station, which had been bought by a local drug company and renamed WBAW. It was while working for WBAW that Stone got his first inkling of the popularity of down-home music. Lebeck's, a downtown department store, had sponsored a series of live shows broadcast from their own shop windows. The guest star each day was none other than the

Opry's irrepressible Uncle Dave Macon, who so charmed passersby that he brought all motorcars, buggies, and even streetcar traffic to a standstill. It didn't take very long before the police tired of the daily traffic snarls and demanded that Stone cancel Uncle Dave's streetside serenading.

Thus, when Stone joined WSM, he had some idea of the power of hillbilly music. Over the next couple of years, Harry Stone gradually wrested control of the Opry away from Judge Hay. In 1930 Stone replaced Hay as program director, making the switch in their roles official. Hay's motto for the Opry had been "Keep her close to the ground, boys." The Solemn Old Judge liked the down-to-earth sound of string bands, and banned jazzy horns and drums from the Opry stage. Stone didn't exactly disagree with these limitations, but he nevertheless worked to broaden the Opry's appeal.

The first act he signed on—the Vagabonds—did just that. Organized in Chicago by Dean Upson, the smooth harmony trio included Curt Poulton and Herald Goodman by the time they joined the Opry in 1931, having previously honed their skills at the WLS Barn Dance and KMOX in St. Louis. College-educated and skilled in musical arranging, the Vagabonds trio brought a newfound urbanity to the Opry stage. They were careful to frame

their barbershop harmonies simply with the strumming of a single guitar and to offer up rewrites of sentimental folk songs rather than the jazzy singing that they were quite capable of. Stone was vindicated when the Vagabonds quickly became one of the show's more popular acts with tunes like "When It's Lamplighting Time in the Valley" and the prison lament "Ninety-Nine Years."

Seeing the value of sentimentality, Stone ushered in a cute father-and-son act, Asher & Little Jimmie Sizemore, in 1932. That was the year four-year-old Shirley Temple made her film debut. Little Jimmie, also four years old when he and his father began on the Opry, tugged on the heartstrings just as expertly. Even at that tender age, the little tyke knew more than 200 songs, or so his father claimed. Mr. Sizemore would strum the guitar and sing in a soft tenor while Little Jimmie sang cute

In their ten years at the Opry (1932–42) Asher Sizemore and son Little Jimmie appealed to fans' sentimental side with sweet songs and gentle humor.

During the thirties, the Opry's mixed bag included the "Talking Blues" of Robert Lunn (left) and the minstrel antics of vaudevillian 'Lasses White (right) as well as hoedowns from musicians like fiddler George Wilkerson and mandolinist Glen Stagner.

best and most broadly influential of these brother acts, the Delmore Brothers, from Athens, Alabama, who joined the cast in the spring of 1933. Blending soft vocal harmonies learned from Southern gospel and intricate dual guitar parts derived from the blues, the Delmore Brothers developed a rhythmic yet hushed old-time sound unlike any other of the time. Thanks to gifted elder brother Alton—who dreamed of becoming a writer of books—the Delmores had truly original songs that joked ("Brown's Ferry Blues"), evoked sadness ("Gonna Lay Down My Old Guitar"), and celebrated romance ("Beautiful Brown Eyes"). "Brown's Ferry Blues," probably their best-known record of the period, sold more than 100,000 copies. Within months of joining, the Delmores ascended to the top rank of performers at the Opry, frequently mentioned in Opry press releases as drawing mail second only to Uncle Dave Macon. Though they would leave the Opry in 1938 to work at other stations, the Delmores would continue as one of country music's best-loved acts through the late forties.

Perhaps the most significant development at the Opry in the early thirties wasn't musical

novelties like "Chawin' Chewin' Gum," sentimental songs like "Silver-Haired Mother," or heartrending ballads like "The Death of Jimmie Rodgers." In those innocent times, the act was hard to resist; during their heyday, Asher and Little Jimmy performed on WSM radio three days during the week as well as Saturdays at the Opry. In 1933 Asher Sizemore published a book of the songs they sang; that first twenty-seven-page 25¢ book sold in the hundreds of thousands.

During the late twenties and into the thirties, a number of hillbilly brother duet acts emerged on radio and records. The new electrical microphones, which continued to be improved, allowed harmony singing to flourish. As anyone who's heard good family singing can attest, blood harmonies are the closest. The Allen Brothers, the Lone Star Cowboys (Bob and Joe Attlesey), the Blue Sky Boys (Bill and Earl Bolick), the Shelton Brothers, the

Dixon Brothers, the Callahan Brothers, and the Monroe Brothers all came to prominence on radio and records in the thirties. Fortunately the Grand Ole Opry signed one of the

With a rhythmic yet hushed old-time sound, the Delmore Brothers—Rabon (left) and Alton—became one of the Opry's most popular acts during the thirties.

The Opry's first touring troupe, 1931: Sam McGee and Uncle Dave Macon (seated); Kirk McGee, Dr. Humphrey Bate, Dorris Macon, Buster Bate, Alcyone Bate, and Lou Hesson (standing).

but technological. In October of 1932 WSM built the world's largest radio tower—878 feet tall—to broadcast at the new rating of 50,000 watts. Assigned a clear channel by the government, WSM now reached into every U.S. town and hamlet east of the Rockies and north from Florida into southern Canada.

Led by veterans Uncle Dave Macon and Dr. Humphrey Bate, Opry cast members undertook their first tour of RKO vaudeville theaters in hopes of cashing in on their Opry stardom. Joining the two veterans on a railroad tour across the Midwest for two months in 1931 were Macon's son and accompanist Dorris, Bate's sister, son Buster and daughter Alcyone, and brother act Sam & Kirk McGee. By all accounts, they played to packed houses at every whistle-stop. Their success opened some eyes back at the Opry. Touring—not radio fees of $5 a week, not recording at a roy-

alty of half a cent a side—was the best way a hillbilly musician could earn a decent living. Radio and records merely offered a fancy soapbox for plugging upcoming show dates.

Around 1933 the seemingly insatiable demand for Opry music plus the musicians' own financial needs prompted WSM to organize its own office to book artists on tours. The Artists Service Bureau opened under the aegis of Judge Hay with WSM taking a 15 percent commission for bookings. Through personal appearances in schoolhouses, movie theaters, and mining camps during the depths of the Depression, the Opry's bond with its audience strengthened immeasurably—although at an untold personal cost to the performers who drove hundreds of miles each week on unlit, poorly paved, two-lane highways. Every Saturday night without fail every act had to return to the Opry. Advertisers were by now

counting on acts to appear and were paying the station handsomely for the privilege of being associated with the Opry. And the show always went on. In 1937 a WSM press release boasted that the show had been interrupted only twice, each time for a half hour for one of President Franklin Roosevelt's "Fireside Chats."

Progress for the Opry didn't come without growing pains. By the end of 1933 the overflow crowds at the National Life Building every Saturday necessitated yet another expansion, in February 1934, to Studio C in a new wing of the National Life Building; this studio seated 500. Even then there weren't enough seats to fill the demand, so for the first time WSM began issuing tickets, in three different colors. Each color allowed the bearer to be admitted to one hour of the Opry. Tickets could be obtained only through WSM and National Life's 3,000 insurance agents.

But the crowds continued to swell. When chairman of the board C. A. Craig and his second-in-command Runcie Clements, who

George D. Hay, the Opry's first master of ceremonies, was also its most gifted myth-maker.

The Opry cast onstage at the Hillsboro Theater, the show's home from 1934 to 1936.

were on the way to their offices one Saturday night in July 1934, had difficulty pushing through the crowd of good country people, audiences were banned temporarily from the show. In the fall, though, the crowds came back bigger than ever. It was time for the Opry to move again, this time away from National Life and the downtown, a couple miles southwest to the Hillsboro Theater, which seated 800. Again the three-color ticket system was used to accommodate 2,400 people each Saturday. It was here that the Opry divided the show into fifteen-minute segments that were sold to advertising sponsors. The mineral laxative Crazy Water Crystals was the first product thus advertised on the Opry.

Almost inevitably, overflow crowds forced a move once again. On June 13, 1936, the show moved to the Dixie Tabernacle on Fatherland Street in East Nashville. Though it was drafty as a barn (which it resembled) and had rude wooden benches for seats and sawdust on the floor, the audience didn't mind. The Dixie

Tabernacle seated 3,500 and every seat was filled that first June night.

Judge Hay would experience the first of several mysterious protracted illnesses in December of 1936 which would keep him from the Opry and allow even more control of the show to pass into Harry Stone's hands. Though Hay resumed announcing at the Opry in March 1938, by then David Stone, a WSM announcer and Harry's brother, had assumed his duties in booking acts through the Artists Service Bureau. The Solemn Old Judge would remain the Opry's favorite master of ceremonies for many years, but the Opry's founder had become little more than a figurehead.

★ THE NATIONAL BARN DANCE

Without doubt the Grand Ole Opry was a hit. But it wasn't the most popular country radio show. That honor went to the WLS Barn Dance. Even without the ingenious

Judge Hay, the show continued to thrive. Initially the show emphasized a mellower kind of old-time music than the Opry, with trained singers like Grace Wilson and harmonizers Ford & Glenn sounding more urbane than down-home.

One of the Barn Dance's most popular performers of the late twenties was Bradley Kincaid. Raised in the Kentucky farm town of Lancaster, nestled in the foothills of the Cumberlands, Kincaid had learned from his parents dozens of old folk songs, many of them centuries old. He received his first guitar as a boy when his father traded a foxhound for it. Becoming a regular cast member in 1926 he delivered mournful folk songs in a smooth, pleading tenor, backed with his strumming on the acoustic guitar. Some 2,000 cards and letters a week deluged the station, clamoring for more old songs like "Barbara Allen," "The Fatal Wedding," and "Fair Ellen" from the "Kentucky Mountain Boy and His Houn' Dog Guitar." In fact, the tragic Elizabethan-

The 1936 National Barn Dance cast, which included Lulu Belle & Scotty, Patsy Montana, Red Foley, Pat Buttram, and Little George Gobel.

era tale of "Barbara Allen" proved so popular that Kincaid sang it for nearly every WLS Barn Dance broadcast for five years.

Performing at theaters and schools, Kincaid made $150 to $500 per appearance. Listeners often asked for copies of the songs. In 1928 he obliged his fans by printing up a songbook of these requests to sell on the air. Priced at 50¢ and titled *My Favorite Mountain Ballads and Old-Time Songs,* the songbook sold out its initial print-run of 10,000 within a week. During Kincaid's tenure at WLS, that songbook eventually sold 100,000 copies in six different printings, and over the next few years Kincaid would publish a total of thirteen different songbooks to sell on the air. Coupled with his personal appearances, these staked him to a small fortune by the time he graduated from college in June 1928. Though Kincaid would record for a number of labels, he probably reached far more listeners through radio. Leaving WLS in 1931, he would go on to work on nearly every major barn dance in America. Next to the Carter Family, he probably did more than any other old-time act to preserve and popularize ancient British folk songs.

While Kincaid was charming millions of American listeners each Saturday, WLS was undergoing an expansion program of its own. On October 1, 1928, the nation's oldest farm paper, *The Prairie Farmer,* purchased a controlling interest in the station from Sears. The

A major star at WLS from 1926 to 1931, Bradley Kincaid preserved and popularized old folk songs like "Barbara Allen" and "The Fatal Wedding." He came to the Opry in 1944.

following year, station offices moved from the Sherman Hotel to *The Prairie Farmer*'s new Studio A on West Washington Boulevard in Chicago. The new location allowed for a studio audience of 200, double the number that could be accommodated at the hotel. Just as at the Opry, the demand quickly exceeded the studio capacity. When the requests for free tickets had backed up to six months' worth of shows, the WLS management began renting the 1,200-seat Eighth Street Theater in Chicago, holding two shows each Saturday night and charging 50¢ admission for adults, 25¢ for children. The Barn Dance moved there on March 19, 1932, and stayed for the next twenty-five years.

In September 1933 the NBC Blue Network picked up a full hour of the WLS Barn Dance for broadcast over eighteen stations, and about a year later the network had expanded to thirty stations coast to coast. Sponsored by Alka Seltzer, the show became known, quite rightly, as the National Barn Dance. In 1934 the Barn Dance reported receiving over 1 million fan letters. They repeated the feat the following year.

Though Bradley Kincaid had left WLS by then, the National Barn Dance cast still could boast some of the top talent in the hillbilly field. The Barn Dance's "Hayloft Sweethearts," the husband-and-wife team of Lulu Belle and Scotty Wiseman, charmed audiences with Lulu Belle's sassy, gum-chewing antics and Scotty's shy but always winning responses. To give some idea of their enormous popularity at the time, Lulu Belle topped a 1936 readers' poll in *Radio Digest* for the title "Radio Queen of America." Romantic songs like "Have I Told You Lately That I Love You" and "Remember Me When the Candle Lights Are Gleaming" and novelties like "Does the Spearmint Lose Its Flavor on the Bedpost Overnight" were some of their enduring hits.

★ GENE AUTRY AND THE COWBOY SOUND

The National Barn Dance's most influential performer broke into the music business, as so many young men did in those days, imitating Jimmie Rodgers. But by 1933 Gene Autry had begun to establish his own style, and it wouldn't be very long before thousands of hopefuls were emulating him.

Orvon Gene Autry could not have had a better background for his eventual career. Born in Texas, the son of a horse trader and livestock dealer, he grew up on an Oklahoma ranch. But he was captivated by movies and song, and by age ten he was already working as an usher in the local movie house. Two years later he bought his first guitar from a Sears mail-order catalog for $12. It was a foreshadowing of things to come. After graduation from high school he took a job with the St. Louis & Frisco railroad as a telegrapher. As he was strumming his guitar and softly singing in the railway office one night, a telegraph customer passing through town took notice and even joined in singing. The stranger turned

Gene Autry, the first big singing cowboy star, as he appeared in the early 1930s when he was still at WLS in Chicago.

Gene Autry's Cowboy Code

Part of what made Gene Autry so popular with young and old alike was that he stood for more than mere entertainment. Gene Autry stood for what was right. And he made millions of youngsters in the 1930s and 1940s proud to be Americans. Autry was never wishy-washy. He spelled out for his fans his ethics in his famous "Cowboy Code," a sort of western Ten Commandments:

1. A cowboy never takes unfair advantage—even of an enemy.
2. A cowboy never goes back on his word.
3. A cowboy always tells the truth.
4. A cowboy is kind to children, elderly people, and animals.
5. A cowboy does not possess racially or religiously intolerant ideas.
6. A cowboy helps people in distress.
7. A cowboy is a good worker.
8. A cowboy is clean about his person, and in thought, word, and deed.
9. A cowboy respects women, parents, and his nation's laws.
10. A cowboy is a patriot.

out to be famous humorist Will Rogers, and he encouraged young Gene to go to New York and try his luck as a recording star. With that push Autry headed off to New York. Though he failed to land a recording contract on his first foray to the concrete canyons of Manhattan, Autry didn't give up. He went back to Oklahoma and brushed up on his act at Tulsa's KVOO before returning to New York.

The year was 1929, and by this time Jimmie Rodgers was one of the hottest singing sensations around. Like so many others his age, Autry was completely smitten with the Blue Yodeler's style. Imagine his excitement, then, when at the age of twenty-two, he began recording for Rodgers's label, Victor. Years later his recordings would sound so uncannily like those of his idol that RCA Records would accidentally reissue a couple of Autry's tracks instead of the Blue Yodeler's. In April of 1931, he signed a new record-

ing contract with the American Record Corporation (which would be bought out by Columbia in 1938), and he quickly notched a major hit with a sentimental piece of nostalgia called "That Silver Haired Daddy of Mine," a duet with his old boss on the Frisco line, Jimmy Long. When the record sold very well through Sears catalogs, Sears moved to get the young Oklahoman on WLS, initially for a limited thirteen-week engagement. Billed as "Oklahoma's Singing Cowboy," Autry soon had his own WLS show, "Conqueror Record Time," as well as frequent appearances on the Barn Dance. A Gene Autry "Roundup" guitar (just $9.95) for youngsters marketed in Sears catalogs further boosted his public visibility.

The mastermind behind the rise of Gene Autry was a dapper, silver-haired Englishman named Art Satherley, who was the head record scout at the ARC label and Gene Autry's record producer. Forty-two years old in 1931, Satherley had been working in the American record business since 1923 and understood the hillbilly market better than most of his American competitors. It had been his idea to bill Autry as "Oklahoma's Singing Cowboy" at WLS, and it was he who steered Gene Autry toward western songs. Anything to boost his exposure was worth a try, Autry figured. At WLS he was making the princely salary of $35 a week. With his initial recording session of the year in 1933, Autry tried cowboy songs for the first time. In fact, three of the five sides he cut were western numbers. Though he would record several tributes to Jimmie Rodgers hot on the heels of the Blue Yodeler's passing in the summer of 1933, increasingly Autry went western.

Hollywood clinched it for him. The firm that owned his record company also owned a film studio, Republic

Pictures. Thanks again to the persuasive powers of record man Art Satherley, Autry got his break in movies. In the fall of 1934 he appeared in his first film, *In Old Santa Fe*, alongside established singing cowboy star Ken Maynard, who had been making movies since 1924. "I'd never even seen a movie camera," Autry later confided, "and I was scared to death the first couple of days." Autry didn't have to do much—just sing a little (notably his big seller "Silver Haired Daddy"), and by all accounts he did it better than Maynard, who excelled more at roping and riding. Next, Autry was cast in the lead role of the bizarre science fiction–Western serial *The Phantom Empire*, in which he played a cowboy radio entertainer (what a stretch!) who discovers an underground kingdom of evil alien beings. A twelve-part serial like that might have sunk many careers, but audiences immediately took to the smooth-singing, down-to-earth young Oklahoma cowboy. By the following fall, he had left WLS to star (and sing of course) in his own full-length feature, *Tumbling Tumbleweeds*. It was a hit, and Autry's screen cowboy persona took the nation by storm.

His movies were pure formula. From *Tumbling Tumbleweeds* on, he always rode Champion, his clever, trusty steed. Autry also had his loyal, goofy sidekick around for comic relief. Roly-poly, with a croak of a voice, Smiley Burnette played that role to the hilt, as the awkward, well-meaning, ever-present Frog Millhouse. Each plot invariably involved Gene foiling bad guys and helping the downtrodden, with time out for a lighthearted song here or there. Significantly, Autry's pictures usually depicted not a West of days gone by but the modern West of the 1930s and 1940s. The evildoers that Autry confronted might be crooked businessmen, corrupt politicians, even Nazis,

Gene Autry with Art Satherley, the dapper English record producer who first steered him to cowboy songs—which explains the inscription in the photo's upper left corner.

and they often had the benefit of cars and machine guns. It made it all the more satisfying, then, when Autry would beat them with Champion, his six-gun, or—even better—his two fists. The contemporaneous scripting technique gave Autry's movies a kind of immediacy and realism that other Westerns lacked, and Autry underscored it by performing many of his own stunts. Autry further narrowed the distance between himself and his audience by always playing himself. It was a brilliant move. What was the name of the hero in any given Gene Autry movie? Why, Gene Autry, of course.

Through some ninety pictures over the next two decades, Gene Autry epitomized the best in the American character: fairness, honesty, kindness to the weak and needy, two-fisted bravery, all tied up with a catchy, carefree, picturesque song. In spite of a depressed record market, his recordings—"South of the Border," "Mexicali Rose," "Back in the Saddle Again"—sold in the millions. It's also worth noting that Bing Crosby, the most popular singer of the thirties, recorded a number of Autry-style western songs through the thirties and into the forties, including such top hits as "The Last Roundup" (1933), "Empty Saddles" (1936), and "Tumbling Tumbleweeds" (1940).

In 1939 Autry gained his own CBS radio show, "Melody Ranch," sponsored by Wrigley's gum; the show would run for seventeen years. From 1935 until he enlisted in the Army Air Corps in 1942, Gene Autry would regularly show up at the top of Hollywood's box office lists. (In 1940, for example, he placed fourth behind heavyweights Mickey Rooney, Spencer Tracy, and Clark Gable.) Like his early inspiration Jimmie Rodgers, Autry would leave an indelible impression on those who followed.

The singing cowboy was an idea whose time had come—and seemingly occurred to many singers at almost the same time. It was as if a dam had burst. Within the space of a year or two, dozens of western acts hit the airwaves, the record stores, and the silver screen. By the time Autry was embarking on his movie career in the fall of 1934, the Sons of the

Cincinnati, Ohio, would become the most famous of them all, eventually rivaling Gene Autry in popularity.

Today we know Leonard Slye by his marquee name: Roy Rogers. Despite growing up in Cincinnati, he learned how to ride horses at an early age and yearned for a life out West. In 1930, at age eighteen, he and his family moved

after working with several similar groups, Slye joined forces with Bob Nolan and Tim Spencer to form the Pioneer Trio, which eventually became the Sons of the Pioneers. Specializing in creamy harmonies and evocative western songs, the Sons of the Pioneers quickly gained a reputation as the top cowboy group in L.A., debuting on record in 1934 and

Roy Rogers on guitar (center) with his old band, the Sons of the Pioneers in The Man from Music Mountain *(1943).*

Pioneers in Los Angeles had just finished their first sessions for Decca Records, which would yield "Tumbling Tumbleweeds," soon to be the title song for Autry's first starring feature. The ultimate western harmony group, the Sons would provide a training ground over the next two decades for western singers who cycled in and out of the lineup—ace songwriters Bob Nolan and Tim Spencer, Pat Brady, Lloyd Perryman, Ken Curtis (Festus on the TV show "Gunsmoke"). Leonard Slye from

out to California, where he did migrant labor, picking peaches for the Del Monte Company and driving trucks, before stumbling into a music career. At the urging of his sister, he sang on the late-night Los Angeles radio program "Midnight Frolic," which featured amateur talent. There, his smooth, resonant voice got noticed by a local hillbilly group, the Rocky Mountaineers, who had been doing strictly instrumentals. With Len Slye, they gained a handsome, distinctive singer. In 1933,

appearing right alongside Gene Autry in *Tumbling Tumbleweeds* the following year.

The Sons of the Pioneers were riding high in 1937 when a twenty-six-year-old Len Slye looked for a solo career in the movies. He passed an audition at Republic Studios (where Gene Autry was the leading cowboy star), was renamed Dick Weston, and was given a bit part in the studio's next Western. Then, a dispute between Gene Autry and Republic Studios opened the door to stardom. When Autry walked off the studio lot, vowing not to return until his contract was straightened out, Republic plugged Len Slye, again renamed Roy Rogers, into the lead role in the next cowboy picture, *Under Western Stars*. By the time Autry returned to Republic in the fall of 1938, Roy Rogers was heading toward stardom at a gallop. At one point early in his movie career, studio execs expressed concern that Roy's smiling, squinty eyes didn't look quite right. They suggested he use eyedrops to widen them. Luckily, a flood of fan letters—80,000 a month by 1939—convinced the studio to leave well enough alone.

In 1942 advertising for *Ridin' Down the Canyon,* Republic billed Roy Rogers for the first time as "King of the Cowboys." The following year, right after Gene Autry enlisted in the Army Air Corps, the sobriquet became real when Roy slipped past Autry to emerge as the leading western star at the box office, a title he would hold through 1954. (Meanwhile, Roy's golden palomino Trigger challenged Gene Autry's Champion for title of "Smartest Horse in the West.")

In 1944 Dale Evans co-starred with Roy in *The Cowboy and the Senorita*. It was their first of twenty-eight pictures together, and they married on New Year's Eve, 1947. Dale Evans didn't set out to be a cowgirl. "I usually played a reporter or some other kind of smart-alecky girl," she pointed out. "Before I realized what was happening . . . I was being typecast as a western player." Certainly by the time Roy and Dale appeared side by side in the long-running "Roy Rogers Show" Saturday morning NBC-TV series (1951–1964) they had become the epitome of the western hero and heroine.

Dale Evans was not the only cowgirl in the corral. During the thirties, the National Barn Dance could boast the talents of the spunky Patsy Montana, probably the best-known cowgirl star of the decade. Born and raised in

Roy Rogers, who starred in his first Western because Gene Autry was in a contract dispute, then became "King of the Cowboys" when Gene Autry joined the Army Air Corps in 1942.

Arkansas as Ruby Blevins, Patsy Montana had already apprenticed in hillbilly and western music on the West Coast and in Shreveport, Louisiana, by the time she auditioned for the Barn Dance at age twenty-one. Joining the Kentucky Ramblers' string band as the group's vocalist, Montana led the group west—stylistically speaking. Right away, they changed their name to the Prairie Ramblers. Then, in 1935, with their backing, she scored the biggest hit up to that time for a female hillbilly singer with "I Wanna Be a Cowboy's Sweetheart." Contrary to the sound of the title, the million-selling record, driven by a sprightly polka rhythm and punctuated by Patsy's yodels, actually advocated equality out on the range, quite a progressive concept for the time. It was some measure of her stature that in 1940 she rode on-screen with Gene Autry in *Colorado Sunset*.

Fittingly, the first Opry act to capitalize on the cowboy look and to forge a smooth sound to go with it was a Gene Autry protégé. Reared on a farm just north of Green Bay, Wisconsin, the son of second-generation Polish Americans, Julius Frank Kuczynski must have seemed as unlikely a candidate for hillbilly stardom as one can imagine. Though he began playing fiddle as

In 1935, Patsy Montana sold a million copies of her record "I Wanna Be a Cowboy's Sweetheart." It was the biggest hit up to that time for a female hillbilly singer.

a youngster, he switched to accordion at age fourteen. Before long, he was playing waltzes in the Milwaukee area under the adopted name Frank King, in honor of another Polish musician, Wayne King, the then-popular "Waltz King."

Frank's musical career took a dramatic turn, however, in 1934 when Gene Autry—still several months away from a movie career—heard the twenty-year-old accordionist on the radio and hired him for his road band. The road led to Louisville where Autry got the call to Hollywood for his first picture. The deal included room for one sidekick (Smiley Burnette) but didn't include room for a band, so King remained behind in Louisville, where he joined WHAS as a member of the Log Cabin Boys & Girls. King—renamed "Pee Wee" for his five-foot-six-inch height and because there were too many other Franks at WHAS at the time—soon formed his own band, taking a cue from Autry's mellow western sound and sharp cowboy look. By dint of hard touring and a push from Autry's ex-manager Joe Frank, King's Golden West Cowboys ultimately landed at the Grand Ole Opry on June 5, 1937. The popular band proved another coup for Harry

Stone, and another blow to Judge Hay's string band party. Pee Wee King & the Golden West Cowboys were full-time professional musicians and the first to bring musicians' union cards to the Opry. They dressed like professionals too, in flashy western costumes, boots, and hats. With King's accordion and a series of smooth vocalists, they also didn't sound anything like a down-home string band.

Gene Autry and the cowboy singers who came after him showed that rural-looking singers could star in movies and capture the public's fancy. For the most part, though, the songs that the movie cowboys sang were not those of real, working cowboys. Nor were these songs derived from ancient British folk tunes. The actual source for most movie cowboy songs was the professional songwriting establish-

Pee Wee King (seated left) with his first band, the Golden West Cowboys, 1937. An Autry protégé, King helped popularize the western costumes at the Opry.

ment of New York's Tin Pan Alley and later Hollywood. Even if the cowboy songs in Hollywood Westerns weren't usually the genuine, rough-and-ready article, they still often incorporated hillbilly fiddles and the language of rural America.

In addition to a legacy of genuinely popular songs, the movie cowboys left their mark through their distinctive western costumes. Broad-brimmed cowboy hats, embroidered leather boots, and fringed vests carried with them the air of manly authority and romance. Everybody loved cowboys; even President Roosevelt's favorite song was said to be "Home on the Range." Little wonder, then, that many Southern musicians cheerfully exchanged their floppy hats and bib overalls for cowboy garb. It looked sharp—and it didn't elicit snickers. The hillbilly music game would soon be heading uptown—in Nashville, in Texas, on the West Coast—and it was time for a new look to go with the exciting new sounds.

1931—BRADLEY KINCAID LEAVES WLS BARN DANCE; GENE AUTRY JOINS	1932—WLS IN CHICAGO AND WSM IN NASHVILLE ORGANIZE BOOKING BUREAUS TO TAKE THEIR ACTS ON THE ROAD	CHICAGO'S EIGHTH STREET THEATER, SEATING 1,200	SEPTEMBER 30, 1933— WLS BARN DANCE AIRS ON NBC BLUE NETWORK	AUGUST 8, 1934—THE SONS OF THE PIONEERS, FEATURING LEN SLYE, A.K.A. ROY ROGERS, MAKE THEIR FIRST RECORD, "TUMBLING TUMBLEWEEDS," IN LOS ANGELES	AUGUST 16, 1935— PATSY MONTANA RECORDS "I WANNA BE A COWBOY'S SWEETHEART" IN NEW YORK, THE FIRST MILLION-SELLER BY A FEMALE COUNTRY SINGER
1932—U.S. RECORD SALES PLUNGE TO 6 MILLION	MARCH 19, 1932—WLS BARN DANCE MOVES TO	MAY 26, 1933—JIMMIE RODGERS DIES IN NEW YORK CITY AT AGE THIRTY-FIVE	1934—GENE AUTRY'S FIRST MOVIE APPEARANCE, UPSTAGING KEN MAYNARD IN *OLD SANTA FE*		

Jimmie Davis parlayed a string of hit records into a political career that culminated in the governorship of Louisiana.

Country Diversifies

NEW STYLES FOR A NEW ERA

Increasingly, string bands and age-old folk songs were giving way to new forms of hillbilly music. Cross-pollinated by radio and records, hillbilly music was blooming in a dazzling variety of sounds and styles. From the moment Gene Autry hit the silver screen, cowboy music and cowboy clothes were all the rage. Other styles also emerged as America pulled itself out of the Depression and toward responsibilities overseas. By the beginning of the Second World War, country music would begin to show the first evidence of vibrant new sounds like western swing, honky-tonk, and bluegrass. It would also show its clout in a series of remarkable political campaigns from Texas to Tennessee.

★ THE SINGING GOVERNOR

Raised in a sharecropper's two-room shack that he shared with ten siblings, his parents, and his grandparents, Jimmie Davis pulled himself up out of his parents' insular backwoods community with a college education and a subsequent master's degree. Almost simultaneously, he managed to launch careers in Louisiana politics and country music. In 1928, after a year spent teaching at a women's college, he took a job as clerk of Shreveport's Criminal Court. In September of the following year, the twenty-seven-year-old civil servant recorded for RCA Victor. Like Gene Autry (who would make his first records for the same label a month after Davis), Jimmie Davis was completely under the spell of America's biggest hillbilly star of the time, Jimmie Rodgers. For the

four years he recorded for RCA Victor, Davis's records amounted to little more than pale imitations of the Blue Yodeler. But also like Autry, Davis was a quick learner and an adaptable singer and he toned down the bluesy Rodgers honk in his voice and developed a softer, crooning style of his own.

His new sound coincided with a move to the two-month-old Decca label in September 1934. In May 1935 Davis's fourth release for Decca Records, "Nobody's Darling but Mine," took off. With the resulting royalties, he settled his college debts, bought a farm, and married. By April of 1938 Davis had clearly arrived when *Collier's Magazine* declared, "The big stars now are Jimmie Davis, clerk of criminal court in Shreveport, Louisiana, and Gene Autry, the singing cowboy of the movies." With the royalties and newfound celebrity from his next big hit, "It Makes No Difference Now," released that November, Davis was in position to advance his political career yet again. Campaigning with his band in tow in 1938, he was elected Shreveport's commissioner of public safety, in charge of the city's fire and police departments.

Two years later—on Monday, February 5, 1940, in Chicago—Davis cut the song that would be his calling card for the remainder of his career. Released a month later, "You Are My Sunshine" sold over a million copies in America. The record even crossed the Atlantic to England, where King George VI declared that the breezy, clarinet-embroidered number was his favorite song. Davis had done so well with "It Makes No Difference Now" and "You Are My Sunshine" that both were covered by Gene Autry and Bing Crosby. In addition to a

JUNE 5, 1937—PEE WEE KING & THE GOLDEN WEST COWBOYS JOIN THE OPRY

FALL 1937—ROY ACUFF & THE CRAZY TENNESSEANS TOUR WITH THE DELMORE BROTHERS

FEBRUARY 5, 1938—ROY ACUFF'S FIRST APPEARANCE ON THE OPRY

JULY 1939—THE OPRY MOVES TO THE WAR MEMORIAL AUDITORIUM, SEATING 2,200; AN ADMISSION FEE OF A QUARTER IS INSTITUTED

OCTOBER 14, 1939—OPRY APPEARS ON NBC RADIO NETWORK WITH THE HALF-HOUR "PRINCE ALBERT SHOW," SPONSORED BY R. J. REYNOLDS TOBACCO

OCTOBER 28, 1939—BILL MONROE JOINS THE OPRY

JUNE 28, 1940—THE MOVIE GRAND OLE OPRY PREMIERES IN NASHVILLE

NOVEMBER 1940—MINNIE PEARL JOINS THE OPRY

JANUARY 16, 1943—ERNEST TUBB JOINS THE OPRY

handsome income and Hollywood movie appearances, Davis's hits also propelled him into the highest office in his home state. In March 1944, after campaigning again with his five-piece band, he was elected governor of Louisiana by a margin of 37,000 votes.

★ THE KING OF WESTERN SWING

Davis's astonishing success with a handful of songs certainly points to the power that hillbilly music had gained through the 1930s. But Davis's political triumphs were by no means unprecedented. Down in Texas, a hillbilly impresario by the name of Pappy O'Daniel twice won his state's gubernatorial elections (in 1938 and in 1940) using little more than hillbilly songs as his platform. The magazine *Rural Radio* reported that when radio listeners urged him to run for his first governor's race, O'Daniel stated: "I am no politician—merely a plain citizen of humble birth. What would you do in my case?" In reply he received 54,900 letters begging him to run. In 1941, he defeated a young Lyndon Johnson for a seat in the U.S. Senate.

It was about ten years earlier that O'Daniel, then in his early forties, first got involved with hillbilly musicians, not so much out of a fondness for the music as for the hold it had on listeners. As the sales manager of the Burrus Mill & Elevator Company in Fort Worth, he had hired on a four-man Texas string band to advertise Burrus Mill's Light Crust Flour over Fort Worth's WBAP in January 1931. That band, soon dubbed the Light Crust Doughboys, convinced Pappy O'Daniel of hillbilly music's power. Soon he was reading poetry while the

band played behind him, even venturing to sing once in a while. O'Daniel was cagey, all right. But the leader of the Light Crust Doughboys was a man whose vision far outstripped that of O'Daniel. Long after O'Daniel's political accomplishments became yesterday's news, Bob Wills would be remembered.

When Bob Wills landed his string band on WBAP in 1931, he was not quite twenty-six years old and was itching to get something going with music. Already in his short life, he had farmed, worked in construction, sold insurance, tried preaching and barbering, and performed in a medicine show in travels around his native Texas and New Mexico. Wills found he liked show business the best, so he set off with his fiddle and Herman Arnspiger, a guitarist from the medicine show, to set hillbilly music on its ear.

Bob Wills knew old-time fiddle breakdowns backwards and forwards. He had grown up in a family full of fiddlers; as a matter of fact, his father had defeated Eck Robertson in

Pappy O'Daniel (standing) & the Light Crust Doughboys, October 1933. Although Milton Brown and Bob Wills had left his band by the time of this photo (Wills just two months before), O'Daniel did all right: five years later he was governor of Texas.

Bob Wills (standing, with fiddle) combined fiddle tunes and big-band arrangements to arrive at his popular western-swing sound.

fiddle contests on more than one occasion. But young Bob had also absorbed much more. As a youth, he had heard blues from black migrant workers; while working in New Mexico, he had played alongside Mexican musicians in dance bands. Like so many musicians coming of age in the 1920s and 1930s, the new sounds on radio and records enthralled him. During the mid-1920s, when he was in his late teens, he had once ridden fifty miles on

horseback to see the "Empress of the Blues," Bessie Smith. Years later he described the experience as "the greatest thing I ever heard."

The Wills Fiddle Band (in truth, just Wills and Arnspiger, but then Wills always thought big) took up residence in Fort Worth, playing at a dance hall whose customers included Bonnie and Clyde. Wills made his first big connection playing one night in 1931 at a schoolhouse on the outskirts of Fort Worth. Years later Wills recalled that a man "dressed like he just walked off a movie screen" came up to the bandstand between songs and asked to sing a number. Wills asked if the dapper fellow, a cigar salesman named Milton Brown, knew W. C. Handy's "St. Louis Blues." Did he ever! Wills was impressed. Weeks later, when Brown was no longer selling cigars, Wills hired him and eventually Brown's teenaged brother Derwood as well.

By the time Wills signed on with Pappy O'Daniel and WBAP, his little quartet had

begun imaginatively expanding on old-time fiddling and string-band music. Their polished best they saved for their daily radio broadcast, while in the evening the band played local dances to make extra money. In those days, hot jazz, the music of Louis Armstrong, was the thing among the young, modern folks of Fort Worth. So the Light Crust Doughboys—Wills on fiddle and vocals, Arnspiger on guitar, Milton Brown on lead vocals, and Milton's brother Derwood on second guitar—obliged, jazzing up their string-band music to the hilt. As the string band jammed and improvised, as Milton Brown and Wills crooned and scatted, the seeds of hot string music and, ultimately, western swing were sown. Meanwhile, the Light Crust Doughboys gained such a loyal following that O'Daniel moved the show to prime time—high noon.

Pappy O'Daniel learned how to exploit music effectively, but he never really understood musicians. From the beginning, the ebullient Wills had a habit of tossing high-pitched vocal commentary into the band's numbers, his most common interjection being a cartoony falsetto AH-*haaa!* At one point, O'Daniel forbade Wills to dispense this sort of running commentary. "We got better than 250,000 letters wanting to know what become of the little animal that was on the show," Wills said years later. O'Daniel relented in this case but he couldn't stop interfering. He ordered the band to rehearse eight hours a day. He fired Arnspiger, replacing him with another guitarist. The last straw for Milton Brown was the edict prohibiting the band from playing dances at night. Brown, who needed the money, quit on the spot, taking his brother Derwood with him to form his own band, Milton Brown & His Musical Brownies, in September 1932. Almost a year later, O'Daniel fired Wills, figuring the ol' Pappy knew a little bit about the hillbilly business himself by then.

Wills soon rustled up radio work in Waco, then in Oklahoma City, and finally in Tulsa, by February 1934. At Tulsa's 25,000-watt KVOO, Bob Wills & His Texas Playboys found a home for the next nine years, broadcasting a popular noontime show. All along the way, Wills drew musicians to him by sheer force of personality. One night when he heard Smokey Dacus playing drums in a hotel dance band, he offered the musician a job. "What the hell do you want with a drummer in a fiddle band?" asked a skeptical Dacus. Said Wills: "I want to play your kind of music and my kind of music—put it together and make it swing."

Dacus came on board in 1935. It was an audacious idea. Hillbilly bands—string bands, whatever you called them—simply didn't have drums in 1935. But Bob Wills earned his bread and butter keeping people dancing, and drums were the next logical step. After he got drums, Wills added more to his musical palette. He brought in eighteen-year-old Leon

Milton Brown (at the mike in this 1935 photo) initially made a bigger splash than Bob Wills with western swing music. But his promising career ended prematurely with his death in a 1936 auto crash.

McAuliffe to handle electrified steel guitar and Jesse Ashlock to play fiddle swing-style. He added a horn section with trumpet, saxophone, and trombone. Arriving in Tulsa with a fairly conventional six-piece string band, Wills eventually built up to a sixteen-piece orchestra, capable of an authentic fiddle breakdown one moment and full-tilt big-band swing the next.

Back in Fort Worth, Wills's old pal Milton Brown had initially made a bigger splash with hot string band music. At one point before Wills left O'Daniel and the Burrus Mill, Brown even invited Wills to join His Musical Brownies. Though they remained the best of friends, Wills had his own ideas about hot string band music. Wills, at least in the beginning, preferred to jazz up older tunes while Brown tackled the hot jazz and blues of the day string-band-style. Although it sounds like merely a matter of semantics, there really was an audible difference between the two outfits.

In fact, Milton Brown & His Musical Brownies are generally acknowledged by historians to have been the first band to record western swing, which they did for Bluebird Records in April 1934. The band scored another first in early 1935 when the Brownies recorded with steel guitarist Bob Dunn using his newly electrified steel guitar to coax trumpet-like phrases onto wax. Within months, bands across the Southwest figured out ways to plug in as well. Today Milton Brown might have been remembered in the same breath as Wills, were it not for an untimely automobile accident one night after a dance. Brown died five days afterward, on April 18, 1936; he was thirty-two.

After Milton Brown's passing, two of his Musical Brownies—steel man Bob Dunn and fiddler Cliff Bruner—carried on with their own successful bands in Houston. Their brand of hillbilly music evolved rapidly to fit the times. Prohibition had been repealed in

1933 and bars reopened for a nighttime crowd. Jukeboxes began appearing in bars, restaurants, and truck stops around 1935, spreading the good-time dance music. For a nickel you could hear six songs. Even by Depression standards that was a bargain. By 1940 some 300,000 jukeboxes were spinning tunes nationwide.

The demand for jukebox music affected the hillbilly music business. In a little more than a decade after hillbilly music had begun to be recorded, profound changes were taking place in the music. Nowhere were the changes more pronounced, nor happening more rapidly, than in the little taverns and roadhouses of the Southwest—the honky-tonks—where a new brand of hillbilly music grew out of the experiments of Bob Wills and his contemporaries. Sentimental old folk songs of mother and home would no longer do in the loud, dark honky-tonks. New songs that acknowledged carousing and playing around—and paying for those sins—better reflected the tenor of the times.

★ THE TEXAS TROUBADOUR

One Sunday afternoon in 1935, as he was listening to some Jimmie Rodgers records, it suddenly occurred to Texas musician Ernest Tubb that his idol had been a resident of San Antonio when he died just two years previously. Tubb checked a city directory, and—sure enough—there was a phone number for Carrie Rodgers. Putting his courage to the sticking place, Tubb dialed the number and nervously poured out the full measure of his admiration for Carrie Rodgers's departed husband, and stammered a request for an autographed photo. Many fans had contacted Carrie Rodgers since the passing of America's Blue Yodeler, but something about the sincerity of this twenty-one-year-old aspiring musician touched her. A week later she invited Ernest Tubb to her house—Jimmie's house!—to pick up the photo and lingered over scrapbooks with him. He told her about the fifteen-minute radio show he did (for free) twice a week at 5:30 A.M. on little 250-watt KONO. A couple of months later, out of the blue, Carrie Rodgers called Tubb. She'd been listening to his show. She wanted to help him.

Not many hillbilly musicians during the Depression could claim the support of a wealthy patron. Carrie Rodgers arranged a recording session in October 1936 with Jimmie's old company, RCA Victor. She persuaded her sister, Elsie McWilliams, who used to write for Jimmie, to provide new songs for Ernest. She even lent Ernest her car to get to the afternoon recording session at San Antonio's Texas Hotel. The largesse of Carrie Rodgers seemingly knew no bounds. Afterward, she arranged for Tubb's first publicity pictures. When he didn't have a suit, she lent him her husband's tuxedo (because the pants didn't fit, he was photographed from the waist up). She gave him one of Jimmie's personalized guitars. She helped arrange his first tour, making sure that the theaters billed the newcomer properly: "Mrs. Jimmie Rodgers Presents Ernest Tubb Playing Jimmie Rodgers on Guitar."

As it turned out, Tubb could play Jimmie Rodgers very well, right down to the guitar runs and the yodels. Perhaps too well. His imitative recordings didn't sell, and his tour just

Ernest Tubb received more than inspiration from Jimmie Rodgers; he also had use of the Blue Yodeler's guitar.

Three Ernest Tubb song-books, 1941–43. On the cover of No. 1, he's wearing the tuxedo jacket of his hero, Jimmie Rodgers.

broke even. Despite the grand send-off, it would take Tubb four years of climbing the ladder of radio stations in Texas before he simply learned the importance of being Ernest. It was adversity that taught him best: When a botched tonsillectomy robbed him of his falsetto and his ability to yodel, Tubb had to change his style and work even harder on his songwriting. Finally in November 1940, he landed his first full-time radio job at Fort Worth's 5,000-watt KGKO. It paid $20 a week, and the twenty-six-year-old singer needed every penny of it to support his wife and two small children. A new song written about his wife ("Blue Eyed Elaine") and recorded for the Decca company got him the spot; after much cajoling, Universal Mills, makers of Gold Medal Flour, agreed to sponsor him for $75 a week on the condition that he would put in a half-day working in the mill after his early-morning broadcast.

One day in early 1941 while his wife and children were out of town, Tubb paced the floor of his small second-floor apartment and got an idea for a song. In short order (it came so quickly, he later said, "I could hardly get the words down on paper"), he turned his longing for his family into a song that would make his career.

From the start, Tubb felt that "Walking the Floor over You" was one of his strongest writing efforts to date. But what made the song stand out in its day was its sound on record. As luck would have it, a Fort Worth jukebox operator pointed out to Tubb that records with acoustic guitars didn't stand a chance in loud taverns when pitted against the big-band sounds of Bob Wills. Tubb took the hint and brought along the staff guitarist from WBAP for his April 26, 1941, Dallas session. Tubb's lazy, wobbly baritone came across carefree and sunny, in synch with the bouncy, jazzy electric guitar of Smitty Smith. "Aww, do it purty, son," Tubb drawled just before a horn-like guitar solo; Smitty did and the record did.

"Walking the Floor over You" changed Ernest Tubb's life. From the beginning he knew he had a winner. Record producer Dave Kapp had wanted to release another song from Tubb as a single. But Tubb pleaded: "Mr. Kapp, do me a favor and release 'Walking the Floor over You' next. I'll never ask for another favor." In its first year out the record sold 400,000 copies and eventually sold over a million. Bing Crosby gave the record his seal of approval: He recorded it himself.

Cards and letters addressed to "The Gold Chain Troubadour" poured into little KGKO at a rate of 10,000 a week. Within a year of the fall release of "Walking the Floor," Tubb had starred in two Hollywood Westerns for Columbia Pictures and received an invitation to guest at the Grand Ole Opry. With offers coming in from Hollywood and Nashville, Tubb began to realize that he had made it. Even so, the night of his first Opry appearance in December 1942, Tubb was so nervous he could hardly remember any of it afterward. But others confirmed that the crowd called him—and Pee Wee King's band, who accompanied him—back for three encores of "Walking the Floor." The Opry was suitably impressed. The following month, on January 16, about three weeks shy of his twenty-ninth birthday, Ernest Tubb joined the Grand Ole Opry cast, expanding the show's style and regional flavor to include his Texas honky-tonk.

Judge Hay liked Ernest Tubb just fine, calling him "a very courteous and generous young man, a straight shooter and a mighty fine friend to have." And how could a show-man like Hay resist Tubb's ever-ready reply for an applauding audience: the words THANK YOU painted in big block letters on the back of his guitar, which Tubb would flip around and flash to the audience along with his big, winning smile. But the Solemn Old Judge reportedly just couldn't cotton to Tubb's electric guitar sound, though he did allow in a press release that "his voice carries a Texas drawl and a vibrant note which goes over in a big way with those who love the music which is close to the soil."

★ ACUFF ARRIVES

Judge Hay preferred his music even closer to the soil. The old-time string band sound of Roy Acuff from May-nardville, Tennessee, was certainly more to his purist taste. Initially, for some unknown reason, Judge Hay wasn't too fond of Acuff—at least not interested enough to hire the young musician whose fondest wish was Opry membership. Acuff had estab-lished himself as a performer at Knox-ville's WROL in 1934 when he began regularly making the 200-mile trip to Nashville to beg Judge Hay for an op-portunity to join the Opry. Acuff and his Crazy Tennesseans band played good old down-home string-band music. Yet over and over Hay would simply say that the show al-ready had enough acts. But Acuff, who had settled on music as a career rather late in life, was determined to see it through.

Roy Claxton Acuff had been a standout athlete at Knoxville's Central High School, where he earned twelve varsity letters in foot-ball, basketball, and baseball. Right up through his twenties, he harbored hopes of becoming a professional baseball player. To

make ends meet, he took temporary jobs working construction, on assembly lines, and on the Louisville & Nashville railroad, just so he could play semi-pro baseball in the sum-mers. In the spring of 1929 at the age of

Roy Acuff, looking the part of a matinee idol in this 1940s photo, starred in eight feature films between 1940 and 1949.

twenty-five, Acuff finally managed a tryout for scouts from the New York Yankees, only to fall unconscious in the field from sunstroke. The Yankees passed on him. With his dreams of ballplaying in ruins, Acuff suffered a nervous breakdown, coinciding

with the country's own deep Depression. Licking his wounds at his parents' house, he gradually turned to music as an alternative. His father gave him tips on playing the fiddle and gave Roy a $12 model to practice on. Roy studied the records of Fiddlin' John Carson and Gid Tanner over and over on the family Victrola, practicing on that $12 fiddle.

In the summer of 1932 a neighbor who owned a traveling medicine show, Doc Hauer, heard some potential in Roy's playing and hired him. Helping Doc Hauer sell patent elixirs and nostrums, which supposedly cured everything from constipation to corns, taught Acuff in-valuable lessons on how to sell himself as an entertainer. In trips to Appalachian towns throughout south-west Virginia and east Tennessee, Acuff performed in comic skits, dressing sometimes as a little girl, an old woman, or a black man. He fiddled. He did yo-yo tricks. He balanced his fid-dle bow upright on his chin. And during the year he spent with the show, he learned to project his voice without the aid of a micro-phone so that it "would reach people standing as far as you could see out there into the night."

Emboldened by his experi-ence with Doc Hauer, Acuff hired his own band, the Crazy Ten-nesseans, and cracked Knoxville radio, first at WROL in 1934 and then at WNOX, before returning to WROL for a regular noontime show. While in Knoxville he heard a gospel group called the Black Shirts singing an unusual hymn, "The

Great Speckled Bird." Its peculiar, allegorical lyrics derived from the biblical passage Jeremiah 12:9 ("Mine heritage is unto me as a speckled bird, the birds round about are against her"), in which the Christian church is compared to a bird with unique plumage, assailed by its enemies.

Completely taken with the song, Acuff was thrilled to hear that the gospel act was leaving Knoxville. He asked if he could sing the song and paid one of the Black Shirts to copy down the lyrics. The tune he sang it with was virtually identical to the Carter Family's "I'm Thinking Tonight of My Blue Eyes," which had ancient British beginnings. Singing the strange metaphorical lyrics plainly and with utter conviction, Acuff soon made the song his own, regardless of who wrote it.

That number proved to be the anchor that finally hooked Acuff to the radio show of his dreams, the Grand Ole Opry. Having heard that Pee Wee King's Golden West Cowboys had joined the Opry from faraway Louisville (and, if he only knew, Wisconsin), Acuff contacted King's manager, J. L. Frank, about getting on the Opry. Frank talked to David Stone (Harry's brother and the new head of the Artists Service Bureau) and persuaded him to give Roy Acuff & His Crazy Tennesseans an audition. Although Stone was no more impressed with Acuff than Judge Hay had been, he needed another act, at least temporarily, and the Delmore Brothers, whom Acuff had befriended months earlier, wanted Acuff's group to join their road show. A bargain was struck. The Crazy Tennesseans did some touring with the Delmores during the fall of 1937 and performed a few times on WSM.

Acuff and his band finally received an invitation to perform a guest spot on February 5, 1938. When the time came, Acuff led his band through a fiddle tune and then launched into "The Great Speckled Bird." At one point Acuff was so nervous that for a moment he forgot the words. He sold the song nevertheless and was called back for several encores. The following week mail began streaming in. By midweek when it got to the point that letters addressed to Acuff were filling up baskets, David Stone wired Acuff to join the show for February 19. At the age of thirty-four, Roy Acuff had found the job of a lifetime.

Ever since he had taken over management of the Opry, Harry Stone had been salting the show's cast with professional performers who had star quality. Roy Acuff fit the bill perfectly. He and his band (renamed the more

Roy Acuff (calling the tune on the fiddle) as he and his band appeared just before they joined the Opry in 1938.

Onstage at the Opry in the forties: Roy Acuff on fiddle with Smoky Mountain Boys Lonnie "Pap" Wilson on guitar, Jimmy Riddle on accordion, and Bashful Brother Oswald on dobro.

dignified Smoky Mountain Boys at Judge Hay's suggestion) could play fiddle breakdowns, or Roy could step out in the spotlight and deliver an impassioned rendition of "The Great Speckled Bird." Uncle Dave Macon was still the program's undisputed No. 1 star, but Acuff brought a new energy to singing at the Opry. Acuff poured himself body and soul into his songs, letting his emotions carry him like a method actor. "I like to get into the mood of a song," Acuff explained. "If you

don't feel it, you can't sing it. You can't fool a person out there. I've cried onstage, not just for that audience, but I've cried because I wanted to cry, because it was hurting."

Not only did Acuff deliver a song with sincerity, he also took care to project his voice as he had with Doc Hauer's medicine show—powerfully and clearly enough to be heard in the back row. "I didn't realize how different my singing was from the rest until mail started coming in," Acuff recalled. "The letters I got would mention how clear I was coming through and how distinct my voice was and how they could understand my words."

Entirely unbeknownst to Acuff, forces behind the scenes were at work that would soon

offer him a truly national stage. In January of 1939 the New York advertising firm of William Esty & Company convinced the R. J. Reynolds Tobacco Company to sponsor a half hour of the Opry to promote its Prince Albert Smoking Tobacco ("The National Joy Smoke"). The clout of a major sponsor like R. J. Reynolds helped convince the NBC network to pick up the show for broadcast, from 8:30 to 9:00 P.M. Central Time.

On October 14, 1939, six weeks after Hitler's invasion of Poland touched off the firestorm that would become World War II, NBC broadcast the first "Prince Albert Show." Judge Hay served as the colorful master of ceremonies. Also on hand for that

Bill Monroe at WSM in the early forties. Note that he's holding a guitar instead of his usual mandolin.

twenty-six stations, it ensured that the Opry—and Acuff—could be heard from the Southeastern Seaboard all the way to Arizona.

★ THE FATHER OF BLUEGRASS

Even as Roy Acuff was emerging as the vocal star in his Knoxville string band, another Opry newcomer was remaking the string-band tradition in his own image. Bill Monroe debuted on the Grand Ole Opry on October 28, 1939, two weeks after the network hookup. At age twenty-eight Monroe had over a decade of music-making experience behind him. Like Acuff, he had already made records before auditioning for WSM. In contrast to Acuff, the records that Bill and his brother Charlie Monroe made had sold fairly well, particularly the chilling gospel side "What Would You Give in Exchange for Your Soul." But the inevitable friction that comes between ambitious brothers pulled the harmony act apart

in early 1938 after popular stints on radio stations throughout the Midwest and Southeast. Charlie Monroe headed to Knoxville and formed the Kentucky Partners. Bill lit out west for Little Rock, Arkansas, then headed to Atlanta, and finally Greenville, North Carolina, before bringing his Blue Grass Boys band to WSM.

It was a confident, laconic young man who led his quartet up to the National Life's fifth-floor studios to audition for Judge Hay and the brothers Stone one morning in October 1939. Steadying his broad shoulders and barrel chest, Monroe looked the auditioners straight in the eye and told them that his band—named the Blue Grass Boys after his native state of Kentucky—would do folk music "the way she should be sung and played." With that, Monroe kicked his band into breakneck versions of the Carter Family's "Foggy Mountain Top" and Jimmie

inaugural half hour were Uncle Dave Macon, singer Ford Rush, and Roy Acuff & the Smoky Mountain Boys. Acuff became a regular headline attraction on the "Prince Albert Show," a testament to his growing popularity in his year and nine months with the show. Though that first network broadcast of the Opry was initially limited to a regional network of

Bill Monroe & His Blue Grass Boys, ca. 1940: bassist Bill Wesbrooks, fiddler Tommy Magness, Monroe, and guitarist Clyde Moody.

The Opry cast at the War Memorial Auditorium, the show's home from July 1939 until June 1943.

Rodgers's "Muleskinner Blues." This was string band music but with a difference. Monroe made the tempos faster, he sang higher, and he demanded that each of his band members match his dazzling solos on the mandolin. After finishing up with the fiddle breakdown "Fire on the Mountain," Monroe was told in no uncertain terms that he had a job at the Opry for as long as he wanted it.

That Saturday, Bill Monroe and his band —fiddler Art Wooten, bassist Amos Garen, and guitarist-singer Cleo Davis plowed the audience flat with their supercharged, sky-high rendition of "Muleskinner Blues." The band came back three times for encores. It was the beginning of a long and beautiful friendship between Bill Monroe and the Opry, one that would last well into the nineties.

Bill Monroe & His Blue Grass Boys made their Grand Ole Opry debut in the plush confines of Nashville's War Memorial Auditorium. The handsome granite-and-marble edifice, located just across the street from the National Life Building, had been the new home of the Opry since that July. Because of complaints from East Nashville residents about the hullabaloo surrounding the Dixie Tabernacle every Saturday night, Harry Stone had gone looking for yet another home for the Opry. He went all the way to the governor to gain admittance to the 2,200-seat facility. To control the crowds, Stone authorized the Opry to charge admission: 25¢ for adults, 9¢ for children. Crowds remained just as thick, all the same.

A little over a year after Bill Monroe arrived at the Opry, a young actress joined the show to do a rural comedy act. She showed promise right from the start, but few would have predicted the enormous contribution that Minnie Pearl would make to the Opry over the next fifty years. She was born Sarah Ophelia Colley in Centerville, a quiet Tennessee town of about 500 souls, located fifty miles southwest of Nashville, a good two-hour drive in the days before interstate highways. Her parents were educated, cultured people: her father a prosperous lumberman, her mother a civic leader. They encouraged young Ophelia and her four older sisters to read the classics. Although Mr. Colley dearly loved listening to the Grand Ole Opry, his sophisticated daughters left him to it on Saturday nights.

Since Ophelia showed a flair for drama, her parents enrolled her in Nashville's elite finishing school for young ladies, Ward-Belmont College. There she studied speech and drama for two years. Upon completing her studies in 1932, she returned to Centerville. Despite dreams of Broadway stardom, she opened a small studio in town, where she taught drama, dance, and piano. Desperate to explore the wider world, she left two years later to join the Wayne P. Sewell Producing Company of Atlanta. For about a dollar a day,

A young Ophelia Colley in street clothes . . .

the Sewell Company hired young women to travel from one small town to another organizing amateur theater productions—written by Mrs. Sewell. "They were musical come-

dies," the young teacher recalled years later, "and they were just terrible. I'd go into a town and have to persuade people to be in a play I knew wasn't any good." But it was the Depression and her father's lumber business had been crippled by the flagging economy. She had to support herself somehow. So she traveled across the rural Southeast, she fretted, and she dreamed.

"I wanted to be a serious actress like Helen Hayes, Katharine Hepburn, Lynn Fontaine," she recalled. "My whole idea was to get away from the country, not knowing that the country was going to be my salvation."

In January of 1936, in the north Alabama town of Baileyton, Miss Colley had arrived to put on another in an endless string of mediocre productions, and somehow the Sewell Company had failed to arrange its usual lodging for her. Luckily, a poor but hospitable country family offered to take her in for the next ten days. Something about the woman of the house warmed Ophelia Colley's heart and tickled her all the same. "She was funny, like Granny on the 'Beverly Hillbillies,'" Colley recalled. "A sprightly, brittle, hardy woman with a bun of hair on top of her head. She told me once: 'I've had sixteen young'uns. Never failed to make a crop.'"

Living with that funny old woman, her husband, and their youngest son, whom they called Brother, planted the germ of an idea in

COUNTRY MILESTONES	SEPTEMBER 1932—MILTON BROWN FORMS OWN GROUP, THE MUSICAL BROWNIES	1934—ROY ACUFF BEGINS PERFORMING AT WROL IN KNOXVILLE	JULY 1934—JACK KAPP FOUNDS U.S. BRANCH OF DECCA RECORDS AND OFFERS HILLBILLY RECORDS AT THE LOW PRICE OF 35¢	1935—JUKEBOXES BEGIN APPEARING ACROSS THE UNITED STATES	OCTOBER 26, 1936—ROY ACUFF'S FIRST RECORDING SESSION TAKES PLACE IN CHICAGO; HE SINGS "THE GREAT SPECKLED BIRD"
JANUARY 1931—THE LIGHT CRUST DOUGHBOYS (BOB WILLS, MILTON BROWN, DERWOOD BROWN, AND HERMAN ARNSPIGER) BEGIN BROADCASTING OVER WBAP IN FORT WORTH	AUGUST 1933—FIRED FROM WBAP, BOB WILLS FORMS OWN GROUP, THE TEXAS PLAYBOYS	FEBRUARY 1934—BOB WILLS BEGINS WILDLY SUCCESSFUL NINE-YEAR STINT AT KVOO IN TULSA		APRIL 18, 1936—MILTON BROWN DIES FIVE DAYS AFTER AN AUTO ACCIDENT	

Ophelia Colley's theatrical imagination. When she later offhandedly imitated the old woman and passed along her countrified stories, she got laughs. "For the rest of the time I was with the Sewell Company traveling to these rural towns, I collected country humor and country songs." Gradually, a character emerged so full of life that Ophelia Colley had to give her alter ego a name. "I took Minnie and Pearl because everybody in the country knows Minnies and Pearls. They are the most wonderful names, soft and euphonious to say."

In the fall of 1940, back home in Centerville, Ophelia Colley managed to impress a local businessman when she did her Minnie Pearl routine at a Lion's Club show. The following week Harry Stone of WSM called her on the businessman's recommendation and asked if she'd like to audition for the Grand Ole Opry. She passed that audition, though barely. "They were scared of me," she said, referring to her audition panel of Harry Stone, Judge Hay, and a couple of other WSM officials. "They didn't think I was country. They said, 'The Grand Ole Opry will go to any extent to keep from having anybody think that we're putting a phony up, and we're afraid they'll think you're a phony.' " It seems they had done some checking up on Miss Colley and knew all about her high-toned finishing school education. Somehow she managed to convince them it would not be a hindrance.

. . . and onstage at the Opry as Minnie Pearl.

Still, they booked her at 11:05, because, they said, there weren't as many people listening then.

On a Saturday night in November 1940 Minnie Pearl made her first appearance at the Grand Ole Opry. Though redheaded, blue-eyed, and slender, even then Ophelia Colley wasn't a belle of the ball, and she dressed as homely as she could manage to fit the part: "a crisp yellow cotton dress, white cotton stockings, an old pair of black one-strap Mary Janes, and a flat straw sailor's hat with flowers on the front."

She didn't have a lot of experience to draw on. Up to this point, she had only worked with people who knew less about entertaining than she did. Standing in the wings, Judge Hay noticed that the new comedienne was literally quaking with stage fright. "You're scared, aren't you?" he asked. Yes, she admitted. "Just love 'em, honey," he offered, "and they'll love you back."

She barely remembered those first few minutes she spent on the Opry stage; they just went by in a blur. She figured she must have been satisfactory, for Judge Hay called her the following Wednesday asking her to come back for that Saturday. When she arrived on Friday to show him the script that she and her sister had worked up, she saw just how well she had followed the good Judge's instructions: in the week since that first Opry appearance, WSM had received two bulging sacks of mail addressed to Minnie Pearl—some 250 cards and letters. She was hired at the salary of

OCTOBER 27, 1936—ERNEST TUBB'S FIRST RECORDING SESSION TAKES PLACE IN SAN ANTONIO

1938—THE CARTER FAMILY APPEAR ON BORDER STATION XERA FOR TWO YEARS

1938—PAPPY O'DANIEL ELECTED GOVERNOR OF TEXAS

1940—JUKEBOXES NOW NUMBER 300,000 ACROSS THE UNITED STATES

1940—PAPPY O'DANIEL RE-ELECTED

FEBRUARY 5, 1940—JIMMIE DAVIS RECORDS "YOU ARE MY SUNSHINE," HIS MILLION-SELLING THEME SONG

1941—PAPPY O'DANIEL DEFEATS LYNDON JOHNSON IN TEXAS FOR U.S. SENATE SEAT

APRIL 26, 1941—ERNEST TUBB RECORDS "WALKING THE FLOOR OVER YOU" IN DALLAS (ONE OF THE FIRST COUNTRY NUMBERS TO FEATURE A PROMINENT ELECTRIC GUITAR)

MAY 9, 1944—JIMMIE DAVIS BEGINS HIS FIRST TERM AS GOVERNOR OF LOUISIANA

$10 per Opry appearance, which worked out to about $80 a month, with two Opry shows every Saturday.

Minnie Pearl would have some setbacks over the next few years. In one particular disheartening instance, Roy Acuff hired her for his road show beginning January 1, 1941, but fired her in early March. "Roy fired me because I was not willing to turn loose and act silly," she always maintained. Still, she persevered and went to work on the road with Pee Wee King the following fall. In February 1942 she began appearing on the NBC portion of the Opry, which was a big vote of confidence. Minnie Pearl gradually developed into a distinctive act—arguably the single most memorable act on the program. She always arrived onstage with a big "How-dee! I'm just so proud to be here," and a $1.98 price tag dangling conspicuously from her flower-covered straw hat. Dressed in her hopelessly styleless clothes, she would go on about "ketchin' fellers" with an endearing balance of awkwardness and self-assurance. In time, the regular cast of characters she gossiped about back in her mythical hometown of Grinder's Switch—Brother, Uncle Nabob, her sometime boyfriend Hezzie—became as familiar and as real to Opry audiences as their own neighbors. Very quickly, "Minnie Pearl" became synonymous with the Grand Ole Opry and heartwarming Southern entertainment.

★ HOORAY FOR HOLLYWOOD

In 1938 Republic Pictures—the same studio that had signed Gene Autry and Roy Rogers—began scouting the Grand Ole Opry for a possible feature film to expand its reach to rural audiences. It was the NBC hookup that ultimately convinced Republic to clinch a deal for a picture to be titled simply *Grand Ole Opry*. Filmed during two weeks in April and May 1940, the picture offered a hokey Hollywood take on the origins of the Opry: The show is founded as a way to get a character named Abner Peabody elected governor. That's show business. Nobody from the Opry got top billing; the Weaver Brothers & Elviry, vaudeville veterans who had already made several movies, got that honor, but genuine Opry stars also filled out the bill. Uncle Dave Macon was as entertaining as always, appearing with his son Dorris. Judge Hay was along for the ride. Although he didn't have a big starring role, Roy Acuff made the most of his screen moments, singing stirring versions of his hits "Great Speckled Bird," "Wabash Cannonball," and "Down in Union County."

Of the bunch who appeared in the film, it was Roy Acuff who vaulted into a long-term movie contract. Between 1942 and 1949, he would go on to star in seven more feature films, including *Hi Neighbor* (1942), *My Darling Clementine* (1943), *Night Train to Memphis* (1946), and *Smoky Mountain Melody* (1948). As might have been expected, Republic's directors wanted Acuff to wear cowboy clothes in the movies. But with the exception of *My Darling Clementine*, Acuff adamantly refused to dude up. "I told them my music was mountain music, not western music," Acuff explained, and that was that.

Acuff could afford to take the hard line with Hollywood. He had clout. In mid-October 1943, satisfied by the show's success, NBC

Big wheels at the Opry in the forties: the Duke of Paducah, Minnie Pearl, and Roy Acuff.

extended the Opry's coverage from coast to coast, reaching 143 stations—and some 10 million listeners. With the nation as his stage, Acuff's recording career kicked into high gear, turning out one hit after another. Mostly they were unabashedly sentimental numbers, delivered in his inimitable, heart-in-the-throat style: "The Precious Jewel" (1940), "Wreck on the Highway" (1942), and "The Prodigal Son" (1942). But the former L & N railroad hand also excelled in upbeat train songs like "Wabash Cannonball" (1936), "Fireball Mail" (1942), and "Night Train to Memphis" (1942).

Record charts did not exist to cover country music in the early 1940s, but we can get some idea of Acuff's popularity from a poll of U.S. servicemen in 1945, that ranked Acuff first with Frank Sinatra a distant second. Ear-

lier that year, war correspondent Ernie Pyle reported that Japanese troops on Okinawa charged American positions, hurling what they considered the ultimate insults to American culture: "To hell with Roosevelt, Babe Ruth, and Roy Acuff!"

Perhaps the ultimate indication of Roy Acuff's popularity, at least within his home state, was that the Republican party offered him the gubernatorial nomination twice (in 1944 and 1946) before he finally accepted it in 1948. "I'm running for governor of Tennessee, and I'm running to win," he declared at last. "I'm running like the Wabash Cannonball and the Night Train to Memphis rolled into

one!" That fall, he barnstormed across the state, concentrating on singing and keeping speeches to a minimum. Though he didn't win the election in the traditionally Democratic state, he did manage to collect more votes than any previous Republican candidate. Even better, he didn't have to trade his six-figure earnings for the governor's $8,000 salary.

Hillbilly music may not have gotten Roy Acuff elected, as it had Jimmie Davis and Pappy O'Daniel, but it clearly had a power to move people. The term "hillbilly" now encompassed a wide range of sounds and styles, from the stark backcountry laments of Roy Acuff and the high-energy string-band music of Bill Monroe at the Opry to the bluesy bounce of Ernest Tubb and the big-band rhythms of Bob Wills from out of the great Southwest. As America pulled out of its Depression and girded itself for the threat of world war, hillbilly music would grow right along with the nation and it would soon find its rightful home in Nashville.

A cast shot from the film Grand Ole Opry *(1940), which featured Roy Acuff (with fiddle in hand), Uncle Dave Macon (in car with banjo), and Judge Hay (right of car, waving).*

From June 1941 to Christmas 1942, a group of Opry performers—including Pee Wee King, Eddy Arnold, and Minnie Pearl (right)—entertained U.S. troops in the States and the Canal Zone in a tour sponsored by Camel cigarettes.

Music City, U.S.A.

COUNTRY AND THE WAR

Until 1942 most Americans weren't concerned with the war that had been raging across Europe and Asia since 1939 and the business of hillbilly music, like the rest of American life, went on pretty much as usual. But two days after the Japanese bombing of Pearl Harbor on December 7, 1941, the largest American audience ever—estimated at some 90 million people—listened intently to their radios as President Roosevelt outlined U.S. plans to fight the Axis powers of Japan, Germany, and Italy.

Beginning early in 1942, musicians of every stripe—indeed all Americans—felt the effects of waging world war. With rationing in effect, musicians on the road found gasoline and tires particularly hard to come by. "The hardest thing was finding bootleg tires," said Ernest Tubb. Minnie Pearl agreed: "I remember during the war, we were on the road and had our thirteenth flat of the tour—using those old war retreads. And Pee Wee King threw a jack stand through the windshield and started cussing in Polish!" Meanwhile, the War Production Board restricted the use of aluminum and shellac, cutting into the pressing of records. As a result, the jukebox was virtually the only place for people to hear the latest releases. And then there was the draft, calling on every able-bodied man from ages eighteen to thirty-eight.

As if the war itself weren't enough of a strain on musicians, the leader of the American Federation of Musicians union, James Petrillo, chose August of 1942 as the moment to call a nationwide strike against record companies. This meant that no recording sessions were held in

Pee Wee King and bassist Joe Zinkan ham it up during the wartime Camel Caravan tour.

the United States from August 1942 through October 1943, after which the record companies one by one came to terms with the musicians union. In the interim, record companies simply released stockpiled recordings and made their profits just the same. But with the strike

JUNE 5, 1943—THE OPRY BEGINS A THIRTY-YEAR RUN AT THE RYMAN AUDITORIUM, SEATING 3,000

OCTOBER 1943—NBC EXTENDS NETWORK COVERAGE OF "THE PRINCE ALBERT SHOW" TO 143 STATIONS

1943—EDDY ARNOLD, FORMERLY A MEMBER OF PEE WEE KING'S BAND, BECOMES A SOLO ACT AT THE OPRY

JUNE 6, 1944—GRANT TURNER, LATER KNOWN AS "THE VOICE OF THE OPRY," BEGINS WORK AS AN OPRY STAFF ANNOUNCER. COINCIDENTALLY, IT'S D-DAY—THE DAY THE ALLIED INVASION OF NORMANDY BEGINS

JULY 15, 1944—COMEDIAN ROD BRASFIELD JOINS THE OPRY CAST

DECEMBER 30, 1944—BOB WILLS & THE TEXAS PLAYBOYS INTRODUCE DRUMS TO THE OPRY STAGE

1944—BRADLEY KINCAID, WHO STARRED AT WLS-CHICAGO IN THE LATE 1920S, JOINS THE OPRY CAST

MARCH 1946—GRANDPA JONES JOINS THE CAST OF THE GRAND OLE OPRY

APRIL 1946—RED FOLEY ASSUMES HOST DUTIES OF "THE PRINCE ALBERT SHOW" ON NBC; A YOUNG CHET ATKINS IS A MEMBER OF HIS BAND

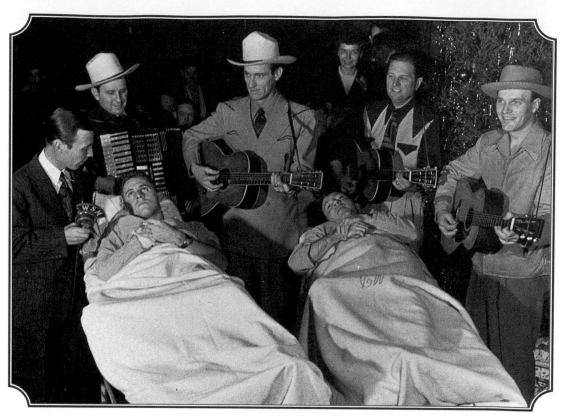

Strong medicine: Opry stars Milton Estes (on mike), Pee Wee King, Ernest Tubb, Bradley Kincaid, and Eddy Arnold serenade patients at the Veterans Hospital in Nashville for Christmas 1947.

taking away the opportunity to record, many musicians must have felt they might as well enlist. Who knew when they would have a chance to make records again?

For as much distress as the war caused hillbilly musicians, it also proved ultimately to be a great help. The farm-to-city population shift that America had been experiencing since the beginning of the century accelerated greatly during World War II. With the nation gearing up for war production, millions of workers migrated from fields to factories. Many rural transplants brought with them their love for hillbilly music. A March 1943 story in *Billboard* magazine headlined "Hillbilly Tunes Gain Popularity" pointed out that in Baltimore the songs were "especially popular in spots patronized by West Virginians, North and South Carolinians, and other na-

tive Southerners who have virtually invaded the defense plants." As country boys entered the armed services, they too helped spread a taste for their music.

Roy Acuff's meteoric ascent marked him as the brightest star in country music during the 1940s. Yet for all Acuff's fame and the Opry's growing audience, Nashville could hardly lay claim to being the fountainhead of hillbilly music during the genre's first two decades. Bob Wills was the King of Western Swing in the Southwest. Gene Autry and Roy Rogers ruled the Hollywood corral. The WLS National Barn Dance continued to compete with the Opry for talent, although they shared much the same NBC radio audiences on Saturday nights, with the Opry's network slot coming at 8:30 P.M. Central Time and the Barn Dance airing at 9:00 P.M. New York, Chicago, and Los Angeles remained the nation's recording centers, with field recording teams working in many cities from time to time throughout the Southeast and Southwest.

During the thirties, radio barn dances had sprouted like dandelions after a spring shower, encouraged by the enormous success of the Grand Ole Opry and the National Barn Dance. St. Louis had KMOX's Old Fashioned Barn Dance (beginning in 1930), Des Moines had WHO's Iowa Barn Dance Frolic (1932), West Virginia had WWVA's Jamboree (1933), Richmond had WRVA's Old Dominion Barn Dance (1938), and Cincinnati had the Boone County Jamboree (1939), to name only a few of the most prominent.

Hillbilly music was becoming a truly national phenomenon. During the early 1940s, however, Nashville began to emerge as the preeminent center of the hillbilly music business. Because of NBC's decision to broadcast the Grand Ole Opry over its network, the Opry gained a national audience. A shrewd man, Roy Acuff figured out a way to capitalize on such widespread exposure. Thus, even as the Opry attracted top hillbilly musicians, Acuff established a business that ultimately attracted ambitious songwriters. In the process, Nashville would benefit enormously.

Nashville and Chicago didn't have a monopoly on barn-dance talent. Here the cast of Wheeling, West Virginia's Radio Jamboree shows off some mighty fine western duds.

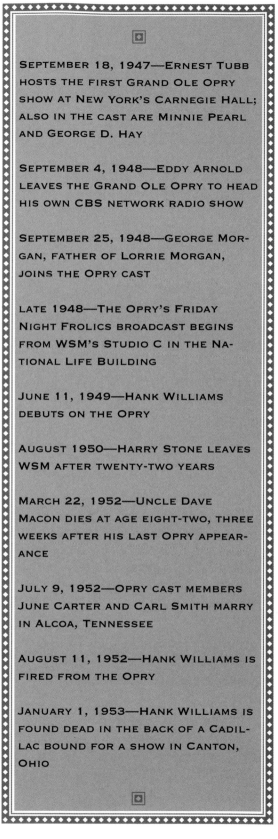

SEPTEMBER 18, 1947—ERNEST TUBB HOSTS THE FIRST GRAND OLE OPRY SHOW AT NEW YORK'S CARNEGIE HALL; ALSO IN THE CAST ARE MINNIE PEARL AND GEORGE D. HAY

SEPTEMBER 4, 1948—EDDY ARNOLD LEAVES THE GRAND OLE OPRY TO HEAD HIS OWN CBS NETWORK RADIO SHOW

SEPTEMBER 25, 1948—GEORGE MORGAN, FATHER OF LORRIE MORGAN, JOINS THE OPRY CAST

LATE 1948—THE OPRY'S FRIDAY NIGHT FROLICS BROADCAST BEGINS FROM WSM'S STUDIO C IN THE NATIONAL LIFE BUILDING

JUNE 11, 1949—HANK WILLIAMS DEBUTS ON THE OPRY

AUGUST 1950—HARRY STONE LEAVES WSM AFTER TWENTY-TWO YEARS

MARCH 22, 1952—UNCLE DAVE MACON DIES AT AGE EIGHT-TWO, THREE WEEKS AFTER HIS LAST OPRY APPEARANCE

JULY 9, 1952—OPRY CAST MEMBERS JUNE CARTER AND CARL SMITH MARRY IN ALCOA, TENNESSEE

AUGUST 11, 1952—HANK WILLIAMS IS FIRED FROM THE OPRY

JANUARY 1, 1953—HANK WILLIAMS IS FOUND DEAD IN THE BACK OF A CADILLAC BOUND FOR A SHOW IN CANTON, OHIO

The Mother Church of Country Music

Although the Grand Ole Opry began in 1925 in the fifth-floor studios of the National Life Building, in the minds of many fans it will be associated forever with the Ryman Auditorium. Located in downtown Nashville, the Ryman was the Opry's home from 1943 to 1974—longer than any other site. Often referred to as "The Mother Church of Country Music," it was in fact originally built in 1892 as the Union Gospel Tabernacle, a place for religious revival meetings, by a reformed riverboat captain, Tom Ryman. After the captain's death in 1904, the Tabernacle assumed his name, although the name change did not become official until 1944.

Because of its large seating capacity and downtown location, the red-brick, barn-shaped structure very soon played host to a number of secular events. One of the first was a reunion of Confederate veterans in 1897, which necessitated the building of the sweeping, scimitar-shaped balcony, thereafter known as the Confederate Gallery. With the balcony addition, the Ryman could seat 3,574 in its semicircular hard oak pews. Before the end of the nineteenth century, symphonies from New York, Chicago, and Boston—as well as John Philip Sousa's celebrated U.S. Marine Corps band—played at the Ryman. Famed stage actress Sarah Bernhardt performed there in March 1906. Carrie Nation lectured on prohibition at the Ryman the following year. Nijinsky and the Ballet Russe danced there in 1917. In April 1919 the great Enrico Caruso sang at the Ryman, with general admission tickets priced at $2 to $6, while box seats went for the unheard-of price of $10.

There had been occasional performances of country music at the Ryman at least as early as November 1925, when Uncle Dave Macon and Dr. Humphrey Bate's string band performed for a policeman's benefit. But the Grand Ole Opry's tenure there dates from June 5, 1943, when the Opry began renting the space for $100 per night. That first summer, tickets were 25¢ for adults, 9¢ for children. Although the Saturday evening show began at eight o'clock, lines would begin forming outside well before, often by mid-afternoon. Outside, vendors sold their captive audience peanuts and hot dogs, songbooks, seat cushions, and programs. During the summer months, paper fans and soft drinks sold especially well in the stuffy, unair-conditioned hall. Typically, fans brought their own picnic suppers of fried chicken or ham sandwiches, which they ate right inside. "The cheapest seats were always those under the

★ ACUFF BECOMES A MUSIC PUBLISHER

Roy Acuff was nothing if not a realist. He was hardly a youngster when he joined the Opry, and he doubted that the run would last for decades. Sensing his growing popularity and seeing his opportunity, Acuff and his wife, Mildred, printed up a postcard-sized souvenir book of his hits to sell on the air (even though Harry Stone warned him that Asher & Jimmie Sizemore had probably pumped the songbook well dry). As Acuff told it, "I had it figured that I could have the folders printed for 5¢ apiece and sell them for a quarter, and I got a fifteen-minute spot on the Opry to advertise them with. I got on there that first Saturday night and really made a pitch about how these little folders had all the songs and pictures and were sized so they could be carried in your shirt pocket. . . . The Wednesday of the next week, the first song-folder mail arrived—2,500 letters, every one with a quarter enclosed. . . . I got 10,000 letters a week for over a year on the song-folders, and the boys had to haul the quarters to the bank in bushel baskets so big one man couldn't carry them by himself. Then I had me a 50¢ songbook printed up."

Given this kind of firsthand experience in the publishing business, when New York music publishers approached Acuff with offers to buy out his songs for $1,500 apiece, he rebuffed them. Acuff had already seen how the quarters from the hinterlands could add up. In the summer of 1942, he approached songwriter and sometime WSM pianist Fred Rose with a proposal to start their own music publishing firm.

Acuff could not have picked a better partner to start a publishing house with than the forty-five-year-old professional tunesmith from Evansville, Indiana. By 1942 Fred Rose had been writing songs for more than twenty years. Sophie Tucker and Paul Whiteman's Orchestra had cut his pop numbers; beginning in 1938 Gene Autry recorded one Fred Rose song after another, including "Tweedle O'Twill," "At Mail Call Today," and "Be Honest with Me," which was nominated for a 1941 Academy Award for best motion-picture song. But in mid-summer 1942 Autry enlisted in the Army Air Corps, leaving Rose without his most reliable outlet for his songs.

In June 1942 Rose moved back to Nashville and his job as a staff pianist with WSM, where he had worked off and on since 1933. Acuff approached Rose with "an offer I hoped he couldn't refuse." Acuff put up $25,000 to get the company started and suggested that Rose should be in charge of the publishing

Fred Rose, a veteran pop songwriter, joined forces with Roy Acuff in 1942 to form the South's first music publishing company, Acuff-Rose Publications.

decisions. Basically, Rose would write new songs and find new songwriters, and Acuff would be available to sing them, if no one else did.

On October 13, 1942, Rose and Acuff struck a deal, establishing Acuff-Rose Publications. It was the first music publishing house in the South. Although Roy provided name recognition for the venture, legally the company began as a partnership between Mildred Acuff and Fred Rose. The little firm started in Fred Rose's Kirkman Avenue home in Nashville, but within two months the business had expanded enough to prompt a move to more businesslike quarters at 220 Capitol Boulevard.

Helping Acuff-Rose Publications get off the ground was a behind-the-scenes battle in the music business, which pitted radio stations on one side against the established songwriters and music publishers represented by the American Society for Composers, Authors, and Publishers (ASCAP) on the other. ASCAP collected royalties for songwriters and publishers based on public performance of their works on radio, in the movies, and in theaters. In theory, ASCAP protected songwriters from exploitation. But in 1939, when ASCAP was the only game in town, only about 1,100 songwriters and 140 publishing houses made up the membership of this select society. Almost all these members were connected with Hollywood or New York's Tin Pan Alley establishment. Blues and hillbilly songwriters were almost

balcony," remembered Loretta Lynn. "And you'd have popcorn and stuff falling on your head, and if somebody spilled a Coke, it would leak on your head. At least I hope it was a Coke."

Accommodations for performers weren't much better. The old tabernacle already had accumulated fifty years' worth of soot by the time the Opry moved in. Whenever a curtain or backdrop fell a little too hard, dust clouds would go swirling. With only two genuine dressing rooms, both cramped, the men's and women's restrooms were also pressed into service. "Most people came already in costume," said former announcer Hal Durham, now the Grand Ole Opry's president. "They would change on their bus or at home because of the lack of facilities." With more than three times as many male cast members as females, the Opry relegated the women to a single restroom for getting made up. Somehow performers made the best of it. "You know what I recall most about the old Ryman?" mused Barbara Mandrell. "It's dressing and getting made up in the toilet, which was the women's dressing room. That was really close, and warm and friendly, sharing that crowded space with Loretta Lynn and Connie Smith and Dolly Parton and Jeannie Seely." Pipes had a distracting tendency to groan and rattle during performances. And yet performers and audiences alike always swore by the acoustics of the Ryman. "It's a great voice launcher," said Porter Wagoner. Marty Stuart agreed: "It's like playing inside a big bass fiddle. You don't have to sing very hard to be heard."

Across the alley from the back door of the Ryman was Tootsie's Orchid Lounge, which opened in 1960, where musicians and songwriters would gather between performances to grab a beer and shoot the breeze. Early in their careers, Kris Kristofferson slept upstairs when he had nowhere else to go and Willie Nelson swept the floors to make a little extra money. Though owner Tootsie Bess passed away in 1978, her bar is still there, and its walls, papered with autographed publicity photos, bear mute testimony to the number of stars who have stopped in over the years.

In September 1963 the National Life & Accident Insurance Company (owners of WSM and the Opry) bought the Ryman for $200,000, renaming it the Grand Ole Opry House. Improvements continued to be made: The famous stained-glass windows, for example, were installed in 1966 to give the hall an even more spiritual atmosphere. From 1969 to 1971 Johnny Cash taped his ABC-TV show from the Ryman. When the Grand Ole Opry left the Ryman in March 1974 for the spacious new Opry House on the Opryland properties, the old hall became a shell of its former self.

The Ryman Auditorium, ca. 1900.

Occasionally, special performances took place there, such as filming for the 1980 movie *Coal Miner's Daughter* and the 1991 recording of Emmylou Harris's *At the Ryman* album. Mostly, though, the hall was a museum piece, a stop for tourists.

In June 1994, after twenty years of silence, the Ryman Auditorium reopened for performance, launched with a special broadcast of Garrison Keillor's "Prairie Home Companion." The $8.5 million renovation project added state-of-the-art sound and climate control systems. Two hundred fifty original oak pews were refinished and the hall's original color scheme of pale mint green with gold, dark green, and brown accents was faithfully restored. Today the Ryman is once again playing host to a wide range of entertainment events— from a regular series of bluegrass concerts to musical theater and dance. No one is happier about the renovation than the old Opry veterans, though. "It has the same personality," said Porter Wagoner. "It's just better."

uniformly denied admission. In fact, Gene Autry tried for eight years to be admitted to ASCAP; he finally prevailed in late 1938, when he was clearly a leading box-office attraction.

Thinking themselves in the catbird seat, the directors of ASCAP put the screws to radio in 1940, calling for a 100 percent raise in their royalty rates. Radio broadcasters countered by forming their own licensing organization, Broadcast Music Incorporated. By necessity, BMI opened its doors to the blues and hillbilly songwriters and independent publishing firms that ASCAP had long snubbed. Significantly, whereas ASCAP had only paid royalties on live radio performances emanating from New York, Chicago, and Los Angeles, BMI quickly developed a system to track airplay all across the country, tallying record play as well as live performance.

Acuff-Rose Publications immediately benefited from BMI's presence when BMI advanced Fred Rose $2,500 for ten new songs that the firm licensed for airplay through BMI. More important, though, was the fact that BMI paid for airplay wherever it occurred, giving Acuff-Rose a brand-new, virtually unrivaled opportunity. Instead of merely relying on sales of sheet music and songbooks, Acuff-Rose could count on substantial income from airplay as well. Thus, when Acuff-Rose entered the music publishing business, the playing field had finally been leveled for country songwriters and publishers. In the twenties Ralph Peer had nudged hillbilly music away from genuine folk songs by paying royalties for new tunes. With the coming of BMI, the foundation had been laid for country songwriting to become a legitimate, and potentially lucrative, profession.

★ THE OPRY STARTS AT THE RYMAN

Right around the same time, the Grand Ole Opry made a move of its own. Unfortunately, the Opry's boisterous, fun-loving crowds had put a lot of wear and tear on the plush War Memorial Auditorium—at least, that's what the hall's management thought. After much haggling, Harry Stone arranged a rental agreement with Lula Naff, house manager of the Ryman Auditorium, for, Stone admitted later, "more rent than we had ever paid." Although it was already over fifty years old in 1943 and had definitely seen better days, its audience capacity of 3,574 fit the Opry's needs. Even if it wasn't air-conditioned or heated properly, and even if its wooden church pews could be hard on the spirit, music did sound wonderful in the Ryman. In fact, many compared its acoustics to that of fabled Carnegie Hall. So, beginning Saturday, June 5, 1943, National Life began renting the Ryman for $100 a month. As time would tell, the Ryman proved to be a very appropriate home for the Grand Ole Opry—in fact, its home for the next thirty years.

Even though the Opry had moved to new facilities, some things remained the same as ever. Judge Hay still wanted the cast to keep the show down to earth. When Bob Wills & the Texas Playboys pulled into town in their chartered Trailways bus for an Opry show December 30, 1944, a collision was inevitable. Wills had never played the Opry before. It was high time; Wills had about the most popular hillbilly band in the land. His "New San Antonio Rose," with its smooth big-band sound, had proved a particular favorite, hitting both the pop and country charts before Bing Crosby covered it, selling a million copies and making it a chart item all over again. That danceable sound put the band on top and brought them to the Opry. Ironically, the horns and drums that made the sound so easy to dance to were taboo on the Opry stage. Opry officials ordered Wills to set up his drum kit behind a curtain. Wills would have none of the compromise. At the last moment he told drummer

The old interior of the Ryman, showing the curved oak pews and the balcony, which was added five years after opening.

Street scene outside the Ryman in the 1940s.

Monte Mountjoy to move his kit onstage. When the band stepped out and struck up the introduction to "New San Antonio Rose," they received thundering applause. "They just stopped the show cold," recalled singer Eddy Arnold. "They had a good heavy dance beat. And in that old building, which had great acoustics, it was just overpowering." Wills won that round, but the Opry officials avenged themselves by refusing the band an encore. It would be thirty more years before full drum kits appeared regularly on the Opry stage.

★ THE JOURNEY OF MERLE TRAVIS

Though the Opry was growing in strength in the 1940s, it didn't corner the market on talent. One of the most influential musicians and songwriters to emerge out of hillbilly music got his start at Cincinnati's WLW. His story epitomizes the lives of many hillbilly musicians of the forties—even if his talent marked him as something much more unusual. A gospel string band called the Drifting Pioneers brought a twenty-year-old fleet-fingered guitarist to the station. The son of a coal miner, Merle Travis came from Rosewood, Kentucky, where he learned a distinctive style of syncopated fingerpicking in which he used his thumb to play a thumping rhythm while picking out a melody with his index finger. To add to his skill with the guitar, Travis had a knack for words as well.

In Cincinnati the draft broke up the Drifting Pioneers, leaving Merle Travis without a band and WLW program director George Biggar without a gospel act to fill the Pioneers' early-morning half-hour program each day. In June 1943, on Biggar's suggestion, Alton Delmore of the Delmore Brothers assembled an ad hoc gospel group with his brother Rabon, Merle Travis, and a newcomer to the station named Louis Jones, already

Country renaissance man Merle Travis popularized a style of guitar finger-picking that bears his name, wrote timeless songs, acted in Hollywood, refined recording and guitar-making techniques, and always kept audiences entertained.

better known as "Grandpa" for his old-time act, even though he was just twenty-nine years old. Calling themselves the Brown's Ferry Four (after one of the Delmores' hits), the new quartet took to the airwaves, singing hymns, Southern gospel, and spirituals. To keep stocked with material—particularly black spirituals—the bunch would head down to Central Avenue on the black side of town. There a used-record store had all they wanted. Syd Nathan, the store's owner, got to know the group from their regular visits. One day,

the pudgy, asthmatic, forty-year-old businessman with the Coke-bottle eyeglasses asked Travis: "Why don't you boys make your own records?"

"Ain't nobody asked us," replied Travis.

"Well, I'm asking you," said Nathan. "I'm going to start me a company."

The company was King Records, and its first act was the Sheppard Brothers—in actuality Merle Travis and Grandpa Jones doing their best Delmore Brothers impression. Fearing reprisal from their bosses at WLW, Travis and Jones recorded incognito at a studio in Dayton that was just a little room over the local Wurlitzer Piano Company. They made that first recording in September 1943. King's second release was by one Bob McCarthy—actually a solo outing from Merle Travis entitled "When Mussolini Laid His Pistol Down," a topical number celebrating the recent lynching of Il Duce in July 1943.

Shortly afterward, Grandpa enlisted in the Army, Merle went into the Marines, and Alton Delmore joined the Navy. Though the original Brown's Ferry Four had scattered, WLW recognized a good name brand and continued to feature the group by filling the gaps with station regulars like Rome Johnson, Ray Lanham, and Dolly Good of the Girls of the Golden West. Meanwhile, inspired by his first artists, Syd Nathan plunged into the record business, incorporating King Records in August 1944. With the 1944 opening of Earl T. Herzog's recording studio on Race Street in downtown Cincinnati, Nathan no longer had to go to Dayton to make records. Drawing on the talented musicians who worked at WLW, Nathan developed a strong roster of hillbilly talent for the King label, including Clyde Moody, Moon Mullican, Wayne Raney, T. Texas Tyler, and, upon their return from the service, the Delmore Brothers and Grandpa Jones.

Nathan also formed a subsidiary label named Queen for rhythm and blues talent around the time he incorporated King, and in 1948 he hired Henry Glover, a twenty-seven-year-old musical arranger from Lucky Millinder's jump blues band to be his A & R man. Though less heralded than Jackie Robinson, who became the first black baseball player in the major leagues the year before, Glover helped break the color barrier in record producing, supervising both R & B and country sessions for King and Queen. Guided by Glover and Nathan, the Cincinnati labels produced a fusion of blues and hillbilly styles in records like the Delmore Brothers' "Blues Stay Away from Me" and Wayne Raney's "Why Don't You Haul Off and Love Me." These No. 1 hits would fuel the boogie craze that led directly to the development of rock and roll in the fifties.

With WLW and King Records both going strong, Merle Travis naturally headed back to Cincinnati in March 1944 after discharge from the Marines. But he didn't stay long. Gene Autry's sidekick Smiley Burnette, in Cincinnati for a tour, gave the twenty-six-year-old Travis a piece of advice that struck a nerve: "I'd rather live in California and live on lettuce than live in Cincinnati and eat caviar." Travis figured a successful movie star ought to know what he was talking about and left for Hollywood on the next train.

Travis headed west at an opportune time. In girding for war, U.S. industries expanded dramatically, and nowhere was the industrial growth more apparent than in California. While the most dramatic business vitality occurred in shipbuilding and aircraft manufacturing, the music business continued to do well in Hollywood, in spite of the war shortages. Bob Wills, upon his discharge from the Army in July 1943, headed for the West Coast and reorganized his Texas Playboys in Los Angeles. Former movie extra and Roy Rogers stunt double Spade Cooley had been leading his own western swing band—an even larger and smoother outfit than Wills's—at local hotspots like the Venice Pier and Redondo Beach. The Venice Pier alone drew crowds of well over 5,000 on the weekend swing shift.

Soon after arriving in Los Angeles, Travis landed enough occasional work in bands and playing bit parts in singing cowboy movies to get a foothold. To hear Travis tell it, getting work in pictures was a snap: "To work a picture out there was nothing more than working a recording session in Nashville," he recalled. "The phone would ring and they'd say, 'You want to do a picture? Get yourself together three guys that can ride.' "

He also got recording work at a new record label called Capitol Records. His first session found him playing lead guitar on a Tex Ritter record called "Jealous Heart," in late 1944. Tex Ritter was the first hillbilly star signed to Capitol, formed in April 1942 by pop songwriter Johnny Mercer, music-store owner Glenn Wallichs, and Paramount Pictures production chief Buddy DeSylva. The label concentrated exclusively on pop music at first. But once Tex Ritter's records started connecting in 1944, the label eagerly brought on new hillbilly talent. Travis got his chance as a Capitol artist in 1946. His first session yielded the double-sided hit "Cincinnati Lou"/ "No Vacancy." Between 1946 and 1949 Travis was rarely off the charts, proving to be probably the hottest hillbilly artist from coast to coast, thanks to No. 1 hits like "Divorce Me C.O.D." and "So Round, So Firm, So Fully Packed."

Travis would have been the first to admit that he was no great shakes as a singer. Surprisingly, his early records didn't compensate by spotlighting his

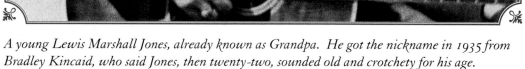

A young Lewis Marshall Jones, already known as Grandpa. He got the nickname in 1935 from Bradley Kincaid, who said Jones, then twenty-two, sounded old and crotchety for his age.

tricky guitar picking either. His records were built mostly around a jaunty studio band that spotlighted an accordion and a muted trumpet. More than anything, audiences probably responded to Travis's clever and topical wordplay. "So Round, So Firm, So Fully Packed," for example, took its title from an advertising slogan for Lucky Strike cigarettes; Travis turned it around and made it a winking tribute to his ladyfriend's physical attributes. In 1947 Travis's way with words gave Capitol Records its first million seller on the record of another artist, Tex Williams. As a favor to his friend, Travis cooked up a humorous, high-octane tongue twister about the frustrations of cigarette smokers. "Smoke, Smoke, Smoke (That Cigarette)" topped both the country and the pop record charts in the summer of 1947.

Ironically, Merle Travis's best-remembered numbers were ones he wrote almost against his will. His producer at Capitol, Cliffie Stone, asked Merle to record an album of folk songs. Travis protested that Bradley Kincaid and Burl Ives had already recorded every folk song he knew. "Then write some new ones," replied Stone.

"You don't write folk songs," Travis countered logically.

"Well, write some that sound like folk songs."

Performing under pressure, that's exactly what Travis did. Among the eight tracks he recorded for his *Folk Songs of the Hills* album, Travis turned out such immortal gems as "Dark As a Dungeon" and "Sixteen Tons." He also managed to rework a few traditional folk songs, such as "Nine Pound Hammer" and "I Am a Pilgrim" into such memorably new forms that they might as well have been written by him. Though Travis later claimed the album was a commercial flop, its songs are now acknowledged classics.

Merle Travis's creative fires burned fiercely for the next several years. He drew up

Movie cowboy Tex Ritter was the first country act to be signed to Capitol Records in 1942. This photo dates from around 1965, when he joined the Grand Ole Opry.

the prototype for Fender's line of electric guitars. He helped develop the vibrato bar for guitars. In the studio, he helped pioneer multitrack recording—the new engineering technique of layering one musical track over another—around the same time as guitarist Les Paul. (The innovative "Merle's Boogie Woogie" was released in July 1947, some seven months before Les Paul's first multitrack single, "Lover.") In the meantime, Travis appeared on local TV shows, in some forty Westerns, and earned critical plaudits for his role in the feature *From Here to Eternity* (1953) singing "Re-Enlistment Blues." Sadly, a chronic problem with alcohol dogged Travis, preventing him from achieving the wider renown his many talents deserved. Nevertheless, he helped pave the way for Capitol Records' enormous growth in the country music realm during the 1950s and 1960s with future stars like Tennessee Ernie Ford and Hank Thompson, while his influence as a guitarist and songwriter remains incalculable.

★ NASHVILLE'S RISE TO POWER

Hollywood, Cincinnati, and Chicago all vied with Nashville to be the headquarters for the growing hillbilly music business during the forties. But a number of forces came together toward the end of World War II to push Nashville to the top. One was the National Barn Dance's loss of its sponsor and subsequently its network hookup in May 1946. For years the show had been slowly faltering; most of the original cast had grayed considerably, and its biggest stars had all left. Gene Autry was in Hollywood, Lulu Belle & Scotty went to WLW, and Bradley Kincaid joined the Grand Ole Opry, having arrived at the show in 1944. In a way, the arrival of the great folksinger symbolized the passing of the torch from Chicago to Nashville. The biggest loss to WLS, and the biggest gain to the Opry, came in the person of Red Foley, who had left the

Merle Travis (left) with producer–bass player Cliffie Stone, 1940s. In 1947, Stone asked Travis to write some new folk songs. Travis came up with modern standards "Sixteen Tons" and "Dark As a Dungeon."

didn't need the Opry anymore to publicize his name. So he left to do more movies, to tour, and to count the money coming in from the publishing company he and Fred Rose had founded. On the road he soon found he was earning nightly what he had wanted from the Opry as an annual salary. But Acuff belonged on the Opry. After playing shows across the country, Acuff had had his fill of traveling for a while. When the Opry asked him to return, Acuff obliged. On April 16, 1947, almost

National Barn Dance to take over Roy Acuff's spot hosting "The Prince Albert Show" on the Opry in April 1946.

Clyde Julian Foley, nicknamed "Red" for his shock of red hair, had joined WLS in 1931 when Bradley Kincaid and Gene Autry were its biggest stars. He himself played bass and guitar in John Lair's Cumberland Ridge Runners and also traded wisecracks and silly songs with Lulu Belle before Scotty Wiseman came on the scene. Signing with Decca Records in 1941, Foley had a hit almost immediately with the sentimental tribute to a boy and his dog, "Old Shep." Foley wrote the song, in fact, in memory of his own German shepherd, Hoover, and he sang the heart-tugging lyrics with a light touch, reminiscent of Bing Crosby, that endeared him to listeners. During World War II, he scored a direct hit in 1944 with the patriotic "Smoke on the Water," a vow of revenge for the attack on Pearl Harbor. *Billboard* touted him on the cover of the May 26, 1945, issue as "Air, Disk Folk Topper."

Red Foley fit perfectly into the increasingly modern makeup of the Grand Ole Opry cast when he arrived in April 1946. But few would have expected anyone to replace Roy Acuff at the time. The problem, it seems, was that Acuff had noticed his stock rising in the entertainment world. He had several movies on his resume, his records continued to sell well, and since 1943 he had stepped into Judge Hay's role as emcee for "The Prince Albert Show." Somehow, Acuff felt underappreciated for all the attention he felt he brought the Grand Ole Opry. When he and the Opry couldn't come to terms, he walked away not only from "The Prince Albert Show" but also from the Opry and WSM. Acuff, quite rightly, reasoned that he really

From 1946 to 1954 Red Foley hosted the Opry's "Prince Albert Show" over the NBC radio network. Note the tobacco can.

exactly a year after his departure, Acuff rejoined the Opry as host of the "Royal Crown Cola Show."

For Red Foley, the appointment as host of "The Prince Albert Show" proved a tremendous boost to his career. Over the next ten years, his name was rarely off the record charts, as he racked up thirty-nine Top Ten country hits. Among them were some of that era's best-remembered songs, such as "Peace in the Valley," "Chattanoogie Shoe Shine Boy," and "Mississippi." The presence of both Ernest Tubb and Red Foley in Nashville, Decca's two best-sellers in the hillbilly market, didn't escape the notice of Paul Cohen, head of Decca's hillbilly recording division.

At age twenty-seven, Cohen started at Decca when it first opened in 1934, and was promoted to branch manager of the Cincinnati office a year later. After becoming head of Decca's hillbilly division in 1945, he decided that it was foolish to bring Tubb, Foley, and his other Decca artists to studios in New York, Chicago, and Los Angeles, when once a week most of his label roster was working at the Opry. Nashville, he reasoned, would be a good place to record.

As luck would have it, by early 1946 Nashville had a recording studio up and running with three experienced engineers from WSM at the helm. Aaron Shelton, Carl Jenkins, and George Reynolds, moonlighting from their regular station jobs, built their recording studio in a high-ceilinged, forty-by-sixty-foot dining room in the downtown Tulane Hotel, located on Church Street, just a couple blocks south of the National Life Building. "We saw the need for a recording studio because of the great talent the Opry attracted," Shelton later explained. "The old Tulane dining room was a natural because it was close to WSM, close to the downtown operations, and easy to get to in a hurry." They called the place Castle Studio, playing on the motto of WSM ("Air Castle of

Two fellows who helped make Nashville "Music City, U.S.A.": Opry star Red Foley on guitar and WSM announcer David Cobb, who coined the famous name.

the South"). Cohen quickly made use of the new facility, lining up an Ernest Tubb session there in August 1947. A & R men from other labels soon followed suit.

What put Nashville recording on the map, though, was a pop recording made at Castle in January 1947 by Francis Craig & His Orchestra, who had been playing at WSM since the first night it went on the air. Set off by a rollicking, barrelhouse piano and balanced by a smooth vocal of singer Bob Lamm, the record, released on the local Bullet label, shot up to No. 1 and stayed there for four months. Within a year the record had sold 3 million copies. In 1948 Milton Berle adopted it as the theme song for his "Texaco Star Theater" television variety show. Craig had one follow-up to "Near You," titled "Beg Your Pardon," which was nearly a carbon copy of the big hit, right down to the signature piano intro. It sold a cool half million, reaffirming Nashville's emergence as a recording center.

★ THE TENNESSEE PLOWBOY

If "Near You" had been the only big record to come out of Nashville, little would have come of Castle Studio. But country artists soon began coming close to duplicating that pop record's success. The frontrunner during the 1940s was Eddy Arnold, a former vocalist for Pee Wee King's band. Nicknamed the "Tennessee Plowboy," Arnold looked the part—square-jawed, broad-shouldered, and a stout six feet tall. He also lived the part, having grown up the youngest of four children on a 200-acre cotton farm near the west Tennessee town of Henderson. When Arnold was eleven his father died, leaving the family to scrape by as sharecroppers on land they had once owned. Music offered young Eddy a way out, and by the age of eighteen he was performing professionally, first in Jackson, then in Memphis and St. Louis.

At some point in 1939, while visiting his

mother in Jackson, Arnold heard Pee Wee King's band on WSM and noticed its lack of a strong male singer. He wrote to King, enclosing a photo and offering to send a radio transcription recording to show off his voice. King's manager and father-in-law, J. L. Frank, followed up quickly and offered Arnold a job. Arnold accepted without even asking about the salary (it was $25 a week). In January 1940, at the age of twenty-one, Eddy Arnold took his guitar to Nashville to be a Golden West Cowboy.

By his own admission, Eddy Arnold never became a very proficient guitar player. For King, he strummed an unobtrusive rhythm and mostly concentrated on his singing. Every time he did the latter, anyone within earshot knew what he was made for. After three years of apprenticing at a sideman's low wages, Arnold began a solo career.

WSM's Harry Stone saw potential in the young singer with the honey-smooth voice, giving him his own spot on the Opry as well as brief morning and noon programs at the station. In August 1943, with support from Stone, Arnold signed a recording contract with RCA Victor. At the time, though, the American Federation of Musicians union still had their strike on against the record companies. RCA Victor and Columbia Records, the two biggest labels, were also the last to negotiate with the union and begin recording again. They finally reached terms with the union in

Eddy Arnold concentrates on composing another big hit while his wife, Sally, holds the good luck charm—his first songbook, published in 1944.

November 1944. As a result, Eddy Arnold didn't stand in front of an RCA microphone for more than a year after signing his contract. During the interminable interim, Arnold studied welding, just in case his shot at recording glory didn't work out. "I always had the feeling in those days that maybe it wouldn't last," Eddy wrote years later. "I always had the horror of winding up a pauper. . . . I guess maybe that goes back to seeing my daddy's farm sold out from under us."

When his first session finally took place, RCA Victor scheduled it in Nashville, on December 4, 1944, probably in the WSM studios at the National Life Building. As far as historians have been able to determine, this was the first commercial recording session in Nashville since Ralph Peer made a disappointing visit in 1928. (As one might expect, Ralph Peer did try to record some Grand Ole Opry talent. During one week in the fall of 1928 he cut sixty-nine songs by nine acts, including De-Ford Bailey and the Crook Brothers. Victor released a few records from the Nashville session, but none were hits, and Peer never returned.) And it proved to be the first of countless sessions to come for Arnold and for other artists. Among the four numbers Arnold cut at that historic session were two that RCA quickly released: a sentimental tune in the manner of Roy Acuff, "Mommy, Please Stay Home with Me," and a cowboy number, "Cattle Call." The latter, though it had been written nearly a decade earlier by cowboy singer Tex Owens, had the distinction of getting a few deft, late additions from the pen of Fred Rose. "Mommy, Please Stay" sold a very respectable 85,000 copies, and Arnold soon took "Cattle Call," a lilting piece that allowed Arnold to slide his smooth baritone into a gentle yodel, as his theme song.

Perhaps the first sign of the public's reaction to Eddy Arnold, RCA Victor recording artist, came in late June 1945 when the twenty-seven-year-old singer went to Memphis to help plug war bonds at a downtown rally. For a series of fifteen-minute broadcasts over WMPS during a twelve-hour period, Arnold pushed a million-dollars' worth of E bonds to the Memphians thronging Victory Square, causing automobile and trolley traffic to come

COUNTRY MILESTONES	FEBRUARY 15, 1940— BMI OPENS AND BEGINS LICENSING COUNTRY SONGS FOR AIRPLAY	APRIL 1942—CAPITOL RECORDS FOUNDED IN HOLLYWOOD; TEX RITTER IS SIGNED AS THE FIRST OF MANY HILLBILLY ACTS	GOES ON NATIONAL STRIKE, WHICH CONTINUES THROUGH MUCH OF THE FOLLOWING YEAR; RECORD LABELS RELEASE STOCKPILED RECORDINGS DURING THIS TIME	OCTOBER 13, 1942— FRED ROSE AND ROY ACUFF ESTABLISH ACUFF-ROSE PUBLICATIONS, THE FIRST MUSIC PUBLISHING HOUSE IN THE SOUTH	JUNE 1943—THE BROWN'S FERRY FOUR (MERLE TRAVIS, GRANDPA JONES, AND THE DELMORE BROTHERS) BEGIN BROADCASTS OVER CINCINNATI'S WLW
1940—THE U.S. CIRCUIT COURT OF APPEALS CONCLUDES THAT RADIO STATIONS MAY PLAY RECORDS ON THE AIR FOR FREE		AUGUST 1, 1942— AMERICAN FEDERATION OF MUSICIANS UNION			

to a standstill. At the end of that month, Arnold saw his name on *Bill-board*'s record charts for the first time, as "Each Minute Seems a Million Years" went to No. 5 on the Juke Box Folk Records chart.

At about this point, a very colorful character entered Eddy Arnold's life—Colonel Tom Parker. A round, bald-headed fellow who punctuated his talk with drags on stogies, Parker had all the bluster and palaver of an experienced huckster, which he was, having worked as a carnival barker before meeting Arnold. He had never been a military officer; the title was merely honorary, bestowed as a favor by Governor Jimmie Davis. His name wasn't really Thomas A. Parker either, for he had been born in Holland as Andreas van Kuijk and had emigrated to the United States just seventeen years before Arnold met him. Whoever he was, the thirty-five-year-old Parker knew how to play a hand and how to drive a bargain. Arnold soon realized that. After signing on as Arnold's manager, Parker got the singer the sponsorship of the Ralston Purina Company for a segment of the Opry, plus a Saturday noontime show, called "Checkerboard Square Jamboree," over the Mutual network. Eddy hosted the first half hour; Ernest Tubb, the second. In 1948 Parker arranged for even more Eddy Arnold—fifteen minutes over the Mutual network *every day*.

With lots of network exposure, Eddy Arnold's career skyrocketed. Beginning in late 1947 and running through early 1949, he dominated the country charts as no one has before or since. During that period, his records held the top spot on the country charts continuously, except for three weeks in December 1948. The records in that string of hits— "I'll Hold You in My Heart (Till I Can Hold You in My Arms)," "Bouquet of Roses," "Anytime"—became standards for the country audience and for the wider popular audience as well. For the first time, a hillbilly artist's records regularly "crossed over" to pop radio shows and appeared high on the pop record charts.

Positioned for maximum exposure by Tom Parker, Eddy Arnold gave America a breath of fresh air as clean as a mountain breeze. With his good looks and smooth, strong voice, Eddy Arnold epitomized the

With his good looks and smooth, straightforward sound, Eddy Arnold was the first country artist to hit the pop charts consistently.

JULY 1943—UPON HIS DISCHARGE FROM THE ARMY, BOB WILLS RE-FORMS THE TEXAS PLAY-BOYS IN LOS ANGELES

AUGUST 1943—EDDY ARNOLD SIGNS WITH RCA VICTOR RECORDS

SEPTEMBER 1943—MERLE TRAVIS AND GRANDPA JONES MAKE THEIR FIRST RECORD-INGS FOR THE KING LABEL AS "THE SHEP-PARD BROTHERS"

DECEMBER 1944—HANK AND AUDREY WILLIAMS ARE MARRIED IN ALABAMA

DECEMBER 4, 1944—EDDY ARNOLD RECORDS IN NASHVILLE, THE FIRST COMMERCIAL SESSION IN TOWN SINCE 1928

APRIL AND DECEMBER 1945—GUITARIST-VO-CALIST LESTER FLATT JOINS BILL MONROE'S BLUE GRASS BOYS, FOLLOWED BY BANJOIST EARL SCRUGGS

SEPTEMBER 1945—ROY ACUFF BESTS FRANK SINATRA IN A POLL OF U.S. SERVICEMEN STA-TIONED IN GERMANY

1946—CASTLE STUDIO OPENS FOR RECORDING SESSIONS IN NASHVILLE

all-American boy. When he sang hillbilly music, it didn't twang, it didn't sound Southern; it sounded simply unaffected and straightforward, in the best American tradition. Like Roy Acuff, Eddy Arnold conveyed absolute sincerity with every song, but without any taint of regional twang.

Inevitably, Arnold proved to be too big a star for the Grand Ole Opry. In September 1948 he jumped to a new radio program, "Hometown Reunion," originating from a different city each week. In 1949 Parker maneuvered him into two movies, *Feudin' Rhythm* and *Hoedown*—a trick that Parker would duplicate a few years later with another country singer named Elvis Presley. Though the movies were flimsy and forgettable vehicles, they did no damage to Arnold's growing reputation—or to his annual income, pegged at $250,000 by *Newsweek* in 1949. He continued to dominate country's record charts. By the end of 1949 Eddy Arnold was once again voted in *Billboard* as America's No. 1 Folk Artist.

★ THE HILLBILLY SHAKESPEARE

While Eddy Arnold showed how big country music could be when the music veered toward the middle of the road, *Billboard*'s No. 2 Folk Artist for 1949 showed what the music could do when it stayed true to its basic nature. Hiram Williams—known to all the world as Hank—sang with a thick Alabama twang, filled out his western suits like a scarecrow, and had a terrible reputation (at least among his employers and fellow musicians) for being an obnoxious, irresponsible drunk. He also had charisma and a natural-born knack for writing songs that sounded like pages from his diary. They called him the "Hillbilly Shakespeare."

He once explained his secret to a magazine writer. "You ask what makes our kind of music successful. I'll tell you. It can be explained in just one word: sincerity. When a hillbilly sings a crazy song, he feels crazy. When he sings, 'I laid my mother away,' he sees her a-laying right there in the coffin.

Hank Williams onstage at the Opry with Chet Atkins on guitar, ca. 1950.

"He sings more sincere than most entertainers because the hillbilly was raised rougher than most entertainers. You got to know a lot about hard work. You got to have smelt a lot of mule manure before you can sing like a hillbilly."

Williams often recycled melodies, a point driven home for songwriter Vic McAlpin when they were working on the song "Long Gone Lonesome Blues." After they had worked out the words, McAlpin asked what Hank had in mind for a melody. "My slow one," Hank replied. "I got two—a slow one and a fast one."

Yet somehow Hank Williams had a way of making every recorded performance stand up as a unique moment. In fact, judging from the radio transcriptions and demo recordings that survive, not to mention the personal testimony of eyewitnesses, it seems that Hank Williams threw himself body and soul into the music every time he sang. And short fuse that he was, he burned out quickly.

Hank proved a precocious talent in every way. He started singing in church, sitting beside his mother, the organist for the Mount Olive West Baptist Church, in south Alabama. "My earliest memory," he once said, "is sittin' on that organ stool by her and hollerin'. I must have been five, six years old, and louder'n anybody else." From hymns, he gained a sense of fatalism and of events being foreordained. By age eleven he had begun drinking hard liquor and performing in the streets for loose change. In his early teens he met a fiftyish black street musician by the name of Rufus Payne. Tee-Tot, as he was commonly known, played the blues and captivated young Hank Williams. "All the music training I ever had was from him," Williams would later confess. "I was shinin' shoes, sellin' newspapers and followin' this old Nigrah around to get him to teach me to play the guitar. I'd give him 15¢, or whatever I could get a-hold of for the lesson."

At thirteen, Hank was singing for his supper twice a week in fifteen-minute programs over WSFA in Montgomery, Alabama, and known to listeners as "The Singing Kid." He quit high school after the ninth grade, having warned his relatives in advance, "I ain't goin' to school always. I'll sing my song and make more money than any of you." Though he got a head start on his chosen profession, he still had to pay years of dues in crummy joints and honky-tonks around Alabama. There were times as a teenager when his drinking got so bad that his friends and associates figured he would never amount to anything.

In the summer of 1943, just before he turned twenty, Hank met the woman who would inspire his greatest songs and push him to the very pinnacle of hillbilly stardom. She also, many maintained, pushed him over the edge into unremitting alcoholism. Audrey Sheppard Guy—blond, slinky, and seven months his senior—had already been through

Hank Williams, country's tortured, tragic genius in an uncharacteristically statesmanlike pose.

one brief marriage and had a child when she and Hank met. It was just about love at first sight, at least for Hank; he proposed to her that first day. A little over a year later, in December 1944, they were married by a justice of the peace at a Texaco station. From the beginning, they mixed like oil and water, and fights were the norm in their household. They would divorce in 1948, reconcile, have a son together in 1949, then divorce for good in 1952.

Bolstered by the ambitious Audrey, Hank realized his first inkling of success as a songwriter when he sold the topical tune "I Am Praying for the Day Peace Will Come" in December 1943 to Pee Wee King.

Three years later a batch of his songs came to the attention of Fred Rose, then on the lookout for material for a new Columbia artist, Molly O'Day. Rose had O'Day record four tunes written by Williams and signed him as an Acuff-Rose writer before placing him with, first, Sterling Records (in 1946) and, then, MGM Records (in 1947).

Fred Rose's experience in songwriting, record producing, and the ins and outs of the music business came to glorious fruition with Hank Williams. Rose recognized in Williams a fertile imagination and nurtured it. He gave Hank advice on shaping his songs and steered him in profitable directions. When necessary he even edited and co-wrote with Hank to make sure the songs fulfilled their potential. In 1948, looking for a radio show with the wattage capable of properly promoting Hank's music, Rose placed Hank with the Louisiana Hayride. Broadcast over KWKH from the Municipal Auditorium in Shreveport, Louisiana, at 50,000 watts, the Hayride covered almost as much territory as the Grand Ole Opry, even without the benefit of a national network hookup. More to the point, as a brand-new show having begun in April 1948, the Hayride was in a position to gamble on a

Hank Williams with his classic Drifting Cowboys band, 1951: (from left) Cedric Rainwater, Sammy Pruett, Hank's wife Audrey, Hank, Jerry Rivers, and Don Helms.

FEBRUARY 13–14, 1946—DECCA'S PAUL COHEN RECORDS ERNEST TUBB FOR THE FIRST TIME IN NASHVILLE AT WSM'S STUDIOS

MAY 1946—THE NATIONAL BARN DANCE LOSES ITS NBC NETWORK CONNECTION

JULY 1947—MERLE TRAVIS BECOMES THE FIRST ARTIST TO RELEASE A HIT MULTITRACK SINGLE WITH "MERLE'S BOOGIE WOOGIE"

JULY 19, 1947— "SMOKE, SMOKE, SMOKE (THAT CIGARETTE)," RECORDED BY TEX WILLIAMS, TOPS BOTH THE COUNTRY AND POP CHARTS, CAPITOL RECORDS' FIRST MILLION SELLER

AUGUST 1947—ERNEST TUBB RECORDS FOR THE FIRST TIME AT CASTLE STUDIO IN NASHVILLE

NOVEMBER 1, 1947— EDDY ARNOLD BEGINS A SEVENTY-TWO-WEEK RUN AT THE TOP OF THE COUNTRY CHARTS

young, unknown artist with the reputation of being a problem drinker. The established hillbilly showcases—the Opry, WLW's Boone County Jamboree, the National Barn Dance—simply wouldn't give Hank Williams a second thought at the time. Arriving in August 1948, Hank quickly made good at the Hayride, joining a strong cast of up-and-comers that included Johnnie & Jack and a then largely unknown Kitty Wells.

Ironically, Hank Williams, the consummate country songwriter, purchased his ticket to the next level with a song he didn't even write. In fact, "Lovesick Blues," which he recorded in the Herzog Studios in Cincinnati on December 22, 1948, wasn't even a country song to begin with, but a show tune that vaudeville and fringe country performers had somehow kept kicking around until Hank Williams claimed it for his own. As styled by Hank, though, the song was pure country, right down to his own personalized blue yodels. By early May 1949 "Lovesick Blues" stood atop the country hit parade, where it would remain for the rest of the summer. And on June 11, 1949, it provided Hank the password for entry to the Grand Ole Opry.

Those in attendance at the Ryman Auditorium that hot June night would never forget the moment Hank hit the Opry stage. It came during the 9:30 to 10:00 P.M. segment sponsored by Warren Paint and hosted by Ernest Tubb. Following performances by Tubb and Bill Monroe & His Blue Grass Boys, Hank came out to do his "Lovesick Blues." Although there was a polite smattering of applause at his entrance, most of the crowd apparently didn't recognize the grinning twenty-five-year-old hayseed until he kicked into the song. Then the audience's buzzing began to swell as Hank hunkered down and bobbed to the beat in his easy-going style. Offstage, Uncle Dave Macon turned to Minnie Pearl and said, "Who *is* that boy?"

The audience called him back to reprise chorus after chorus of "Lovesick Blues." As Minnie Pearl recalled, "They wouldn't let that man off the stage." On another occasion she summed up the essence of Hank's appeal: "He had real animal magnetism. He destroyed the women in the audience. And he was just as authentic as rain."

In the June 25, 1949, issue of *Billboard* Hank Williams still ruled the charts with "Lovesick Blues," but there was a change. The magazine no longer called the music "folk" or "hillbilly." Now the charts were titled "country and western," reportedly because Ernest Tubb had lobbied *Billboard* editor Paul Ackerman for the change. "In the old days, it was called 'hillbilly music,'" Tubb said years later. "But if you called somebody a hillbilly, you were making fun of him. Hillbilly meant inferior. I started telling record companies, 'Let's not call it hillbilly; let's call it something else.' And I thought, Why not call it 'country'?

JANUARY 1, 1948—AMERICAN FEDERATION OF MUSICIANS UNION GOES ON NATIONAL STRIKE AGAIN, WITH A SETTLEMENT COMING LATE IN THE YEAR; RECORD LABELS AGAIN COPE BY RELEASING STOCKPILED RECORDINGS

JANUARY 1948—LESTER FLATT AND EARL SCRUGGS LEAVE BILL MONROE AND FORM THEIR OWN BAND

APRIL 3, 1948—THE LOUISIANA HAYRIDE GOES ON THE AIR AT KWKH IN SHREVEPORT, LOUISIANA

JUNE 21, 1948—COLUMBIA INTRODUCES THE 33 1/3-RPM LONG-PLAYING (LP) RECORD

JULY 24, 1948—ROY ACUFF ANNOUNCES HIS INTENTION TO RUN FOR GOVERNOR OF TENNESSEE

AUGUST 1948—CAPITOL RECORDS BECOMES THE FIRST LABEL TO BEGIN USING MAGNETIC TAPE IN RECORDING

AUGUST 1948—HANK WILLIAMS JOINS THE LOUISIANA HAYRIDE

MARCH 1949—RCA VICTOR INTRODUCES THE 45-RPM SINGLE

MAY 7, 1949—HANK WILLIAMS HAS HIS FIRST NO. 1 HIT, "LOVESICK BLUES"

The name stuck. Nobody calls it hillbilly anymore."

With the Opry as his launching pad, Hank Williams blazed across the country firmament like a shooting star. His records consistently broke high into the country charts, many of them settling at No. 1. Most of them he wrote, delivering country wit and wisdom in a delightful variety of ways. His records included the pointed joshing of "Mind Your Own Business" and "Why Don't You Love Me"; harrowing stories from life's other side such as "Honky Tonk Blues" and "I'm So Lonesome I Could Cry"; classic hurtin' tunes like "Cold, Cold Heart" and "I Can't Help It If I'm Still in Love with You"; and good-natured romps like "Hey, Good Lookin'" and "Jambalaya."

With the help of Fred Rose (whom he affectionately called "Pappy"), Hank broke through to the pop music market in a way that no single country music songwriter had before him. Although Bing Crosby and other pop artists recorded many country songs, beginning in the summer of 1951 Hank had his songs *consistently* recorded by pop singers. First came "Cold, Cold Heart," which gave Tony Bennett a No. 1 pop hit, in spite of the fact that Bennett begged his Columbia producer Mitch Miller not to saddle him with what he derisively labeled "cowboy songs." Miller reassured him: "Tony, listen to the *words*." Following that trailblazing success, Mitch Miller had a standing arrangement

with Fred Rose that he would get first crack at any Williams compositions for his pop roster at Columbia Records. In 1951 alone, Mitch Miller doled out "Jambalaya" to Jo Stafford, "I Can't Help It If I'm Still in Love with You" to Guy Mitchell, and "Hey, Good Lookin'" to the duet team of Frankie Laine and Jo Stafford. In the fall of 1952 Joni James and Frankie Laine each notched Top Ten pop hits with "Your Cheatin' Heart," while Williams had sold more than 10 million of his own records, earning about $200,000 a year.

But Hank Williams was living on borrowed time. A chronically bad back begged to be soothed with liquor and pills. A bad marriage pushed him deeper into a bottomless well of drink and self-pity. By 1952, more often than not, Hank showed up onstage woozy from drink, in no condition to sing, and his rickety marriage to Audrey splintered for good. In August he was fired from the Grand Ole Opry for failing to show up for scheduled shows. Though he quickly regained a berth at the Louisiana Hayride and found himself a nineteen-year-old October bride in Billie Jean Jones, his days were numbered.

On New Year's Day, 1953, Hank Williams was discovered dead in the back of a car headed for the next gig in Canton, Ohio. The coroner's report indicated that he "died of a severe heart condition and hemorrhage." It didn't say anything about his having lived too

much in too few years—just twenty-nine years on this earth. As 1953 dawned, Hank's latest hit record, "I'll Never Get Out of This World Alive," still hung on the charts.

In death as in life, Hank Williams was a showstopper. Three days after his demise, his memorial service at the Municipal Auditorium in Montgomery, Alabama, drew almost 20,000 mourners, although only 2,750 could squeeze inside for the hour-long ceremony. (Two hundred were seated in the segregated black section.) Despite Hank's recent dismissal from the Opry, the entire cast turned out for the send-off. Ernest Tubb sang "Beyond the Sunset," Roy Acuff weighed in with Hank's own "I Saw the Light," and Red Foley, his voice cracking with emotion, offered up his hit gospel song, "Peace in the Valley." Hundreds filed by the open casket to see the deceased, a little white Bible clasped in his hands. Despite the solemnity of the occasion, Opry manager Jim Denny couldn't resist remarking to Horace Logan, his counterpart at the Louisiana Hayride, "If Hank could raise up in that coffin, he'd say, 'See, I told you I could draw more folks dead than you SOBs could alive.'"

Macabre jokes aside, as the outpouring of grief in Montgomery pointedly underlined, Hank Williams had a unique talent. He struck an emotional chord in listeners. Yet, rather than marking the end of country music's ascendancy in Nashville, his death

| JUNE 25, 1949—*BILL-BOARD* MAGAZINE RETITLES ITS HILLBILLY MUSIC CHART "COUNTRY & WESTERN" | 1950—WSM ANNOUNCER DAVID COBB OFFHANDEDLY CALLS NASHVILLE "MUSIC CITY, U.S.A." FOR THE FIRST TIME DURING A BROADCAST | FEBRUARY 11, 1950—RED FOLEY'S RECORDING OF "CHATTANOOGIE SHOE SHINE BOY" TOPS THE *BILLBOARD* POP CHART; IT IS ALREADY NO. 1 ON THE COUNTRY CHART | DECEMBER 16, 1950—PATTI PAGE'S RECORDING OF "TENNESSEE WALTZ" BY PEE WEE KING AND REDD STEWART TOPS THE *BILLBOARD* POP CHART | NOVEMBER 3, 1951—TONY BENNETT'S RECORDING OF "COLD COLD HEART" BY HANK WILLIAMS TOPS THE *BILLBOARD* POP CHART | |

The last roundup for ol' Hank, with pallbearers Fred and Wesley Rose, among others, January 4, 1953.

merely marked a beginning. Nashville and the Grand Ole Opry had so much momentum that even the death of the greatest communicator hillbilly music had ever known couldn't slow the city's ascent.

★ ★ ★

With country hits scoring high on the pop charts, it was only a matter of time before someone coined the right term to describe Nashville's new dominance in the country music market. It happened in 1950 on WSM, when David Cobb was announcing "The Red Foley Show," a morning program broadcast over the NBC network. Cobb always opened the show with the typical: "From Nashville, Tennessee, the National Broadcasting Company presents . . ." One morning, Cobb tried a new twist: "From Music City, U.S.A., Nashville, Tennessee . . ."

"It felt right," Cobb recalled, "and fell trippingly from the tongue, like a good billboard should."

Like Grand Ole Opry, it was a name that captured the meaning perfectly. Now it was up to Nashville to live up to it. The formation of BMI made country songwriting a potentially lucrative profession. Acuff-Rose Publications ably demonstrated the fact not only by signing top writers like Hank Williams and Pee Wee King ("Tennessee Waltz," "You Belong to Me") but also by promoting their work to the wider pop market. All the while, the Opry, with its 50,000-watt clear-channel signal and NBC half hour, continued to act as a magnet for topflight musicians. With the opening of Castle Studio, ambitious musicians began coming to Nashville for country recording sessions. Easing Nashville's transition as a recording center was the far-sighted George Cooper, head of the Nashville musicians union. For years the American Federation of Musicians had required potential members to pass a music reading test. It was a rule that stood in the way of hundreds of country boys who had learned to play by ear rather than through formal lessons. After Cooper successfully lobbied the national office to waive the rule for Nashville, country musicians could work in the studio for union wages. The numbers speak for themselves. In 1950 the Nashville musicians union had 526 members; over the next twenty years, that number would more than triple. Nashville was on its way.

Waiting in the wings: manager Hubert Long, WSM program director Jack Stapp, unidentified, Little Jimmy Dickens on fiddle, unidentified, Opry manager Jim Denny, and Faron Young.

All Shook Up

WINDS OF CHANGE

Even without Hank Williams, the country music business was booming in the early 1950s, paralleling the growth in the postwar economy. More than 1,400 radio programs featured country music on an average of eleven hours a week. By 1953, according to the *Wall Street Journal*, the country music business was pumping $25 million a year into Nashville's coffers. That year, attendance at the Opry hit an all-time peak of 243,721.

Looming on the horizon, though, were enormous changes. Technological developments would profoundly affect the way country music was played and recorded. During the 1950s magnetic tape would become the standard medium for recording, allowing a previously undreamed-of flexibility in the studio. Meanwhile, thanks to a technical innovation and a key recording session, the electric steel guitar would quickly supersede the fiddle as the quintessential country music instrument. The fifties would also see televisions crowd radios out of nearly every living room in the United States. In 1948 only 1 percent of American homes had the newfangled idiot boxes; by 1960 that figure had swelled to 90 percent, and it was still growing. Television's hegemony spelled the end of live radio; the Grand Ole Opry would be one of the few survivors, as stations turned increasingly to disc jockeys and records (supplied free of charge to stations by record companies)—a big savings over the cost of live performance.

In the social realm, three decades of voting and five years of defense-plant work had given women a newfound confidence in the workplace and a louder voice in American society. That voice would make its way into country music thanks to the breakthrough record of a shy but talented singer by the name of Kitty Wells. Finally, the most momentous upheaval of all came from America's youth. Beginning in 1946 the nation experienced an unprecedented rise in births. Fueled by the feeling of relief following a hard-won war and a spectacularly prosperous economy, America experienced what we have now grown accustomed to calling the "Baby Boom." Before the decade was out, the taste of American teenagers would come to dominate the pop record market. The aftershocks of that youthquake would affect country's course for years to come.

★ MAN OF STEEL

When the Opry dismissed Hank Williams in August 1952, Opry manager Jim Denny and WSM program director Jack Stapp quickly began laying plans for finding Hank's replacement. They found a good candidate at the Louisiana Hayride (where, ironically, Hank returned to lick his wounds) in a six-foot raven-haired thirty-one-year-old Louisianian, Webb Pierce. Signed to Decca Records in 1951, Pierce had slugged two hits to the top of the country charts when the Opry tapped him to join the cast, and he would prove an able replacement, and an innovator in his own way.

As it happened, his third straight No. 1 hit was a song that Hank

Webb Pierce with wife, Audrey, in their Nashville home. During the fifties, Pierce had more No. 1 records than any other country artist.

Williams had originally wanted to cut. While guesting on the Opry in the summer of 1952, Webb Pierce heard Hank sing "Back Street Affair" and liked the style of the song, which offered a first-person account of an extramarital affair. Cheating songs were the new thing in country music, ever since Floyd Tillman's "Slipping Around" had become a massive hit in the fall of 1949, topping both the country and pop charts for Jimmy Wakely and Margaret Whiting. "Back Street Affair" was just racy enough for the brash Pierce, and he asked Hank if he intended to record it.

"It ain't my new record," said Hank. "Fred Rose won't let me record it. Too risky. I think anyone's got guts enough to record it has got themselves a No. 1 hit."

Pierce recorded the song in July and, sure enough, it did go to No. 1 that fall. A few months after his cheating-song triumph, he found a song about drinking that didn't exactly glorify getting drunk but didn't condemn having a drink either. Delivered in Pierce's shrill, nasal tenor, "There Stands the Glass" simply presented a vivid picture of the drinking life, nonjudgmental and not one bit sentimental.

"Both Jim Denny of the Grand Ole Opry and Fred Rose said recording it would ruin my career because it tolerated drinking," Pierce later recalled. Rose, a reformed alcoholic, was against the song. He complained to Pierce that "it doesn't even have a moral!" To which Pierce, the canny businessman, replied, "Well, Fred, 75 percent of the people in this world take a drink ever' once in a while." Although several stations did ban the record, it nevertheless became Pierce's fifth No. 1 hit.

Not only did Pierce look for new controversial subject matter, he also kept his ear cocked for interesting new sounds. In September 1953 Pierce guested on Kate Smith's network TV show where he heard Nashville steel guitar player Bud Isaacs playing his new toy, a steel guitar with pedals, enabling Isaacs to bend notes—even entire chords—dramatically, with just the tap of his foot. Pedal steel guitars had been around for a few years by then, but most folks considered them a gimmick. Pierce liked the sound, though, and told Isaacs that he had just the song for it.

November 29, 1953, turned out to be a historic day, for it was that evening that Pierce unleashed Bud Isaacs and the pedal steel sound on "Slowly," which opened with the atmospheric swoop of Isaacs's steel. Isaacs kicked off the leisurely love song with a four-note phrase that made his six steel strings toll like six bells in a belfry, each swinging tantalizingly in and out of key. Then, when his mutant steel picked up the solo from Tommy Jackson's fiddle, he bent full chords with his quavering, slightly discordant phrases. Three weeks after its release, "Slowly" hit No. 1 on the country best-seller chart. Within weeks, pickers nationwide were rigging their guitars with coat hangers, chicken wire, even Model T gas pedals in an effort to simulate the new, full sound.

"I had no idea it would skyrocket like it did," Isaacs later said. "When we came in off the road a couple of weeks later a big surprise was waiting in the mailroom of WSM. There was a huge pile of laundry bags stuffed with mail. Everyone wanted to know how I got the new sound. They were tuning their guitars this way and that, trying to figure out how I did it." Not surprisingly, with his new signature sound, Isaacs remained much in demand as a sideman and studio musician, and he would go on to work with many of the brightest stars in country music during the fifties and sixties.

For his part, Webb Pierce became a major star in country music. During the 1950s he had more No. 1 songs on the country charts—thirteen in all—than any other artist. He also set the standards for hillbilly style with his flashy rhinestoned costumes. In 1953 he went into partnership with Opry manager Jim Denny to form Cedarwood Publishing. As with Acuff-

Rose, the firm had its own star as a ready outlet for getting songs recorded; ultimately, Cedarwood would sign a number of talented writers, including Mel Tillis and John D. Loudermilk. Like Eddy Arnold, Webb Pierce eventually found that he could do without the Grand Ole Opry, leaving the show on a trial basis in 1955–56 and permanently in February 1957. Though his popularity tapered off in the sixties, he remained for many fans the epitome of the country star, with a silver-dollar-studded convertible and guitar-shaped swimming pool to prove it.

★ Lefty

Even though Webb Pierce amassed the most hits during the decade, the most influential

Lefty Frizzell in 1951: He made his lazy Texas drawl a distinctive vocal style that has influenced innumerable country singers, including Randy Travis, Merle Haggard, and Willie Nelson.

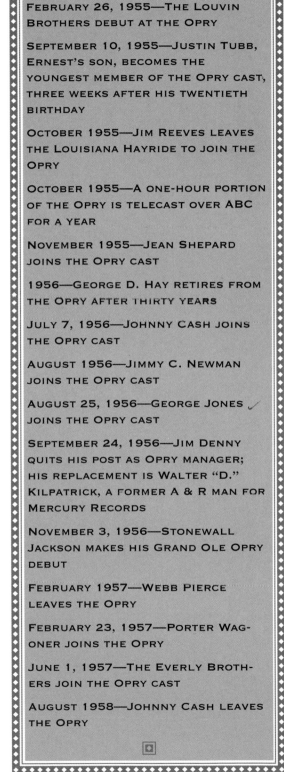

FEBRUARY 26, 1955—THE LOUVIN BROTHERS DEBUT AT THE OPRY

SEPTEMBER 10, 1955—JUSTIN TUBB, ERNEST'S SON, BECOMES THE YOUNGEST MEMBER OF THE OPRY CAST, THREE WEEKS AFTER HIS TWENTIETH BIRTHDAY

OCTOBER 1955—JIM REEVES LEAVES THE LOUISIANA HAYRIDE TO JOIN THE OPRY

OCTOBER 1955—A ONE-HOUR PORTION OF THE OPRY IS TELECAST OVER ABC FOR A YEAR

NOVEMBER 1955—JEAN SHEPARD JOINS THE OPRY CAST

1956—GEORGE D. HAY RETIRES FROM THE OPRY AFTER THIRTY YEARS

JULY 7, 1956—JOHNNY CASH JOINS THE OPRY CAST

AUGUST 1956—JIMMY C. NEWMAN JOINS THE OPRY CAST

AUGUST 25, 1956—GEORGE JONES JOINS THE OPRY CAST

SEPTEMBER 24, 1956—JIM DENNY QUITS HIS POST AS OPRY MANAGER; HIS REPLACEMENT IS WALTER "D." KILPATRICK, A FORMER A & R MAN FOR MERCURY RECORDS

NOVEMBER 3, 1956—STONEWALL JACKSON MAKES HIS GRAND OLE OPRY DEBUT

FEBRUARY 1957—WEBB PIERCE LEAVES THE OPRY

FEBRUARY 23, 1957—PORTER WAGONER JOINS THE OPRY

JUNE 1, 1957—THE EVERLY BROTHERS JOIN THE OPRY CAST

AUGUST 1958—JOHNNY CASH LEAVES THE OPRY

voice belonged to a young Texan, William Orville Frizzell, known to friends and fans as Lefty. Of all the country singers of the 1950s, Lefty Frizzell is the only one regularly spoken of in the same breath as Hank Williams. "I feel he was the most unique thing that ever happened to country music," Merle Haggard has said. "In the beginning," said Randy Travis, "I would learn Lefty Frizzell songs and try to copy them note for note." Not surprisingly, the sound of Lefty Frizzell's voice colors the vocal styles of both Haggard and Travis as well as numerous other country singers, including George Jones and Willie Nelson.

What accounts for this sort of pervasive influence and reputation? Everyone seems to understand the legend of Hank Williams: an untimely death, a charismatic stage presence,

an unadorned, plaintive singing style, and, most of all, songs that became nationwide pop smashes in his lifetime and that have shown a remarkable durability. Unlike Hank, Lefty remains almost unknown outside of country music and its most devoted fans. He too died before his time—though unromantically—felled by a stroke at forty-seven after years of hard living. He wrote more than twice as many songs as Hank had—some 300—but most of them were such idiosyncratic extensions of his own voice that they have been less often recorded by other artists.

What set Lefty apart from other singers was what he did with his voice. He bent notes as if his vocal cords were guitar strings, stretched single syllables into several, pushed against the upper and lower edges of his warm

baritone for effects both rough and tender. Like a blues singer, he took his good sweet time singing each and every line. In short, he took the quintessential lazy Southern drawl and made it a distinctive vocal style.

"What I sing, to me every word has a feeling about it," he said in an interview just before his death. "I had to linger, had to hold it, I didn't want to let go of it. I want to hold one word through a whole line of melody, to linger with it all the way down. I didn't want to let go of that no more than I wanted to let go of the woman I loved."

The impact of Lefty Frizzell's voice was swift. His first record was the double-sided hit "If You've Got the Money I've Got the Time"/ "I Love You a Thousand Ways." The record sold so quickly that seventeen days after its re-

Tall, blue-eyed, and handsome, Carl Smith capitalized on his good looks by singing romantic ballads like "It's a Lovely Lovely World" and playful up-tempo numbers like "Hey, Joe" and "Back Up, Buddy." A member of the Opry cast from 1950 to 1956, he sold some 15 million records during his nearly thirty-year recording career.

lease in September 1950, Columbia Records asked Lefty to return to the studio for more records. Both sides became No. 1 hits in late 1950 and early 1951. In April of 1951 he spent a week on tour with Hank Williams. In July, at age twenty-three, the hottest star in country music, he was invited to join the cast of the Grand Ole Opry. Welcomed to the show on July 21, 1951, by "Prince Albert Show" host Red Foley, Lefty sang "I Love You a Thousand Ways" and his third No. 1 hit, "I Want to Be with You Always." That October he slugged four hits in *Billboard*'s Top Ten country chart during a single week—"Always Late" (No. 1), "Mom and Dad's Waltz" (No. 2), "I Want to Be with You Always" (No. 7), and "Travellin' Blues" (No. 8).

By February 1952, after only eight months in Nashville, Lefty was through with the Opry. Unlike Hank, he left of his own accord, and initially he seemed to continue on course. But a messy, protracted lawsuit with his manager shortly afterward sent his career into a tailspin. His road band broke up, and as he drank his sorrows away, his hits dried up. He didn't manage another No. 1 hit for twelve years, but his influence far outlasted his brief 1950–52 heyday.

Besides breaking new ground with his vocal style, Lefty Frizzell was the first country singer to wear rhinestones onstage. Today we take the sparkle of country costumes for granted, but in Lefty's day it was a big deal for a man to wear rhinestones. It happened around 1953 after Lefty had relocated to Los Angeles and was working a local country music TV show. One of the best western tailors in the area was a fifty-year-old Russian-Jewish immigrant by the name of Nudie Cohen. Formerly a maker of lingerie for New York burlesque shows, Nudie (anglicized from Nutya) became established as a cowboy clothier in L.A. in 1946 when he outfitted Tex Williams's band. Those suits were little more

than businessmen's suits with a western accent in the cut and the contrasting piping. It was far more audacious to outfit Lefty Frizzell in a costume with his initials in rhinestones on the lapels. Although he liked sharp clothes, Lefty certainly didn't want to risk looking like a sissy. Nudie had a ready-made argument for him: Only a really tough guy could carry off wearing rhinestones. Besides, Nudie added, women love men who look flashy—and what could be flashier than rhinestones? Lefty was convinced. He wore the suit and got rave reviews from bedazzled fans and envious performers. Within weeks he was back, telling Nudie Cohen not to skimp on those rhinestones.

★ TATER AND THE SINGING RANGER

Despite losing both Lefty Frizzell and Hank Williams in 1952, the Grand Ole Opry rolled along unaffected. Indeed, on the day Hank Williams died, the Opry could boast the strongest cast of any radio program in country music—if not the strongest in all of American radio. In addition to dependable mainstays Red Foley, Roy Acuff, Minnie Pearl, Ernest Tubb, and Bill Monroe, the show continued to recruit a wave of talented newcomers. Two of the most memorable were Little Jimmy Dickens and Hank Snow.

As a singer, Little Jimmy Dickens was cut right out of the Roy Acuff mold. That may explain, in part, why Acuff was so taken with Dickens when he first heard the four-foot-eleven-inch belter in 1947. But Acuff also noticed the diminutive singer's undeniable energy. "The first time I saw Jimmy Dickens," Acuff recalled, "was in Cincinnati, Ohio, at the Music Hall. I was supposed to be the star of the show, but when I introduced Jimmy Dickens to the stage, that was all she wrote. He took the show."

The twenty-six-year-old West Virginia

Little Jimmy Dickens, standing all of four foot eleven, joined the Opry in 1948 and quickly made a name for himself with comic novelty numbers like "Take an Old Cold Tater (and Wait)."

farm boy already had a decade of performing experience behind him at several radio stations when Acuff invited him for a guest appearance at the Opry in 1947. The following year Dickens joined the Opry cast without the benefit of a hit record—or for that matter even a recording contract. Not long after bringing Dickens into the Opry fold, Acuff introduced him to his partner Fred Rose and to veteran A & R man Art Satherley, who signed the diminutive singer to Columbia Records in November 1948. Blessed with a powerful voice that belied his size, Dickens could wring tears from any good ballad. But he'd always had success with a comic number from the 1920s called "Take an Old Cold Tater (and

Hank Snow had worked for fifteen years to gain his Opry membership in 1950. He cemented it in 1950 with the massive hit "I'm Movin' On."

Roy Acuff. Through the fifties he would capitalize on a string of such numbers (known in the business as "novelty songs"), many of them trading on his stature or his country ways: "A-Sleepin' at the Foot of the Bed," "I'm Little but I'm Loud," "Bessie the Heifer," "Out Behind the Barn."

Like Dickens, Hank Snow was also a veteran performer when he joined the Opry in 1950, but he had been scuffling from one station to another for nearly fifteen years. Hank Snow's odyssey began in a fishing village in Nova Scotia, Canada, where among the first records he'd listened to as a child were those of Vernon Dalhart. At age sixteen, after hearing Jimmie Rodgers, Hank was inspired to be a singer. He began his career at a Nova Scotia radio station in 1935. A year and a half later, at the age of twenty-two, he made the first of some ninety recordings for RCA Victor's Canadian branch. Up until 1949 those records were rarely heard in the United States—which may have been just as well, since it took

Snow years to break free from the Rodgers style. Nevertheless, he tried to crack the American market. Between 1945 and 1950 he tried a number of blind alleys: a stint at the WWVA Jamboree in West Virginia, cowboy movies in Hollywood, another stint at Dallas's Big D Jamboree, even a shot at the Louisiana Hayride in June 1949 after the departure of Hank Williams. Finally in March 1949 the U.S. branch of RCA consented to record him.

Throughout this time, Snow kept up a regular correspondence with Ernest Tubb in which they expressed their mutual admiration for Jimmie Rodgers. Those letters eventually led to Tubb's recommending Snow to the Opry. He got his first shot on January 7, 1950, working for $75 a week. Snow didn't exactly bowl over the Opry audiences with his first appearances. In fact, he so underwhelmed them that Opry manager Jim Denny was seriously considering letting the thirty-five-year-old Hank go to make room for younger blood. Then Snow caught fire with a big hit. In his

Wait)" that made light of his "puny ways." It didn't take much convincing for Art Satherley to let him record it at his first session in January 1949. In the spring, it broke into the country charts and earned him the nickname "Tater," which Hank Williams himself bestowed.

Fred Rose took note of the hit and brought Dickens another comic tune called "Country Boy." When that second release climbed into the charts as well, Satherley saw a pattern developing and kept Dickens recording humorous songs. As a result, Little Jimmy developed an identity quite apart from that of his mentor

Celebrating: RCA executive Steve Sholes (left), Hank Snow, and WSM station manager Harry Stone (right) in 1950.

Women didn't have much of a voice in country music until Kitty Wells came along and opened the doors with her big hit "It Wasn't God Who Made Honky Tonk Angels" in 1952.

though, he developed a catchy country sound all his own that prefigured rock and roll with his tongue-twisting wordplay, his high-velocity guitar picking, and steady beat on bouncy numbers like "Rhumba Boogie" and "Music Makin' Mama from Memphis."

★ A WOMAN'S VOICE

During the early fifties no one who listened to country music doubted that the Grand Ole Opry represented the pinnacle of achievement. Yet something was lacking not only at the Opry but also in country music in general. In the summer of 1952, just as Hank Williams was falling from grace with the Opry, the first great female singer took her place alongside the men at the Ryman.

Few performers of her stature have had as unheralded an arrival as Kitty Wells. She was born Muriel Deason, in Nashville of all places, and began visiting the Opry as a youngster, visits which inspired her to sing professionally. She performed as a teenager on radio, not at WSM but at WSIX. At age eighteen she married local musician Johnnie Wright and became part of his traveling show, headlined by Johnnie's duet act with his brother-in-law, Jack Anglin. Between her 1937 wedding and settling in at the Opry in 1952, Muriel and Johnnie & Jack worked a dizzying string of radio stops—Greensboro, North Carolina; Charleston, West Virginia; Knoxville, Tennessee; Raleigh, North Carolina; Memphis; Nashville and the Grand Ole Opry for a solid year; then Shreveport and the Louisiana Hayride; Decatur, Georgia; Birmingham, Alabama; and then Shreveport again. One station job was very much like the next: low pay, usually early-morning or noontime hours, and touring the broadcast area to make some decent money from shows. It was in Knoxville that Muriel became known as Kitty Wells.

second stateside session on March 28, 1950, Snow recorded a driving train song inspired by—who else?—Jimmie Rodgers.

In July "I'm Movin' On" began its inexorable drive up the charts. By late August it rolled into the No. 1 spot on the country best-seller charts, where it would remain off and on for the next six months, long enough for Snow to match it with yet another No. 1 song about riding a train, "The Golden Rocket." Hank Snow was off and running, gaining in the process a permanent membership in the cast of the Grand Ole Opry. Even more importantly,

The program director thought "Muriel" wouldn't stick in people's minds, so Johnnie Wright suggested a name from an old folk song, "Kitty Wells," that had been popularized by the Vagabonds and the Pickard Family on the Opry. A star was born. Eventually.

By the time Johnnie & Jack returned to the Grand Ole Opry in January 1952, the constant traveling and the challenge of raising three young children had cooled Kitty's ardor for the music business. With Johnnie & Jack firmly established as a hit duo on the Grand Ole Opry, Kitty Wells slipped quietly out of the music business and focused more on her home and her children. But Johnnie Wright didn't give up on his wife's career so easily. From Shreveport, he sent a demo record of hers up to Decca's Paul Cohen. Weeks later, back in Nashville, Cohen ran into Wright and told him that he liked Kitty's singing. Actually, Cohen was trying to reel in Johnnie & Jack for Decca by signing Kitty Wells first, but he did have an interesting song for her. It was an answer to Hank Thompson's current No. 1 hit, "The Wild Side of Life." Delivered in first

Hank Thompson has artfully blended western swing and honky-tonk styles for fifty years. But it was his first No. 1 record, "The Wild Side of Life" (1952), that inspired Kitty Wells's famous answer song.

person, the lyrics of "Wild Side of Life" castigated a woman for leaving a faithful husband. It was a song that appealed to those who thought the world was going to hell and that faithless women deserved a good deal of the blame.

The song just begged for an answer from a woman. Ironically, the person who penned the rebuttal, "It Wasn't God Who Made Honky Tonk Angels," turned out to be a man, J. D. Miller. It was Kitty Wells, though, who gave voice to its sentiments, but not without some elbow twisting. When she heard the demo recording, Kitty Wells didn't think much of it. "If you want me to record it," she told her husband, "we'll do it. At least we'll get a session fee out of it." The song turned out to be worth a lot more than the $125 standard fee of the day.

Even if she didn't love the song, Wells tackled it with real enthusiasm at the May 3, 1952, recording session at the Castle Studio. Since Paul Cohen was out of town, he asked Owen Bradley to preside for him. The band—Jack Anglin on guitar, Shot Jackson on steel, Paul Warren on fiddle, and Johnnie Wright on string bass—took the identical melody of "Wild Side of Life," but at a slightly faster clip. The tempo suited Kitty perfectly, making her recording sound vibrant and feisty, as she called Hank Thompson's bluff. "Too many times married men think they're still single," she sang, her voice wringing with indignant vibrato. "That has caused many a good girl to go wrong." "It Wasn't God Who Made Honky Tonk Angels" hit the country charts in June. By August it had sold a half million copies, and, in a nice

Even after she became a star in her own right, Kitty Wells continued to perform with her husband Johnnie Wright (left) and his duet partner Jack Anglin.

comeuppance, it elbowed "Wild Side of Life" out of the No. 1 spot in the best-seller chart. Kitty Wells had notched the first No. 1 country record by a woman since Billboard had begun tracking country records in January 1944.

"I was shocked," Kitty said years later. "Women never had hit records in those days.

Very few of them ever even recorded. I couldn't believe it had happened."

The record's breakthrough did not come without some resistance. The NBC radio network banned "It Wasn't God Who Made Honky Tonk Angels" for being "suggestive." For a brief time Kitty Wells was barred from singing the song not only on NBC's "Prince Albert" spot but also on the entire Opry as well. Jim Denny and program director Jack Stapp questioned the wisdom of even having Kitty Wells perform on the show. The record had an audience however. Minnie Pearl remembered that "fans went wild over Kitty. When she did 'Honky Tonk Angels,' they'd scream and holler and carry on." The problem, as Denny and Stapp saw it, was that Kitty didn't do very much to whip up that kind of enthusiasm. She just stood stock still and sang. It took the intercession of another performer who sang much the same way—Roy Acuff—before Kitty Wells had a regular role in the Opry.

Acuff, of course, recognized a good tune when he heard one. "It Wasn't God Who Made Honky Tonk Angels" and "Wild Side of Life" had both been based on the old folk melody that Acuff had used for "The Great Speckled Bird." Acuff knew full well that that same melody went back to the Carter Family's "I'm Thinking Tonight of My Blue Eyes," and beyond. The publishers of "Wild Side of Life" didn't, though, and tried to sue for copyright infringement. Naturally, the lawsuit fell apart when it was pointed out how much both songs owed to the Carters' "I'm Thinking Tonight of My Blue Eyes."

Fittingly, Kitty Wells harked back to the rustic beauty of Sara Carter when she sang. Though she was a soprano and Sara Carter an alto, Kitty Wells had that same authentic gritty twang. Like Sara Carter, Roy Acuff, and Hank Williams, like all the best country singers, Kitty Wells sounded as though she was telling the truth.

Although the success of "Honky Tonk Angels" built a new career for Kitty Wells, it did not change her views on the traditional roles of men and women. "I've always worked with my husband," she said. "And I like having somebody around to look after me. Woman was put on earth for man to look after."

Despite the stature she attained, Kitty Wells remained a quiet, in many ways retiring performer. Nevertheless, she kept knocking out hits. During one incredible stretch of 161 weeks, her recordings were never off the charts. Right into the mid-sixties, Kitty Wells remained by far the biggest female star in country music, and her influence on women extended many years beyond that.

★ BEGINNINGS OF MUSIC ROW

Business moves behind the scenes strengthened Nashville's claim as Music City, U.S.A. In 1951, taking a cue from Roy Acuff and Fred Rose, WSM program director Jack Stapp founded his own music publishing company, Tree Publishing, along with Lou Cowan, an old New York buddy from CBS-TV, who had developed the TV game show "$64,000 Question." Two years later Jim Denny and Webb Pierce got in the act with their own publishing outfit, Cedarwood.

By the mid-1950s Nashville was develop-

Goldie Hill was the first woman in country to capitalize on the breakthrough of Kitty Wells. She first hit the charts in 1953, but she married Carl Smith in 1957 and left the business soon after.

ing almost everything it needed to become a major music center. National Life gave WSM and the Grand Ole Opry enormous reserves of capital to draw on, allowing the Opry to thrive even as other live radio shows were disappearing. The Opry, in turn, with its powerful clear-channel signal and network hookups,

acted as a magnet for musical talent. Even though the Opry still didn't pay musicians very much, it offered greater exposure to plug tours than any other country music outlet. With the rise of publishing firms like Acuff-Rose, Tree, and Cedarwood, songwriters no longer had to work in New York, Chicago, or Los Angeles; now they could live in Nashville and pitch their latest tunes directly to the country singers. The last piece in the puzzle to establish Nashville was recording studios.

Luckily for Nashville's music business, just around the time Castle Studio was phasing out, Owen Bradley was gearing up in the recording business. From the time he got his first professional gig at age fifteen, all Owen Bradley ever wanted to do was play music. He took jobs playing piano with Nashville dance bands, at stations WLAC and WSM, even at the speakeasies and gambling casinos outside Nashville in Cheatham County ("It was wide open—like a little Reno out there," Bradley remembered). He just couldn't get enough music. When Fred Rose needed a copyist to write out arrangements of Acuff-Rose songs, he called on Bradley. Upon returning from the Navy after World War II, Bradley joined WSM as one of two staff bandleaders and musical directors. On the side he made instrumental records with his own band, most of them pop versions of country hits, such as "Blues Stay Away from Me."

He met Decca's Paul Cohen in January 1949 when Cohen was in town to record Red Foley. Bradley had been working as Red

Owen Bradley— musician, record producer, and the first to open a recording studio on what is now known as Music Row in Nashville.

When the landlord tripled the rent, they moved to a small warehouse building behind the Woolworth's store in west Nashville. Although Kitty Wells cut a couple of sessions there and Fred Rose used the studio as well, its low ceiling cramped the Bradley brothers' style. By late 1954 Paul Cohen was threatening to take his country recording business to Dallas where Jim Beck, an enterprising engineer and studio owner, had been cutting great records by up-and-comers like Lefty Frizzell, Marty Robbins, and Ray Price for Cohen's archrival, the Columbia label. Owen and Harold Bradley made Cohen a proposition: They would build a new studio and stock it with the most up-to-date equipment. They just needed a little money to get started. Cohen promised them a hundred Decca sessions a year if they could do it and put up $7,500 toward the building of the new studio.

In a run-down residential neighborhood that had just been zoned commercial, located about ten blocks southwest of the Ryman, the Bradleys bought a two-story wooden frame house on Sixteenth Avenue South that they would turn into Paul Cohen's dream studio. The Bradleys moved in around Christmas of 1954, promptly tore out the house's ground floor, set up an office on the second story, and installed a small studio in the basement, which had an eighteen-foot ceiling now that the first floor was gone. By April 1955 Bradley Film and Recording Studios was open for business

Foley's part-time arranger. Cohen liked the smooth, rhythmic sounds Bradley coaxed out of Foley and his band, particularly the jivey organ flourishes on a Latin-flavored number called "Tennessee Border." As Bradley remembered it, "Paul took it to New York, and they thought it was great." The record hit the No. 3 spot on the *Billboard* Country Juke Box charts that spring. Shortly afterward, the A & R man recruited the thirty-four-year-old Bradley as his assistant.

The first big success Bradley helped bring Cohen came with Red Foley's "Chattanoogie Shoe Shine Boy." Recorded in November 1949 at Castle Studio, the song topped both the pop and country charts, selling a million copies.

The record owed a lot to Bradley's swinging arrangement and the novel shoe-shine rag rhythm that Bradley got drummer Farris Coursey to slap out on his thigh. Emboldened by successes like that and inspired by Cohen's example, Bradley and his younger brother Harold began working their way into the recording business as well, opening their first film and recording studio on the third floor of an old Teamster's building in downtown Nashville. They concentrated mostly on making two- to three-minute films of bands playing songs. The Bradley brothers thought that with the advent of TV, there ought to be a big demand for "filmed records." Their music video idea was about three decades too soon.

at the corner of Sixteenth and Hawkins, the first recording studio on what is now known as Music Row. The Bradleys later added a portable Quonset hut to the site for filmmaking, although they soon realized it worked as a recording studio as well. "It had an arched ceiling," Bradley recalled, "and that's terrible for acoustics. . . . We had problems with the sound rolling around in there, so I got a bunch of old velour curtains. It wasn't scientifically worked out; we just kept going till it sounded all right to us."

In the fall of 1955 as they put the finishing touches on their new studio, the Bradleys seemed well positioned to capitalize on Nashville's new profile. That September, however, just 200 miles west, a rough beast was slouching toward the top of the country charts for the first time.

★ THE HILLBILLY CAT

When Elvis Presley's "I Forgot to Remember to Forget" entered the country charts in September 1955, he was two years out of high school and had been recording for a little over a year. He confided to his friends his vague dreams of being a movie star like his favorites Dean Martin and James Dean. He had already made a trial appearance on the Grand Ole Opry the previous October, singing his hopped-up version of Bill Monroe's "Blue Moon of Kentucky." It was not one of Presley's

Young Elvis Presley basks in newfound stardom.

greatest triumphs. Although popular legend has it that Opry manager Jim Denny told him he ought to go back to his day job—driving a delivery truck for the Crown Electric Company—the truth seems to be that Presley just didn't make much of an impression on the

Opry or its audience. So he went instead to the Louisiana Hayride where his wildly gyrating hips and his pink pegged suits fit in just fine. By 1955 the Hayride was being carried on nearly 200 stations over the CBS radio network every third Saturday of the month. Like

PROMINENCE WITH WEBB PIERCE'S RECORDING SESSION FOR "SLOWLY"; BY FEBRUARY 1954 THE RECORD IS NO. 1, AND THE STEEL GUITAR IS THE HOT NEW INSTRUMENT IN COUNTRY	JANUARY 19, 1954— GEORGE JONES, AGE TWENTY-TWO, MAKES HIS FIRST RECORDINGS FOR STARDAY RECORDS IN BEAUMONT, TEXAS	JULY 5, 1954—ELVIS PRESLEY, AGE NINE- TEEN, MAKES HIS FIRST RECORDINGS FOR SUN RECORDS IN MEMPHIS

JULY 17, 1954—IN SPRINGFIELD, MISSOURI, THE OZARK JUBILEE DEBUTS AS A RADIO | BARN DANCE WITH RED FOLEY AS HOST

OCTOBER 16, 1954— ELVIS PRESLEY BEGINS A YEAR OF RADIO APPEAR- ANCES AT THE LOUISIANA HAYRIDE | DECEMBER 1, 1954— SONGWRITER AND ACUFF-ROSE CO- FOUNDER FRED ROSE DIES | JANUARY 22, 1955—THE OZARK JUBILEE, HOSTED BY RED FOLEY, MAKES ITS TV DEBUT ON THE ABC NETWORK |

the Opry, the Hayride broadcast at a far-reaching 50,000 watts. Having graduated Hank Williams and Webb Pierce, the Hayride was known as the Cradle of the Stars, the unofficial farm team of the Grand Ole Opry. Embarking upon his first of a year's worth of appearances at the Hayride in November of 1954, Elvis was asked by announcer Frank Page where his unusual brand of country music came from: "I'd like to know how you came up with that rhythm and blues style," he asked, "because that's all it is."

"Well, sir," Presley replied humbly, "to be honest, we just stumbled upon it."

"You're mighty lucky, you know," said Page. "They've been looking for something new in the folk music field for a long time now. I think you've got it."

Truer, more prophetic words are rarely ever spoken. Though the Opry apparently didn't hear it, twenty-year-old Elvis Presley had that certain something that would transform the entire music industry. He thought he was singing country music with rhythm and blues, mixing the two in whatever way felt comfortable. Even Elvis Presley himself didn't realize he was unleashing the full gale force of rock and roll upon the slumbering populace of 1950s America.

Elvis Presley didn't create rock and roll; he simply proved to be the most potent popularizer of it. By 1955 what we call rock and roll had been brewing for at least a decade. Just after World War II it began to spill forth in the joyously hopped-up jump blues of black musicians like Louis Jordan and Big Joe Turner, in the hillbilly boogie of the Delmore Brothers and Moon Mullican. All through the late forties and early fifties, white country singers and black R & B singers recorded each other's tunes and copped each other's licks.

When Bill Haley, a not very well-known country musician from Pennsylvania, cut "(We're Gonna) Rock Around the Clock" and "Shake, Rattle and Roll" in April 1954—two months before Elvis Presley began recording for Sun Records in Memphis—the stage was set for a quaking. "Shake, Rattle and Roll," previously an R & B hit for Joe

Tennessee Ernie Ford had one of the biggest pop hits of the year in 1955 with Merle Travis's "Sixteen Tons." Over the next ten years, he would become an even bigger star on TV with shows on NBC and ABC.

SPRING 1955—OWEN AND HAROLD BRADLEY OPEN BRADLEY FILM AND RECORDING STUDIOS ON SIXTEENTH AND HAWKINS IN NASHVILLE	NOVEMBER 20, 1955—RCA RECORDS BUYS ELVIS PRESLEY'S CONTRACT FROM SUN RECORDS FOR $40,000	JANUARY 10, 1956—ELVIS FIRST RECORDS IN NASHVILLE; FROM THIS SESSION COMES "HEARTBREAK HOTEL," HIS FIRST MILLION SELLER AND POP NO. 1	JANUARY 26, 1956—BUDDY HOLLY'S FIRST RECORDING SESSIONS, SUPERVISED IN NASHVILLE BY OWEN BRADLEY AND PAUL COHEN	MAY 1956—DALLAS RECORDING STUDIO OWNER JIM BECK DIES AND THE CITY'S HOPES OF BECOMING A RECORDING CENTER DIE WITH HIM	JULY 21, 1956—JOHNNY CASH'S FIRST COUNTRY NO. 1 WITH "I WALK THE LINE"

Turner, climbed into the pop Top Ten for Haley. But that was small change compared to "Rock Around the Clock." The record had no impact in 1954, but the following year, when it was revived to open and close the popular movie of teen unrest, *Blackboard Jungle*, the record crashed the charts and stormed to the No. 1 slot on June 19, 1955. It was the first rock and roll song to top the record charts, and at year's end it capped *Billboard*'s list of the year's best-selling singles, just ahead of Tennessee Ernie Ford's rendition of "Sixteen Tons," one of Merle Travis's instant folk songs. "Rock Around the Clock" was the most successful of a shower of rock and roll records that poured out in 1955. Bo Diddley's first record, "Bo Diddley," with its infectious shave-and-a-haircut Latin rhythm, hit the market in March; Fats Domino's first pop chart hit, "Ain't That a Shame," came out in April; Chuck Berry's first hit, "Maybelline," was released in July; Little Richard's first hit, "Tutti-Frutti," was released in November. The age of rock and roll was dawning, unbeknownst to almost everyone working in country music.

Everyone except Colonel Tom Parker, that is, who had split with Eddy Arnold in August 1953. Since then, he had been working with the popular Opry star Hank Snow. In early 1955 Jamboree Attractions, the firm owned jointly by Parker and Snow, began booking Presley on tour dates across the Southwest and Southeast. Bob Luman, who would later become a Nashville recording artist himself, recalled one of those early tour dates for writer Paul Hemphill:

> This cat came out in red pants and a green coat and a pink shirt and socks, and he had this sneer on his face, and he stood behind the mike for five minutes, I'll bet, before he made a move. Then he hit his guitar a lick and broke two strings. I'd been playing ten years and hadn't broken a total of two strings. So there he was, these two strings dangling, and he hadn't done anything yet, and these high school girls were screaming and fainting and running up to the stage, and then he began to move his hips real slow like he had a thing for his guitar. That was Elvis Presley when he

Colonel Tom Parker, an ex-carnival barker, had a nose for talent and knew how to drive a bargain: He managed Eddy Arnold from 1944 to 1953, then guided Elvis Presley from 1956 until the singer's death.

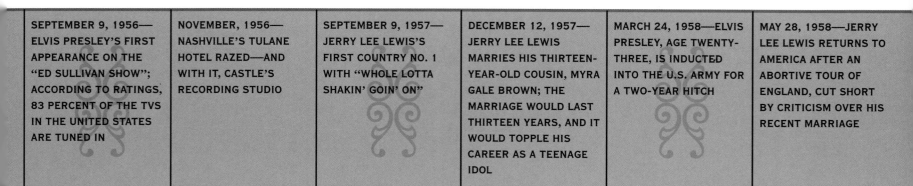

SEPTEMBER 9, 1956—ELVIS PRESLEY'S FIRST APPEARANCE ON THE "ED SULLIVAN SHOW"; ACCORDING TO RATINGS, 83 PERCENT OF THE TVS IN THE UNITED STATES ARE TUNED IN

NOVEMBER, 1956—NASHVILLE'S TULANE HOTEL RAZED—AND WITH IT, CASTLE'S RECORDING STUDIO

SEPTEMBER 9, 1957—JERRY LEE LEWIS'S FIRST COUNTRY NO. 1 WITH "WHOLE LOTTA SHAKIN' GOIN' ON"

DECEMBER 12, 1957—JERRY LEE LEWIS MARRIES HIS THIRTEEN-YEAR-OLD COUSIN, MYRA GALE BROWN; THE MARRIAGE WOULD LAST THIRTEEN YEARS, AND IT WOULD TOPPLE HIS CAREER AS A TEENAGE IDOL

MARCH 24, 1958—ELVIS PRESLEY, AGE TWENTY-THREE, IS INDUCTED INTO THE U.S. ARMY FOR A TWO-YEAR HITCH

MAY 28, 1958—JERRY LEE LEWIS RETURNS TO AMERICA AFTER AN ABORTIVE TOUR OF ENGLAND, CUT SHORT BY CRITICISM OVER HIS RECENT MARRIAGE

Elvis Presley mixed together everything that he loved—country, blues, pop, and gospel. Here he records with his favorite gospel quartet, the Jordanaires, ca. 1956.

one show after another from any established country entertainer who headlined, the wily ex–carnival barker moved into position to become the phenom's new manager. Throughout 1955, as Parker leaked word that Presley's contract would soon be up and available to the highest bidder, record labels began making offers to buy Presley's contract from Sam Phillips at tiny Sun Records in Memphis. On August 15, 1955, Colonel Parker bought a controlling interest in Presley's management contract from Memphis DJ Bob Neal for what then seemed a hefty $2,500. Then Parker proceeded to engineer the most expensive deal ever for a pop artist, bankrolled in part by country music publishers Hill & Range in return for a 50 percent publishing cut of whatever Presley recorded. In mid-November 1955, in return for $40,000, Sam Phillips released Elvis Presley to RCA Victor Records. With that deal Colonel Parker cemented his management relationship with Presley.

The A & R man who signed the Hillbilly Cat to RCA in November 1955 didn't quite know what he had. It was not for lack of experience. The son of an RCA Victor man, Steve Sholes had been working for the company since he was a teenager. Now forty-four years old, he had been managing the country and R & B divisions of RCA Victor for a decade. After seeing Presley perform at Nashville's annual Disc Jockey Convention on November 11, 1955, Sholes commented that he "hadn't seen anything so weird in a long time." In less than a week, he nevertheless signed the deal that brought Elvis to his label. Then he just had to figure out what to do with him.

The first single to emerge from his first RCA session in January 1956 turned out to be a song that Elvis, who didn't write, found during that DJ convention in Nashville. Penned by the country writers Mae Axton and Tommy Durden, "Heartbreak Hotel" had a

was about nineteen, playing Kilgore, Texas. He made chills run up my back. Man, like when your hair starts grabbing at your collar. For the next nine days, he played one-nighters around Kilgore, and after school every day me and my girl would get in the car and go wherever he was playing that night. That's the last time I tried to sing like Webb Pierce and Lefty Frizzell.

★ ★ ★

As reports filtered back to Parker of Presley driving teenage girls into frenzies and stealing

stark, haunting sound unlike anything Presley had yet recorded. Already, with the sound of this first RCA release, Presley confounded all the usual expectations for a hillbilly singer. With his television appearances over the next few months he would completely explode them and blaze a new path.

Between 1949 and 1955 Americans bought some 44 million television sets; well over 50 percent of all U.S. homes owned televisions. America was ripe for Elvis Presley. Every Saturday for six weeks in February and March 1956, Elvis appeared on the Dorsey Brothers' CBS-TV "Stage Door" show in prime time, strutting his stuff, showing off his cat moves for the nation. At the end of his stint on the show, "Heartbreak Hotel" had sold more than 300,000 copies and topped not only the country chart but also the pop chart. In its April 26, 1956, issue *Billboard* reported that Elvis was selling 50,000 singles a day and 8,000 copies of LPs and EPs, accounting for half of RCA's total sales. Elvis appeared on one prime time TV showcase after another: Milton Berle's show in April and June; Steve Allen's Sunday night show, July 1; and finally on September 9, the first of three appearances on Ed Sullivan's top-rated Sunday night variety program—in spite of Sullivan's initial announcement that he would never allow Presley on his show. Though seen only from the waist up, Elvis drew 82.6 percent of the viewers in America, some 50 million people.

Six months into his RCA contract, Elvis was the biggest act in RCA Victor's history. By the year's end he had sold 12.5 million singles and 2.75 million albums, an astounding begin-

ning to what would be an even more incredible career. Years later Parker would succinctly sum up his role in the transformation of Elvis Presley from country singer to national idol: "When I first met Elvis he had a million dollars' worth of talent. Now he has a million dollars."

Soldier boy: Thanks to the behind-the-scenes machinations of Colonel Tom Parker, Elvis continued to release hit records and movies during his two-year hitch in the army from 1958 to 1960.

★ AFTER ELVIS, THE DELUGE

Down in Lubbock, Texas, a bespectacled teenager named Charles Hardin Holley had been listening to the new sounds with his best friend, Bob Montgomery. As Buddy & Bob, they had played the local roller rink and sock hops, doing their best renditions of Hank Williams, Bill Monroe, and Gene Autry. On the side they listened to and fooled around with the blues of Muddy Waters and Howlin' Wolf. When Elvis rolled into their hometown in early 1955, he stood before them as the very embodiment of what they'd been stumbling toward. With Elvis having shown the way, Buddy grew bolder and bolder in his rockabilly experimenting, eventually catching the ears of record scouts with a demo record.

Paul Cohen and Decca were looking to jump on the new music trend, and in late 1955 Cohen signed Buddy Holly (he shortened his name) as one of the label's first rockabilly cats. On January 26, 1956 (the day after RCA released Elvis's "Heartbreak Hotel") Holly had his first Decca sessions in Nashville at the Bradley Film and Recording Studios. At that session and two others in Nashville in July and November, Cohen and Decca couldn't figure out how to get what they wanted out of Holly. After twice allowing him to record with his own band with little result, they saddled him with Nashville studio musicians for his November 1956 sessions. The resulting tracks were plodding and tentative versions of Presley's ferocious bop.

As Owen Bradley later recalled to journalist Chet Flippo: "Paul and I felt we should

Buddy Holly (top) with his band the Crickets, (from left) Joe B. Mauldin, Jerry Allison, and Niki Sullivan, 1957.

that Cohen and Decca wouldn't release—"That'll Be the Day"—and with the help of producer Norman Petty in Clovis, New Mexico, spun it into a No. 3 pop hit the very next summer. Because Holly thought that his Decca contract restricted him from rerecording songs with new companies, he and his band came up with a group name, the Crickets, for him to hide behind. As it turned out, his new record company, Brunswick, was actually a subsidiary of Decca, so there was no legal hassle. When Holly proved to be a prolific writer, he soon had a solo career on Coral Records (another Decca label) *and* with the Crickets on Brunswick. Holly and his Crickets went on a two-year chart tear that stopped only when Holly's heart was stilled in the wreckage of a plane crash in February of 1959.

Meanwhile, back in Memphis, for a brief period it appeared that Sam Phillips, the man who had discovered Elvis, had found the fountainhead of rock and roll talent. Everyone he touched turned to gold. Though he had parted with Elvis, Phillips and his Sun Records label came right back in 1956 with Carl Perkins, whose jivey, self-penned "Blue Suede Shoes" zoomed up the charts right behind Elvis's "Heartbreak Hotel," nestling in at No. 2 on both the country and pop charts. It was Sun Records' first million seller. Perkins lodged two more country hits in 1956, with "Boppin' the Blues" and "Dixie Fried."

Perkins seemed to have an especially bright future ahead of him. Sam Phillips fervently believed that Carl Perkins was "someone who could revolutionize the country end of the business," which was part of the reason he was willing to let Elvis Presley go. At that point, no one was certain that Elvis was the one. In fact, in late January 1956, Steve Sholes of RCA was so uncertain that, on the day that Elvis recorded a cover version of "Blue Suede Shoes," Sholes called Sam Phillips long distance from New York to get reassurances that

record him country. . . . Paul said, 'Look, just call our regular guys and do it country.' We'd go in to record him, but Buddy had a feeling to go in a different direction; he heard a different drummer."

After two lackluster singles over the course of the year that saw Elvis explode into a supernova, Decca lost interest in Holly. But the twenty-year-old from Lubbock rebounded dramatically when he took a song

he had signed the real hillbilly cat. Phillips told him not to worry, he had the right boy.

Elvis was a naturally gifted singer, but he didn't write his own material, and he wasn't a talented guitar picker. Carl Perkins, on the other hand, wrote vivid original songs and played a mean electric guitar. When Perkins became the first country artist to hit R & B charts in March 1956, the music industry took notice. Perry Como booked the rising star to be on his Saturday night NBC-TV show. But on the way to the Como taping, disaster overtook Carl Perkins. Speeding to New York late at night, with his manager at the wheel, the car carrying Perkins and his band collided with a truck somewhere near Dover, Delaware. Perkins sustained a broken shoulder, cracked skull, and cuts; his two brothers, Jay and Clayton, also suffered extensive injuries. While they mended in the hospital, "Blue Suede Shoes" topped the pop charts in April, and sold its millionth copy shortly after. But they missed the Como show, and somehow Carl Perkins never quite got on the same track again. He continued to write memorable songs and make

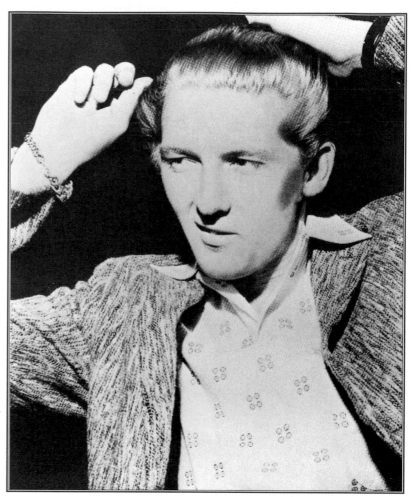

Jerry Lee Lewis, a.k.a. the Killer. Unlike every other guitar-toting rockabilly cat to come down the pike, Lewis played piano, and he did it brilliantly. For a brief moment or two, he even threatened to usurp Presley's throne.

The Sun King: Sam Phillips, ca. 1954. Within less than five years, he discovered and recorded Elvis Presley, Carl Perkins, Johnny Cash, Jerry Lee Lewis, Roy Orbison, Charlie Rich, and many others for his upstart Sun Records label in Memphis, Tennessee—and sent Nashville into a tizzy trying to compete with his rockabilly rebellion.

great records, but the momentum was gone. Though he landed a contract with Columbia Records in 1958, his rockabilly career had peaked. For the next several years, Perkins would think of himself as a failure until one night in 1964 when he met the Beatles during a tour of England. As it turned out, the world's most popular rock and rollers idolized Perkins and invited him to the studio with them the next day to hear them cover his old Sun record "Matchbox." Later that year, the Fab Four also recorded his "Honey Don't" and "Everybody's Trying to Be My Baby." It was a sweet vindication for Carl Perkins, and the beginning of his role as one of rock and roll's admired elder statesmen.

Meanwhile, Sam Phillips unleashed an even bigger sensation in 1957, when the irrepressible Jerry Lee Lewis surpassed the achievements of Perkins and even threatened to usurp Presley's throne. Unlike every other guitar-toting rockabilly cat to come down the pike, Lewis played piano, and he did it brilliantly, turning up the heat on boogie-woogie rhythms and throwing all manner of wild flourishes into his playing. Lewis had tried to break into Nashville in 1955, only to be told to come back when he learned to play guitar. He headed to Memphis in 1956 when he read an article about Elvis Presley in the *Country Song Roundup* fan magazine. Setting foot in the studio where Elvis got started, Lewis boasted that he could play the piano "like Chet Atkins." Nashville record honchos hadn't taken the time to find out what that bizarre brag meant. It took a man with Sam Phillips's golden ears to hear what Lewis had.

In the late summer of 1957, after a July 28 appearance on Steve Allen's network TV show during which he unleashed a new kind of rock and roll fury, Lewis climbed to the pinnacle of both the pop and country charts with "Whole Lotta Shakin' Goin' On." He did it again later that year with "Great Balls of Fire." In the spring of 1958, with Elvis Presley in the army for two years, Jerry Lee Lewis looked ready to conquer the pop world and take the King's throne. Seemingly, he could be as licentious as he wanted to onstage and do no wrong. But offstage, Lewis miscalculated his popularity enormously when he married his thirteen-year-old cousin, Myra Brown. In May 1958, six months after the wedding, the news broke loose while he was in England just beginning a thirty-date tour. Hounded by the press and heckled unmercifully by audiences, he cut short the tour after only three shows. But he was no more welcome at home than he had been abroad. Disc jockeys refused to play his records. Atten-

Johnny Cash's records sounded like nothing else on the radio in the fifties—country or pop. The arrangements were stark, and Cash's deep voice was instantly recognizable.

dance at his performances dwindled. His performance fees dropped from $10,000 per night to $250. A has-been at age twenty-two, he fell off the charts and remained in obscurity for a decade, until he returned singing straight country.

Sam Phillips discovered other singers who would go on to fame after they left the Sun label (Roy Orbison, Charlie Rich) and others who arguably had the talent to make it but never got the breaks (Billy Lee Riley, Warren Smith). These early rock and rollers were really just country boys, singers who loved country music but couldn't be contained within its confines. It was the teen craze for rock and roll that set them free.

The one artist Sam Phillips discovered who took root from the beginning in country and remained there was Johnny Cash, a twenty-three-year-old ex-serviceman who was selling vacuum cleaners door to door when he auditioned for Phillips. Ironically, Cash came to Sam Phillips hoping to sing gospel music. Phillips quickly set him straight on that score: Gospel isn't going to sell; your sound is pretty good, though; come back with some more commercial songs. Desperate not to lose his chance, Cash scratched out a new song overnight and returned to Phillips the next day with band mates Luther Perkins and Marshall Grant. Phillips recorded Cash's rag-tag trio without any augmentation. As Cash remembered, "Luther had a little secondhand Sears amplifier and a six-inch speaker. Marshall Grant had a bass that was held together with masking tape, and I had a little $4.80 guitar I had brought back from Germany. Phillips had to be a genius to get something out of that conglomeration." In short order he did, and by November of

1955, as Sam Phillips was selling Elvis Presley's contract to RCA, he was watching Johnny Cash's first record, "Cry! Cry! Cry!," hit the country charts. Thanks to Sam Phillips's intuition, Johnny Cash's records sounded like nothing else on the radio—country or pop. There was no fiddle. There was no steel. The sound of a Johnny Cash record consisted only of the string bass of Marshall Grant, the simple *boom-chicka-boom* picking of lead guitarist Luther Perkins, Johnny Cash's rhythm guitar with paper woven between the strings for a more percussive sound, and of course, Cash's voice, deep and sonorous as a cavern. Instantly recognizable, it could have been the bass part in a gospel quartet or the word of a biblical prophet.

Johnny Cash didn't play rockabilly really (though he tried to write a rocker for Elvis that he ended up cutting himself, called "Get Rhythm"). He played country. In the summer

Though the Everly Brothers started out as a country harmony act, they quickly graduated from the Opry to ABC-TV's "American Bandstand" and wider pop stardom. Between 1957 and 1960, Don and Phil sold 15 million records. This photo dates from November 1960.

of 1956 Elvis may have been the hottest thing anywhere, but Johnny Cash topped the country charts with his unique declaration of fidelity "I Walk the Line"; Dick Clark even featured the record on "American Bandstand," and it broke into the pop Top Twenty. It earned him his first appearance on the Grand Ole Opry that very summer and soon won him membership in the cast. Over the next couple of years, Cash would continue to place records consistently on top of the country charts and high up on the pop charts, even if Sam Phillips softened his sound with background vocalists to ensure success in the teen market. In late 1958 he moved over to Columbia Records in Nashville. He had left the Opry that August, wanting to keep as many of his weekends free for lucrative touring as he could.

Though Cash was just one artist out of an Opry cast of 125 at that point, it did not bode well for country's premier showcase that one of the hottest, most distinctive stars of the moment was leaving. The Grand Ole Opry had adjusted well to the losses of Hank Williams and Lefty Frizzell. Potent new stars like Little Jimmy Dickens, Hank Snow, and Kitty Wells had filled the gaps admirably. But Elvis Presley had tapped a volatile market no one had realized was there—America's youth. Elvis and rock and roll represented the spirit of rebellion. Country music represented tradition. Something had to give.

The Grand Ole
Opry cast at the
Ryman Auditorium
in 1956. Sitting on
platform (from left
to right) are Ernest
Tubb, Little Jimmy
Dickens, and Webb
Pierce; Hank Snow
is standing. Judge
Hay is at the ladder.

A Nashville Sound

UPHEAVAL IN NASHVILLE

By 1958 Nashville was truly shaping up as Music City, U.S.A. Thanks to the influx of new rock and roll talent, Nashville's recording studios were doing better than ever with more than 500 sessions taking place that year. From the outside, the Grand Ole Opry *seemed* to be doing well. After a visit to the show one Saturday night in 1958, the nation's most famous gossip columnist, Walter Winchell, noted that the cars parked in the Ryman's lot bore license plates from thirty-nine different states. Furthermore, that year the Opry could point to more than 69 percent of the country records played on radio and more than 62 percent of the records played on jukeboxes as being recorded by Opry artists.

But there were chinks in the brickwork of the Opry. The show's audience had been steadily diminishing. From a peak of 243,721 in 1953 (the year that began with the death of Hank Williams), attendance fell to 144,464 in 1958. In September 1956, a couple of weeks after Elvis's first Sullivan appearance, Jim Denny left his post as manager of the Opry and its booking agency, the Artists Service Bureau, opening his own booking agency. Twenty-seven Opry acts—including Minnie Pearl, Little Jimmy Dickens, Kitty Wells, and Webb Pierce—jumped from WSM's in-house booking agency to Denny's. The Opry responded with an ultimatum: Leave Denny or leave the Opry. Most stayed with Denny, who promptly booked several of them on the Philip Morris Country Music Show, which ran for sixteen months and toured more than one hundred cities and towns across the South and Midwest.

Because the tour was underwritten by Philip Morris (for more than a half million dollars, according to the *Wall Street Journal*), admission was free, and the show aired every Friday over the CBS radio network. Not surprisingly, it consistently drew packed houses.

By mid-1958 things returned to some semblance of normality at the Opry. Most of Denny's charges were readmitted to the cast, but some never returned. Red Foley, Webb Pierce, and Carl Smith all left the Opry to star on Springfield, Missouri's Ozark Jubilee. Even more galling, the competing show was not on radio, but on ABC-TV every other Saturday night. Opry management had been trying to break into television since the early 1950s, briefly succeeding from October of 1955 to September of 1956 with hour-long broadcasts over ABC. But the Ozark Jubilee had a commanding head start, which it would hold for the next few years.

Aside from dissension within the ranks, the Opry's other major problem was the pull of rock and roll on the hearts and minds of Amer-

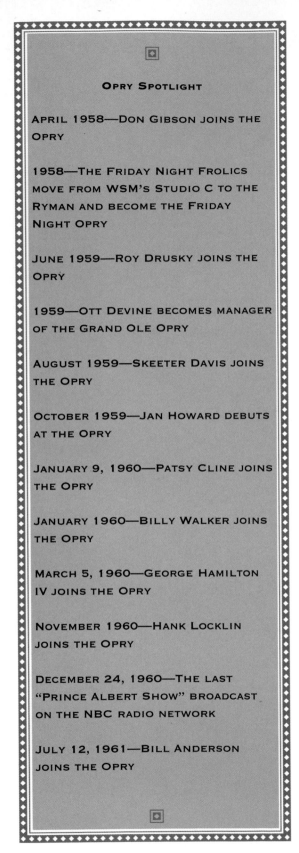

Jim Denny, the Opry's manager from 1946 to 1956, established his Cedarwood music publishing and booking firm while working for the Opry. When WSM officials asked him to cease his moonlighting, he left to run his lucrative business full-time.

ican teenagers. Why would they want to listen to performers like Roy Acuff, Ernest Tubb, and Kitty Wells—all old enough to be their parents—when Elvis Presley and Jerry Lee Lewis spoke to them as peers and rebellious role models? Of course, country music records were still being made, but they were being played less often on radio and bought in disturbingly dwindling numbers.

In general, record execs of the day and Presley's less-talented imitators noticed only Presley's gimmicks—the cat clothes, the greasy pompadour, the hiccuping intro to "I Wanna Play House" or the high and low vocal swoops of "Love Me." What most of these performers and their handlers didn't see was that Elvis Presley performed with supercharged

sincerity. He had, in fact, the same sort of sincerity that audiences responded to again and again, the sincerity that had made stars of Jimmie Rodgers and Hank Williams.

★ THE RESPONSE

Not everyone in Nashville cowered at Elvis's staggering success. In truth, it affected the town's music business unequally. While the Opry and many older country performers were groping for ways to adapt to the new sounds, over at RCA Steve Sholes was celebrating. He had gone out on a limb to sign Elvis and by the end of 1956 he looked like a genius. Thanks to the millions of records that Elvis was selling, Sholes got the green light from New York to commit to building a new studio and country headquarters in Nashville. Taking a cue from the Bradleys, Sholes decided to build just one street over from the Bradley Film and Recording Studios. They were at Sixteenth and Hawkins; Sholes chose Seventeenth and Hawkins as his site. Boosted by his success with Presley, Sholes got a promotion. In turn, he then promoted his part-time A & R assistant, Chet Atkins, to manage the new office and studio beginning in 1957.

It was an incredible opportunity for the thirty-two-year-old Atkins, a brilliant guitarist who was finally coming into his own after fourteen years of struggling in the music business. Starting out as an eighteen-year-old fiddler and guitarist from the tiny East Tennessee hamlet of Luttrell, Atkins had bounced from one radio station job to another—eight radio station jobs in eight years, a string of failure stretching from Richmond to Denver—throughout the 1940s. The problem was never with Chet's playing. His syncopated finger-picking, modeled on Merle Travis's style, dazzled anyone within earshot. Yet he was shy and diffident, and audiences just didn't easily warm up to him. "A lot of people

Chet Atkins (left) with the man who hired him to run RCA Records in Nashville, Steve Sholes. "I had no fear of his capability as a producer," Sholes once said. "I knew his ability better than he did."

thought I was stuck-up," he said, "when actually I was just scared to death. Back then, on radio stations and shows, your value was determined on how well you drew mail, and I didn't draw mail."

Upon returning to WSM in June 1950 as guitarist for Maybelle Carter and her three daughters, Atkins hooked up with Fred Rose and Steve Sholes on recording sessions, backing Hank Williams and Webb Pierce on such big hits as "Jambalaya" and "There Stands the Glass." In the studio, Chet particularly impressed Sholes with his musical knowledge. The young guitarist played more than straight country, modeling his style on the playing of jazzy guitarists like Les Paul and Django Reinhardt as much as Merle Travis. "Right away I started telling everybody else what to do," Chet has said. "I've always been that way, because most of the time I knew four chords and the other guys knew three." Sholes came to rely increasingly on Atkins to assemble and even lead Nashville sessions. In 1952 Sholes hired him as a part-time A & R assistant for $75 a week. All of this led up to early 1957 when Atkins got the opportunity to run the

Nashville show for RCA. It was a wonderful opportunity. But in the wake of Elvis Presley, Atkins wondered, what sort of country records should he record?

Atkins had an idea. He could play rock and roll; as a matter of fact, he had played on Elvis's first RCA records as well as those of other teen idols like the Everly Brothers. But at thirty-two he was far from a teenager and felt more comfortable making music for adults. Though born in a small country town and schooled on country radio shows, he was also quite a sophisticated musician who loved jazz and classical music. Atkins decided to please himself and go with his instincts. If pop music was being turned over to the teenagers, he would make country music that could appeal to the adult audience that was left behind. He would revive the pop vocal style of the forties and early fifties and adapt it for the country market.

His first choice for this venture was Jim Reeves, who had a crooner's voice every bit as smooth as Red Foley's or Eddy Arnold's. In July 1956 Atkins experimented with a hushed arrangement when Reeves recorded a pensive

NOVEMBER 29, 1961—A GRAND OLE OPRY TROUPE, INCLUDING PATSY CLINE, JIM REEVES, BILL MONROE, AND MINNIE PEARL, ENTERTAINS A SELL-OUT CROWD AT CARNEGIE HALL

OCTOBER 27, 1962—SONNY JAMES JOINS THE OPRY

MARCH 5, 1963—PATSY CLINE, HER MANAGER RANDY HUGHES, HAWKSHAW HAWKINS, AND COWBOY COPAS DIE IN A PLANE CRASH

MARCH 7, 1963—JACK ANGLIN OF JOHNNIE & JACK DIES IN A CAR ACCIDENT

MARCH 29, 1963—TEXAS RUBY OWENS DIES IN A FIRE AT HER TRAILER HOME

AUGUST 1963—THE BROTHER-SISTER VOCAL GROUP THE BROWNS—JIM ED, MAXINE, AND BONNIE—JOIN THE OPRY

NOVEMBER 28, 1963—WILLIE NELSON JOINS THE OPRY

JULY 8, 1964—DOTTIE WEST JOINS THE OPRY

JULY 31, 1964—JIM REEVES DIES IN A PLANE CRASH ALONG WITH BAND MEMBER DEAN MANUEL

The Big Finish

One of the Opry's grandest traditions for nearly twenty years was the final 11:30 P.M. segment hosted by Marty Robbins. From the moment he bounded onto the Opry stage, everyone knew it was Marty's show. Cradling his miniature Martin guitar in the crook of his right arm, unfurling a strong and soulful tenor voice, Robbins was one of the most versatile and dynamic entertainers in country music. In a career that spanned thirty years, Robbins racked up nearly a hundred hits encompassing rockabilly, calypso, teenage pop, folk, Tex-Mex, Hawaiian, and western styles. Among his enduring classics are "Singing the Blues," "A White Sport Coat (And a Pink Carnation)," "El Paso," and "Devil Woman." Yet even though he had been an Opry member since 1953, Robbins didn't carve his special niche in Opry history until a dozen years later. And it was all because of a hobby.

A tireless, adventurous man, Robbins had taken up competitive auto racing in 1959. By 1965, he had graduated to the professional stock-car circuit, racing every chance he got in Nashville and out on tour. Robbins loved racing so much he worked out a deal with Opry manager Ott Devine that allowed him to play the Opry's final half hour. That way, he could spend the early part of the evening racing at the Nashville Speedway. "That's kind of the way he drifted into that spot," recalled Opry president Hal Durham, then the show's junior announcer. "Later on, that's the only show he would work. He didn't want to do anything else. In fact, it kind of became his show if he was in town."

Once he became ensconced in his role as the Opry closer, Robbins began stretching out the end of the show. Always the crowd pleaser, he couldn't bear to stop playing if the audience wanted more. "As the eleven-thirty segment became more and more his show, so to speak," said Durham, "he began to take liberties with the time. Instead of running over five minutes, he'd run over fifteen minutes."

The late endings didn't much matter to WSM and the Opry management. But fellow performers sometimes wished that Robbins didn't always have to put his fans first. "When he started closing the show, we were still doing live commercials with jingles provided by our artists," recalled Hal Durham. "The sponsor for the last segment in those days was Lava Soap, and the Willis Brothers did their jingle. . . . So when Marty would run late, they'd have

In a career that spanned thirty years, the versatile Marty Robbins racked up nearly one hundred hits encompassing rockabilly, calypso, teenage pop, folk, Tex-Mex, Hawaiian, and western styles.

ballad he'd written, "Am I Losing You?" True, the record had the requisite fiddle and steel that identified it as country, but they were pushed way back in the mix until they were just whispers. Reeves's voice came across as intimate and relaxed, because Atkins allowed the singer to get up close to the microphone. This arrangement took advantage of Reeves's velvet-soft baritone. Reeves had first broken into the entertainment business as a disc jockey and announcer for stations in east Texas, and his measured, clearly enunciated diction would remain one of his hallmarks. The song hit the charts in January 1957 and became a solid Top Ten hit.

One month later when they headed back into the studio, Atkins thought he had found a strong follow-up for "Am I Losing You?" The song, "Four Walls," had initially been written for a woman to sing, with lyrics that spoke of being left alone at home with four walls to hear the singer's disappointment while the lover is out on the town. Chet wasn't sure of the lyrics for Reeves, but he knew that the words and melody lent themselves to an intimate treatment. If Reeves could pull it off, the lyrics offered a nice twist having the man at home missing his lover. Chet decided to give it a try.

Though he's wearing cowboy duds here in this mid-fifties shot, Jim Reeves would soon be wearing dinner jackets to match the uptown ballad sound of hits like "He'll Have to Go."

"We made that record, and he got right in the mike," Chet recalled, "and when he sang 'Four Walls,' man, what a sound. I remember Steve Sholes called me from New York and said, 'How did you get that sound? How did you do it?' "

The answer lay in the simple, understated arrangement that resembled "Am I Losing You?" in its focus on the singer's voice. In place of fiddle and steel this time, Atkins balanced Reeves's vocal with Floyd Cramer's lazily tinkling piano and the voices of the Jordanaires gospel quartet echoing softly behind Reeves, who sang as close to the mike as possible. The resulting production was not quite country and not quite pop but a hybrid of the two styles. Released in March the record gradually picked up momentum until late May when it topped the country

to wait around to sing that last commercial. It used to upset Vic Willis quite a bit—until we finally put the commercials on tape."

The late endings also presented a problem for acts anxiously waiting to perform down the street from the Ryman at the Midnite Jamboree, which was broadcast on WSM radio immediately after the Opry live from Ernest Tubb's Record Shop. Though he was the host of the Jamboree, Tubb himself didn't begrudge Marty the late endings. He and Marty were good friends, and Tubb would roll with the punches.

"He would talk to Ernest on the air," said Durham. " 'Just a couple more songs, Ernest, and we'll turn it over to you.' Finally one night we taped a thing with Tubb so that, when Marty said something like that, we'd punch on that tape, with Tubb saying 'OK, Marty, you've had your time. Now it's my turn.' "

Eventually the Opry pretaped a closing for Marty's segment for WSM radio. "We'd punch in this closing of him singing 'El Paso' and the sign-off," recalled Durham, "but it just went to the radio audience. Here in the house they were still seeing a Marty Robbins concert. He could go another thirty minutes. We finally told him what we were doing. He didn't realize it, but he didn't mind." Even after entertaining the folks he affectionately referred to as "my people," Robbins often remained to sign autographs until two or three o'clock in the morning.

The talent of Marty Robbins burned out all too quickly as he threw himself into every waking moment. He handled his own management and tour bookings. He toured ceaselessly. He slept an average of only two or three hours a night. The intensity and drive must have taken its toll. Though he abstained from smoking and drinking, he had his first heart attack in August 1969 at the age of forty-three. Five months later, he had triple-bypass heart surgery. He rebounded quickly, devoting himself once more to music and racing. But following a severe heart attack in December 1982, he underwent a second bypass operation. This time he didn't pull through, and on December 8, 1982, Marty Robbins passed away. He was just fifty-seven. Two months earlier, he had been admitted to the Country Music Hall of Fame.

"He kept everybody loose," said Hal Durham. "He had fun with Hank Snow. He'd go into Hank's dressing room and do an impression of Hank singing. Even Hank thought it was funny. Talk about missing somebody. The Opry has really missed what Marty has brought to it."

Jim Reeves with Opry announcer Grant Turner in the early sixties.

This time, the new sound clicked for Gibson. Released on the same single in February 1958, both songs zoomed up the country charts. Two weeks after his thirtieth birthday in April, Gibson had his first No. 1 country hit with "Oh, Lonesome Me," which crossed over to the pop charts at No. 7. "I Can't Stop Loving You" followed its flip side right into the country Top Ten at No. 7, held back from climbing higher by Kitty Wells's version of the song, which held the No. 3 position. Thanks to the momentum generated by his two-sided hit, "Blue, Blue Day," an earlier Gibson single that was already more than a year old, was pulled up to the No. 1 spot on the country charts as well. Membership in the Grand Ole Opry followed shortly after.

"After I made those hits with Jim and Don," said Atkins, "I had a lot of luck. I think that every artist that was at RCA then eventually had a hit, if they stayed on long enough." The self-effacing modesty is typical of Atkins; in truth, he had an incredible string of successes for the next few years. By smoothing out country's rough edges, Chet Atkins had found a way for country to hold its own against rock and roll.

Chet Atkins was not the only producer scoring pop-inflected coun-

charts, surfacing amid No. 1 hits by Elvis Presley, Webb Pierce, and the Everly Brothers, and crossed over to the pop charts where it went to No. 11. Reeves had discovered his sound, one he would hone to perfection two years later on his million seller "He'll Have to Go." And Atkins had discovered a way around having to make rock and roll records.

Using similar principles—smooth out the country influences, keep the arrangement simple—Atkins felt even more confident when he launched the first new artist he signed as RCA's Nashville Manager of Operations in 1957.

Atkins had known Don Gibson back in Knoxville and had played on one of Gibson's early RCA sessions in 1951. The RCA records had sold poorly, but Atkins had noticed Gibson's husky but smooth voice and his knack for coming up with good original songs. Gibson got a shot at recording for RCA again on December 3, 1957, bringing two new songs he wanted to record—a big, sorrowful ballad ("I Can't Stop Loving You") and a bouncy lament at being left behind ("Oh, Lonesome Me"). Again Atkins aimed for a clean break with old-timey country, sticking with the small modern-sounding combos that had worked for Jim Reeves. For the up-tempo song, Atkins miked drummer Troy Hatcher's bass drum to get a fresh propulsive sound—a bold innovation for a country session.

Between 1958 and 1962, Don Gibson consistently had Top Ten country hits that crossed over to the pop charts. Two of his biggest were "Oh, Lonesome Me" and "I Can't Stop Loving You."

Hard-country stalwarts of the fifties: Faron Young (center), who joined the Opry in 1952, and the Louvin Brothers, who joined in 1955.

On the surface, the method of recording resembled pop sessions in New York or Los Angeles. Unlike trained pop musicians, however, Nashville's A Team didn't work with written sheet music during sessions. Instead, the A & R man would play a demo recording of a song, then work with the musicians on coming up with a spontaneous "head arrangement"—all the while aiming to do this at a clip of four songs recorded in three hours. This loose style of working and the new sophisticated sound it engendered gradually became known as the Nashville Sound. The name quickly gained popular currency after *Time* magazine used the term in a Nashville story published in November 1960.

The producer who did the most to further the kind of country-pop experimentation that succeeded for Chet Atkins was the man operating just one street over—Owen Bradley. As the fifties drew to a close, Decca's country chief Paul Cohen left more and more of the ac-

try hits. Don Law at Columbia had dependable hitmakers in Johnny Cash and Marty Robbins. Ken Nelson continued to do well with Faron Young and Ferlin Husky. Although the artists differed, the same cast of musicians played on nearly every record out of Nashville. The days of a self-contained group like the Carter Family popping into a makeshift studio in Bristol to cut a few quick tracks had long gone. A & R men looked for efficiency in a modern studio, dependable tracks cut like clockwork.

With its network radio affiliation and broad coverage, the Grand Ole Opry had been serving as a magnet for musicians for years. The cast of regulars, backing nearly every artist, became known as "The A Team" and included guitarists Grady Martin, Hank Garland, Harold Bradley, and Ray Edenton; bassists Bob Moore and Floyd "Lightnin' " Chance; pianists Floyd Cramer and Hargus "Pig" Robbins; drummer Buddy Harman; and choral groups the Jordanaires and the Anita Kerr Singers. For the most part these musicians were unabashed fans of pop and jazz, and they did not hesitate to insinuate their favorite uptown sounds into country records.

An A-Team recording session in RCA's Studio B with Opry star Hank Locklin, Chet Atkins, and Floyd Cramer.

While the smooth Nashville Sound was on the rise, Ray Price (center) and his Cherokee Cowboys carried on the legacy of his mentor Hank Williams and kept the hard-core honky-tonk sound on the charts.

tual record producing in Bradley's hands. As Bradley recalls it, Cohen would say: "Why don't you go in and do this song and that song, and anything else you want to do." Or: "Here's three; see if you can find another one." And eventually: "Here's one; find three more." On April 15, 1958, almost a year after Atkins made a similar move a block away at RCA, Owen Bradley stepped into Cohen's job as head of Decca's Nashville division.

Bradley didn't immediately initiate any sweeping changes. For the most part, he let his established traditional stars stick with their usual formulas; the records of Ernest Tubb, Bill Monroe, and Kitty Wells continued to sound very much as they always had. As he later put it: "With a great artist like Ernest Tubb, you just go in the studio and be real quiet and learn how to work a stopwatch."

But Bradley wasn't at all averse to experimenting with his newer artists. He had noted the slick triumphs of artists like Jim Reeves and had been working in that direction himself even before assuming the Decca reins. By the spring of 1957 he was trying the new pop-country blend himself. The strategy paid off that fall when the twangy voice of twenty-one-year-old Bobby Helms put over the massive pop-country hit "My Special Angel," followed a few months later by what would be a new holiday favorite, "Jingle Bell Rock."

Once Bradley assumed command at Decca, he scored his biggest triumphs with two female singers—Brenda Lee and Patsy Cline. Born Brenda Mae Tarpley, Lee was all of eleven years old when she began recording for Bradley in July of 1956. She already had a distinctive style—a blending of gospel fire and country warmth learned from the records of Mahalia Jackson and Hank Williams—that belied her years. Out of her diminutive frame (she eventually reached all of four foot nine), Brenda threw a husky voice that could scorch a microphone. She had come to Bradley's attention through Red Foley, who had discovered her at a show in her hometown of Augusta, Georgia, in early 1956. Thoroughly impressed by the energy and professionalism of the little girl, Foley brought her to his Ozark Jubilee TV show, where she remained a regular into 1957.

On her first Decca record, she growled and hiccuped her way Elvis-style through Hank Williams's "Jambalaya" and then really turned up the rockabilly flame on the flip side, a teen number called "Bigelow 6-200." In that very first session on July 30, 1956, Brenda Lee showed she had a precocious understanding of the music business to match her mature voice. Owen Bradley recalled Brenda's first session: "I remember when we started rolling on the first take, all of a sudden she yelled; 'Stop, stop, he missed a note,' and she pointed straight at the bass player. The bass player said yes, he had. Nobody else had caught it." At that same session Paul Cohen tried to explain something to Brenda using baby-talk. "Suddenly," Bradley recalled, "she cocked her head back, looked him straight in the eyes, and said, 'Well, goo, goo.' Everybody in the studio cracked up."

In the fall of 1959, Brenda proved to be more than an interesting novelty when she cracked the upper reaches of the pop charts with another telephone song, the rockin' "Sweet Nothin's." Only fourteen years old, she growled and purred the teen song in a way that sounded positively lustful. European fans were certain that she was an adult. "I was still playing with paper dolls at the time," recalled Lee. "I didn't even know what a boy looked like. I really sang like I knew what I was talking about. . . . I mean, I cried my eyes out when I was fourteen years old over a Tiny Tears doll that my mom wouldn't buy me."

For her follow-up record, a lachrymose ballad called "I'm Sorry," Bradley aimed for a sophisticated treatment and surrounded Lee

Only eleven years old when she began recording, Brenda Lee had a husky voice that belied her years. Here she holds a program for the Ozark Jubilee, where she was a cast member in 1956 and 1957.

with a string quartet. " 'I'm Sorry' was one of the first sessions in Nashville to use strings," recalled Bradley in 1966. "We used four strings—now we use ten. . . . On Brenda's sessions, we usually get Bill McElhiney or Cam Mullins to

do the arranging, and we have the Anita Kerr Singers on most of them. On 'I'm Sorry,' Anita had the voices going along well and everybody else was faking along, but the fiddle players were a team and needed something very specific to do. We decided to let the fiddles answer—when Brenda sang 'I'm Sorry,' the fiddles would answer 'I'm Sorry.' So Bill came up with some notes for them and wrote them down, and we were off and running."

The gambit paid off handsomely as Brenda lodged the first of her many million sellers. It topped the pop charts for three weeks in June 1960 and remains a beloved standard more than thirty years later. It established a thoroughly comfortable style for the teenage singer that would launch her as the best-selling female singer of the sixties, with such popular heart-rending ballads as "I Want to Be Wanted," "Emotions," "You Can Depend on Me," and "Break It to Me Gently." For the rest of the decade, Brenda Lee would be considered a teenage pop star, competing with Connie Francis and Paul Anka, even though she recorded in Nashville and worked for Decca's country division. "I never said, 'I want to be rock and roll,' or 'I want to be pop,'" maintained Lee. "The only thing that says that you're a rock or pop singer is sales. Owen and I always just went into the studio and cut the songs that we thought were good, gave 'em the treatment that we thought they needed, and put 'em out."

While Owen Bradley was launching Brenda Lee as the biggest female star of the decade, he also had high hopes in the summer

Though she looked like a rodeo queen (in western outfits sewed by her mother) and cussed like a sailor, Patsy Cline possessed one of the most sophisticated vocal talents ever to come out of Nashville.

any sailor with her salty language. "She could say some words," her young friend Brenda Lee tactfully put it. But Patsy had a deep understanding and love of country music, which poured out in a full, warm, smooth voice. To listen to her sing was to hear the golden sound of coins dropping into jukeboxes and cash registers ringing.

Patsy had a particular knack for putting over songs of heartache. You might say it came naturally to her. She was born Virginia Patterson Hensley in the sleepy Shenandoah Valley town of Winchester, Virginia, six days after her parents married. Her father, the proud scion of a rich family fallen on hard times, was forty-three; her mother was a fifteen-year-old farmer's daughter. It was a bad match from the start, destined for failure. Almost from birth Patsy was a show-off, always trying to catch her father's fleeting attention. By the age of four she had won a local tap-dancing contest, and she was singing soon after. A near-fatal childhood illness seemed to stir something in her, as she once explained: "You might say it was my return to the living that launched me as a singer. In childhood I developed a serious throat infection, and my heart stopped beating. I was placed in an oxygen tent, and doctors brought me back to life. I recovered from the illness with a voice that boomed forth like Kate Smith's."

But even if she sang her heart out, she couldn't hold on to her father. He left the family shortly after she turned fifteen. To make ends meet, Patsy's mother became a seamstress and Patsy quit high school to work in a local drugstore. Absolutely determined to make it as a singer, Patsy made time for music whenever she could. "On Saturdays I worked all day in Hunter Gaunt's drugstore in Winchester, and then at night my mother drove me to Front Royal where I sang pop tunes in a supper club from 10 P.M. to 1 A.M. We wouldn't get home and in bed until about three o'clock in

of 1960 for twenty-eight-year-old Patsy Cline, who seemed to have at least as much potential for crossover success as Brenda Lee. Patsy Cline wasn't a pinup girl. She was big boned, and her five-foot-six-inch frame tended toward matronly stockiness. When she smiled, one could see that her front teeth were slightly chipped. She talked tough and could match

Patsy Cline onstage at the Opry. Backing her on guitar is her manager Randy Hughes, who later piloted the plane in which she died.

ing to find a winning formula. From 1955 to 1960 they had tried hard-core country weepers, western swing tunes, rockabilly boppers, cocktail lounge ballads, even gospel numbers. As Bradley later put it, "We'd try anything that might stick." Decca might have given up entirely on Cline, except that in one instance they connected. In early 1957, boosted by a winning CBS-TV appearance on Arthur Godfrey's "Talent Scouts" contest, Patsy Cline took a lazily swinging country number, "Walkin' After Midnight," up both the country and pop charts. That was her sole hit in five years of recording. Bradley, of course, understood that there were extenuating circumstances. Until 1960 Cline was actually signed to 4 Star Records, and her recordings had merely been leased to Decca. It was more than a business technicality, for 4 Star's owner, Bill McCall, allowed Cline to record only songs for which he controlled the publishing, and many of those songs were eminently forgettable. Fettered by this restrictive arrangement, Cline was remarkably lucky to land at least one good song in "Walkin' After Midnight." Patsy Cline's talent was obvious in spite of her lackluster material.

Amidst all this career disappointment, Patsy rid herself of Gerald Cline and married Charlie Dick, a printing-press operator. Charlie served two years in the Army at the beginning of their marriage. Despite his discharge in February 1959, the U.S. government continued to send Patsy subsistence checks. After seven $137 checks arrived, Patsy and Charlie cashed them, using the money to finance a move to Nashville and

the morning. A few hours later I was up, getting ready to return to work in the drugstore."

In addition to the high-toned supper club engagements, Patsy sang country music over the local radio station, at local VFWs and Moose Clubs, always wearing the flashy, fringed cowgirl outfits her mother sewed for her. In 1949 sheer chutzpah got the sixteen-year-old an audition with Jim Denny at WSM. Along with a family friend, Patsy, her mother, and Patsy's little sister and brother made the 700-mile trip down from Winchester to Nashville, hoping for what they weren't quite sure. Although Denny and Roy Acuff were impressed enough with the big-voiced youngster to give her a one-time test spot on Roy Acuff's noontime show, no one suggested bending the child-labor restrictions to make room for her at the station. It would take her another ten years of hard work before she returned to Nashville and WSM to stay. During the ensuing decade, she built a following in the Washington, D.C., area, leapt into an ill-advised marriage at age twenty with Gerald Cline, who was eight years her senior, and landed a recording contract at age twenty-two that brought her into the studio to work with Owen Bradley. Then the going really got tough.

Bradley and Cline struggled for years try-

hoping for a new start. In the spring of 1960, freed from her 4 Star contract, she and her husband ran into Chet Atkins at a Nashville nightclub. When Patsy asked Atkins for an autograph, he obliged, adding the telling postscript: "When are you coming over to RCA?"

All along, though, Cline placed her trust in Bradley. And in November of 1960, having signed with Decca outright, she returned to Bradley Studios with re-newed enthusiasm. Of all the singers in his sta-ble, Patsy Cline had the style, Bradley thought, that could compete suc-cessfully with the new sound Chet Atkins and Jim Reeves were ex-ploiting, a sound that could simultane-ously win over fans of country and pop without alienating either audience. All Bradley needed was the right kind of song.

The song he had the most faith in had al-ready been rejected by Brenda Lee and a couple of other singers when he brought it to Patsy. When she heard that other singers had passed on "I Fall to Pieces," she tried to do the same. But Patsy was never the best judge of material. She had originally dismissed "Walkin' After Midnight" as "nothin' but a little old pop song. I hate it." She recorded that eventual hit because Bill McCall let her record the less memorable "Poor Man's Roses" as well. This time, Owen Bradley placated the headstrong singer the same way, letting her record the bouncy "Lovin' in Vain" along with the number Bradley favored. "Lovin' in Vain" al-lowed Patsy to in-dulge her penchant for pulling out all the stops, as she growled and belted her way through the up-tempo tune. "I Fall to Pieces," though, was something else. The song took shape with the rhythm section playing a standard country shuffle. On top of that rhythmic foundation, Bradley reworked the architecture of this simple country song. From the plaintive chimes of Hank Garland's guitar on the opening, the track set a distinct mood— Garland's echo-treated guitar cascading on the chorus, the Jordanaires hovering in the background like spirits of regret, Ben Keith's steel wafting in, Pig Robbins's piano shower-ing notes like so many teardrops, all propelled by an undeniably catchy shuffle rhythm. Above it all, Patsy's voice floated, forlorn and inconsolable. The song was a ballad but it had a beat.

"I Fall to Pieces" was far from an instant hit. Released at the end of January 1961, it didn't appear on the charts until April. Thanks to some dedicated record promotion at Decca, the single reached the No. 1 spot on the coun-try charts in August and cracked the pop charts as well, ultimately peaking at No. 12— three notches above Elvis's "Little Sister" and four above Roy Orbison's "Crying"—for the week of September 12. The record rode the country charts from April through the end of 1961—a good thing for Patsy's career, since she was involved in a head-on automobile col-lision in mid-June that laid her up for the rest of the summer. The impact had sent her through her car's windshield and nearly killed her. As it was, she sustained a jagged cut across her forehead that required stitches, a broken wrist, and a dislocated hip.

But Patsy was indefatigable. With a come-

COUNTRY MILESTONES	JANUARY 21, 1957— APPEARING ON ARTHUR GODFREY'S "TALENT SCOUTS," A PRIME-TIME CBS-TV TALENT CON-TEST, PATSY CLINE WINS BY DEBUTING "WALKIN' AFTER MIDNIGHT," WHICH BECOMES HER FIRST HIT	SPRING 1957—CHET ATKINS IS HIRED TO MANAGE RCA'S NASHVILLE OPERATION	DECEMBER 3, 1957— DON GIBSON RECORDS HIS TWO-SIDED HIT "I CAN'T STOP LOVING YOU"/"OH, LONESOME ME" 1958—STEREO LPS INTRODUCED IN THE U.S.	JANUARY 1, 1958— JOHNNY CASH PERFORMS FOR THE INMATES AT SAN QUENTIN PRISON; IN THE AUDIENCE IS PRISONER AND FUTURE STAR MERLE HAGGARD	MARCH 1958—BMI OPENS NASHVILLE OF-FICE HEADED BY FOR-MER WSM RECEPTIONIST FRANCES WILLIAMS (LATER BETTER KNOWN BY HER MARRIED NAME, PRESTON)
NOVEMBER 7, 1956— FERLIN HUSKY RECORDS THE FIRST NASHVILLE SOUND HIT, "GONE," PRODUCED BY CAPITOL'S KEN NELSON AT BRADLEY STUDIOS					

back hit under her belt, she was not the sort of person to let even a near-fatal accident stand in her way. When she returned to Bradley's studio in mid-August, it was with a renewed sense of purpose and confidence. Focusing not on her injuries but on her triumphant chart comeback, Patsy told Owen Bradley: "I think I've found out who I am and what we've been looking for. We don't have to search for my identity anymore. This is it! We're doing it right."

Over the next year and a half, Cline and Bradley cut some of the most memorable country hits of the era, carefully selected from Nashville's top tunesmiths: Willie Nelson's "Crazy," Hank Cochran's "She's Got You," Wayne Walker's "Leavin' on Your Mind," and Don Gibson's "Sweet Dreams." Her two Decca albums released in that period, *Showcase* and *Sentimentally Yours*, tackled a number of old pop and country standards: Cole Porter's "True Love," Bob Wills's "New San Antonio Rose" and "Faded Love," Hank Williams's "Your Cheatin' Heart" and "I Can't Help It If I'm Still in Love with You," Irving Berlin's "Always." Although she did continue to record the occasional up-tempo tune, for the most part Patsy concentrated on singing slow, sorrowful ballads that allowed her to play her tough but tender persona to the hilt and show off the nuances in her style. She didn't put together a string of No. 1 pop hits to match Brenda Lee, but in her own way, Patsy

Few performers have ever balanced the common touch and a regal talent as naturally as Patsy Cline did.

was managing to bridge the gap between country and pop music.

She could never be anything but down to earth. "Honey, I'm not New York material," Patsy told Ray Walker of the Jordanaires when she heard that a Grand Ole Opry troupe would be flying to New York for a benefit concert at Carnegie Hall. "I couldn't be with

APRIL 1958—OWEN BRADLEY SUCCEEDS PAUL COHEN AS HEAD OF DECCA'S NASHVILLE OFFICE

NOVEMBER 1958—COUNTRY MUSIC ASSOCIATION FOUNDED TO PROMOTE COUNTRY MUSIC; FORMER WSM STATION MANAGER HARRY STONE IS ITS FIRST EXECUTIVE DIRECTOR

JULY 1959—EARL SCRUGGS APPEARS AT THE FIRST NEWPORT FOLK FESTIVAL

OCTOBER 1959—IN AN ARTICLE FOR *ESQUIRE* MAGAZINE, FOLKLORIST ALAN LOMAX DESCRIBES THE MUSIC OF FLATT & SCRUGGS AS "FOLK MUSIC WITH OVERDRIVE"

MARCH 28, 1960—PRODUCER OWEN BRADLEY EMPLOYS STRINGS FOR A NASHVILLE SESSION FOR THE FIRST TIME ON BRENDA LEE'S RECORD "I'M SORRY"; IT BECOMES A NO. 1 POP HIT THAT JUNE

MARCH 29, 1960—TOOTSIE'S ORCHID LOUNGE, FAVORITE WATERING HOLE FOR NASHVILLE'S MUSIC CROWD, OPENS FOR BUSINESS ACROSS THE ALLEY FROM THE RYMAN AUDITORIUM

that bunch long. If there's one pile of dogshit in New York, I'd be found standing in it!"

It's some measure of Patsy's standing at the Opry that she did take part in that concert after all, along with Jim Reeves, Minnie Pearl, Bill Monroe, Grandpa Jones, Marty Robbins, the Jordanaires, and Faron Young. Playing to a packed house, the Opry troupe raised $11,000 for the Musicians Aid Society of New York. Patsy went over well (as did the whole cast), but she was still a country girl at heart.

Three days later, during a concert in Atlanta, she gave some idea of how she had felt up there in the Big Apple: "You talk about a hen out of a coop—I really felt like one up there. I'm tellin' ya. But you know what? We made 'em show their true colors. We brought that country outta them if anybody did. They's sittin' up there stompin' their feet and yellin' just like a bunch of hillbillies, just like we do. And I was real surprised: Carnegie Hall is real fabulous but, you know, it ain't as big as the Grand Ole Opry."

Few performers have ever balanced the common touch and a regal talent the way Patsy Cline did. We'll never know for certain what else Patsy Cline might have accomplished. On March 5, 1963, one month after her last recording session, thirty-year-old Patsy Cline died in a plane crash along with her manager Randy Hughes, who was piloting the plane, and Opry stars Cowboy Copas and Hawkshaw Hawkins.

★ ★ ★

The crash took place on a Tuesday, and by the end of Wednesday, everyone at the Opry knew the full extent of the tragedy and prepared for a hasty memorial service in Nashville the next day. On Thursday, on his way to the memorial service, Jack Anglin of Johnnie & Jack lost control of his car in a driving rainstorm and lost his life in the crash. On the

Cowboy Copas, a former singer for Pee Wee King, was forty-nine when he died in the plane crash that also killed Patsy Cline.

| NOVEMBER 14, 1960—THE TERM "NASHVILLE SOUND" APPEARS IN *TIME* MAGAZINE, GAINING POPULAR CURRENCY | NOVEMBER 3, 1961—THE CMA ANNOUNCES JIMMIE RODGERS, FRED ROSE, AND HANK WILLIAMS AS THE FIRST INDUCTEES FOR THE COUNTRY MUSIC HALL OF FAME | FEBRUARY 1, 1962—COLUMBIA RECORDS BUYS OWEN BRADLEY'S MUSIC ROW RECORDING STUDIO FOR $300,000 | JANUARY 1963—FLATT & SCRUGGS'S "BALLAD OF JED CLAMPETT" BECOMES THE FIRST BLUEGRASS SINGLE TO TOP THE COUNTRY CHARTS | 1963—ASCAP, THE MUSIC LICENSING AGENCY, OPENS A NASHVILLE OFFICE | 1963—BMI, ASCAP'S RIVAL, BREAKS GROUND FOR A NEW OFFICE BUILDING ON SIXTEENTH AVENUE IN NASHVILLE |

evening of Saturday, March 9, the dark cloud of grief hung heavy and low over the Grand Ole Opry. Opry manager Ott Devine stepped out onstage and called for a moment of silent prayer for the deceased. Then he asked everyone "to keep smiling, and to recall the happier occasions. I feel I can speak for all of them when I say . . . Let's continue in the tradition of the Grand Ole Opry."

The show went on, but the next weeks, indeed the next few years, would be extremely rocky. Three weeks after the horror of the airplane crash, on March 29, Texas Ruby Owens died in a fire at her trailer-park home. Then, in an eerie reenactment of Patsy Cline's death, Jim Reeves perished as well. In an interview just before he died, Reeves talked about the constant traveling he had to do: "I book one hundred personal appearances a year because I like to perform before people. But what I dislike most is the traveling. The main trouble and danger with tours is getting there and getting back." Like Cline, he was flying in a small, one-engine passenger plane, a Beechcraft, in this case piloting the plane himself and returning from closing a real estate deal in Batesville, Arkansas. He checked in at the airfield in Dyersburg, Tennessee, where he was warned about inclement weather. He went ahead anyway. He and band member Dean Manuel crashed in a driving rainstorm near Brentwood, just ten

Hawkshaw Hawkins (left) had been with the Opry for almost two years when Wilma Lee & Stoney Cooper joined the cast in January 1957. Hawkins, the husband of Opry star Jean Shepard, died in the plane crash that also killed Patsy Cline.

miles south of Nashville's Berry Field airport, on July 31, 1964. Twelve planes, two helicopters, and nearly 400 people searched for forty-eight hours before finding the wreckage. Reeves was forty years old.

It's often said that a recording artist's work never dies, but the work of Jim Reeves showed a remarkable vitality after his death. During the next three years he would go on to post six more No. 1 hits.

The Nashville Sound probably reached its artistic and commercial peak in the work of Jim Reeves and Patsy Cline. Few performers in country music have ever managed to captivate pop audiences so thoroughly and yet retain the loyalty of country fans. Owen Bradley and Chet Atkins would continue to launch hit records after the loss of their two great stars, but increasingly their pop-influenced solution was becoming formulaic and repetitive. Even an extremely talented cadre of musicians like the A Team could only come up with so many variations on a theme. The pendulum was swinging back again. While the Opry regrouped and the Nashville Sound ran efficiently, many die-hard country fans were cocking an ear westward.

Johnny Cash did it his way: He recorded best-selling live albums at prisons; he championed new songwriters like Bob Dylan, Kris Kristofferson, and Shel Silverstein; he stretched the boundaries of country wide enough to bring new fans in.

From Fields of Bluegrass to the Streets of Bakersfield

The Grand Ole Opry reeled from the deaths of Patsy Cline and Jim Reeves; in between those two deaths, the world mourned the assassination of President John F. Kennedy in Dallas, on November 22, 1963. Barely two months later the nation had much happier headlines to contemplate as the Beatles arrived in America. When they appeared on the "Ed Sullivan Show" on February 9, 1964, to a nationwide viewing audience of 73 million, they topped the record that Elvis had established eight years before. The Beatles would forever transform popular music with the notion of the self-contained band that had no need for outside musicians or songwriters. Ironically, the Beatles, who led the British Invasion that held the top spot on the American pop charts for nearly half the year in 1964 and 1965, had been inspired by American music. Among the Beatles' admitted favorites were Elvis Presley, Buddy Holly, the Everly Brothers, and Roy Orbison, all of whom had recorded in Nashville.

Meanwhile, the Opry had weathered the first storm of rock and roll in the fifties and attendance was rebounding. After years of competition, suddenly the Opry stood alone, having outlasted and outclassed all the other barn dances. In a show of confidence, National Life and Accident bought the Ryman Auditorium from the city of Nashville in September 1963 for $200,000 and renamed it the Grand Ole Opry House, which people had been calling it informally anyway for twenty years. The Ryman got a much needed sprucing up—it was rewired and

given new sprinklers, new exits, and new plumbing. Things seemed to be looking up at the Opry and in Nashville. In newspapers and national magazines the city was universally acclaimed as the center of the country music universe and the nation's second leading recording center after New York. Bob Dylan went there to record his *Blonde on Blonde* album in March 1966. Perry Como recorded there. In 1967 a rock band called the Lovin' Spoonful

In 1963, after twenty years of Opry performances at Ryman, National Life bought the old gospel tabernacle and officially named it the Grand Ole Opry House.

sang about "Nashville Cats," celebrating "the thirteen hundred and fifty-two guitar pickers" who made the Nashville Sound.

But the world was changing enormously, and Nashville as a whole was slow to respond to those changes. As the Baby Boomers born between 1946 and 1964 grew to maturity, they clamored for music of their own. While the Nashville Sound didn't speak to most of them, there were still country performers who seemed relevant.

★ BLUEGRASS MEETS THE FOLK REVIVAL

Between the coming of Elvis and the Beatles, the youth of America embraced, of all things, folk music. Or at least a kind of folk music.

The folksingers who became popular during the 1950s and early 1960s were almost exclusively middle-class city dwellers who admired the old folk songs and their singers. At first they were merely content with reviving these old songs. That's what Pete Seeger and his popular folk group the Weavers did with their million sellers "Goodnight Irene" (1950) and "On Top of Old Smokey" (1951). The Kingston Trio did the same with "Tom Dooley" in 1959. By the early sixties this popular movement gave rise to singers who wrote their own songs in the folk idiom, such as Tom Paxton, Phil Ochs, and one who transcended the genre, Bob Dylan.

In their search for unsung traditional artists, the folk revival movement took special interest in the traditional-sounding acoustic

Bill Monroe and His Blue Grass Boys onstage at the Opry, 1976. The finest pickers in bluegrass have passed through his band, including the ace fiddler pictured here, Kenny Baker.

Bill Monroe with his former protégé Earl Scruggs. After Scruggs and Lester Flatt left Monroe's band in 1948, the fiery bluegrass patriarch didn't speak to the two for twenty years.

banjo faster than bullets from a machine gun, and he slayed audiences from the very first time he hit the Opry stage with Monroe in early 1946. Judge Hay liked to introduce Scruggs as "the boy who makes the banjo talk."

With Earl Scruggs as a catalyst, Bill Monroe's Blue Grass Boys began making music so lively and memorable that to this day fans still mourn the breakup of that band. It came swiftly. Scruggs left Monroe in January 1948 along with the band's lead singer and guitarist, Lester Flatt. Together they formed their own group and soon they had a recording contract with Mercury Records. By 1953 the Martha White Flour Company had begun sponsoring the act on an early-morning WSM radio show—although Flatt & Scruggs would have to wait two more years to join the Opry, because Monroe used his considerable influence to keep them out of his sight. (Monroe's grudge against his former protégés was so great, in fact, that after their departure he didn't speak a word to them for twenty years.) Even without Monroe's blessing, the former Blue Grass Boys continued to move from one triumph to the next. In 1954 they began a Martha White–sponsored television show that aired in Nashville and five other cities in the

music of Bill Monroe and Flatt & Scruggs. By the early fifties the music had acquired the name "bluegrass," after Bill Monroe's band, the Blue Grass Boys. Bluegrass was not really folk music, but because Monroe kept the music acoustic and because he incorporated the old music forms of the backwoods church and the string band into his high-energy hybrid, it *seemed* to be as old as the hills.

Monroe didn't single-handedly invent bluegrass. In fact, a good argument can be made that the music didn't really take shape until December 1945 when a twenty-one-year-old banjo player from North Carolina joined the Blue Grass Boys. His name was Earl Scruggs, and he would revolutionize banjo playing with his dazzling three-finger style. Before Scruggs, most banjo players strummed, or "frailed," their instruments for a thick, old-timey sound.

Using his thumb and index and middle fingers, Scruggs attacked each string individually, in rapid-fire syncopated bursts that were positively jazzy. Notes showered out of his

Lester Flatt (on guitar) and Earl Scruggs (on banjo) at the Opry in the 1950s. By the end of the decade, the dynamic duo had become the most popular act in bluegrass, eclipsing even their old boss, Bill Monroe.

Flatt & Scruggs (here with Irene "Granny" Ryan) were a big hit on the popular "Beverly Hillbillies" TV show. They not only provided the theme (a No. 1 country hit) but made several guest appearances on the long-running, top-rated CBS comedy (1962–70).

Southeast. Since videotape was not yet available, Flatt & Scruggs had to appear live at studios in each of those cities on a different day of the week. It was an incredible undertaking: Each week for two years their band covered 2,500 miles. But they built up a very loyal audience, and when videotape did come into use in 1956, Flatt & Scruggs got an even wider syndicated market and one of the largest TV viewing audiences in country music.

By the late fifties Flatt & Scruggs had stolen Monroe's thunder. They were the best-known act in bluegrass, and the folk revival movement embraced them. In July 1959 the first Newport Folk Festival invited Earl Scruggs (without Flatt) to perform along with young folk favorites like Joan Baez. In the October 1959 issue of *Esquire*, folklorist Alan Lomax hailed the music of Flatt & Scruggs as "folk music with overdrive." A year later Flatt & Scruggs joined Baez and blues musician John Lee Hooker for a national TV special, "Folk Music USA." The May 1962 cover story of *Sing Out!* magazine, the folkies' *New York Times*, proclaimed Earl Scruggs "the undisputed master of bluegrass music." It was almost inevitable, then, when CBS-TV debuted a brand-

new cornpone comedy called "The Beverly Hillbillies" in the fall of 1962 that it would include some bluegrass music. Sure enough, when the show's producer saw Flatt & Scruggs at a Los Angeles folk club, he signed them to perform the theme song (although Hollywood singer Jerry Scoggins was brought in to sing the vocal). Flatt & Scruggs subsequently had their own version on the record market—this time with Flatt singing; it did the unthinkable, and became the first bluegrass record ever to top the country charts.

As Flatt & Scruggs ascended into the firmament of folk stardom, their old boss struggled to keep his act on the road. A proud, taciturn man, Monroe did not court the folk movement as Flatt & Scruggs did. In fact he repeatedly snubbed overtures from knowledgeable folk fans who tried to seek him out. On one occasion, Monroe threatened to break his mandolin over the head of a writer if he even mentioned Monroe's name in a book.

In August 1962 a young folklorist, Ralph Rinzler, managed to crack Monroe's wall of silence. A true Monroe fan and a bluegrass mandolin picker himself, Rinzler felt that Flatt & Scruggs were unfairly being trumpeted as the founders of bluegrass, when, if anyone deserved that title, it was Bill Monroe. After three months of negotiation, Rinzler got a rare interview with Monroe and published it in the January 1963 issue of *Sing Out!* Rinzler also undertook to arrange tour bookings for Monroe at folk venues across the United States. With Rinzler's help, Monroe's career revived. He too appeared at the Newport Folk Festival, in 1963 and 1965. Through the 1960s, folk and country fans began gradually to realize the enormous role Bill Monroe had played in the genesis of bluegrass music. Not only had he provided the name for the style and dictated the basic musical course, he also had tutored within his band, at one time or another, virtually every important bluegrass musician to come down the pike. In addition to Flatt & Scruggs, the list of former Blue Grass Boys includes Don Reno (of Reno & Smiley), Carter Stanley (of the Stanley Brothers), Jimmy Martin, Mac Wiseman, Sonny Osborne (of the Osborne Brothers), Peter Rowan, and Vassar Clements.

★ THE MAN IN BLACK

Another country performer who made great inroads with the folk crowd was Johnny Cash. After leaving the Opry in 1958, Cash moved out to Los Angeles hoping for film and television opportunities. He got a few jobs, notably appearing on the ABC-TV Western series "The Rebel" and singing its title song. Mostly, though, he continued as a singer. In 1963 he notched a Top Twenty pop hit (and his first country No. 1 hit in four years) with "Ring of Fire," a song written by June Carter (Mother Maybelle Carter's daughter) and Merle Kilgore. After June's sister Anita got first crack at recording the song, Cash waited politely, then cut his own version in March 1963. It included the unusual touch of mariachi-style horns, despite the protests of his producer Don Law. Cash said the idea came to him in a dream; it might have stuck in his head from listening to the radio as well, since Herb Alpert's mariachi-styled "Lonely Bull" was a Top Ten pop hit the previous fall.

Sometime in late 1962 Cash heard Bob Dylan's first album and became an instant fan. He sent Dylan a fan letter in care of the folksinger's producer John Hammond. Gradually the two singers struck up a correspondence and a friendship. When Columbia Records, for whom Cash recorded, made noises about dropping Bob Dylan after a disappointing first album, Cash made it clear that he was a Dylan supporter. "Johnny Cash was one of Dylan's big boosters at Columbia," remembered Hammond. "Cash was behind Dylan every which

Johnny Cash drives on: For years he seemed bent on self-destruction, but music has always redeemed him from his darker impulses.

The Night the Opry Was Canceled

For seventy years the Opry has always gone on unfailingly, with the exception of one night. There was good reason to cancel the show scheduled for Saturday, April 6, 1968. Two days earlier, Dr. Martin Luther King Jr. had been assassinated in Memphis, touching off a firestorm of riots in Memphis, Chicago, Baltimore, Washington, D.C., and Cincinnati the following day. Local officials in Nashville imposed a 7:00 P.M. curfew in an effort to head off any potential problems. For the Opry, this meant no studio audience and no live show. They had to broadcast a tape of a previous show.

Because events had transpired so quickly, no advance announcement had been made to inform out-of-town visitors about the cancellation. When a small crowd gathered outside the Ryman that afternoon, Roy Acuff couldn't bear to turn them away without at least some kind of show. So he invited everyone to his museum just around the corner on Broadway. Acuff had owned the building since 1965 and used the first floor to house his museum and to provide dressing space for himself and his band. Upstairs was a space used for square dances. That's where Acuff and other Opry performers put on an impromptu show for those lucky enough to be on hand. Afterwards, everyone who had purchased a ticket to the Opry got a backstage tour of the Ryman.

Despite the prevailing spirit of goodwill among performers and fans, it was a disappointing night for Opry officials. They had planned a special tribute to Lester Flatt & Earl Scruggs in honor of their twentieth year together and their fifteenth year of sponsorship by Martha White Flour. The night was also disappointing for E. W. "Bud" Wendell, for it was to be his inaugural show as the Opry's new manager, having succeeded the retiring Ott Devine. Wendell, who hailed from Akron, Ohio, had followed in the footsteps of his father, a National Life Insurance salesman. With an economics degree from Wooster College, he joined National Life in 1950, becoming administrative assistant to WSM President Jack DeWitt in 1964.

Wendell immediately endeared himself to the Opry cast by announcing that all performers who had been scheduled to perform April 6 would be paid for that evening. A few weeks later, someone asked Grandpa Jones what he thought of the new manager. "He's great," said Grandpa, who had his own measure for a good boss. "He's brought in some coffee and lemonade backstage."

Johnny Cash with his wife June Carter Cash. Cash and Carter married in 1968 after the Man in Black had the audacity to make his marriage proposal onstage at a show they were doing near Toronto.

way, and everybody in the company knew it. Cash made it known he thought Dylan was a giant."

Cash recorded Dylan's "It Ain't Me Babe" in 1964, about a month after appearing at the Newport Folk Festival with Dylan. By then Joan Baez had recorded Cash's "I Still Miss Someone," and Cash was building a strong folk music following. He had earned it, not only through his friendship with Dylan and Baez but also by recording adventurous albums through the sixties that explored American history and culture. *Ride This Train* (1960) offered a travelogue in song. *Blood, Sweat and Tears* (1963) dealt with America's heritage of work songs like "John Henry." *Bitter Tears* (1964) was his protest album, confronting the sad history of Native Americans. When disc jockeys proved slow to play the lead single, "The Ballad of Ira Hayes" (a true story about the tragic life of a Native American war hero), Cash took out a full-page ad in *Billboard* chastising the D.J.s with the question: "Where are your *guts?*" The song did eventually climb to No. 3 on the country chart.

Just looking at the charts and the following he was building, one would have thought Cash was on top of the world. But for seven years, from 1960 to 1967, Johnny Cash was addicted to pills—an insidious upper-downer cycle of amphetamines and barbiturates. In his worst moments he would wreck hotel rooms. Seven times he ended up in jail. During one

COUNTRY MILESTONES	OCTOBER 1960—MERLE HAGGARD IS A FREE MAN AFTER SERVING TWO YEARS AND NINE MONTHS FOR ROBBERY AND ESCAPE	JUNE 1965—MERLE HAGGARD MARRIES BONNIE OWENS, BUCK'S EX-WIFE	MARCH 25, 1966—BUCK OWENS PLAYS SOLD-OUT SHOW AT CARNEGIE HALL AND RELEASES A LIVE ALBUM OF THE PERFORMANCE	SEPTEMBER 1966— "THE ROGER MILLER SHOW" DEBUTS ON NBC-TV AND RUNS THROUGH JANUARY	APRIL 1, 1967—THE COUNTRY MUSIC HALL O[F] FAME MUSEUM OPENS I[N] NASHVILLE
MAY 1, 1960—THE NATIONAL BARN DANCE COMES TO AN END AT WLS IN CHICAGO AS NEW STATION OWNER ABC/ PARAMOUNT CHANGES THE STATION FORMAT TO ROCK AND ROLL		MARCH 1966—BOB DYLAN RECORDS HIS *BLONDE ON BLONDE* ALBUM IN NASHVILLE		MARCH 1967—MERLE HAGGARD HAS HIS FIRST NO. 1, "THE FUGITIVE"	

bad period in 1964, he accidentally set fire to a forest in a U.S. National Park. The U.S. government sued him and collected $120,000. In 1965 he was busted in El Paso for crossing the Mexican border carrying hundreds of Dexedrine and Equanil pills. A big-boned six-foot-two-inch man who normally had a healthy appetite, Cash found himself down to 140 pounds. One evening in 1965 when he guested on the Grand Ole Opry, the pills definitely got the better of him. In trying to pull the microphone from the stand, he got frustrated. "I took the mike stand, threw it down, then dragged it along the edge of the stage, popping fifty or sixty footlights," Cash wrote in his autobiography. "The broken glass shattered all over the stage and into the audience.

"The song ended abruptly, and I walked offstage and came face to face with the Grand Ole Opry manager [then Ott Devine]. He kindly and quietly informed me, 'We can't use you on the Opry anymore, John.' "

Later that evening Cash woke up in a hospital emergency room with a broken nose and broken jaw. He had wrecked his car in a rainstorm.

In 1967 Johnny Cash was ready to end it all at age thirty-five. He pulled off a highway around Chattanooga and went into a nearby cave called Nickajack. His flashlight ran out of power, and he told himself he was just going to die there too. But somehow he felt a warmth and a presence calling him back out

Among the many guests Johnny Cash (right) welcomed to his 1969–71 ABC-TV show were Grand Ole Opry cast members Bill Anderson and Jan Howard, who in addition to their solo careers were then enjoying a string of duet hits together.

into the light. He left the cave and, later with the help of June Carter whom he married in March 1968, he kicked his drug habit.

Earlier in 1968 he made his biggest album up to that point. For five years, he had pleaded with Columbia Records to let him record a live album at a prison. He had been performing for prisoners since 1958, and he knew it would be a good work all the way around. On January 13, 1968, he played for an hour and forty-five minutes at California's Folsom Prison for an audience of more than 2,000 inmates. This

JANUARY 13, 1968—JOHNNY CASH RECORDS A LIVE ALBUM AT FOLSOM PRISON IN CALIFORNIA; IT SUBSEQUENTLY SELLS OVER A MILLION COPIES

MARCH 1, 1968—JUNE CARTER AND JOHNNY CASH MARRY

AUGUST 5, 1968—LUTHER PERKINS, JOHNNY CASH'S GUITAR PLAYER SINCE 1955, DIES FROM BURNS SUSTAINED IN A FIRE AT HIS HOME TWO DAYS EARLIER

NOVEMBER 20, 1968—THE FIRST TELEVISED COUNTRY MUSIC ASSOCIATION AWARDS SHOW AIRS ON NBC-TV, HOSTED BY ROY ROGERS AND DALE EVANS, AND BROADCAST FROM THE RYMAN. IT WAS ACTUALLY THE SECOND YEAR

OF AWARDS (THE FIRST YEAR'S CEREMONIES WEREN'T TELEVISED)

MARCH 1969—JOHNNY CASH JOINS BOB DYLAN TO RECORD "GIRL FROM THE NORTH COUNTRY" FOR DYLAN'S NASHVILLE SKYLINE ALBUM

JUNE 7, 1969—JOHNNY CASH'S SATURDAY NIGHT ABC-TV SHOW DEBUTS AND RUNS THROUGH MAY 5, 1971; BOB DYLAN AND JONI MITCHELL ARE THE FIRST GUESTS

Johnny Cash entertains at the Ryman Auditorium, 1971. For a while in the sixties Cash was persona non grata at the Opry—after he smashed out the footlights with his microphone stand during a show in 1965.

time Columbia ran the tape and in July they released an album. Its first single, appropriately, was "Folsom Prison Blues," a hit for him a dozen years earlier on Sun Records and the first number he played in that Folsom Prison concert. The single shot to No. 1; the album quickly sold a million copies. Just over a year later, in February 1969, he did a follow-up live

album, this one at San Quentin prison. It included probably his biggest hit ever, a song that just fell into his lap.

"The week before I went to play San Quentin, we had a party at my house, a guitar pull," Cash recalled for journalist Bill Flanagan. "One right after the other, Bob Dylan sang 'Lay, Lady, Lay,' Graham Nash sang 'Marrakesh Express,' Joni Mitchell sang 'Both Sides Now,' and Kris Kristofferson sang 'Me and Bobby McGee,' and Shel Silverstein sang 'A Boy Named Sue.' I asked Shel to write down the lyrics to it. When I went to San

Quentin, June asked if I had it. I said, 'Yeah, but I haven't had a chance to rehearse it; I can't do it.' She said, 'Take the lyrics, put it on the music stand and read it off as you sing it. They'll love it.' That was the one and only recording of 'A Boy Named Sue.'" The comical novelty tune about the disgruntled son who goes searching to avenge himself against his insensitive father sold a million copies. Released in June 1969, *Live at San Quentin* was the No. 1 pop album in America (ahead of the original cast album of *Hair* and *The Best of Cream*) when 400,000 of the Woodstock generation gathered at Max Yasgur's farm in mid-August 1969. That year Johnny Cash outsold the Beatles in America.

Riding that incredible momentum, Johnny Cash landed his own ABC-TV series. Cash insisted the show needed to be taped from the Ryman Auditorium rather than a Hollywood studio. "I love that old building, I love the feeling it gives me, and I love the people," he said. By then he had made his peace with the Opry, and he got his wish—even though the Screen Gems production company had to bring in remote equipment trucks, set up a scenery shop nearby, and build and tear down an extension for the stage each week. Cash also got his way when it came to the show's guest list. In the two years the show aired, from 1969 to 1971, Cash managed to bring on (among others) Pete Seeger, Louis Armstrong, Linda Ronstadt, Mahalia Jackson, the Who, Joni Mitchell, Neil Young, James Taylor, Stevie Wonder, Roy Orbison, Eric Clapton, Merle Haggard, and of course Cash's friend Bob Dylan. It was probably the hippest guest list for a prime-time network TV show ever.

One of Cash's greatest discoveries was a former Rhodes scholar and Army helicopter pilot who was trying to break into the music business as a songwriter. In the late sixties, Kris Kristofferson was working as a janitor at the CBS Records studio in Nashville. For weeks he had been passing tapes of his songs to June Carter Cash, but somehow her husband hadn't managed to hear them. One Sunday morning Johnny Cash was startled to look out the window of his Nashville home and see a helicopter landing on his lawn. It was Kristofferson, with a beer in one hand and a tape in the other. How could Cash resist that kind of style? Cash invited him inside and listened to two songs that would soon be hits: "Sunday Morning Coming Down" (which Cash would record on the stage of the Ryman, July 10, 1970) and "Me and Bobby McGee" (a massive posthumous hit for rock singer Janis Joplin in 1971). With a boost from Cash, Kristofferson soon set about rewriting all the rules for conventional country songs. "For the Good Times" and "Help Me Make It Through the Night" dealt with sex realistically and yet poetically. Kristofferson had been inspired by Bob Dylan, and he in turn in-

Kris Kristofferson—influential songwriter, marginal singer, successful actor, and bon vivant—with his wife, pop singer Rita Coolidge, to whom he was married from 1973 to 1980.

| JUNE 15, 1969—"HEE HAW" DEBUTS ON CBS AS A SUMMER REPLACEMENT FOR THE "SMOTHERS BROTHERS COMEDY HOUR"; LORETTA LYNN AND CHARLEY PRIDE ARE THE FIRST GUESTS | AUGUST 1969—CHARLEY PRIDE HAS HIS FIRST NO. 1 HIT, "ALL I HAVE TO OFFER YOU IS ME" | NOVEMBER 1969— "OKIE FROM MUSKOGEE" BECOMES MERLE HAGGARD'S EIGHTH NO. 1 HIT | 1974—LORETTA LYNN AND THE WILBURN BROTHERS DISSOLVE THEIR PARTNERSHIP | JULY 17, 1974—DON RICH, BUCK OWENS'S RIGHT-HAND MAN, DIES IN A MOTORCYCLE CRASH | | |

spired a whole generation of country songwriters coming up to look for new ways to make meaningful music.

★ BUCK FROM BAKERSFIELD

While Cash and Kristofferson were busy rewriting the rules in Nashville, out in California folks were also trying to renew country music. In the 1940s Bob Wills had provided an alternative to Southeastern country music with his danceable blend of big-band sounds and old-time fiddling. In the 1960s two bandleaders stepped forward to offer a hard-edged alternative to the relaxed intimacy of the Nashville Sound.

Because they both came out of the southern California town of Bakersfield, Buck Owens and Merle Haggard were names that ran together frequently in the conversations of country fans. Although they didn't plan a joint insurrection against the Nashville Sound, by going their own ways they effectively did revolt. And they did have a lot in common. Each recorded in Hollywood for Capitol Records. Each used his own, hand-picked road band for work in the studio. (Merle, in fact, was the one who gave Buck's band the fitting name Buckaroos.) Each was even married (one at a time) to the same woman. Perhaps most importantly, each was born of Okie-Texas stock and came to prominence in Bakersfield—a dusty, flat, sunscorched oil-and-cotton town of 60,000, located one hundred miles north of bustling Los Angeles. Buck Owens made his mark first. Born to sharecroppers in the dusty Texas town

For an entire decade before he began hosting "Hee Haw" in 1969, Buck Owens was making a big noise out in Bakersfield, California.

of Sherman, near the Oklahoma border, Alvis Edgar Owens always longed for a better life. His family home had no electricity and their floors were dirt; outside, the dirt they tilled often blew away. When Buck (who took his name from the family mule) was eight, the family loaded up their '33 Ford sedan and trailer and headed for the greener pastures of California's fertile San Joaquin Valley. But the

car broke down on the outskirts of Phoenix, and Buck's father made do in Mesa, Arizona, picking cotton and digging ditches. Buck quit school in the ninth grade to do the same; already he was a strapping six-footer.

"That was where my dream began to take hold, of not havin' to pick cotton and potatoes, and not havin' to be uncomfortable, too hot or too cold," Owens has said. "We'd go to bed with just cornbread and milk, and I remember wearing shoes with holes in the bottom. I remember having twine for shoestrings. . . ."

In May 1951, at age twenty-one, determined to make it as a musician, Buck moved west to Bakersfield, which had become a refuge for thousands of Dust Bowl migrants during the Depression. He had a couple of uncles there, and they suggested that he might find steady work as a musician in the town's beer joints. He soon did, joining the Orange Blossom Playboys of local bandleader and nightclub owner Bill Woods. He already had responsibilities to think of, having married at seventeen; by twenty-two he and his wife, Bonnie, had two young sons.

What he learned, first of all, was how to keep people dancing at Bill Woods's clubs, first the Corral and then the Blackboard. Then the top nightclubs in Bakersfield, the two clubs drew working-class audiences who just wanted to drink and dance. Working in Woods's Orange Blossom Playboys, Buck got a graduate-level course in playing virtually all styles of dance music.

"We played rhumbas, we played sambas,

we played tangos, we played polkas," said Buck, "whatever the crowd wanted to hear. I sang 'Bony Maronie' by Larry Williams, 'Long Tall Sally' by Little Richard, 'Blueberry Hill' and 'I'm Walkin'' by Fats Domino. I sang 'Johnny B. Goode' and all the Chuck Berry songs. . . . We used to play with no intermission. If we had a four-hour dance deal, we'd play all four hours and never stop."

Meanwhile, to supplement the $12.50 a night he made at the Blackboard, Buck began spending his days in Hollywood, playing sessions for A & R man Ken Nelson at Capitol Records. Though it was a four-hour round trip, the $41.50 he made per three-hour session was too good to pass up. His first studio work came as a guitar player for another Bakersfield favorite, Tommy Collins, in September 1953. Beginning with that first session, Buck lent a distinctive lead guitar touch to "You Better Not Do That," a No. 2 hit in early 1954. Subsequently, Buck played on virtually all Collins's sessions. As Ken Nelson grew familiar with Buck's work, he invited the young picker back to work on sessions for Sonny James, Wanda Jackson, Gene Vincent, Faron Young, and others.

It was only a matter of time before Buck got a chance to make records of his own. He hit the charts for the first time in May of 1959 with "Second Fiddle," done in the loping 4/4 shuffle style popularized by Ray Price. It was a danceable style of country with an emphasis on fiddle, steel, and a pulsing bass. Its impact in the marketplace convinced Buck to work on this up-tempo style in earnest. A month after his first chart showing,

he returned to Capitol's Hollywood studios for his third session. This one was the charm. A new shuffle, "Under Your Spell Again," climbed all the way to No. 4 on the country charts in the fall of 1959—landing one notch over Ray Price's cover version of the song. For the next three years, Buck continued to explore variations on that shuffle theme, regularly smacking hits into the country Top Ten, including "Above and Beyond," "Excuse Me (I Think I've Got a Heartache)," and "Foolin' Around," the last of which Patsy Cline even covered.

Ken Nelson gave Owens almost complete freedom to go his own way in the studio. In contrast to Chet Atkins and Owen Bradley in Nashville, Nelson didn't concern himself with arranging music; instead he put himself in the place of the audience and listened for mistakes: instruments out of tune, botched lyrics, and such.

So Buck Owens essentially produced his own records and chose

or wrote his own songs. As his stature as a recording artist grew, Buck began to build a top-notch road band, which he also expected to employ in the studio. His band began with a sixteen-year-old fiddler by the name of Don Rich whom he met in 1958 when Buck briefly relocated to the Seattle area. Two years later, after graduation from high school, Rich joined Buck permanently. Fifteen years Buck's junior, Rich at first became something of a younger brother to Buck, and then gradually, as his musical skills blossomed on fiddle and then guitar, he became Buck's trusted second in command. He supplied the tenor harmonies, rehearsed and led the band, worked on finding and writing new songs with Buck, and of course handled fiddle and lead guitar.

With Don Rich as his cornerstone, Buck Owens went about building a band that could play anything from shuffles to old-fashioned tearjerkers to a countrified version of rock and roll. Taking that band into the studio, Buck clicked off one hit after another: from "Act Naturally" (summer 1963) to "How Long Will My Baby Be

Buck Owens with his classic Buckaroos band from the mid-sixties. From left: Owens, guitarist-fiddler Don Rich, drummer Willie Cantu, steel player Tom Brumley, and bassist Doyle Holly.

Gone" (early 1968), Buck Owens & the Bucka-roos reeled off sixteen No. 1 hits. During that run they recorded some of the enduring classics of country music: heart songs like "Together Again" and "Cryin' Time"; rollicking good-time tunes like "My Heart Skips a Beat" and "I've Got a Tiger by the Tail"; even the signature instrumental, "Buckaroo," which also amazingly became a No. 1 country record.

Rock and roll had a new sound and so did he. Owens recorded "Act Naturally" without the familiar fiddle and steel. Instead, he gave it more the feel of an up-tempo folk song, with drums in the background and a gutsy electric guitar. It was, Owens maintained, "a plain old drivin' country sound with a hell of a beat and bunch of twangy guitars.... I had always had a lot of driving-type music in my bones."

Buck's records from then on often had the rhythmic drive and the guitar aggressiveness of rock and roll, but the arrangements retained country's essential twanginess. And Buck's vocals always came across as unrepentantly country.

By the end of the sixties, there was no doubt that Buck Owens was cool. The Beatles covered "Act Naturally" and Ray Charles cut "Cryin' Time," both in 1965; five years later Creedence Clearwater Revival sang about the pleasures of "listenin' to Buck Owens" in "Lookin' Out My Back Door." Buck Owens & the Buckaroos played sold-out engagements at New York's Carnegie Hall (in 1966) and the London Palladium (in 1969); both performances were recorded for best-selling live albums. By 1969 he had sold more than 8 million records. That summer, as he turned forty, Buck Owens joined the cast of

Newcomer Merle Haggard (left) with wife Bonnie Owens and guitarist Roy Nichols at the Opry in 1967. Two years later he would be the toast of country music with "Okie from Muskogee."

the new CBS television show "Hee Haw," developed as a country version of "Laugh-In." He would co-host with Roy Clark for the next seventeen years and bring country music right into America's living rooms. Though his music would lose its bearings after the death of right-hand man Don Rich (at thirty-two) in a July 1974 motorcycle crash, Buck Owens was well on his way to being set for life financially. Among his many lucrative investments (including real estate and radio stations), Buck could count running the music publishing house and the booking agency that handled Bakersfield's newest star, Merle Haggard.

★ THE POET OF THE COMMON MAN

In October of 1960, when Buck Owens was riding up the charts with his third straight Top Ten hit, "Excuse Me (I Think I've Got a Heartache)," Merle Haggard was returning

to Bakersfield after serving two years and nine months in San Quentin for burglary and escape. He was twenty-three years old then and up to that point everything in his life had gone wrong.

Like Buck Owens, Merle Haggard came of transplanted Dust Bowl stock. His parents hailed from Checotah, Oklahoma. Two years before he was born, James and Flossie Haggard and their first two children left Checotah and moved out to Oildale, near Bakersfield, where Flossie's sister lived. James Haggard got work with the Santa Fe railroad and moved his family into an abandoned railroad boxcar that he and Flossie turned into a habitable abode. Merle was born April 6, 1937, and he remembers his childhood as filled with love and laughter and music (the family regularly tuned in to the Opry) until shortly after he turned nine, when his thirty-three-year-old father died of a stroke. When his mother went to work as a bookkeeper to keep the family fed and clothed, ten-year-old Merle turned truant and began riding the rails. In the eighth grade he quit school for good.

"The trouble with me," Haggard has said, "was that I started taking the songs I was singing too seriously. Like Jimmie Rodgers, I wanted to ride the freight trains. As a result, I was a general screwup from the time I was fourteen." At fourteen, he and a friend hitchhiked into Texas, partially to track down his favorite singer, the then red-hot Lefty Frizzell. On the return trip Merle's troubles with the law began when the boys were arrested for carrying a pistol and a switchblade and were jailed for five days in Los Angeles. For the next several years he was in and out of reform schools (seven times), did odd jobs, and crossed the law regularly with petty theft and passing bad checks. He made his big mistake at age nineteen when he and a couple of friends hatched a scheme to burglarize a bar after hours. The problem was that they got drunk beforehand, lost track of time, and tried to break in the

Merle Haggard acquired the sobriquet "Poet of the Common Man" for the working-class truths of songs like "Mama Tried," "Working Man Blues," "I Take a Lot of Pride in What I Am," "If We Make It Through December," and many more.

back door while the bar was still open. Merle was sentenced to one to fifteen years at San Quentin State Penitentiary; he stepped inside the prison walls in late December 1957. A few days later Haggard was in the audience when a twenty-five-year-old Johnny Cash performed in a 1958 New Year's Day concert for the inmates. Years later Haggard would recall how much that performance meant to him.

Haggard did not start out as a model prisoner. Infractions got him locked up in solitary, next door to Death Row inmate Caryl Chessman, a convicted rapist who would die in the gas chamber after twelve years of appeals. Being so close to death and hopelessness, Haggard has said, turned his life around; he made up his mind to put his life right. With encouragement from fellow inmates, Haggard honed his musical skills in the warden's country band, worked in the prison textile mill, got his

high school equivalency degree, and served out his appointed sentence.

In October 1960 he took the first bus back to Bakersfield, wearing ill-fitting prison clothes, with $15 in his pocket. At first he worked for his older brother Lowell, an electrical contractor, digging ditches and wiring houses, though he was itching to get into the music scene. Musically, Bakersfield was in high gear at the time. The Blackboard was jumping; Wynn Stewart, Tommy Collins, and Buck Owens were all recording for the Capitol label; local songwriter Dallas Frazier had written the silly "Alley Oop" for the Hollywood Argyles, and it hit the pop charts the summer of 1960. Of course Haggard, an ex-con with no professional experience, had to start at the bottom, which was a club called High Pockets, where he made $10 a night, four nights a week. Little by little, he made

inroads in Bakersfield, graduating to the Blackboard, appearing regularly on Cousin Herb Henson's local country TV show, and cutting singles for Tally Records, a small local label run by cousins Lewis Talley and Fuzzy Owen. From there he graduated to playing bass in Wynn Stewart's band.

It was Wynn Stewart who gave him his next leg up in the business by giving Haggard a song he'd written. "Sing a Sad Song," issued on the tiny Tally label, managed to crack the country charts for three weeks as 1963 turned to 1964, peaking at No. 19. Haggard found his next big hit when he visited songwriter Liz Anderson (mother of future country star Lynn Anderson) at home to hear a few of her songs. When she sat down at an old pump organ to play them, Haggard was certain he'd wasted his time—until he heard the songs. "There must have been four or five No. 1s there," he said in his autobiography. At the very least, there was a hit for him. In January 1965, a year after his first chart appearance with "Sing a Sad Song," he took Liz Anderson's "(My Friends Are Gonna Be) Strangers" into the country Top Ten, his first appearance there. And he named his road-studio band the Strangers because of it, although the name certainly suited his moody, diffident personality. That June, Merle married Bonnie Owens, who had been divorced from Buck since 1953.

(Merle and Bonnie would remain married until 1978.)

People had begun to take notice of the young ex-con. Ken Nelson signed him to Capitol Records, as he had just about every

Though Merle Haggard has always lived near Bakersfield, he does visit Nashville now and then. In this 1970s shot he's joined backstage by Opry manager Hal Durham. "The girls were always crazy about Merle," remembers Durham.

artist in Bakersfield, it seemed; in the deal Capitol bought up Tally Records and all of Merle's early recordings. Buck Owens took notice too, sending word that he wanted to record one of Haggard's songs, a barroom lament called "Swingin' Doors." Haggard's response: "To hell with that, I'll record it myself. I didn't like the song even when I wrote it, but if Buck wants to record it, it must be

good." That record was his highest charting yet, No. 5 on the *Billboard* charts. He followed it up with yet another self-penned drinking song, "The Bottle Let Me Down"—and it went to No. 3.

It took yet one more song from Liz Anderson to put Haggard on the top of the charts and to point him in a new direction for songwriting. Anderson had been inspired to write "The Fugitive" partially by the popular TV series of the same name. When she showed it to Haggard, at first he wasn't sure he ought to record it. The song hit too close to home for a young man who had spent his childhood in and out of reform schools, then in and out of jail, frequently on the run. But he finally did cut it, and it became his first No. 1 song in March of 1967. When Haggard realized that he could sing songs that alluded to his past, maybe even revealed it, and still be accepted by the public, he jumped in with both feet. He wrote his own song that dealt more explicitly with being an ex-con, "Branded Man." Another No. 1. Then he really began opening up, spilling out all the memories and hopes and fears he'd ever had in song after No. 1 song. He sang of his wayward youth in "Mama Tried" (1968), of prison life in "Sing Me Back Home" (1967), of Depression-era struggles in "Hungry Eyes," of keeping his nose to the grindstone in "Workin' Man

Blues" (1969). Haggard's personal songs had critics hailing him as the most interesting new "folk" songwriter around.

Then he wrote a song as a lark, kind of a gentle joke, and it made him the biggest star in country music. "We were driving out of Arkansas on our bus, and there was this sign that said, 'Muskogee, thataway' or whatever, and somebody said, something like, 'I bet they don't smoke marijuana in Muskogee.' I thought it was a funny line, and we—me and my drummer at the time, Roy Burris—just started making up some more.

"A week or so later, I was listening to [radio commentator] Garner Ted Armstrong. He was saying how the smaller colleges in the smaller towns don't seem to have many problems—you know, drugs, riots. Well, I got to wondering if Muskogee had a college, and it did, and they hadn't ever had any trouble—no racial problems and no dope problems. The whole thought hit me in about two minutes, and I did one line after another. It probably took twenty minutes to write the thing, if you add it all up."

His first hint of how the song would go over came before a crowd of Green Berets at the NCO Club of Fort Bragg, North Carolina. And this audience's reaction unnerved Haggard: "They started comin' up after me on the stage, and I didn't know what was gonna happen next until they said we'd have to do it again before they'd let us go. . . . Boy, I tell you, I didn't realize how strong some people felt about those things."

Without thinking, without really meaning to, Haggard touched a nerve with the song. In a delivery that was completely straight, just like his earlier personal songs, without a hint of irony, Haggard sang about living life in the slow lane, being an unabashed patriot, and dressing conservatively.

In the fall of 1969 "Okie from Muskogee" struck home for country fans who had been watching the news on TV and seeing race riots after the assassination of Martin Luther King Jr. the previous April, student takeovers at Columbia University and California Berkeley in May, riots at the Democratic Convention in August, and 250,000 antiwar protesters marching on Washington that November. Haggard seemed to be extolling the virtues of simpler times. Whether he intended to or not, he had joined a trend in country music commentary on the Vietnam War that had been going on since Kitty Wells's husband Johnny Wright scored a No. 1 hit in October of 1965 with the stoic soldier's story "Hello Vietnam." That trend included Staff Sergeant Barry Sadler's "Ballad of the Green Berets," a No. 1 pop hit (No. 2 country) record that celebrated "fighting soldiers from the sky." Ernest Tubb weighed in with the self-explanatory effort "It's for God and Country and You, Mom (That's Why I'm Fighting in Vietnam)," which hit the charts in early 1966.

The live *Okie from Muskogee* album quickly sold nearly a million copies and stayed on the charts for seventy-five weeks. Haggard's concert price tripled to about $10,000 a show. Everywhere he played, audiences greeted him by waving little American flags. President Nixon sent him a letter commending him for "Okie from Muskogee." Predictably, Haggard's next single was an even more emphatic espousal of patriotism, "The Fightin' Side of Me." It too went to No. 1 and stayed on the charts through May of 1970. Remarkably and tellingly, though, Haggard *wanted* to release "Irma Jean," a song about an interracial love affair. Capitol Records balked.

"They just weren't ready for a black and white love song at that time," Haggard said years later. "I think it would have been good. But they [Capitol's execs] were still more in charge than I was at that time, so I went along. But I think it would have let people understand that 'Okie' is *music*, not necessarily a person standin' on a box makin' a speech."

He could have easily cashed in more songs like "Okie" or "Fightin' Side"; instead he cut tribute albums full of songs by a couple of his idols: Jimmie Rodgers (*Same Train, A Different Time*) and Bob Wills (*A Tribute to the Best Damn Fiddle Player in the World*). When he returned to songs about the war, he preferred to meet it obliquely, as in his cover of Ernest Tubb's sentimental World War II–era "Soldier's Last Letter" (1971) and his first-person tale of a prisoner of war, "I Wonder If They Ever Think of Me" (1972).

Inspired by the sounds of Bob Wills, Jimmie Rodgers, and Lefty Frizzell, Merle Haggard forged his own inimitable style. He wrote songs filled with personal detail that spoke universal truths to a wide audience. In songs as diverse as "Workin' Man Blues" and "I Take a Lot of Pride in What I Am," he not only admitted to being from the country and from the working class, but he also extolled the virtues of the common way of life in ways that hadn't been articulated as forcefully in country music before.

The sixties were a turbulent decade for America and a stern test for country music. Would it continue to speak to Americans? Thanks to the contributions of Owens, Haggard, Cash, Kristofferson, and the bluegrass contingent, it did. Cash, Owens, and Haggard also kept country music rough and edgy, while Monroe and Flatt & Scruggs kept the faith with the music's old-time acoustic traditions. For all their achievements, though, these men were only part of country's story of renewal in the sixties. For the other side of the story, it's important to turn back to Nashville and consider the hard-fought triumphs of three strong-minded women.

In song after song Loretta Lynn spoke up for women. She was not a card-carrying feminist, though; in fact, she once fell asleep on a talk show as Betty Friedan (author of The Feminine Mystique) was speaking!

Woman to Woman

A COAL MINER'S DAUGHTER

Country has always reflected the mood of America. It was only a matter of time before women got the opportunity to express themselves not just as voices but also as songwriters of the first rank. In October of 1960, the Grand Ole Opry got its first opportunity to see a woman who would prove as revolutionary during the sixties as Kitty Wells had been in the previous decade. Loretta Lynn stepped out nervously onto the Ryman stage on that autumn evening and sang her one and only record at the time, "I'm a Honky Tonk Girl." She was a twenty-five-year-old housewife from Custer, Washington, who thought she had reached the very pinnacle of success. In a way, she had. But she still had a long way to go.

Loretta Lynn's up-by-the-bootstraps story, filled as it is with coincidences and lucky breaks, sounds like the stuff of Hollywood. And in fact, it did inspire a very true-to-life movie called *Coal Miner's Daughter* (1980), starring Sissy Spacek and Tommy Lee Jones. Loretta Lynn grew up in the hill country of eastern Kentucky in an isolated coal-mining hamlet known to locals as Butcher Holler. The second of eight children born to Ted and Clara Webb, Loretta was named after the Hollywood star Loretta Young. To cheer up their rough, small cabin home, Clara Webb papered the walls with pictures from movie magazines and mail-order catalogs. Saturday nights, by the light of oil lamps, the family listened to the Grand Ole Opry on a battery-powered radio. Ted Webb worked in the coal mines and did a little farming on the side. All the children pitched in to keep the household together; as the eldest girl, Loretta learned domestic responsibilities early. Loretta Webb might never have been heard from by the wider world had it not been for a twenty-one-year-old ex-GI named Oliver "Mooney" Lynn who took a shine to Loretta at a schoolhouse social. Mooney Lynn didn't realize at first that the headstrong little brunette was just thirteen years old. Nevertheless, they married within a month, and after Mooney found work in Washington state, he sent for Loretta, pregnant with their first child.

By the time she turned eighteen Loretta had four children. It was hard work, not only keeping house for her new family but also picking strawberries (with her kids beside her all the while) to supplement Mooney's income as a lumberjack. She needed a little relaxation, her husband thought. Mooney noticed that Loretta liked to sing along to country songs on the radio. For her eighteenth birthday he gave her a $17 Sears guitar. The year was 1953; the previous summer Kitty Wells had broken through as a woman's voice in the Hit Parade. With just a little prodding from her husband, Loretta learned to play that guitar.

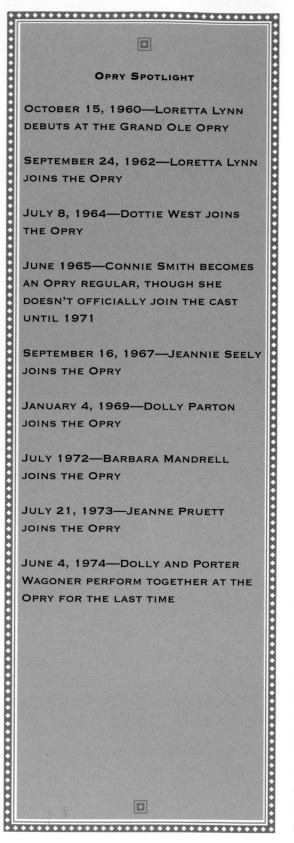

OPRY SPOTLIGHT

OCTOBER 15, 1960—LORETTA LYNN DEBUTS AT THE GRAND OLE OPRY

SEPTEMBER 24, 1962—LORETTA LYNN JOINS THE OPRY

JULY 8, 1964—DOTTIE WEST JOINS THE OPRY

JUNE 1965—CONNIE SMITH BECOMES AN OPRY REGULAR, THOUGH SHE DOESN'T OFFICIALLY JOIN THE CAST UNTIL 1971

SEPTEMBER 16, 1967—JEANNIE SEELY JOINS THE OPRY

JANUARY 4, 1969—DOLLY PARTON JOINS THE OPRY

JULY 1972—BARBARA MANDRELL JOINS THE OPRY

JULY 21, 1973—JEANNE PRUETT JOINS THE OPRY

JUNE 4, 1974—DOLLY AND PORTER WAGONER PERFORM TOGETHER AT THE OPRY FOR THE LAST TIME

Singing to the children helped stave off the loneliness that the young wife and mother felt, two thousand miles away from her Kentucky home. After picking up a copy of *Country Song Roundup* magazine, which reprinted lyrics to the hits of the day, Loretta felt songwriting was within her grasp as well. "It looked easy to me," she later remarked. In 1959 Mooney finally managed to push Loretta out onstage at the Delta Grange Hall in Custer. In a matter of months, she graduated from a regular slot at the Delta Grange Hall to winning a talent contest on Buck Owens's Seattle-area TV show. As luck would have it, a lumber tycoon named Norm Burley, watching the show on his TV at home in nearby Vancouver, spotted Loretta and offered to finance an independent record.

Following a February 1960 recording session, Burley pressed up 3,500 copies of Loretta's first single, "I'm a Honky Tonk Girl," on his none-too-confidently named Zero label, and the Lynns, despite their inexperience, plunged into their own homemade promotion campaign: They mailed out hundreds of records, personalized with a short note from Loretta and a photo taken by Mooney, to disc jockeys across the country. Then, in a stroke of guileless brilliance, Mooney and Loretta left the kids with her brother and set out on the road to talk up the record in person.

"We set out in our old Mercury to promote the record," she recalled. "Because we were too poor to stay in hotels, we slept in the car and ate bologna and cheese sandwiches in parks. When we were driving, I'd just wear jeans or something. When we got near a radio station, I would jump in the backseat and change into my only dress, cowboy hat, and boots. Then we'd go into the radio station and pester the DJ to play my record. We

Two Lorettas: Loretta Lynn and actress Sissy Spacek together at the Opry in 1979. Spacek won a 1980 Oscar for portraying Loretta in the biographical movie Coal Miner's Daughter.

didn't care if it was a 500-watt local station or a 50,000-watt clear-channel station. We'd hit them all. We were on the road three months."

In 1960 the disc jockey was king on radio. He picked the records he wanted to play. Period. There were no consulting firms, no tightly formatted program lists. The DJ just had to keep his listeners happy. That summer, America's country DJs were absolutely

Hootenanny: Loretta Lynn on the road with mentors Teddy and Doyle Wilburn (on guitars). The Wilburns not only got Loretta signed to their record label but also featured Loretta prominently on their syndicated TV show, beginning in May 1963.

Wilburns had placed a dozen hits on the charts, had established a successful tour-booking agency (Wil-Helm), and had a publishing company (Sure Fire Music) to boot. The Wilburns helped to arrange Loretta's first Opry appearance. They encouraged the Lynns' move to Nashville in mid-1961, and they set about securing a contract for her with a major record label. Both the Columbia and Capitol labels turned Loretta down cold. So in the late summer of 1961 Doyle Wilburn turned to Owen Bradley at Decca, the Wilburns' own label. Bradley liked the sound of the demo recording that Doyle brought him, though more for the song than for Loretta's singing. He had an upcoming recording session scheduled for Brenda Lee and thought the tune was a possibility. The Wilburns were the publishers of "The Biggest Fool of All," written by their staff tunesmith

charmed by the spunky twenty-five-year-old from Butcher Holler. They played the little record right alongside the latest from Jim Reeves, Kitty Wells, and Buck Owens. In July of 1960 "I'm a Honky Tonk Girl" hit No. 14 on the country charts and Loretta got an invitation from the Grand Ole Opry.

With such astonishing success the first time out, Mooney and Loretta soon decided to move to Nashville and make a real go of a career in music. Their biggest boosters there were the Wilburn Brothers, Teddy and Doyle, who had first played the Opry briefly when they were children in the family band. After apprenticing in Webb Pierce's band, they moved on to a career as a duo that earned them membership in the Opry cast. By the time the Lynns met them in 1960, the

Loretta Lynn at home with husband Oliver "Mooney" Lynn and their twin daughters Peggy and Patsy, 1969. Patsy was named after Loretta's dear departed friend Patsy Cline.

Honky Tonk Angels

Connie Smith (ca. 1969) and her powerful voice have been a part of Opry shows since 1965. Dolly Parton once said, "There's really only three real female singers in the world: Streisand, Ronstadt, and Connie Smith."

Best known for her 1962 crossover smash "The End of the World," Skeeter Davis (formerly Mrs. Ralph Emery) was the first artist to devote an entire album to Dolly Parton's songs with Skeeter Sings Dolly (1972).

Loretta Lynn recording a duet with Ernest Tubb, 1965. "I never ever dreamed that I would ever see Ernest Tubb," she told journalist Alanna Nash, "let alone record with him." In 1970 she took on a new duet partner in Conway Twitty.

Kathryn Fulton, and Doyle Wilburn played the song like a trump card. Without a contract for Loretta Lynn, he wouldn't give Bradley the song for Brenda Lee. Bradley must have thought a lot of the song, for he agreed to the deal, signing Loretta to a six-month contract on September 3, 1961. Brenda Lee had already recorded the song as "Fool #1" three days earlier, and it became a No. 3 pop hit for her late that fall.

Loretta got her chance to record for Owen Bradley nine days after Brenda Lee's session. The first record—"The Girl That I Am Now"/ "I Walked Away from the Wreck"—didn't make the slightest dent in the charts, despite the provocative titles. But her next release—"Success," recorded in that same first session and released in February 1962—lived up to its title, breaking into the country Top Ten in the summer of 1962.

Looking back now, that first hit seems an anomaly for Loretta. It's a wife's lament for the way her husband's success has pulled apart their marriage. It was, in fact, a typical woman's song for country music in the early sixties.

Loretta's next couple of singles continued in the same vein, with Loretta singing songs much in the style of Kitty Wells, in a countrified voice that even echoed Kitty. Gradually, though, Owen Bradley began to notice that Loretta was writing some strong material. "One day in my office she was singing her new songs," Bradley recalled, "and I remember telling her, 'That's wonderful. That reminds me of Hank Williams. You sound like a female Hank Williams, Loretta.'"

Bradley had a point. Hank Williams had connected with listeners because he sang about the trials and tribulations in his life, particularly the struggles with his wife, Audrey. What Loretta Lynn discovered was a way to tell a woman's side of marital relations in frank, plain-spoken, and often amusing songs. It was as if she had picked up where Kitty Wells had left off with "Honky Tonk Angels" in 1952. In 1964 Loretta tested the waters with "Wine, Women and Song" and "Happy Birthday"—songs that humorously warned her man that he couldn't cheat and get away with it. Each song climbed to the No. 3 spot on the charts, her best showing there yet. Embolded by success, she pushed further. She tackled women who might compete for her husband in "You Ain't Woman Enough" (1966), "Fist City" (1968), and "Woman of the World (Leave My Man Alone)" (1969). Meanwhile, she laid down the law for her man as well in "Don't Come Home a-Drinkin' (With Lovin' on Your Mind)" (1966) and "Your Squaw Is on the Warpath Tonight" (1968). All of these singles were Top Ten hits, and several of them topped the charts.

So successful was Loretta Lynn in defining her musical persona with these songs that soon other writers offered her similarly forthright material. Two of the most memorable of these tailor-made tunes were "One's on the Way" (1971), the wry grumblings of a woman who's had one child too many, and "The Pill" (1975), in which Loretta celebrates gaining control of her sexuality. "The Pill" was considered so controversial that her record company didn't even release it as a single until two years after she recorded it. Then, numerous radio stations banned the record for its frankness. But Loretta never backed down or apologized for singing what she felt. "If they'd had the Pill when I was having babies," she said, "I'd have been eatin' 'em like popcorn." Ultimately, "The Pill" became a Top Ten hit.

Loretta didn't restrict herself simply to material about war between the sexes. Taking a cue from Merle Haggard, she stood up for being from the working class. In "Coal Miner's Daughter" (1969), she told the story of her youth back in the Kentucky hills and proclaimed herself

Jean Shepard (pictured at the Opry in 1961) anticipated the later artistic breakthroughs of Loretta, Tammy, and Dolly with her 1954 concept album Songs of a Love Affair.

A duet partner of Jim Reeves, Don Gibson, Jimmy Dean, and Kenny Rogers, Dottie West is best remembered for her award-winning Coca-Cola jingle "Country Sunshine," which in 1973 became a hit record for her as well.

Jeannie Seely preceded Dolly as Porter Wagoner's featured "gal singer" for a brief period in 1966. After her recording of "Don't Touch Me" hit No. 2 on the charts, Seely moved on to a solo career and Opry membership in 1967.

You've come a long way, baby: Tammy Wynette pulled herself and three daughters out of poverty with a hit recording career.

proud to be a coal miner's daughter. In "You're Looking at Country" (1970), she pledged her unswerving allegiance to country music and country living. "Coal Miner's Daughter," in particular, was a landmark. "It told everybody that I could write about something else besides marriage problems," she said in her autobiography. "Coal Miner's Daughter" not only became a No. 1 hit; it also became her theme song.

In spite of her outspoken style, Loretta Lynn received accolades from the music industry. The Country Music Association's first awards gathering in 1967 honored her as the year's top Female Vocalist. She won the award again in 1972 and 1973. For four years running (1972–1975), she and Conway Twitty won the CMA's Vocal Duo of the Year award for their passionate singing on No. 1 records like "After the Fire Is Gone," "Lead Me On," and "Louisiana Woman, Mississippi Man." (Their singing sounded so emotional, in fact, that many fans erroneously suspected that the two were carrying on an affair. Regardless, she remained married to Mooney Lynn.) In October 1972 she virtually swept the CMA Awards show, winning the Female Vocalist and Duo trophies, plus the CMA's highest accolade, the

Entertainer of the Year award. It was the first time that a woman had won it. The following year a Gallup poll placed her among the top twenty most admired women in the world.

★ HEROINE OF HEARTBREAK

If Loretta Lynn spoke for women who longed for liberation, Tammy Wynette spoke for those who preferred the status quo. In marked contrast to Loretta, Tammy played the role of the patient, devoted wife in song after song. Like Loretta Lynn, Tammy Wynette grew up in grinding poverty. She was born Virginia Wynette Pugh in Itawamba County in the northeast corner of Mississippi, near the Alabama border. Her father died of a brain tumor when she was just nine months old; her mother moved away to work in a defense plant, leaving little Wynette Pugh to be raised by her cotton-farming grandparents. She grew up picking cotton, baling hay, harvesting corn, milking cows, and daydreaming that one day she would be onstage singing beside her favorite singer, George Jones.

Determined to find a better life, Wynette impulsively got married at seventeen to Euple Byrd, an unemployed ex-GI. By the time she was twenty-three, she had three little girls and a failed marriage. She moved to Birmingham, Alabama, where she landed a job singing on a local country music TV show from 6 A.M. to 8 A.M., then worked in a beauty salon until seven each night. The money from the two jobs barely exceeded her rent in a government housing project.

A friendship with a Birmingham DJ led to her first trip to Nashville and the annual DJ Convention in October 1965. She didn't get any commitments from the contacts she made there, but Wynette was determined to return. Although she couldn't have quoted the statistics that were being bandied about by major newspapers and magazines—four record-pressing plants, eleven talent agencies, ten recording studios, twenty-six record labels, some 800 songwriters, and more than 1,000 musicians—Wynette Byrd could see that Nashville was the place to be. A trip to the Ryman was the clincher. "When I saw the Grand Ole Opry, the desire to be up on the stage with the performers was like a hunger."

In January 1966 she returned to Nashville with her children and less than $200 figuring she could fall back on hairdressing if music did not pan out. She took to knocking on doors up and down Music Row, the formerly run-down residential district bordered by Sixteenth and Seventeenth avenues, a four-block-by-two-block area where Owen Bradley and Chet Atkins had built their studios in the fifties. Everyone in the music business had followed the two kingpin producers' lead. In 1966 the old 1920s-era wooden houses had been converted into offices for publishing companies and stood side by side with more lavish glass-and-steel structures that housed most of the major record companies. Following a March groundbreaking, a Country Music Hall of Fame was being built at the head of Music Row, next door to BMI's tasteful two-year-old office building.

For months Wynette Byrd pored over her telephone book, made appointments, and knocked on doors. At one point she managed to hook up with Opry star Porter Wagoner for a ten-day trial tour. If she worked out, Wagoner said he would sign her to take the place of the departing Norma Jean Beasler on his top-rated syndicated TV show and on records. "I just knew that after the tour he would ask me to stay on permanently," she recalled. "I could already see myself making records. Porter was a big star and if anybody could get you a

recording contract, he could." But when the tour ended, Wagoner let her go.

In late August she hit the jackpot when she arrived at the offices of Columbia Records located on the site of Owen Bradley's studios,

Producer Billy Sherrill with one of his greatest discoveries, Tammy Wynette, ca. 1967.

which the company had purchased and built its offices around in 1962. She didn't have an appointment and hoped to make one with whoever was in charge. Not finding a secretary in the reception area, she called out and was answered by staff producer Billy Sherrill, who invited her into his office. With his feet

up on his desk and his youthful demeanor, the then twenty-nine-year-old producer didn't look like somebody important. But Sherrill had plenty of experience. The son of a traveling evangelist, Billy had been a key musician in the burgeoning recording studio scene in Muscle Shoals, Alabama, during the late fifties. In the early sixties he helped run Sun Records' satellite studio operation in Nashville, recording among others Charlie Rich. Having joined Columbia Records in Nashville in 1964, he had just begun to prove himself to the record industry. In the summer of 1965 he had co-written and produced a No. 1 country hit for David Houston, "Almost Persuaded."

He asked Wynette if she'd brought any demo tapes. She hadn't. But she borrowed his guitar and sang a couple of songs she'd co-written. "Tell you what," Sherrill said at the end of the impromptu audition. "If you can find a good tune, I'll record you." Wynette thought it was probably just a brush-off. But Sherrill had heard something in her voice. "The songs she sang weren't bad," Sherrill remembered, "but I was more impressed with her voice. There was this 'cry' in it that really got to you."

The next day Sherrill called Wynette. He had just heard a record called "Apartment No. 9" on Bakersfield's Tally label by a guy named Bobby Austin. Sherrill thought Tammy could do a better job with the song. On Friday, September 9, 1966, Wynette Byrd stepped into the old Bradley Studios, now owned by Columbia, and delivered a bravura performance. Every little hurt that she'd been holding inside seemed to pour out with exquisite sadness on that first brilliantly gloomy record about a lonely woman waiting for her faithless lover. Like Loretta Lynn's first record, it featured

Wynette singing overdubbed harmony with herself. On her first try she hit the country charts, even if she didn't crack the Top Forty. And the world was beginning to know her as Tammy Wynette. That was Billy Sherrill's idea. "Wynette just did not seem to get it," she recalled. "One day when I was wearing my hair in dog ears, Billy looked at me and said, 'You look like a Tammy to me,' and it just stuck."

Over the next year Sherrill and his newly christened Tammy searched for a winning formula. A feisty, Loretta Lynn–like turn on "Your Good Girl's Gonna Go Bad" produced a No. 3 hit in the spring of 1967. A duet with David Houston on "My Elusive Dreams," the poignant saga of a nomadic loser and his faithful wife, brought Tammy her first No. 1. It also hinted at what sort of song her throbbing voice, brimming with tears and womanly ache, was best suited for. Sherrill began matching the hurt in Tammy's voice with appropriate material. In swift succession they began racking up one massive No. 1 hit after another. "I Don't Wanna Play House" (1967) and "D-I-V-O-R-C-E" (1968) had Tammy playing the role of a mother whose child brings her crumbling marriage into sharp focus. "Take Me to Your World" offered romantic pliability. But the watershed was "Stand By Your Man." It hit No. 1 in November 1969, almost exactly a year before "Okie from Muskogee" topped the country charts, and its testimony of a woman fulfilled in a traditional marriage role appealed to the same audience that would lionize Haggard. Ironically, Tammy Wynette claimed she didn't really mean for the song to send an antifeminist message.

It happened this way: On August 28, 1968, Tammy was working on a recording session. During a session break Sherrill pulled out a scrap of paper that he'd been carrying with him for more than a year. "The title was an idea Billy had been kicking around for some time," Tammy says. Sherrill asked what she thought of it. "I said I liked the idea of a woman standing by her man. I was raised to believe that way," she replied. "So Billy said, 'Let's work on it.' He gave the musicians a twenty-minute break and we went up to his office and wrote it. It just flowed out. Then we went back downstairs and recorded it immediately."

Even those who can't abide the song's sexual politics must admit that it's a transcendent performance, with Tammy's high notes challenging the steel for supremacy on the choruses. Billy Sherrill knew how to get the most out of Tammy Wynette. On hit after hit he framed her tear-stained voice with weeping steel guitars, softly tinkling pianos, hushed background choruses, and eventually, full string sections. With his background in pop music Sherrill thought nothing of borrowing from Phil Spector's full "wall of sound" pop production techniques. "Stand By Your Man" not only topped the country charts, it also broke into the pop Top Twenty. It quickly sold well over a million copies.

After having struggled so hard to make it, Tammy suddenly found everything she ever wanted coming to her. In the summer of 1968, shortly before she recorded

Tammy Wynette and George Jones were a hot tabloid item during their tempestuous marriage. They also managed to record some of country music's favorite duets, including "We're Gonna Hold On" (1973), "Golden Ring" (1975), and "Two Story House" (1980).

Tammy Wynette had joined the Opry briefly in 1969. Here the First Lady of Country Music rejoins the cast in 1973.

"Stand By Your Man," George Jones asked her to marry him. It was not quite a fairy tale. For one thing she was already married at the time, having wed songwriter Don Chapel in 1967. But Tammy had been performing here and there with Jones over the past several months, and Jones had secretly fallen for her. One night Jones dropped in on the couple to find them in the midst of a heated argument. When Jones interrupted and took Tammy's side, Chapel pointedly told him the discussion was none of his business. "Yes, it is," George retorted. "I love her. And she loves me too. Don't you, Tammy?"

Tammy was stunned by Jones's avowal of love. "We had never even been alone, much less romantic. And yet the minute he asked the question, I answered, 'Yes, *yes*,' realizing for the first time that it was true."

Immediately, George and Tammy gathered up her three daughters and left. She got an annulment, and on August 22, 1968, George Jones and Tammy Wynette announced that they were marrying. Actually, they lived together for several months until the wedding finally took place on February 16, 1969, in the aptly named town of Ringgold, Georgia, known across the Southeast for its no-waiting wedding chapels. It sounded like a dream marriage to fans, who rejoiced when the two quickly combined their road shows into one star-studded affair that offered (in the phrase of an inspired publicist) "The First Lady and the President" of country music. And omens looked good in October 1970 when Tammy gave birth to a daughter they named Tamala Georgette.

Thanks to the marriage, Billy Sherrill had an opportunity to bring Jones to his record company. "She was the catalyst as to why I signed him," Sherrill has said. "They wanted to sing together so bad, and he was just getting off this other label." In April 1971 Sherrill began recording the two superstars in duet sessions, and on October 1, 1971, Jones ended his six-year association with the independent Musicor label, signing with Billy Sherrill's Epic Records, a subsidiary of Columbia. Five days later Epic released George and Tammy's first joint LP, *We Go Together*.

And in song they did. In a case of art imitating life, their records almost seemed to chronicle the cycle of their relationship. Tammy posted "Stand By Your Man" high on the charts for all to see as they began their affair in the fall of 1968. Jones seemed to reply the next spring with "I'll Share My World with You" (a No. 2 hit). Then their duets kept fans informed as to the progress of their marriage—from its first romantic stirrings ("Take Me," 1971) to a hokey reenactment of their wedding vows ("The Ceremony," 1972) to a grim pledge of loyalty ("We're Gonna Hold On," 1973) to a sorry tale of love come full circle ("Golden Ring," 1975). By 1975, the marriage was dead and buried.

Jones's long-standing problems with alcohol and cocaine worsened during the marriage, driving a wedge between them. It's not at all an exaggeration to say that Jones ended up in the papers more often for his drinking escapades than for his singing. Classic stories abound: Fearing that Tammy would leave him, an inebriated Jones tore the high heels off 200 pairs of shoes. On another occasion, when Tammy hid the car keys to keep Jones away from drink, he jumped on their riding lawn mower and drove it ten miles to the nearest bar. For every amusing tale, unfortunately, there seemed to be three that were clearly traumatic. Once, when he accidentally mixed diet pills with alcohol, Jones went on a bender so full of threatening gunplay and household destruction that doctors had him straitjacketed and committed to a padded cell for ten days.

Tammy filed for divorce in April 1973, but they quickly reconciled. However, when Jones walked out on her on Friday the 13th of December 1974, that was it. Tammy filed for divorce again in January and the marriage ended legally in March. Yet despite all the torment, Tammy Wynette persevered. She continued to rack up No. 1 hits throughout the troubled marriage. The Country Music Association honored her four times as the Female Vocalist of the Year—three years running (1968–1970) and then again in 1972. After her divorce from Jones, she dated celebrities like Burt Reynolds and Rudy Gatlin of the Gatlin Brothers. In 1978, after another short-lived marriage to developer Michael Tomlin, she married songwriter George Richey, who remains her husband and manager to this day. Through it all she even managed to maintain amicable relations with George Jones, continuing to record hit duets with him.

Though she didn't endear herself to feminists with songs like "Stand By Your Man," in real life Tammy Wynette was anything but a doormat. She didn't merely play a passive role in Billy Sherrill's lavish productions; she co-wrote many of the songs that made her career. But most impressive of all, she pulled herself and her daughters out of poverty and overcame four sour marriages to arrive on the other side.

★ HELLO, DOLLY

It was in the spring of 1976, a year after Tammy Wynette's divorce from George Jones, that America began noticing country music's newest female star, Dolly Parton. She too was undergoing her own painful split from her longtime mentor and duet partner, Porter Wagoner. For seven years (1967–1974), she had starred on Wagoner's syndicated TV show. By the time of her departure, the show was playing in more than 100 markets with an estimated audience of more than 4.5 million viewers. Parton declared her independence in the spring of '76 with her

A monumental figure: As Dolly likes to say, "You'd be surprised how much it costs to look this cheap."

COUNTRY MILESTONES	LORETTA LYNN AS A FEATURED PERFORMER	FIRST TRIP TO NASHVILLE TO VISIT THE DJ CONVENTION	HER FIRST RECORD, "APARTMENT NO. 9"	OCTOBER 11, 1967— DOLLY PARTON AND PORTER WAGONER RECORD THEIR FIRST DUET SINGLE, "THE LAST THING ON MY MIND"; IT BECOMES A TOP TEN COUNTRY HIT IN EARLY 1968	NOVEMBER 1968— TAMMY WYNETTE'S "STAND BY YOUR MAN" TOPS THE COUNTRY CHARTS
SEPTEMBER 3, 1961— LORETTA LYNN SIGNS WITH DECCA RECORDS	MAY 30, 1964— EIGHTEEN-YEAR-OLD DOLLY PARTON MOVES TO NASHVILLE	MAY 30, 1966—DOLLY PARTON WEDS CARL DEAN	SUMMER 1967—DOLLY PARTON BEGINS TOURING WITH THE PORTER WAG-ONER SHOW; NOT LONG AFTERWARD SHE BEGINS APPEARING ON HIS SYNDICATED TV SHOW		FEBRUARY 16, 1969— TAMMY WYNETTE AND GEORGE JONES MARRY IN RINGGOLD, GEORGIA
MAY 4, 1963—THE WILBURN BROTHERS BEGIN THEIR OWN SYN-DICATED TV SHOW, WITH	OCTOBER 1965—TAMMY WYNETTE MAKES HER	SEPTEMBER 9, 1966— TAMMY WYNETTE MAKES			

own syndicated television show, "Dolly!" airing in 130 markets. Glowing profiles on her began appearing in such previously unlikely spots as *The New York Times Magazine* and *Rolling Stone*. Then in the fall of 1977, her airy soprano was seemingly everywhere as her bouncy rendition of "Here You Come Again" climbed high up the pop charts. She appeared on the "Tonight Show" and had Johnny Carson eating out of her hand. Who was this singer who resembled a young Mae West replete with cascading blond wigs, Fu Manchu fingernails, and prodigious bustline? Where on earth did she come from?

As most Americans now know, Dolly Rebecca Parton came from deep in the heart of Appalachia, born and raised in a two-room mountain shack not so very different from Loretta Lynn's. Like the Webb family back in Butcher Holler, the Partons didn't have electricity, running water, or indoor plumbing. Dolly's father, Lee, was a sharecropper who made moonshine on the sly. The doctor who delivered Dolly on January 19, 1946, had to journey down the dirt road on horseback to the Partons' cabin on the banks of Tennessee's Little Pigeon River. Dolly's parents paid him in cornmeal.

Dolly's mother, Avie Lee, had married at fifteen; she was twenty-two when she had

Dolly was a precocious child: By the age of ten she was already performing professionally on radio and TV.

Dolly, the fourth of her twelve children. Early on, Dolly learned to pitch in as surrogate mother to her younger brothers and sisters. "We had nothin' so far as material things," Dolly recalled. "If you had a nice sweater or a lipstick, you had to be rich, in our mind."

Privacy was simply not available at home: "We slept four and five to a bed, and it didn't matter if you'd stopped wettin' 'cause somebody else was gonna pee on you anyway." Instead, Dolly found her own private world. From her earliest years Dolly loved to sing. Her mother taught her somber old folk songs from the hills: "Barbara Allen," "The Letter Edged in Black," "Little Rosewood Casket." Soon Dolly was making up her own songs. An uncle gave her a guitar when she was eight; by the time she was ten she had been singing enough in churches and theaters to attract the attention of Knoxville radio and TV showman Cas Walker. The year was 1956 and Brenda Lee's career was just beginning. Precocious little Dolly seemed cut right out of the same mold. Initially she leaned heavily on teenage tunes by Brenda Lee and Connie Francis, while appearing regularly with Walker's shows up through her high school years. Her uncle Bill Owens would frequently take her to Nashville during those formative years. In 1957 they went to the Opry. What she

| NOVEMBER 9, 1970— LORETTA LYNN AND CONWAY TWITTY RECORD THEIR FIRST DUET, "AFTER THE FIRE IS GONE"; IT BECOMES A NO. 1 HIT AND WINS A GRAMMY | APRIL 1971—GEORGE JONES AND TAMMY WYNETTE BEGIN THEIR FIRST DUET RECORDING SESSIONS

MARCH 17, 1972—IN HER FIRST SESSION, THIRTEEN-YEAR-OLD TANYA TUCKER RECORDS | "DELTA DAWN," A TOP TEN HIT

APRIL 12–15, 1972— FIRST FAN FAIR TAKES PLACE AT NASHVILLE'S DOWNTOWN MUNICIPAL AUDITORIUM | OCTOBER 1972— LORETTA LYNN TAKES HOME THE CMA'S TROPHIES FOR ENTERTAINER OF THE YEAR, FEMALE VOCALIST, AND DUO OF THE YEAR (WITH CONWAY TWITTY) | FEBRUARY 19, 1974— DOLLY PARTON ANNOUNCES HER SPLIT FROM PORTER WAGONER

MARCH 13, 1975— TAMMY WYNETTE'S DIVORCE FROM GEORGE JONES BECOMES FINAL | NOVEMBER 1975—REBA MCENTIRE SIGNS WITH MERCURY RECORDS

OCTOBER 1978—DOLLY PARTON IS NAMED THE CMA'S ENTERTAINER OF THE YEAR |

Twenty-four-year-old RCA recording artist Dolly Parton gets the red-carpet treatment for Dolly Parton Day in her hometown of Sevierville, Tennessee, April 25, 1970. That evening her concert performance at the Sevier County High School gym was taped for her Real Live Dolly *album.*

saw and heard there clinched her ambitions. "I saw Johnny Cash for the first time on the Opry," she said. "It was when he first came there. . . . That was also my first encounter with what sex appeal was. I was in the audience—I must have been ten or eleven—and I saw Johnny Cash and, I'll tell you, it was a feeling like I had never had before. I found out years later that what he had was called charisma." With the help of Opry cast members Carl and Pearl Butler, a teenaged Dolly even made a cameo appearance of her own on the Opry, introduced by none other than Johnny Cash.

She managed the impressive feat of recording for the Goldband and Mercury labels before she turned seventeen; unfortunately for her, the singles failed to dent the market. Dolly Parton believed nevertheless she had her future all mapped out. She graduated from Sevier County High School (the first in her family to earn a diploma) on Friday, May 29, 1964, and during the ceremonies she announced to her tittering classmates that she was leaving for Nashville to become a singer. On Saturday morning she did exactly that, boarding a bus for Nashville, carrying her clothes and her spiral notebook of song compositions in a cardboard suitcase.

Though a career was all she wanted, she attracted a beau within hours of setting foot off the bus. Carl Dean, a handsome Nashville native, spied her in a local laundromat and introduced himself. They courted for the next two years, most of which Dean spent in the Army, while Dolly kept busy waitressing, singing on Eddie Hill's local early-morning TV show, and making music business contacts. On May 30, 1966, two years to the day after they met, Dolly and Carl Dean married in Ringgold, Georgia (where George and Tammy would wed nearly three years later). By the time of her marriage, Dolly had made considerable headway in her drive toward becoming a star. The week of her wedding she could be heard on country stations singing a very pronounced harmony on a Top Ten country record, Bill Phillips's rendition of her song "Put It Off until Tomorrow." She had signed with Monument Records as a recording artist and with its affiliated publishing company Combine as a writer. Because the folks at Monument had dissuaded her from marrying so early in her career, Dolly kept her marital status a secret for over a year. (As the years would go by, Carl Dean and Dolly would remain married, though Carl would assiduously avoid the spotlight, content to run his thriving asphalt paving business and spend his time quietly with Dolly.)

She had placed two records of her own— "Dumb Blonde" and "Something Fishy"—on

the charts in 1967 when she got an audition with Porter Wagoner, who was looking for a new girl singer to replace the recently departed Norma Jean Beasler—the same job Tammy Wynette went up for and failed to get. Dolly impressed Wagoner from the start. Thirty-nine years old and rail-thin, Porter Wagoner had been in the country music business for twenty years by the summer of 1967 and was nearing the height of his fame. He had starred on the "Ozark Jubilee" TV show and had been a member of the Grand Ole Opry since 1957. His syndicated "Porter Wagoner Show" drew higher ratings than any other syndicated country show, airing in nearly one hundred markets, with some 4 million fans watching each week.

Wagoner has claimed he needed every bit of his clout to persuade Chet Atkins to sign Dolly to RCA, Porter's label. Wagoner remembered his sales job on Chet: "After listening to her demo tape, Chet frowned a little. 'The songs are well written,' he said. 'But her voice—it's just so high, so sharp, so shrill.' " Chet Atkins had been making smooth Nashville Sound hits for a decade by then, and though Atkins himself has denied it, it's just possible he didn't hear stardom in Dolly Parton's demos.

Porter Wayne Wagoner and Dolly Rebecca Parton, 1971, the year they won their second straight CMA Vocal Duo of the Year award. In 1974, after seven years of performing with Porter, Dolly got the itch to move on to a solo career.

Dolly played the role of Doralee in the film 9 to 5. *The theme song, which Dolly wrote, became her biggest hit ever.*

on the heels of Haggard's "Mama Tried," a hit just that summer. Her straightforward depiction of the dignity of working-class life predated "Coal Miner's Daughter" by two years. In 1971, Dolly turned a painful gradeschool memory into the No. 4 hit "Coat of Many Colors." In it, she deftly compared a jacket her mother had made for her from quilt scraps to Joseph's coat of many colors from the Book of Genesis and underlined the inherent dignity in hard work and simple pleasures.

From the outside, Dolly and Porter seemed an impregnable partnership. He produced her records, helped refine her songs, and found her complimentary material from other songwriters. He ran the successful road show and TV empire. But behind the scenes, the relationship seemed more like the movie *A Star Is Born*. As Dolly's star rose, Porter's seemed to set. Between 1967 and 1975 Dolly Parton had five solo No. 1 hits. Porter Wagoner didn't have any. Dolly gradually extricated herself from her working relationship with Porter Wagoner. It was bound to end someday. In early 1974, Dolly informed him that she would no longer appear on either his TV program or his road shows. She began her own TV show two years later and then negotiated her own contract with RCA Records in New York. In July 1976 she signed with the well-connected West Coast management firm Katz-Gallin-Cleary, who were then managing Mac Davis and Olivia Newton-John. The flashy management deal made her bid for wider acceptance official. "Here You Come Again," released the following summer, broadcast the news. That fall of 1978, at the age of thirty-two, Dolly Parton

Wagoner has maintained, and Dolly has affirmed it, that he had to have Dolly signed as a rider to his own contract; that way, if her records lost money, the losses could be taken out of his own royalties.

Wagoner never had to worry about that rider. In December 1967 their first duet, "The Last Thing on My Mind" (written by folksinger Tom Paxton), cracked the country charts, peaking at No. 7. Their next duet, "Holdin' On to Nothin'," hit the same chart position in the spring. Porter and Dolly won their first CMA award that October as Vocal Group of the Year. In 1969 Dolly joined Porter as a member of the Grand Ole Opry cast and fulfilled a childhood dream.

Although her hourglass figure could not help but draw attention, Dolly soon gained a deserved reputation for her songwriting prowess. Like Loretta Lynn and Merle Haggard, she delved confidently into autobiography. Her songs brought the poverty of her youth into sharp focus without sentimentality or moralizing. "In the Good Old Days (When Times Were Bad)," a No. 25 hit in the fall of 1968, followed hard

officially arrived and was soon on a first-name basis with armchair America. In October of that year, she received the CMA's highest honor, the Entertainer of the Year award. She was only the second woman (after Loretta Lynn) up till then to win it.

From magazine covers and television talk shows, it was but a short jump to movie stardom. In 1980 a chance encounter on an air-

Here you come again: It's a Dolly of your very own.

Dolly Parton has certainly left a lasting impression on popular music.

plane flight with actress Jane Fonda led to Dolly's first film role in the office comedy *9 to 5*. Her bubbly yet strong-willed personality translated appealingly as ever to the big screen. Loretta Lynn inspired a movie; Dolly acted in one. The difference in Hollywood clout was considerable. By the end of the seventies, Dolly Parton repeatedly had to reassure her fans in press interviews that "I'm not leaving country, I'm taking it with me." She, and country's women, had come a long way indeed. Women had finally taken a leading role in country music, not just as singers of hit songs, but also as probing songwriters and multimedia stars. Old ways were passing in country music. In many cases it was a change for the better. In one case in particular—the right of an artist to control his or her music in the studio—it was high time for change in Nashville. A couple of scruffy boys from Texas were ready to take the reins themselves.

Willie Nelson wasn't exactly a wanted man when he arrived in Nashville in 1960, but he kept aiming high. By 1980, he was a star not only on record but also in the movies. Here he films the made-for-TV movie Once Upon a Time in Texas.

Outlaws and Rockers

A NEW HOME FOR THE OPRY

In 1971 attendance at the Grand Ole Opry rose above 400,000 for the first time in its history. But the Ryman Auditorium was deteriorating, and National Life officials seriously doubted whether it was worth the time and money to bring the old hall up to snuff. Behind the scenes, executives with National Life and WSM had been planning a move to a new facility for some time. In the fall of 1968, during the Grand Ole Opry birthday celebrations and the excitement over the first telecast of the CMA Awards show, National Life broke the news. As the *Tennessean* reported on October 19, 1968: "The initiation of plans for the relocation of the Opry, possibly as the center of a multi-million-dollar hotel and amusement complex, was announced at a breakfast at Municipal Auditorium sponsored by WSM." Irving Waugh, president of WSM, explained then that, although the site had yet to be determined, National Life had decided to move the Opry away from downtown and the Music Row area.

"Opryland grew out of the need for an Opry house," Waugh told Opry historian Jack Hurst. "When I first started working on the idea, I figured it would take at least $5 million just to house a Friday night–Saturday night radio show. We then started studying whether we could generate other sources of revenue. In my mind the Opry House was always to be the centerpiece of the park, and I think it is. The house wound up costing $15 million instead of five. If we'd known that in the beginning, I guess we'd never have done it."

The entire park—built on 380 acres of land several miles up the Cumberland River from downtown Nashville—cost $66 million. The 217-acre Opryland amusement park offered rides, restaurants, wild and domestic animals, and live music throughout. Located next door was a 614-room Opryland Hotel, built on a gargantuan scale with large murals inside and guitar-shaped swimming pools outside. Ground was broken June 30, 1970, and the park itself opened in the

The Grand Ole Opry House at the Opryland theme park seats 4,424 in air-conditioned comfort. Although tears were shed when the Opry left the old Ryman Auditorium, the new House offered comforts that were impossible in the old facility.

spring of 1972. In its first year attendance topped 1.4 million visitors, exceeding National Life's wildest dreams. Quickly plans were laid for the opening of the new Opry House. But what to do about the Ryman? In 1971 National Life announced their intention to tear down the Mother Church of Country Music and use its bricks to build a new chapel in the Opryland park. Local historical preservation societies immediately incited a groundswell of public opinion, calling for the venerable hall's preservation. Eventually, *The New York Times* and Dinah Shore weighed in with their opinions that the Ryman should be saved. National Life cautiously tabled the plan to raze the building and reassured everyone that the Ryman would remain.

For those who may have doubted the Opry's reverence for its past, the Old Timers' Night of Saturday, February 23, 1974, was a heartwarming affirmation. On hand at the Ryman that evening were hosts Roy Acuff and Minnie Pearl, welcoming Zeke Clements, Dr. Humphrey Bate's daughter Alcyone Bate Beasley, Pee Wee King and Redd Stewart, and DeFord Bailey. The little Harmonica Wizard had not performed at the Opry in more than a decade and had not been a member of the cast since 1941. Without doubt, the highlight of the evening was the appearance of seventy-four-year-old DeFord, playing his trademark harmonica tunes, "Pan American" and "Fox Chase," with all the energy and dexterity of his youth. It was a grand homecoming.

All the same, more than a few tears were shed on Friday night, March 15, 1974, when the Grand Ole Opry played its last performance in the Ryman Auditorium. The Ryman closed with a whole stage full of performers singing "Will the Circle Be Unbroken," including Carl Perkins, Mother Maybelle Carter, Johnny Cash and June Carter Cash, and Hank Snow. When the curtain came down for the last time, many took with them a beautiful, bittersweet memory. Some took a little something more. "Everybody was trying

DeFord Bailey returned to the Opry for the first time in a decade for the Opry's Old Timers' night on February 23, 1974. He's pictured here with Minnie Pearl and Roy Acuff.

to take a souvenir out of that building," recounted Hal Durham, then the Opry's manager. "I'm telling you people actually had hammers and were taking things off walls and pulling stuff off and it was like a wrecking crew had gone through." When the audience left that night, rain was washing down on them, as if the sky itself were crying.

The promise of the next day, though, gave the Opry cast much to cheer about. Not only were they appearing in a luxurious new Opry House—with air-conditioning! real dressing rooms!—but also President Richard M. Nixon was going to be on hand to inaugurate the new facility. It would be the first presidential visit ever to the Opry stage. Coming as it did in March of 1974, however, it had an air of more than just a goodwill gesture, for the previous day a federal grand jury had named President Nixon a co-conspirator in the

President Richard Nixon (left) tries his hand at a little yo-yoing during opening night at the new Opry House, while Roy Acuff offers a pointer or two.

go and be President, Roy." The President finished up his segment, appropriately, with a rendition of "God Bless America" that had the audience singing right along.

It was a gala occasion and everyone in the Opry cast wanted to appear. So they did, in alphabetical order, starting with Roy Acuff. "The first show ran over maybe an hour," recalled Hal Durham. "I think we got all of the acts on. I believe everybody got one number. The President definitely had more time than anybody else that night."

That first show in the new Opry House would prove to be a milestone in ways that weren't immediately apparent. That evening, a shy, thirty-two-year-old, bespectacled reporter, sent by *The New Yorker* to cover the inaugural show, was actually back in his hotel room, listening to the Opry on a cheap transistor radio. Years later, he would voice the

break-in of the Democratic party offices at Washington's Watergate Hotel. On August 8, under the threat of impeachment, Nixon would resign the presidency. But on March 16, the president could soak up the down-home warmth of the Opry and take part in the opening-night spectacle. The Opry staff band ushered him and his wife, Pat, onstage with a string-band version of "Hail to the Chief." As

it happened, it was Pat's birthday, and President Nixon took the occasion to celebrate onstage by playing "Happy Birthday" and "My Wild Irish Rose" on the piano. President Nixon then joined Roy Acuff at the microphone to banter and try a little Acuff-style yoyoing. Struggling with the stringed gizmo, he turned to Acuff and quipped, "I'll stay here and try to learn how to use the yo-yo, and you

thoughts he had had that night, sitting in the balcony: "I thought to myself: That looks like fun down there onstage. And I thought that if I ever finished writing this piece, I'd like to start a show like the Grand Ole Opry back in Minnesota." He published his Grand Ole Opry article in *The New Yorker*, all fourteen pages of it, on May 6, 1974. And in July 1974, four months after his inspiring Opry visit,

A Movie Called Nashville

There have been many movies that treated country music in one way or another, but none of them ever aroused as much intense interest and ire as director Robert Altman's *Nashville,* filmed on location in Music City during the summer of 1974. Composed in the director's characteristically loose, almost plotless style, the film follows twenty-four characters during a five-day period as a third-party presidential candidate prepares to make a public appearance. It sounds innocuous enough. But Altman didn't just present human interest stories; he tried to portray something of Music City's style and, in doing so, reflect on America as a whole. Some viewers thought the movie wickedly insightful, others found it extremely condescending.

After opening in New York in June 1975, the film had a gala Nashville "premiere" on the evening of August 8, 1975, which included visits by cast members Henry Gibson, Keith Carradine, and Ronee Blakely. (Altman, filming a movie in Canada, was unable to attend.) Half of the 740 seats at Nashville's 100 Oaks Martin Theater were filled with invited country music dignitaries; the rest were available to the general public. The local press were on hand to record reactions to the movie. What follows is a sampling, as reported in the *Nashville Banner* and the *Tennessean* the next day:

"I'm not worried about a negative reaction. But I'd be suspicious if *everybody* who came liked it." (Actor Henry Gibson, who played singer Haven Hamilton in the movie)

"Whoever put that thing together must have had a nightmare the night before." (Webb Pierce)

"When you show the anatomy of a man, you should try to show something besides his tail." (Record producer Billy Sherrill)

"I thought it was hokey from start to finish. I can see how they might like it in New York. They think we're a bunch of hayseeds to begin with." (Jeanne Pruett)

"I've had enough. I'm not going to sit in a chair that long and be slapped in the face." (Opry pianist Del Wood, who left in the middle of the movie)

"The only way it will be a big movie is for it to play a long time in the North. That's what the people up there think we look like anyway." (Brenda Lee)

Garrison Keillor started that radio show back in St. Paul, Minnesota. He called it "A Prairie Home Companion."

While the Grand Ole Opry adjusted to its sumptuous new facility, country music once again was feeling an infusion of creative energy from outside the confines of the Opry. In late June 1974, a week after his thirty-seventh birthday, Waylon Jennings notched his first of many No. 1 country hits. At just about the same time, his friend and fellow Texan Willie Nelson, himself forty-one years old, had just cracked the Top Twenty for the first time in years with "Bloody Mary Morning." The world was finally ready for the Outlaws Willie and Waylon.

★ WAYLON

Waylon Jennings grew up in the dusty little West Texas plains town of Littlefield, just northwest of Lubbock. His father drove a truck for a living and picked Jimmie Rodgers tunes on guitar for fun. From the beginning, Waylon turned to music every chance he got. Trying to imitate his favorite singer, Ernest Tubb, he broke off a broomstick so he could play air-guitar. On Saturday nights, Waylon's father would drive his truck to the side of the house and run cables from the car battery to the radio so they could listen the Grand Ole Opry. "It was one of those old battery radios, but they sounded great," Waylon remembered. "When Hank Snow came on, I thought he was six foot five." (Hank stands closer to an even five feet.)

Music pulled Waylon steadily away from Littlefield. He quit high school midway through; by then, he had already landed his own fifteen-minute radio show, written his first songs, and won a local talent contest. Moving on to the big city of Lubbock at age seventeen, he fell in with a band of young musicians who loved country but were definitely feeling the forces Elvis had unleashed. That band included Buddy Holly. "I saw Elvis in 1955, I guess it was in Lubbock," Waylon recalled. "Well, it changed things in a way. I think it changed Buddy too—at least it had a bearing. Actually, it changed almost everything, really. . . . It was like an explosion."

When Buddy's career took off, Waylon stayed in Lubbock, working as a disc jockey and part-time musician. But the two remained friends and kept in touch. Buddy thought a lot of Waylon's gruff, rough, and rowdy singing style. In

Waylon Jennings, man of many parts: ex-DJ, friend of Buddy Holly, former roommate of Johnny Cash, Willie Nelson's most famous duet partner, reformed cocaine addict, survivor.

October 1958 Holly took Waylon just across the New Mexico border to Norman Petty's recording studio in Clovis (where Buddy had recorded his first big hits). There he produced Waylon's first record, a cover of the Cajun standard "Jole Blon"; Holly not only paid for the session, he also flew top rock and roll sax player King Curtis in from New York to play on the cut. Still, it was a beginner's effort. Waylon has since said he hopes the record remains a trivia question, since he didn't understand a word of the Cajun French lyrics and simply sang what he thought the words sounded like.

In December of 1958 when Holly split with his band, the Crickets, he hired Waylon to play bass for him. The fact that Waylon had never played bass before didn't faze Holly in the least. Waylon stayed with Holly for a while at his New York apartment, rehearsing and playing on demo recordings for new Holly songs. In late January they began a winter tour of the Midwest. Within two weeks, though, it was all over. Holly's plane lay in a heap of twisted wreckage in the Iowa snow. Waylon had originally planned to be on that plane with Buddy, but at the last moment he gave up his seat to J. P. Richardson, the Big Bopper, who was known for "Chantilly Lace."

"We'd been on the road for days, man," said Waylon. "The three of us [Holly, guitar player Tommy Allsup, and Waylon] were going to fly from Mason City—we were playing in Clear Lake, a little place out of

"I think the acting was superb. I think the songs were horrible. I think it's a gross oversimplification of what our city's about." (Larry Gatlin)

"I'm just too close to it. Part of it made me very sad, but sometimes I laughed so hard it hurt. I just couldn't say whether I could recommend it or not." (Minnie Pearl)

"I thought it gave a false, rather unkind picture of the Nashville scene, but some segments, some scenes were just perfect. I liked it a lot better than I thought I would." (Bill Ivey, director of the Country Music Foundation)

"I was pleasantly surprised. There was a little exaggeration, but from what I had read, I was prepared for much worse. It's not bad for country music or Nashville." (CMA executive director Jo Walker)

"I loved it. It had great depth. I was not offended in any way. It is a great piece of work." (Buddy Killen, executive vice president of Tree International Publishing)

"I think most people took it for what it is. . . . The people who take it personally are the ones who feel threatened by it. It's a very intense film." (Actor Keith Carradine, who subsequently won an Academy Award for best original song in the film with "I'm Easy")

"I particularly liked the girl singer. She really *is* Loretta!" (Dottie West)

"I just look a little bit like Loretta. Actually, none of the characters in the film are intentional copies of real-life stars." (Actress Ronee Blakely, who played singer Barbara Jean in the movie)

"I don't understand why so many country music people are raving about this film when it's so obviously anti-country. If I were a country music personality, I wouldn't be here." (Armando Gallo, correspondent for the Italian film magazine *Sorrisi E Canzoni*)

"I can see nothing but good come from it for Nashville and country music." (Roy Acuff, who was on hand for the opening festivities but did not remain to attend the screening)

"I could say I didn't see a thing in the film, but that wouldn't be fair." (Ronnie Milsap, who happens to be blind)

Mason City, Iowa—to Fargo. We were going to play in Moorhead, Minnesota, and the airport was between Moorhead and Fargo.

"So we were backstage when the Big Bopper asked me if he could take my place on the plane because he had the flu. I told him it was all right, and he made it all right with Buddy. Then Richie Valens asked Tommy if he could take his place. A lot of people say it was Buddy who took my place but that ain't the way it was."

It took Waylon a couple of years to get over the shock and the loss. "After that I just kind of quit," he told writer Peter Guralnick. "I went back to radio. Back to Lubbock for a couple of years. I wasn't even interested anymore. It was such a ridiculous waste."

Waylon gradually picked up the pieces. He moved on to Phoenix, and it was in a nightclub there that Jerry Moss (the "M" in A & M Records) signed him to the West Coast–based label in 1964. Nothing much came of that move. Moss and his partner Herb Alpert heard Waylon as a pop artist, but Waylon has always maintained, "I couldn't go pop with a mouthful of firecrackers." Still, A & M did raise his profile. Thanks to strong recommendations from RCA artists Don Bowman and Bobby Bare, and Phoenix guitarist Duane Eddy, Chet Atkins signed Waylon to the label in 1965, and in March 1966 released his first RCA LP, titled *Folk-Country*.

Young Waylon Jennings in 1966, back when he was the Errol Flynn of Nashville and the roommate of another dangerous single man—Johnny Cash.

It was not quite a match made in heaven. Atkins at the time was on a roll with his Nashville Sound production style, which relied heavily on studio musicians to produce a smooth sound. Waylon, in contrast, was anything but smooth. He had absorbed a great deal from Buddy Holly during their short as-

sociation. Like Holly, Waylon had wide-ranging musical tastes: He recorded songs by the Beatles and Bob Dylan right alongside those of offbeat country writers like Kris Kristofferson and Shel Silverstein, as well as his own work. And he liked a good tough beat. He also felt more comfortable playing with his own band than with studio musicians. Many artists prospered in that Nashville Sound system, but Waylon Jennings wasn't one of them. He just couldn't abide it. The hits he scored in his first five years or so with the label—and he had several—seemed to come in spite of the production, as if his rough-hewn voice simply bulldozed all slick obstacles thrown in his path.

Waylon made a major breakthrough in 1972 when his manager, Neal Reshen (or as Waylon liked to call him: "My bulldog on a leash"), discovered that RCA had not picked up its contractual option to resign him. Playing off offers from Columbia, Atlantic, Capitol, and Mercury, Reshen was able to negotiate a new contract that gave Waylon much more artistic freedom. He could now produce his own records and record with his own band—arrangements that had meant so much to the Bakersfield sound of Buck Owens and Merle Haggard.

Around the same time, Waylon fell in with a key kindred spirit, singer-songwriter Tompall Glaser. A Nebraska farm boy who joined the Opry during the 1950s in a har-

They dressed in scruffy denim and leather and boots and cowboy hats at a time when many country artists strove for a more urbane look. They wore their hair long and didn't shave and were widely rumored (not without reason, in some cases) to be doing drugs. Outlaw Music: It sounded dangerous and romantic at the same time.

The person who launched the term "Outlaws" into the media stratosphere was RCA executive Jerry Bradley. As the son of Owen Bradley, Jerry was a second-generation Nashville studio man. Joining RCA in 1970 Jerry Bradley apprenticed as an assistant to Chet Atkins. When Atkins had stepped down from running the label's Nashville office in 1974, Jerry Bradley succeeded him. In November 1975 Bradley conceived his masterstroke: an

Waylon Jennings (third from left) at the Opry in 1966 with his band the Waylors, about a year after he arrived in Music City.

mony trio with his brothers Jim and Chuck, Tompall Glaser had grown disaffected with the Nashville Sound system. In 1967 he and his brothers dared to publish a song that broached the subject of "free love"—John Hartford's hobo song for the counterculture, "Gentle on My Mind." During the next few years it became one of the most played records of all time (country or otherwise), and it launched Glen Campbell's career. It also staked Tompall and his brothers to an independent recording studio and production company. There, in a two-story house on Nineteenth Avenue, just west of Music Row, Tompall and Waylon set to work crafting music that stood apart from the standard Nashville formula. Though some called the music "progressive country," really it was a throwback in some ways—just a couple of guitars, bass, drums, steel, maybe a harmonica now and then. No strings. No horns. No care-

fully harmonized background choruses. By making his own kind of driving music, with Tompall Glaser's help, Waylon Jennings began to click on the charts as he never had before.

One fateful day in 1973 a North Carolina disc jockey needed some handle to explain grouping together the music of Waylon, Tompall, Kristofferson, and Willie Nelson. "Call it Outlaw Music," said Tompall's office manager–publicist Hazel Smith. It was perfect. These artists were outsiders in Nashville.

Waylon with wife Jessi Colter (left) and Opry star Jan Howard.

album that would exploit the term Outlaws and its namesakes' newfound visibility. Waylon would be on it, of course; he had just won the CMA's Male Vocalist of the Year award that October. Waylon in turn insisted that Tompall Glaser be represented. Rounding out the group of Outlaws were Waylon's wife, singer-songwriter Jessi Colter (who had topped the country charts the previous spring with "I'm Not Lisa"), and Willie Nelson (who had been with RCA from 1964 through 1971 and was just enjoying his first chart breakthrough with "Blue Eyes Crying in the Rain"). Bradley pulled together some licensed tracks from Tompall and Jessi, some old RCA tracks from Waylon and Willie, even created a synthetic duet on "Good Hearted Woman" by overdubbing Willie's voice with Waylon, gussied up the LP to look like a wanted poster for genuine outlaws, and voilà—he had a hot property. Issued January 12, 1976, *Wanted! The Outlaws* became by the end of December the first country music album to be certified platinum, the new designation for selling a million records. Country records had sold a million before of course; the difference this time was that everybody knew it.

★ THE RED HEADED STRANGER

Like Waylon, Willie Nelson was born in a small Texas town (Abbott, forty-five miles south of Fort Worth), and he got started in music very early, joining his first musical group, John Raycjeck's Bohemian Polka Band, as a ten-year-old guitarist. Willie graduated from high school, served briefly in the Air Force, and even enrolled for a short while at Baylor University. But by the time he entered college he had a wife and daughter; for the next several years, he held a variety of jobs, including door-to-door salesman and guitar teacher, though usually he worked as a disc jockey and part-time nightclub musician.

During these years he was writing songs. He knew they were pretty good because people bought them. He sold "Family Bible" for $50; in 1960, Claude Gray had a Top Ten hit with it, but Willie had forfeited all financial claim to the song by selling it. By the time "Family Bible" became a hit, Willie had moved to Nashville, having driven a ramshackle 1946 Buick that promptly died as soon as it got to town. Luckily, shortly after arriving, Willie met songwriter Hank Cochran at Tootsie's Orchard Lounge behind the Ryman. Cochran liked Willie's songs and introduced him to Hal Smith, co-owner of Pamper Music with Ray Price. The firm was on the way up, with sharp young writers like Cochran and Harlan Howard, both of whom would collaborate on a big hit for Patsy Cline in 1960, "I Fall to Pieces." That year, Willie signed with Pamper for

$50 a week. He also got supplementary work as a musician, joining Ray Price's band as a bass player for $25 a date.

Willie Nelson wasn't meant to remain in the background for long. His songs started to fall into the hands of talented singers. In 1961 alone, Faron Young cut "Hello, Walls"; Billy Walker did "Funny How Time Slips Away"; and Patsy Cline recorded "Crazy." All of them were hits. Willie had tried to sell the first of those hits, "Hello, Walls," to Faron Young, who wouldn't hear of it. He loaned Willie $500 instead. When the struggling songwriter received his first royalty check for a whopping $3,000, he found Faron down at Tootsie's and kissed him on the lips. With the royalties starting to pour in, Willie was riding high: "I got my first royalty check, and I started flyin' to all the dates and rentin' a penthouse. Price was ridin' the bus with the boys." Ray Price didn't seem to mind one bit; he even cut Willie's bluesy "Night Life" in 1963, bringing Willie more royalties. Willie was so cocky at the time that when he decided to go out on the road on his own, he hired away Price's band.

In the fall of 1961, Willie got his own shot at recording with Hollywood-based Liberty

The saga of Willie Nelson has been one of country music's most improbable—and satisfying—success stories. After years of being out of step, the world finally caught up with Willie.

Records. Sessions were split between Nashville, where he recorded with Nashville's A Team, and Hollywood, where he recorded in Capitol Records' studios with a full string section. Right off the bat, he had two Top Ten hits—"Touch Me" and "Willingly," a duet with Shirley Collie, soon to be his second wife. The hits, however, began to taper off after that. He still hit the charts here and there, but he couldn't seem to break through in a big way, even after moving over to the Monument Record label that was notching so many pop hits with Roy Orbison. When Willie's subdued Christmas song, "Pretty Paper," became a Top Twenty pop hit during the 1963-64 holiday season, it was for Orbison.

Though Willie continued to record, he gave up touring. He decided instead to concentrate on songwriting and do a little pig farming on the side. As it turned out, though, Willie was not cut out to be a hog farmer. He lost $5,000 on his hogs, but fortunately, he was making about $100,000 a year from songwriting royalties.

Despite the inertia of his recording career, many people in Nashville saw promise in Willie Nelson. The Grand Ole Opry, for instance, invited him to join the cast, which he did on November 28, 1964. (He later recalled that the Opry paid him $35 for that first appearance.) Ernest Tubb made him a regular on his syndicated TV show beginning in 1965. And Chet Atkins signed him to RCA early in 1965, along with that other young Texan, Waylon Jennings.

Willie and Waylon were at that time two clean-cut, clean-shaven, blazer-wearing acts that just seemed a little too off center musically for RCA to market in a big way. Like Waylon, Willie was a musical eclectic. He liked all kinds of music—blues, old big-band standards, gospel, and of course country music

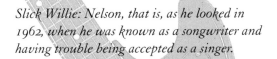

Slick Willie: Nelson, that is, as he looked in 1962, when he was known as a songwriter and having trouble being accepted as a singer.

in its many varieties. The trouble was that he couldn't get the eclectic style down on record. Between 1965 and 1969 Willie had logged just two hits of any consequence—"One in a Row" (1965) and "Bring Me Sunshine"(1968)—and they just barely squeaked into the Top Twenty. "The music I played on a bandstand was better than the music I played in the studio," Willie recalled. "For one thing, I'd be using my own band, and we'd have a better feel for it—be more relaxed." Having put a band back on the road in 1965 (subsidized by his songwriting royalties), Willie began to find his audience.

The year 1969 offered many milestones for

America—men walking on the moon; 400,000 fans descending on Woodstock for a festival of music, peace, and love—but it was a rotten year for Willie Nelson. He wrecked five cars. His marriage to Shirley snapped in November when she opened up a maternity ward bill addressed to Willie—for the birth of a child he'd had with another woman. (That young woman, Connie Koepke, would become his third wife in 1971.) During Christmas week, 1969, Willie and Hank Cochran got together at Willie's house and wrote a song called "What Can You Do to Me Now?"

A day or two later, while at a friend's Christmas Eve party, Willie received a telephone call: His house was burning down. Rushing back, he found firefighters working in vain. The house was a smoking black skeleton. Thankfully, no one was trapped inside, although more than one hundred tapes of unrecorded songs had gone up in smoke. Willie knew this when he darted inside to grab one possession that might have survived. "I ran into the smoking, stinking debris and kicked through the ashes until I found an old guitar case that contained two pounds of Colombian tea," he wrote in his autobiography.

"I stuck the case under my arm and went back to the car and sighed with relief. In 1969, you could get life in prison for being caught by the law with one joint. In Louisiana you could get the death sentence. I was glad to find my stash before the authorities did."

The time had come to move on. After a decade in Nashville, Willie returned to Texas. There in the college town and state capital of Austin, he found the younger audience he'd been searching for, congregating at a former National Guard Armory that had been converted into a cavernous nightclub and dubbed the Armadillo World Headquarters. Taking note of the scruffy stars of the local scene, particularly Jerry Jeff Walker and Michael Murphey, Willie let it all hang out. He let his whiskers and his hair grow long, he wore T-shirts and denim instead of Nashville-style suits and ties. To approximate the tone of jazz picker Django Reinhardt, Willie began playing a Martin classical guitar that soon became so worn it had a hole in it where a pickguard should have been. (That guitar became so much a part of him, he dubbed it "Trigger.") Most important of all, he let his musical inclinations run free.

Between 1971 and 1975 he embarked on a series of ambitious albums that stretched the boundaries of country music. The first of these, *Yesterday's Wine*, was his last for RCA Records. Recorded in 1971, it was a concept album; that is, a thematically related set of songs. Rock bands like the Who, the Moody Blues, and Pink Floyd had been making such albums since the late sixties. But in country, the concept album was still a rarity. "It's about a guy—an imperfect man," said Willie, "watching his own funeral and reviewing his life." The concept was, in the parlance of the times, "heavy." Perhaps a little too heavy. The album didn't sell, though critics took notice as did Willie's new compadres in Austin, and Willie gained confidence from it.

In 1973 he moved to the Atlantic label—a shrewd maneuver on Willie's part. He'd been hemmed into a corner with Nashville Sound production. Atlantic, a label that had specialized in rhythm and blues since the forties and was just beginning to stake a claim in rock, offered a breath of fresh air. Right away, Atlantic won Willie over by giving him creative autonomy. During a week of sessions in New York in early 1973, Willie cut a whole gospel LP in two days (released in 1976 as *The Trouble-*

maker), then recorded enough unrelated tracks for yet another album. This wasn't a concept album, but it was a leap forward, for Willie finally recorded the sort of mix he'd been playing for years in clubs—a couple of Bob Wills tunes, two new songs by rocker Leon Russell, a drinking song ("Whiskey River"), a road song ("The Devil Shivers in His Sleeping Bag"), and the fun-loving "Shot-

Willie Nelson with third wife Connie and daughters Paula and Amy, early 1980s.

gun Willie," which gave the title for the album. *Shotgun Willie* outsold all his previous albums combined.

Next came a second concept album, *Phases and Stages*. "The concept," Willie explained, "is a look at marriage and divorce from the man's point of view on one side and the woman's point of view on the other." He recorded it in Muscle Shoals, Alabama, with the crack session team that had backed soul singers Aretha Franklin and Wilson Pickett on their biggest hits. "Bloody Mary Morning," the album's first single, broke into the country Top Twenty in

the summer of 1974, Willie's first appearance that high on the charts in six years.

In spite of Willie's triumphs, Atlantic folded its country division toward the end of 1974. Still, Willie had made enough of a splash at Atlantic to cause a small bidding war between Warner Bros. and Columbia Records. When he signed with the Nashville division of Columbia, Willie and his attorney were careful to spell out in the contract that Willie would retain full creative control. He had learned how to exercise that control, and he had plans. Willie had yet another concept album up his sleeve. For years he had been singing the old cowboy song "Red Headed Stranger"—in concerts, with his friends, to his children at bedtime. Everyone seemed to relate to the tale of the mysterious hombre who rides into town from nowhere, kills a saloon girl who tries to steal one of his horses, and then rides off. At the suggestion of his wife, Connie, Willie decided to build an album around the song, filling out the narrative with compatible old songs from other writers: Hank Cochran's "Can I Sleep in Your Arms," Lulu Belle & Scotty's "Remember Me," and Fred Rose's "Blue Eyes Crying in the Rain," which had been a hit for Roy Acuff back in the forties.

Instead of doing the usual and heading for Nashville, he went to a recording studio in tiny Garland, Texas, that had been mostly used for recording advertising jingles. There, with his own band he set about recording his *Red Headed Stranger* album. It took him only three days and $20,000 worth of studio costs—a breeze and a pittance by modern standards. When Billy Sherrill and his staff with Columbia Records in Nashville listened to the album, they sat in stunned disbelief. Was this really a finished album? It sounded like no more than

In 1985, old compadres Waylon Jennings, Willie Nelson, Kris Kristofferson, and Johnny Cash joined forces for a hit album, The Highwayman, followed in 1990 by The Highwayman 2 and in 1995 by The Road Goes On Forever.

rough demos to Sherrill. "They thought it was underproduced, too sparse, all those things," said Willie. "Even though they didn't like it, they had already paid me a bunch of money for it, so they had to release it under my contract. And since they had money in it, they had to promote it." Running counter to all expectations, the album sold like nothing Willie had ever recorded before. In October of 1975, his spare, contemplative reading of "Blue Eyes Crying in the Rain" became his first Top Ten hit in thirteen years and his first No. 1 record. At the age of forty-two, Willie Nelson was a genuine star.

Willie's next creative watershed was a trip back into his past. By chance, he lived next door to R & B musician-producer Booker T. Jones in Malibu, and the two became friends.

When they talked about what kind of record they could make together, Willie thought about the classic pop songs of the 1930s and 1940s that he had grown up with, in particular Hoagy Carmichael's "Stardust" and "Georgia on My Mind." Right off the top of his head, Willie came up with eight more—"Blue Skies," "All of Me," "Unchained Melody," "September Song," "On the Sunny Side of the Street," "Moonlight in Vermont," "Don't Get Around Much Anymore," and "Someone to Watch Over Me." In the fall of 1977, Willie recorded the songs at Emmylou Harris's house, in husband Brian Ahern's portable truck studio.

When he played his tapes for his record label, the execs were skeptical once again. "I think you're crazy," the new Columbia

Nashville chief Rick Blackburn told him. "You're a great writer. Go write. Do a 'Luckenbach, Texas' [a hit then riding the charts for Waylon] or some damn thing. Stay with the mood that's hot."

But Willie insisted on releasing the album. "My audience right now is young, college age and mid-twenties," he told Blackburn. "They'll think these are new songs, and at the same time, we'll get the sentiment of the older audience who grew up with these songs but don't necessarily know me as an artist. We will bridge that gap."

Shortly after *Stardust*'s release in May 1978, he was proved spectacularly right. Following hard upon Willie's duet with Waylon, "Mamas Don't Let Your Babies Grow Up to Be Cowboys" (a No. 1 hit that spring), *Stardust* sold in Elvis-like proportions. By the end of the year, sales had passed 3 million copies. "Georgia on My Mind" and "Blue Skies" both topped the country charts, and the album itself remained on the country charts for a decade. When President Jimmy Carter invited Willie and Waylon to visit the White House later that year, it somehow seemed fitting and proper. The Outlaws had arrived in high style. In 1979 Willie tasted sweet vindication when the CMA named him Entertainer of the Year.

Stardust put Willie over the top. He appealed to young and old, pop fan or country. He seemed to transcend categories. So it was a natural transition for him to be acting in movies. In short order, he went from supporting performer, playing Robert Redford's manager in *The Electric Horseman* (1979), to starring roles of his own in the Western *Barbarosa* (1980), in the semiautobiographical *Honeysuckle Rose* (1980), and in the film adaptation of *Red Headed Stranger* (1986).

Willie and Waylon had found a way to reach a young audience that was ready and waiting for country music. And they found that it didn't matter how old the songs were or how sparsely they were produced; what seemed to matter most of all was sincerity and willingness to keep the music's edges rough.

★ BOCEPHUS

In Nashville a young singer was taking note of the changes Waylon and Willie were ringing. That singer was none other than the only son of country's greatest legend: Hank Williams Jr. Randall Hank Williams was three years old when his daddy died. Pictures from Hank Jr.'s earliest years show a smiling, fat baby pawing a toy guitar, while his father, in full western regalia, beams proudly. Hank Sr. dubbed his son "Bocephus," after Rod Brasfield's ventriloquist dummy, and the nickname stuck. Aside from the nickname, Hank the younger was left with only the dimmest memories of his father. From the very beginning, Audrey Williams saw her son as a meal ticket, a way to perpetuate the Hank Williams legend, and more important, the Hank Williams income.

Twenty-one-year-old Hank Williams Jr. was a seven-year veteran of the road by the time of this 1970 photo. And he already was sick to death of singing his father's songs.

COUNTRY MILESTONES	MARCH 1966—RCA RECORDS RELEASES ITS FIRST WAYLON JENNINGS ALBUM, *FOLK-COUNTRY*	AUGUST 7, 1970—AR-MADILLO WORLD HEAD-QUARTERS, A HANGOUT CATERING TO HIPPIES AND COWBOYS ALIKE, OPENS IN AUSTIN, TEXAS	*THE CIRCLE BE UNBRO-KEN*, A THREE-RECORD SET, IN NASHVILLE WITH ROY ACUFF, MOTHER MAYBELLE CARTER, MERLE TRAVIS, AND OTHER MEMBERS OF COUNTRY'S OLD GUARD	1973—HAZEL SMITH, TOMPALL GLASER'S PUBLICIST, COINS THE TERM "OUTLAWS" TO DESCRIBE ALTERNATIVE COUNTRY SINGERS LIKE TOMPALL, WAYLON, WILLIE, AND KRIS KRISTOFFERSON	MARCH 1973—THE GROUP ALABAMA, STILL KNOWN AS WILDCOUN-TRY, BEGINS PLAYING AT THE BOWERY IN MYRTLE BEACH, SOUTH CAR-OLINA
OCTOBER 1958—WAY-LON JENNINGS MAKES HIS FIRST RECORD, "JOLE BLON," PRODUCED BY BUDDY HOLLY	DECEMBER 24, 1969—WILLIE NELSON'S NASHVILLE HOME BURNS DOWN; HE MOVES TO TEXAS	AUGUST 9–14, 1971—THE NITTY GRITTY DIRT BAND RECORDS *WILL*			

Watch out for that ol' Lost Highway, son: Hank Williams Sr. gives baby Hank Jr. a private lesson, May 27, 1950, the day after Jr.'s first birthday.

country hit. In 1965 the fictionalized movie of his father's life, *Your Cheatin' Heart*, may have starred George Hamilton as Hank, but Hank Jr. did all the singing. The sound-track album gave Hank his first gold record.

"At first," he recalled years later, "I thought it was the greatest thing in the world—a ghost of this man that everyone loved. They think I'm Daddy. Mother's smilin', money's rollin' in, seemed ideal."

But he was a prisoner of his success. Though Hank Jr. would experiment from time to time with blues and with rock and roll, the vast majority of his record releases were straitlaced country and often remakes of his father's hits. In an effort to forge an identity of his own in his early twenties, he resorted to cutting pallid country-pop remakes of Slim Harpo's "Rainin' in My Heart" (1970) and Fats Domino's "Ain't That a Shame" (1971). They were Top Ten country hits, but they weren't memorable records. Besides, when he went on tour, the crowd still wanted to hear his

Hank Jr. was eight years old when he sang onstage for the first time. It was 1957. He debuted at the Grand Ole Opry in 1960 at the age of eleven, singing "Lovesick Blues," just as his daddy had his first night there.

Though he revered his father's memory, Hank Jr. really preferred playing blues and rock and roll, which he did in a teenage garage band called Rockin' Randall & the Rockets. But that was just for kicks. He made money—

hundreds of thousands of dollars—for his mother when he went on tour to sing his father's songs. At age fourteen in the fall of 1963, he hit the road for the first time. He did so well that his mother didn't mind one bit when he quit school the following year. He made his first record at fourteen as well. Naturally, it was a remake of one of his father's: "Long Gone Lonesome Blues," released by MGM Records, his father's label. It was a Top Ten

| JULY 4, 1973—WILLIE NELSON'S FIRST FOURTH OF JULY PICNIC CONCERT TAKES PLACE AT DRIPPING SPRINGS, TEXAS, WHERE WILLIE, WAYLON, LEON RUSSELL, AND KRIS KRISTOFFERSON, AMONG OTHERS, ENTERTAIN SOME 25,000 FANS; | IT BECOMES AN ANNUAL EVENT

JUNE 1974—WAYLON JENNINGS HAS HIS FIRST NO. 1 HIT WITH "THIS TIME"

APRIL 1975—WILLIE NELSON RECORDS HIS | BREAKTHROUGH ALBUM *RED HEADED STRANGER* FOR $20,000 IN GARLAND, TEXAS

AUGUST 8, 1975—HANK WILLIAMS JR. FALLS OFF MOUNT AJAX IN MONTANA | OCTOBER 1975—"BLUE EYES CRYING IN THE RAIN" BECOMES WILLIE NELSON'S FIRST NO. 1 SINGLE

NOVEMBER 4, 1975—AUDREY WILLIAMS, HANK JR.'S MOTHER AND HANK SR.'S EX-WIFE, DIES | JANUARY 12, 1976—*WANTED! THE OUTLAWS*, AN RCA COMPILATION OF TRACKS BY WAYLON, WILLIE, TOMPALL, AND JESSI COLTER, IS RELEASED | NOVEMBER 24, 1976—*WANTED! THE OUTLAWS* BECOMES THE FIRST COUNTRY ALBUM TO BE CERTIFIED PLATINUM, FOR SALES OF 1 MILLION UNITS |

This country's rockin': Opry clogger Ben Smathers welcomes big Charlie Daniels to the show, October 1977. Around this time Daniels, a former long-haired rocker and studio musician, was making his move to country music, joining buddies like Hank Williams Jr.

with a mixture of Darvon and Jim Beam. He seemed destined to reenact his father's tragic life right to the bitter end.

The Outlaw music of Waylon and Willie and the Southern rock of the Allman Brothers, the Marshall Tucker Band, and Lynyrd Skynyrd finally pulled Hank Jr. back from the edge. Here, he thought, were Southern musicians blending country, blues, and rock in ways that seemed fresh and meaningful. The first major statement of his new direction came in the fall of 1975: *Hank Williams Jr. and Friends*, recorded with special guests Charlie Daniels, Toy Caldwell from the Marshall Tucker Band, and Dickie Betts and Chuck Leavell from the Allman Brothers. On the album, Hank mixed strong versions of Southern rock (two Marshall Tucker songs) with insightful, introspective new writing of his own. The album got rave reviews from rock critics at *Rolling Stone* and *The Village Voice*, but Hank almost didn't live to enjoy the fruits of his labors.

Immediately after finishing sessions for the album in July, Hank took off with a couple of hunting buddies for the Rockies on the Montana-Idaho border. There, on Saturday, August 8, while hiking up Mount Ajax, Hank stepped on a glacial ridge that crumbled beneath his feet, sending him tumbling and sliding headlong down the mountainside. Some 500 feet below, his fall was broken by a headfirst collision with a boulder. Miraculously, he survived, but the fall smashed his nose and his teeth, broke every bone in his face, and split his skull open. A series of nine operations gradually put him back together. The scars account for at least part of the reason why Hank subsequently grew a beard and took to wearing cowboy hats and dark glasses. But the look also suited the rougher musical territory he was heading for.

It took Hank a good two years to recover fully from his brush with death. Early in his convalescence, on November 4, 1975, Audrey Williams died. The last chain to the past broken, Hank Jr. looked to the future with a renewed sense of purpose. Instead of being in thrall to his father's legend, Hank Jr. began turning it to his advantage. In hit songs like "Family Tradition" (1979) and "The Conversation" (with Waylon,

father's songs, and that's what he gave them. Overwhelmed by having to live up to his father's image, he increasingly resorted to drink and drugs. In late 1973, at the breaking point, he attempted to kill himself

JULY 1977— "I WANNA BE WITH YOU TONIGHT" BECOMES ALABAMA'S FIRST SINGLE TO HIT THE CHARTS	MAY 1978—WILLIE NELSON RELEASES *STARDUST*, A COLLECTION OF POP STANDARDS THAT SELLS MORE THAN 3 MILLION COPIES BY THE END OF THE YEAR	OCTOBER 1978—WAYLON JENNINGS RELEASES "DON'T YOU THINK THIS OUTLAW BIT'S DONE GOT OUT OF HAND," WHICH BECOMES A TOP TEN HIT	OCTOBER 1979—WILLIE NELSON NAMED CMA ENTERTAINER OF THE YEAR APRIL 11, 1980— ALABAMA, THE BIGGEST SELLING COUNTRY ACT OF THE 1980S, SIGNS WITH RCA RECORDS	AUGUST 1980— ALABAMA SCORES THEIR FIRST NO. 1 WITH "TENNESSEE RIVER"	OCTOBER 30, 1982— HANK WILLIAMS JR. HAS NINE ALBUMS ON THE *BILLBOARD* COUNTRY CHART AT THE SAME TIME

The scars from a disastrous 1975 mountain fall account for at least part of the reason that Hank Williams Jr. grew a beard and took to wearing cowboy hats and dark glasses. But the look also suited the rougher musical territory he was heading for.

1979), Hank suggested that his father had been the original Outlaw and that he was just carrying on in his father's footsteps. Hank Jr. openly sang about drugging and drinking and enjoying the pleasures of the flesh in songs like "Whiskey Bent and Hell Bound" (1979) and "Outlaw Women" (1979). His hard-hitting, bluesy, and swaggering sound attracted a proud-to-be-a-rebel crowd. One indication of his popularity came in 1982 when he placed nine albums on the country charts simultaneously. No one had ever done that before. His fans loved his rebellious attitude, and bought his records in the millions. In fact, between

1981 and 1990, nearly every album he released went gold, if not platinum.

During the late seventies and early eighties, in his songs and to the press, Hank often complained that he was an outcast in Nashville. Consequently, he set up headquarters in rural enclaves like Cullman, Alabama, and later Paris, Tennessee—out of earshot of Music Row, but close enough to drive in for recording sessions. In 1987, the CMA finally recognized what industry insiders had been saying privately for years: Hank Jr. was the best all-around entertainer in country music. He packed the biggest auditoriums and outdoor amphitheaters, dazzling his crowds with his full-tilt country boogie and his mastery of half a dozen instruments. When he accepted the Entertainer of the Year trophy, Hank quipped, "I got to looking for this one so long, I thought I was gonna run out of glasses." As if in atonement for sins of omission, the CMA crowned him Entertainer of the Year again the following year.

Hank Jr. arrived when he found a way to be true to himself. "All I'm doing now is Rockin' Randall & the Rockets," he claimed. And that was great for him. But what did it mean for country music when it sounded so much like rock? Just what was country? With the rise to prominence of a certain country-rock quartet, the definition got stretched a little wider.

★ THE BOYS FROM ALABAMA

In August 1980 a bar band working at the seaside resort town of Myrtle Beach, South Carolina, notched their first No. 1 on the country singles charts. Before the decade was out, they would rack up twenty-five more No. 1 hits and sell a whopping forty-five million records. Their sound was upbeat and up-tempo, with rocking guitars and big kick drums, and often a gauzy backdrop of violins. Rather than draw from deep wellsprings of pain, the band's music celebrated love and life in the South. That band was Alabama, and its members couldn't have made music more unlike the hard-core country of Hank Jr.'s dad even if they'd set out to.

Alabama epitomized a new generation of country musicians who had grown up listening to rock and roll as well as country. Their music drew on the country-tinged rock of the Eagles as much or more than the sounds of any genuine country artist. Asked one time to categorize their music, lead singer Randy Owen struggled: "Country. Progressive country, I guess. Southern country. . . ." In sharp contrast to traditionalists like George Jones, Alabama shunned steel guitars. (Lead guitarist Jeff Cook could play fiddle and did—onstage and on record—but usually he preferred to let 'er rip rock and roll style on electric guitar.) They were a quartet: two guitars, bass, drums—the standard rock and roll lineup since the Beatles rewrote the rules for pop music. They sang their three-part harmonies smoothly and without a hint of twangy discordance. Their stage costumes usually consisted of jeans, football jerseys, T-shirts; there was nary a rhinestone in sight. In the grand tradition of rock bands from the seventies, when Alabama took the stage they dressed just like their fans.

The band was born in Fort Payne, a town of about 12,000 nestled in the northeast corner of Alabama at the foot of Lookout Mountain. Cousins Randy Owen and Teddy Gentry (three years younger) grew up on adjoining farms. Both families struggled to make ends meet: Owen's family didn't splurge for a radio until he was twelve; Gentry's family didn't just lack indoor plumbing—they didn't even have an outhouse. Learning harmony and guitar at the local Holiness church, the cousins dreamed of becoming musicians. Randy Owen remembers listening with special devotion to the bands of the British Invasion as a teenager: "Late at night I used to listen to a station out of Cleveland, Ohio, and they had a British Countdown show—that's when the Beatles were coming out. Boy, I really enjoyed that. It was a big thing for me." When they met Jeff Cook, a hot-shot guitar player who turned out to be a distant cousin as well,

Owen and Gentry realized they had found a soulmate and began taking music even more seriously.

In the summer of 1970, after Gentry finished high school and Jeff Cook got a diploma in electronics, the three cousins began working as the house band at Canyonland, a nearby amusement park. For a brief time, they broke up. Teddy Gentry went to work laying carpets, Randy Owen went to college, and Jeff Cook took an electronics job. But around 1971 Owen and Gentry moved in with Cook, determined to give their dreams another shot. When they turned out the lights in their small apartment at night, the three would harmonize until they drifted off to sleep. In the spring of 1973, when Owen got his college degree, the trio moved down to Myrtle Beach and a waterfront bar called the Bowery, where they began playing music full time under the name Wildcountry. Randy Owen played rhythm guitar, Teddy Gentry played bass, Jeff Cook played lead; all sang, with the handsome Owen usually handling the lead vocals. They got whoever they could to handle the drums. They were green, but they were also confident and determined. That fall they incorporated and formed their own music publishing company, Maypop, to handle the songs they were writing. In early 1977 they changed their name to Alabama. Between 1973 and 1980 they released two self-financed

albums, went through at least three drummers, and honed their harmonies to perfection each summer while they served as human jukeboxes for the bar's vacationing patrons.

There was one more piece of the puzzle before Alabama was complete: drummer Mark Herndon, who arrived in April 1979. Born in Massachusetts, the son of a career Marine, Herndon was working with a dance band in Florence, South Carolina, when Alabama rolled into town for a week's engagement. Herndon's mother, a clerk at a local motel, met the band and heard that Alabama's latest drummer had recently given notice. She said she knew a good drummer, not revealing just how well she knew him. A few weeks later, Mark Herndon got the gig in spite of his ignorance of country music. An unabashed rock and roller, Herndon readily admitted that when he'd joined the band, he'd never even heard of Mel Tillis, the CMA's Entertainer of the Year just three years earlier.

Herndon had arrived just in time for the ride. The small GRT label had released the first Alabama single in June of 1977. That summer "I Wanna Be With You Tonight" slipped into the

Three cousins from Alabama: Teddy Gentry, Randy Owen, unidentified, and Jeff Cook, 1982.

Country summit: Alabama (the biggest country act of the eighties) with George Jones (country's all-time leading hit maker).

country singles charts at No. 78. Following Herndon's arrival, the Dallas-based MDJ label released a minor variation on the theme entitled "I Wanna Come Over"; it inched up to No. 33 in the fall of 1979. Then came the breakthrough. "My Home's in Alabama," released by MDJ Records in January 1980, really caught Nashville's attention. Randy Owen and Teddy Gentry had written the song just a couple of years earlier when the band was struggling. Shortened to just under four minutes from its original Lynyrd Skynyrd-ish ten, "My Home's in Alabama" gave the band a theme song and their first Top Twenty country hit. On April 11, 1980, the day before the record officially peaked at No. 17, RCA's Joe Galante signed the band to his label. Galante and RCA were hoping that they might sell 60,000 copies of the band's first RCA album, *My Home's in Alabama*; it went on to sell 2 million. Alabama had their first No. 1 by August with Randy Owen's "Tennessee River." Twenty consecutive No. 1s would follow—including such chart toppers as "Love in the First Degree" (1981), "Mountain Music" (1982), "The Closer You Get" (1983), and "Forty Hour Week"

(1985)—running through 1987. The Country Music Association would go on to name Alabama its Entertainer of the Year three years running—1982–1984.

The unheard-of had happened at last: A rock-style band was on its way to becoming the biggest thing in country music. The young audience that Willie and Waylon had brought into country music just a few years before had made their choice loud and clear. They wanted country music that sounded energetic and fresh. Naturally, in the wake of Alabama's success, record companies scrambled to sign more self-contained country bands with a rock edge: Restless Heart, the Nitty Gritty Dirt Band, and Sawyer Brown all probably owe their record contracts to Alabama. In their rush to satisfy demand, though, record companies completely overlooked the durable appeal of hard-core country music, even to young audiences. It would take a grizzled old veteran, an ex-folksinger, and a bluegrass whippersnapper to remind everyone of what they'd been missing and swing country's stylistic pendulum back to tradition.

After woodshedding in the bands of bluegrass legend Ralph Stanley and Emmylou Harris, Ricky Skaggs took a stand for bringing country music back home to tradition.

Hearts on Fire

URBAN COWBOYS

If the seventies were a heady time when artists like Waylon, Willie, Loretta, and Dolly were gaining control of their music, the early 1980s were when country music went Hollywood. All the artistic breakthroughs that Willie, Dolly, and the rest made in the mid-to-late seventies culminated in a spate of Hollywood movies in 1980—Willie's *Honeysuckle Rose,* Dolly's star turn in *9 to 5,* Loretta's story in *Coal Miner's Daughter,* and *Smokey and the Bandit II,* which featured country picker-singer Jerry Reed as sidekick to hot-rodding Burt Reynolds and had a sound track that was pure country.

Of all the year's country box-office triumphs, the movie that would come to symbolize the era in country music was *Urban Cowboy.* Adapted from a 1979 *Esquire* cover story about days in the Houston oil-fields and nights in a cavernous honky-tonk known as Gilley's, *Urban Cowboy* seemed an ideal vehicle for promoting country music. Its star, John Travolta, had played the lead in *Saturday Night Fever,* the movie that sold Middle America on disco in 1978. In *Urban Cowboy,* Travolta played a struggling oilfield cowboy who found distraction at night at Gilley's, with Debra Winger in the role of his long-suffering girl-friend. The movie featured Gilley's prominently, along with a heaping helping of country music, soft country-rock, and mechanical bull riding. Propelled by *Urban Cowboy,* Gilley's house singer Johnny Lee scored a No. 1 hit with the movie's *Mr. Goodbar*-ish theme song, "Looking for Love." His boss Mickey Gilley, part-owner of the club and cousin of Jerry Lee Lewis, didn't do badly himself in those days either,

racking up ten No. 1 singles between 1980 and 1984.

"Movies like *Urban Cowboy* just did so much to make country music popular," observed Jeff Cook of Alabama. "We don't like to put a label on our music, but after that

The career of Mickey Gilley took off in 1980 when Urban Cowboy *became a hit. The movie prominently featured the Houston dance hall that bore his name. Between 1980 and 1984 he had ten No. 1 singles.*

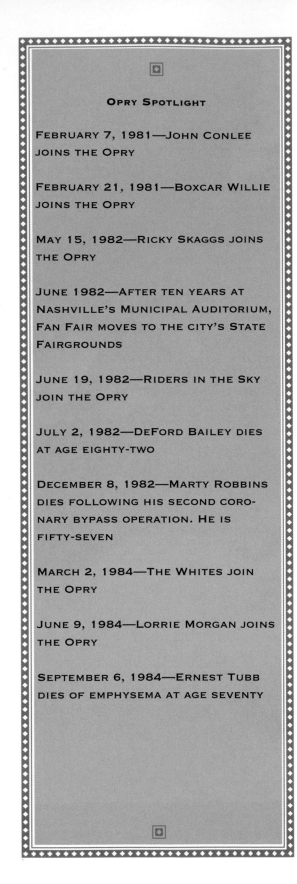

movie, everybody wanted country music." Indeed, buoyed by the cresting publicity tide of *Urban Cowboy,* country music seemed to be everywhere. Country dancing was all the rage, as were mechanical bulls and western attire (designed by the likes of Halston and Calvin Klein, no less). The television networks embraced country as well. CBS had its "Dukes of Hazzard" series, based around the muscle-flexing exploits of would-be country singers John Schneider and Tom Wopat. Waylon Jennings sang the series' theme song.

NBC countered with "Barbara Mandrell and the Mandrell Sisters," hosted by the winner of the CMA's Entertainer of the Year for 1980. She was perfect for the part. At the age of thirty-one, Mandrell had already been playing music professionally for twenty years. A musical prodigy, she spent her teenage years on the road with the Mandrell Family Band— father Irby on guitar, mother Mary on bass, Barbara's eventual husband Ken Dudney on drums, and Barbara herself on a passel of instruments. It seemed she could coax music from anything she put her mind to: steel guitar, saxophone, banjo, guitar, bass, mandolin. As Irby Mandrell liked to say, his little girl was reading sharps and flats before she was reading words. But she gave up her performing career at age eighteen when she married Dudney, then a Navy pilot. She didn't give her early retirement a second thought until one night when she sat in the audience at the Grand Ole Opry:

> When Ken was assigned to overseas duty in 1967, he brought me to Nashville to be with my family while he was gone.

Barbara Mandrell (center) with sisters Irlene (left) and Louise (right). From November 1980 to June 1982, "Barbara Mandrell and the Mandrell Sisters" was top-rated for its Saturday-night time slot. But the show's hectic schedule took its toll on Barbara.

I had never been to Nashville before, and I really had not known a lot about the Grand Ole Opry. . . .

Daddy took me to the old Ryman, and we sat in the balcony and watched the show. And while I was watching I got the idea, 'Hey, I can do that.' I turned to Daddy and said, 'I want to do that. I can't just sit out front here. I want to be up there.'

Her recording career began in 1969 under the tutelage of Billy Sherrill at Columbia Records. There and later at ABC/Dot and MCA Records, she specialized in country remakes of R & B records as well as perky, slightly suggestive pop-country ditties like "Sleeping Single in a Double Bed"; both styles suited her husky, come-hither voice. She joined the Grand Ole Opry in July 1972. When the CMA recognized her as its top entertainer in 1980, its members were acknowledging Mandrell's successful balance of razzle-dazzle showmanship and down-home sincerity.

Within one month of receiving country music's highest award, Barbara and her sisters Louise and Irlene were appearing on their own NBC-TV network show, "Barbara Mandrell and the Mandrell Sisters." The hour-long variety show featured the standard blend of music, dance, and comedy, spiced by the Mandrell sisters' country charm

Barbara Mandrell, ca. 1972. She was just twenty-three when she joined the Opry that year.

and personal chemistry. Plenty of country performers got a showcase there, including Dolly Parton, Marty Robbins, Tennessee Ernie Ford, and Charley Pride. Though the Mandrell TV show drew top ratings for its Saturday-night time slot (some 40 million viewers per week), the intense weekly preparation for taping the shows proved ultimately too grueling for Barbara to continue.

"People say, 'It must have been very difficult for you to decide to give up your television show,'" Barbara recalled in her autobiography. "And I say no, it wasn't difficult at all. The doctor made the decision for me. He said give it up. So I gave it up." The doctor's diagnosis if she continued the TV show? "Vocal suicide." In June 1982, after a year and a half, the Mandrell show ended, even though the Mandrells still had three years left in their five-year contract.

During the height of the show's run, Mandrell managed to nab a second CMA Entertainer of the Year award in 1981 and notch her fourth No. 1 single that summer,

Barbara Mandrell—the Country Music Association's Entertainer of the Year for 1980 and 1981—brought an uptown glamour to country music.

singing a song that would become something of a theme for her: "I Was Country When Country Wasn't Cool." Helping her out at the song's tail end was a very special guest, George Jones, a man who personified the title of the song. At the age of fifty he was then enjoying the peak of his career. It had been a long, hard climb.

★ THE VOICE OF EXPERIENCE

George Jones has been called the greatest country singer who ever lived. The acclaim in part is an acknowledgment of his impressive technical gifts. He's capable of rumbling and hiccuping his way through a rollicking novelty like "White Lightning" (1959) or mimicking the gliding moan of a steel guitar on "He Stopped Loving Her Today" (1980). His voice

No country singer is more revered than George Jones, both for his technical talent and his ability to transform deep sorrow into song.

can reach towering heights or plumb harrowing depths. Technical gifts aside, what distinguishes George Jones from nearly every living singer is his deep understanding of sorrow and his ability to convey its infinite shades and subtleties in song. Those who have met him over the years have invariably described him as a shy, taciturn man, who isn't at all comfortable holding up his end of a conversation. In singing, he found a voice that could entertain strangers. But one can't sing all the time, so he found another comfortable voice at the bottom of a shot glass. George Jones may have learned how to sing country music by imitating his idols—Roy Acuff, Hank Williams, and Lefty Frizzell—but he was born to sing sad songs, one way or another.

His life began in sorrow. "When I was born," he has said, "the doctor dropped me and broke my arm." Though he suffered no lasting physical effects from the accident, it certainly was an omen of things to come. Five years before his birth, his parents' first-born, Ethel, died at age seven of malaria. She was her father's darling and the death of his little girl hit thirty-year-old George Washington Jones hard. He had a weakness for alcohol, and soon he spent all his spare time staying liquored up. By the time little George was born, the whole town of Saratoga, Texas, knew his father as a good-for-nothing drunk. It was George's mother, Clara, who sheltered the boy and introduced him to music through the local Baptist church. There George

learned to sing hymns and strum his first guitar chords.

Music provided solace and escape, wherever he could find it. As a youngster, George sat transfixed in front of the family radio every Saturday evening listening to the Grand Ole Opry. "When I was real little," George recalled, "I'd go to sleep early and have my mother wake me up when Bill Monroe or Roy Acuff came on." By age twelve he was already walking the streets of Beaumont, Texas, strumming a Gene Autry guitar almost as big as he was and singing for spare change. At fifteen he quit school and ran away from home, performing in nightclubs and on small radio stations in towns near Beaumont for $17.50 a week. After he heard a Hank Williams record for the first time, George had a new honky-tonk hero to pattern his singing after. "His style was all in the feeling," Jones has said. "He could sing anything and it would make you sad. But an up-tempo thing could make you happy."

One afternoon in the spring of 1949, around four o'clock, George was doing his regular show at radio station KRIC in Beaumont when his hero walked in the door. "The program director at the station knew him," recalled Jones, "and he got Hank to come by and sing 'Wedding Bells' [his current hit] on our radio show to plug his date that night. It was a big thrill."

Actually, George, then eighteen, was so thrilled he was petrified. He'd been recruited to play lead guitar behind his idol that night, and it didn't go well. "I froze," said George. "I never hit a lick."

But Hank sympathized. They got through the show just fine on Hank's own guitar. Afterward, Hank gave the youngster a little free advice. "He was told that I loved Roy Acuff and that I could sing a lot like him. Hank started telling his story about how much he admired Acuff, that he was his favorite singer too. But he said somebody finally told him, 'Son, they've already got a Roy Acuff.'"

It would take several years for Jones to realize the wisdom in that advice. In January 1954, after a two-year hitch in the Marine Corps, he got his first chance to record for Pappy Daily's Houston-based Starday Records. Daily heard potential in the twenty-two-year-old's voice; he also heard all the undeniable influences.

"When I was in the studio to record my very first session," said Jones, "I was there a couple of hours, just messing around. Finally, Pappy Daily came in and said: 'George, for the last few hours you've sung like Roy Acuff, Lefty Frizzell, Hank Williams, and Bill Monroe. Can you sing like George Jones?'"

He tried. But for years he still slipped into uncanny impressions of Hank Williams and Roy Acuff. Jones experimented briefly in 1956 with the rockabilly style that Elvis Presley had popularized in records issued under the pseudonym Thumper Jones. But those records slipped quietly into obscurity. Luckily, his straightforward country efforts became hits, even if "Why Baby Why" (1955) was pure, moanin'-the-blues Hank and "Just One More" (1956) was pixilated Acuff. In August 1956, after having spent three months on the Louisiana Hayride, Jones joined the Grand Ole Opry.

George soon began drinking heavily and the habit got out of hand all too quickly. One night out on the road, frustrated because the local stores wouldn't sell him a beer after hours, Jones flushed his night's earnings down a hotel toilet. "George came in to see me," recalled Daily, "and I asked him if it was true he'd flushed $2,000 down the toilet. He said, 'Pappy, that's a damn lie! It was only $1,200!'"

Like his self-destructive hero Hank Williams, George Jones could afford to throw away money with both hands; his records and the crowds on the road would bring it right back to him with the sureness of a boomerang. By the late fifties he had forged his own unmistakable gut-wrenching style. He could

Young George Jones as he looked, ca. 1954, when he first began recording and was still searching for his own style.

even record drunk and make great records. As Daily remembered it, "George was so drunk the day he recorded ["Walk Through This World with Me" in 1966], he couldn't have hit the floor with his hat." No matter; it was a towering performance and a No. 1 hit in April 1967. According to the pianist on the session, Hargus "Pig" Robbins, George's success in spite of a few drinks shouldn't have been any

surprise. "He seemed to do especially well with those slow ballad things. There'd be a certain point where, if you caught him before he went too far overboard, he could just moan them out."

Drunk or sober, Jones improved remarkably on record during the late 1950s and 1960s as Pappy Daily shepherded him from one record label to the next (four labels in eight years). To name his biggest hits is to cite landmarks in country music history: the hopped-up moonshine revelry of "White Lightning" (1959), the exquisite disappointment of the cuckolded husband in "Window Up Above" (1960), the studied nonchalance of "She Thinks I Still Care" (1962), the galloping heartache-as-horse-race metaphor of "The Race Is On" (1964). No matter what the arrangement was, no matter what the tempo, his voice made each song a George Jones song.

As his records clearly demonstrated, Jones could control every nuance of his voice in song. Away from the microphone, however, he clung too often to the bottle. In 1967 Jones had himself committed to a hospital in an attempt to come to grips with his alcohol problem. After a short convalescence, he promptly fell off the wagon. Not long afterward he fell in love with Tammy Wynette and they married. It was the third try at marriage for both. Though country fans had high hopes that it would be a match made in heaven, within two years of their 1973 No. 1 hit "We're Gonna Hold On," "Mr. and Mrs. Country Music" had divorced.

The marriage and its breakup wreaked new havoc on Jones's emotional life. As he spun deeper and deeper into alcohol and cocaine, he gained a reputation for missing performances—fifty-four during one stretch—that saddled him with the nickname "No Show

The marriage of Tammy Wynette and George Jones produced a few good things: daughter Georgette (onstage with them here in this 1976 photo), some great duet records, and a working relationship for George with Tammy's producer, Billy Sherrill.

Jones." One positive outcome of the Jones-Wynette relationship, though, was that it brought Jones to the Epic label and Billy Sherrill, a producer who appreciated Jones and knew how to draw the best out of him.

Between 1966 and 1978 Sherrill would produce career-making hits for Tammy Wynette, David Houston, Tanya Tucker, Charlie Rich, and Johnny Paycheck. But his work with George Jones may have been his greatest achievement. In their recordings between 1971 and 1989, Jones and Sherrill proved to be ideal foils for each other's ten-dencies: Sherrill's lush orchestrations of strings and choruses often provided grand counterpoints to Jones's vocal gymnastics; occasionally Jones had to use all his vocal abilities to overcome Sherrill's wall of sound and the struggle was thrilling.

Sherrill was also almost singlehandedly responsible for bringing Jones his biggest song ever—at a point when Jones needed a big hit desperately. During the late seventies, though Jones continued to place hits on the charts, his personal life fell into shambles. Lawsuits for missed shows, for reneging on business deals, for failure to pay alimony and child support became an almost seasonal occurrence. His drinking got completely out of hand, and he began using cocaine as well. His weight plummeted from a healthy 150 down to around 100 pounds. In September 1977, he was accused of shooting at his buddy Peanut Montgomery. That December Jones declared bankruptcy, having accumulated more than $1 million in debts, and later that month he was arrested on charges of assaulting a former girlfriend. Two years later Jones was again hospitalized for alcoholism. In the midst of this incredible turmoil, Billy Sherrill somehow managed to keep Jones's recording career moving forward. Over a two-year period, he brought in a host of famous singers—including Willie Nelson, James Taylor, Linda Ronstadt, Elvis Costello, and even Tammy Wynette—to record duets with Jones for an album called *My Very Special Guests*. Then in 1979 Sherrill stumbled across a Bobby Brad-dock–Curly Putman song called "He Stopped Loving Her Today."

Sherrill liked the concept of the song—a man's unrequited love ending only with his death. Jones didn't like the song and repeatedly confused its melody with "Help Me Make It Through the Night" when he tried to sing it. When they finally finished work on the song on February 6, 1980, Jones was still grousing about the song ("It's too damn depressing. Nobody'll ever play that thing!"). Sherrill bet him $100 that the song would be a No. 1 hit. Five months later, during the July Fourth weekend, Sherrill won the bet, as the sad, soaring strains of "He Stopped Loving Her Today" ruled the airwaves and the record topped the country charts. At age fifty George Jones had his seventh No. 1 song, his fiftieth Top Ten hit. That October, Jones was honored

George Jones and Aaron Neville on camera. Neville had a 1993 hit with "The Grand Tour," which was a No. 1 for Jones in 1974.

Emmylou Harris at the Opry in 1993. Twenty years ago she seemed just about the least likely person to lead a country music movement.

as the CMA's Male Vocalist of the Year—the first time he'd been acknowledged with a CMA award. "He Stopped Loving Her Today" took top honors in the awards as well. In January 1981 he took home a Grammy award for the performance. The following year both Jones and the song won CMA awards again. George Jones had finally achieved, in the autumn of his years, the recognition he so richly deserved. He would continue to struggle with his addictions, however, until his fourth marriage to thirty-four-year-old Nancy Sepulveda, in March 1983, finally set him on the path to recovery. A year later, after yet another prolonged hospital stay, Jones kicked his alcohol and drug habits for good.

★ EMMYLOU

Even as George Jones struggled with his demons during the seventies and early eighties, country music was going through stylistic throes of its own. On the one hand, artists like Alabama and Hank Jr. were pulling country music inexorably toward rock. Meanwhile, other young musicians were determined to hold onto those things that made country a distinct musical style. Ironically, the person who would lead country music back to its traditional strengths was an admitted suburban folkie, who got started professionally in Greenwich Village and failed in a first attempt to stake a claim in Nashville. Her name was Emmylou Harris.

Emmylou Harris's life had started out very promisingly. Born in Birmingham, Alabama, she was the daughter of a career Marine Corps officer. Consequently, her family moved around, living in various parts of North Carolina and Virginia. She went to high school in suburban Virginia, just outside Washington, D.C., and grew up to be a well-scrubbed, attractive academic achiever—valedictorian of her high school class, cheerleader, and winner of the local Miss Woodbridge beauty contest.

Thanks largely to her older brother, Emmylou gravitated to music, particularly folk music and bluegrass. She hit her teenage years just as the folk revival movement was peaking, and at age sixteen got her first guitar, bought by her grandfather at a pawn shop. She became a devout subscriber to *Sing Out!* magazine so she could keep up with folk favorites like Joan Baez, Judy Collins, and Bob Dylan. A peek at the magazine's September 1965 issue reveals the following letter from an eighteen-year-old Emmylou Harris of Woodbridge, Virginia (a letter she apparently wrote that summer just before heading off to college):

I have never voiced my opinions before (lazy, I guess), but perhaps now is just as good a time as any. All I really want to say is that I don't always agree with your opinions, but you have the guts to stand up for them, which very few publications do.

Also, I would like to request an article on John Hammond, Jr.

Just one more thing. How can I go about getting honest criticism on my singing and playing style? I am not interested in becoming a professional, but I do enjoy performing and would appreciate honest help or advice from someone who knows.

Despite her musical inclinations, Emmylou went to the University of North Carolina at Greensboro on a drama scholarship in the fall of 1965. About a year and a half later she dropped out. "I was a pretty lousy actress," she later explained. "I loved music and wanted to do that more than drama." Having played a bit at a Greensboro nightspot called the Red Door, she decided at the end of the fall 1967 semester that it was time to head for the folk-music big time and New York. That's where she really learned about drama. She lived at the Y, played solo gigs at the legendary Gerdes Folk City club (where Bob Dylan had been discovered six years earlier), met influential songwriters like Jerry Jeff Walker and Townes Van Zandt, and then got married to musician Tom Slocum. In 1969 she recorded a decidedly folkie album titled *Gliding Bird* for the tiny Jubilee Records label, done in three quick three-hour sessions. The record soon disappeared, much to Emmylou's later relief. At the time, the much-vaunted Greenwich Village folk scene seemed like a dead end for Emmylou. And then she got pregnant: "The worst thing any girl could do to her budding career," Emmylou later remarked.

Dissatisfied with opportunities in New York, Emmylou and her husband moved to Nashville in May 1970 with two-month-old daughter Hallie in tow. "It seemed to me that there wasn't really room for any country music in New York," she remembered, "although my decision

Emmylou Harris in 1976, when she was just beginning to make records that carrie on the legacy of her mentor, Gram Parsons.

was partly that and partly that it was very depressing in New York. It was very hard. My career was at a standstill, and I guess I just wanted to make a change. And Nashville seemed a lot easier than going out to Los Angeles." Almost immediately, however, the marriage broke up, and Emmylou was forced to scrape together any work she could find—a gig here and there at motel lounges, a little modeling for art classes, but mostly waitressing at a Polynesian restaurant. She and Hallie managed to eke out an existence with the aid of a woman roommate and food stamps. Finally, around Christmastime 1970, thoroughly demoralized by Nashville, Emmylou and her daughter moved back to the Washington, D.C., suburbs to be with her parents.

For the next six months or so, Emmylou played clubs in the area, enjoying the music as a diversion but very skeptical that she'd ever make a real living at it. By day, to hedge her bets, she worked as a hostess in a housing development in Columbia, Maryland, handing out brochures to sell model homes. Then one night in the fall of 1971, members of the Flying Burrito Brothers band discovered her singing in a Georgetown bar and passed word about their find to their friend and former member, Gram Parsons. A good-looking, well mannered heir to a Florida orange-grove fortune and a Harvard drop-out, Parsons had pioneered the country-rock movement. In 1968 while briefly a member of the Byrds, he had been the catalyst behind the group's groundbreaking *Sweetheart of the Rodeo* album. Afterward, he and his fellow Byrd Chris Hillman formed the Flying Burrito Brothers to continue their explorations into what Parsons liked to call "Cosmic American Music," a blend of country, rock, and soul. By the time Hillman and the rest of the Flying Burrito Brothers met Emmylou, the mercurial Parsons was embarking on a solo career and on the lookout for a female harmony singer. Emmylou fit the bill. He met her and sang with her in a small D.C. nightclub one evening in late 1971 and said he'd be in touch.

Months went by, nearly a year, and then, out of the blue, Emmylou got a call from Parsons in August of 1972: He wanted her to come out to Hollywood and record an album with him. Merle Haggard would be producing, he said, and Elvis Presley's band would be backing them. "He was looking for a girl to sing traditional country on his solo album—do male-female duets à la Conway and Loretta, George and Tammy. I thought, Here's a chance to sing and make enough money to buy a new guitar. That's about how high my sights were at that point."

Emmylou flew out to Los Angeles and found out that just about everything Parsons promised was true. He had a record deal with Warner Brothers for his first solo album. At the last moment, Haggard had backed out of the project, so Merle's longtime recording engineer Hugh Davies showed up instead. But Elvis's band—Ronnie Tutt on drums, Glen D. Hardin on piano, James Burton on guitar—was there and rarin' to go. "The sessions seemed very disorganized to me," Emmylou recalled. "Gram didn't seem very together. He was drinking at the time. And L.A. seemed like the most decadent place I'd ever been. But Gram made it work." Emmylou made it work too. She reportedly served as a calming, almost maternal influence during the sessions, always singing her parts with professional aplomb and knitting quietly in the corner of the studio when she wasn't on call. The album that resulted in February 1973, *GP*, didn't sell. The country-rock that did—the Eagles were soaring by early '73 on the strength of "Take It Easy" and "Peaceful Easy Feeling"—owed a lot more to rock than to country. Still, critics generally noted that Parsons was pulling off his blend of rock and country, and Emmylou was hailed as one of the finest new voices on record.

"I really came to country music through Gram Parsons," Emmylou admitted. "That, to me, was like the earth is hit by a meteor—it changes the face of the earth forever. It changed the way I heard music, the way I felt music, the way I perceived it and, ultimately, the way I performed it."

But the time that Parsons and Emmylou had together was short. They toured briefly in early 1973 at the sorts of clubs where

Emmylou Harris had to hold onto her hat when her career took off in a rush with her first Warner Brothers album in 1975.

rock bands usually played (the Armadillo World Headquarters in Austin, for instance), and then they recorded Gram's second album for Warner Brothers that summer with basically the same cast as the first album. The Parsons-Harris harmonies, which they arrived at instinctively, came to full fruition on achingly beautiful renditions of "Hearts on Fire" and the old Everly Brothers–Roy Orbison favorite "Love Hurts." The album was slated for a late fall release; Gram and Emmylou would tour in October. Suddenly, the dream was over. Gram Parsons, who had always played fast and loose with drugs and alcohol, overdosed in a motel in Joshua Tree, California, and died on September 17, 1973. He was twenty-six.

Emmylou got the news at her grandmother's house back east and she was devastated. She's never publicly said whether or not she and Parsons had a romantic relationship, but there was undoubtedly a bond of friendship and love there. One year after they first recorded together, he was gone.

What could she do? She grieved, but she regrouped and carried on with what he'd left her. Duly impressed by her duets with Parsons, Warner Brothers offered her a solo contract and in 1974 she set to work on recording. Parsons would have been proud. She hired his kind of pickers—James Burton, Glen D. Hardin—and she recorded hard-core country songs from Dolly Parton, Merle Haggard, and the Louvin Brothers. She also composed an elegy to her mentor with "Boulder to Birmingham." Her album, *Pieces of the Sky,* released in the spring of 1975, did what a Gram Parsons record had never been able to do: It sold. But what would have pleased Parsons even more was that it broke through to the country audience. Her second single from the album, a remake of the Louvin Brothers' "If I Could Only Win Your Love," climbed to No. 4 on the country singles charts during the summer of 1975. Emmylou was on her way.

She soon became the most in-demand duet partner in popular music, getting calls to sing harmonies with Bob Dylan, Linda Ronstadt, Roy Orbison, and others. During the next five years she released seven studio albums; all but her Christmas collection *(Light of the Stable)* went gold. This was at a time when country albums rarely sold in those numbers, and for a good reason: They were usually records built around a hit single or two and a bunch of quickly recorded filler. Unlike rock albums, country albums (except those of Merle Haggard or Waylon or Willie) simply weren't expected to make artistic statements.

In marked contrast to most country artists, Emmylou called her

Rodney Crowell was twenty-three years old and new to Nashville when Emmylou Harris brought him into her band. Today he's recognized as one of Nashville's finest singer-songwriters with numerous hits of his own.

Longtime mutual admirers Linda Ronstadt, Emmylou Harris, and Dolly Parton had been harmonizing on and off together for more than a decade when they finally recorded an entire album together. Released in 1987 and titled Trio, *it sold more than a million copies.*

own shots. She recorded in Los Angeles with her own handpicked musicians and with her new husband, Brian Ahern, as producer. Emmylou also showed that a woman could really lead a country band. Not just have a band back her, mind you, but *lead* it. Beginning with the original lineup of James Burton on lead guitar, Glen D. Hardin on piano, John Ware on drums, Hank DeVito on steel, Emory Gordy on bass, and a future star named Rodney Crowell on rhythm guitar and harmony vocals, she built her justifiably legendary Hot Band.

From 1975 through 1977 Rodney Crowell harmonized with Emmylou, played rhythm guitar, and supplied her with a string of classic songs: "Bluebird Wine," " 'Til I Gain Control Again," "I Ain't Living Long Like This," "Leaving Louisiana in the Broad Daylight," "Even Cowgirls Get the Blues." Some suggested that Crowell filled the role that Gram Parsons had left vacant, but Crowell denied it. "I was just another musician who could sing and had some real roots in music— someone Emmylou could hit it off with. So I was no surrogate Gram."

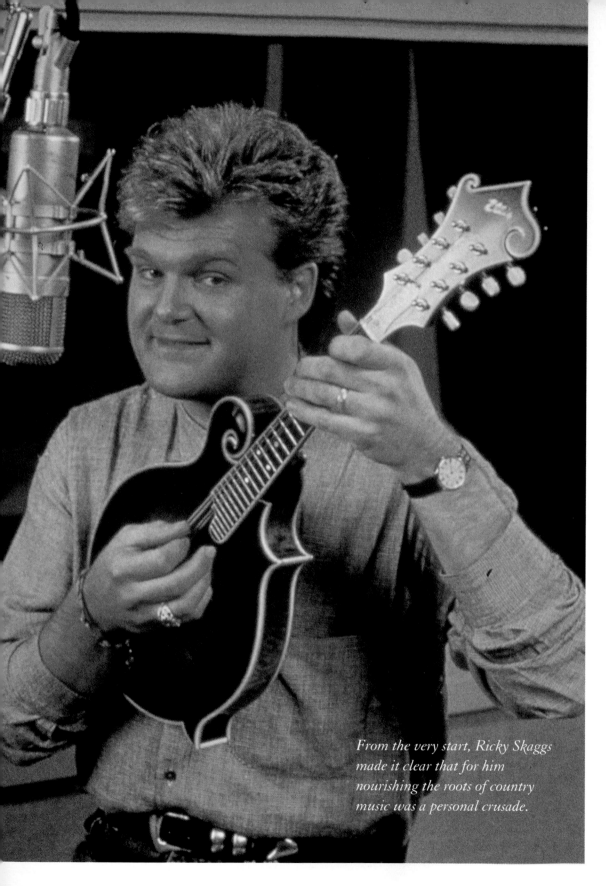

From the very start, Ricky Skaggs made it clear that for him nourishing the roots of country music was a personal crusade.

With the help of fresh talents like Crowell and old hands like Burton and Hardin, the Hot Band developed a reputation for being the hippest outfit in country music. When one musician would leave, another great talent would come in to fill the gap. Thus, upon the departure of James Burton in 1977, English guitarist Albert Lee stepped in and drew raves for his fleet-fingered runs. When Glen D. Hardin left that same year, a young gospel piano player, who had recently worked with Elvis until his death, joined Emmylou. His name: Tony Brown. A decade later he would be hailed as the best record producer in Nashville. "That shaped my whole taste in music," said Brown. "And whatever benchmark was set for me was set by Emmylou Harris and Brian Ahern and Rodney Crowell."

★ THE BLUEGRASS KID

In late 1977 Rodney Crowell left to forge his own solo career in recording and producing (particularly for his wife, Rosanne Cash). Once again Emmylou found an ace to replace him, one who also had very definite ideas about country music. This was twenty-three-year-old Ricky Skaggs from Cordell, Kentucky. Skaggs was a genuine musical prodigy. When he was five years old, his father bought him a mandolin. Within two weeks Ricky had taught himself to play and sing along. During the summer of 1960 the Father of Bluegrass, Bill Monroe, was performing near Ricky's hometown. Already Ricky had made something of a name for himself on local radio, and the audience called for little Ricky to join the venerable bluegrass patriarch onstage. Taking hold of Monroe's mandolin, the six year old delighted the crowd with a rendition of the bluegrass standard "Ruby." He received a standing ovation for his efforts. Once he had a taste of the spotlight, Ricky hungered for more. A year later he had earned his first

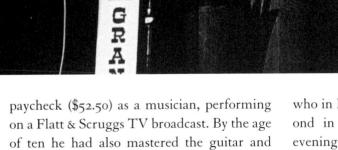

paycheck ($52.50) as a musician, performing on a Flatt & Scruggs TV broadcast. By the age of ten he had also mastered the guitar and fiddle.

At age fourteen he fell in with Keith Whitley, a year younger but just as interested in playing bluegrass music. Together they worked up a repertoire of bluegrass tunes, paying particular attention to duets in the style of the Stanley Brothers, Ralph and Carter,

who in Kentucky were bluegrass legends second in stature only to Bill Monroe. One evening in late 1970 Skaggs and Whitley went to a nightclub in nearby Louisa, Kentucky, to hear Ralph Stanley, who had carried on his act following his brother's death in 1966. When word came that Stanley would be late, the two teenagers were asked to fill in. Imagine Stanley's delight upon stepping into this club and hearing note-perfect renditions of Stanley

Brothers songs. He soon asked them to join his band: Ricky, age sixteen, on mandolin and harmonies; Keith, fifteen, on lead guitar and lead vocals. Skaggs skipped his senior year of high school in order to tour full time, preferring instead to get a crash course in high-grade bluegrass with his idol.

"The Stanley Brothers were my strongest influence," he said years later. "They just had a sound that went through me like a March wind. I listened to 'em all through my teen years, even though I was listening to the Rolling Stones, Beatles, and Hollies. There was a lot about both of those kinds of music that I couldn't see a whole lot of difference in. A lot of the Beatles' music had harmony styles that the Stanley Brothers, Bill Monroe, and Flatt & Scruggs had done, which influenced the Everly Brothers, who influenced the Beatles. It came back over, and this thing just made a cycle."

Although Stanley's outfit was a wonderful training ground, it was grueling work for low wages. By age twenty Skaggs quit the band and went to work as a boiler operator. "I had worked with Ralph Stanley for about two and a half years and I was *burnt up* on the road. I was just *fried*. I wasn't making very much money and the accommodations were terrible—four or five in a motel room together." After taking a little time to consider his options, Skaggs plunged back into music in the fertile bluegrass scene of Washington, D.C., working in a succession of bluegrass bands: the Country Gentlemen, J.D. Crowe & the New South, and his own band Boone Creek in 1976.

It was during Skaggs's Washington stint with the Country Gentlemen in the early seventies that Emmylou had first spotted the young whippersnapper. "I always felt," she

Ricky Skaggs and Sharon White, married in 1982, briefly worked together backing Emmylou Harris on the road and on record. Today both are members of the Opry—Sharon with her family group the Whites and Ricky as a solo act.

said, "that if at some point in time I could afford to have a fiddle player, this is the kid I'd like to have." Of course, Emmylou gained far more than just a fiddler—she got a fiddler-mandolinist-guitarist steeped in the bluegrass styles of Monroe and Stanley, who sang harmony in a high, pure, bracing-as-a-mountain-stream tenor. When Ricky Skaggs joined the Hot Band in late 1977, it was almost inevitable that he would take Emmylou to bluegrass school. That was exactly what she wanted. "I longed to do some bluegrass music," she's said. "I've always had this sonic vision of having more bluegrass instruments in country music."

With Skaggs's help she realized that vision on her next two albums, *Blue Kentucky Girl* (1979) and *Roses in the Snow* (1980). Each found Emmylou and the Hot Band heading deep into traditional country music, with the bluegrass bent becoming obvious on the latter. It was a gutsy move, especially because her record label saw her as poised to win over rock and rollers in a big way. To Warner Brothers, the traditional stylings of those records must have seemed a gigantic, horrifying step backward. But Emmylou knew exactly what she was doing. Surrounded by the Hot Band and joined by such guests as Linda Ronstadt, Dolly Parton, Don Everly, Johnny Cash, and Willie

COUNTRY MILESTONES	JULY 1975—EMMYLOU HARRIS'S FIRST TOP TEN HIT, "IF I COULD ONLY WIN YOUR LOVE," ENTERS THE CHARTS	LATE 1977—TWENTY-THREE-YEAR-OLD RICKY SKAGGS JOINS EMMYLOU HARRIS'S HOT BAND	FEBRUARY 6, 1980—GEORGE JONES RECORDS FINAL VOCALS FOR "HE STOPPED LOVING HER TODAY"	JULY 1980—"HE STOPPED LOVING HER TODAY" HITS NO. 1	OCTOBER 1980—BARBARA MANDRELL NAMED THE CMA ENTERTAINER OF THE YEAR, GEORGE JONES NAMED MALE VOCALIST, EMMYLOU HARRIS NAMED FEMALE VOCALIST
SEPTEMBER 17, 1973—GRAM PARSONS DIES AT AGE TWENTY-SIX					

Nelson, she took a stand for bedrock country traditions. Audiences embraced both records, each of which went gold. Emmylou won a Grammy for *Blue Kentucky Girl*, and in 1980 the CMA named her Female Vocalist of the Year.

After two and a half years of woodshedding in the Hot Band, Ricky Skaggs set out to push the traditional agenda on his own. He had learned how to manage a full, mainstream country band from Emmylou. He also learned how to do a thoroughly modern recording with traditional country material. And he had an inkling from her how far he could push a turbocharged version of bluegrass and honky-tonk-style country. He started quietly, recording an album of old duet songs with acoustic guitar ace Tony Rice, and a slightly more ambitious full-band album of old country favorites. Both of these came out on the North Carolina–based Sugar Hill label in 1980 and 1981. Skaggs then caught Nashville's Music Row by surprise when his version of the Stanley Brothers' "I'll Take the Blame" became a regional hit in Houston. Mildly impressed, Rick Blackburn of Columbia/Epic Records signed him as a sort of experiment, expecting to sell 50,000 copies of Skaggs's first album. After a little contractual wrangling, Blackburn even agreed to let Skaggs produce the records himself. Skaggs recorded the albums for $50,000 apiece, almost guaranteeing a profit before they even went on sale.

In the summer of 1981 Ricky Skaggs released his battle cry: a rousing remake of Flatt & Scruggs's bluegrass classic "Don't Get Above Your Raising." Ostensibly an admonition to a woman not to get too "high-headed," the song sent out a message to Nashville that old Judge Hay would have appreciated: "Stay down to earth with me." It became a Top Twenty hit, the first of four from *Waitin' for the Sun to Shine* (1981), his first Epic album, which sold more than 500,000 copies. The follow-up, *Highways and Heartaches* (1982), did even better, with three No. 1s and sales of over 1 million copies.

What he had managed to do was take the Hot Band approach to traditional country and turn up the flame. As with classic bluegrass, Skaggs's records featured hot pickers swapping hot solos. Rather than focus exclusively on updating bluegrass or relying solely on acoustic bluegrass instruments, Skaggs mixed and matched. In contrast to Emmylou, who excelled in moody, melancholy numbers that showcased the fragility of her voice, Skaggs put together bouncy, punchy remakes of honky-tonk and bluegrass classics. In fact, of his first dozen singles, fully half of them were remakes of forties or fifties tunes. When he cut newer songs, he gave them the same treatment. The result was a seamless blend.

On May 15, 1982, he joined the Opry cast as its youngest current member (then twenty-seven). That October the CMA named him

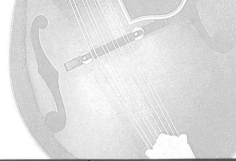

Male Vocalist of the Year. The culmination of Skaggs's string of hits (nine No. 1s) between 1982 and 1985 came on October 14, 1985, when the CMA named him Entertainer of the Year. Holding the award aloft, with tears in his eyes, Skaggs said, "This is everything I've worked for all my life." Then he added: "This is for Bill Monroe, Flatt & Scruggs, the Stanley Brothers, George Jones, Merle Haggard, and Buck Owens—some of my idols and influences. They ran the race and have had to slow down—now a fresh runner has grabbed the torch."

It was a night of triumph for Ricky Skaggs and all those who believed in traditional country music. At long last, the sounds of hard-country had received the biggest accolades at country's biggest showcase of the year. A movement genuinely seemed to be afoot, with Skaggs leading the charge. Yet no one watching the televised show that night could have guessed how quickly Skaggs himself would pass on the torch. Forces were already at work that would change country music in ways that neither Skaggs nor anyone else in country music could foresee. The age of video was dawning.

NOVEMBER 18, 1980—THE HOUR-LONG VARIETY SERIES "BARBARA MANDRELL AND THE MANDRELL SISTERS" PREMIERES ON NBC-TV AND RUNS THROUGH JUNE 1982

SEPTEMBER 1981—RICKY SKAGGS'S FIRST OF SIXTEEN STRAIGHT TOP TEN HITS, "YOU MAY SEE ME WALKIN'," ENTERS THE COUNTRY CHARTS

OCTOBER 1981—BARBARA MANDRELL NAMED THE CMA ENTERTAINER AND FEMALE VOCALIST OF THE YEAR, GEORGE JONES NAMED MALE VOCALIST

MARCH 1983—GEORGE JONES MARRIES NANCY SEPULVEDA

OCTOBER 14, 1985—RICKY SKAGGS NAMED CMA ENTERTAINER OF THE YEAR, REBA MCENTIRE NAMED FEMALE VOCALIST FOR THE SECOND STRAIGHT YEAR, AND GEORGE STRAIT NAMED MALE VOCALIST

After the Judds' farewell tour in 1991, it was time for Wynonna to put aside childish things and step into the spotlight alone.

Back to Basics

WHO'S GONNA FILL THEIR SHOES?

In September of 1985 a front-page story in *The New York Times* pointedly suggested that the Nashville Sound was dead. In the article *Times* music reporter Robert Palmer pointed out correctly that sales for some of country's biggest artists—Waylon Jennings, Barbara Mandrell, Tammy Wynette—were slumping. Those, he said, "whose record sales remain healthy are mostly rockers with a country tinge—Hank Williams Jr. and the four-man band Alabama." The numbers didn't lie. In 1981 country accounted for 15 percent of all record sales; by 1984 country's share of the market had dropped to 10 percent, a decline of more than $200 million in sales. The problem, as Palmer saw it, was that country music performers and their audience were graying. The music, like any human enterprise, needed an infusion of youth to continue. There must always be a chance for a new generation.

Robert Palmer was hardly alone in his opinion that country needed new blood. The week the *Times* article appeared, George Jones was riding high on the country charts with "Who's Gonna Fill Their Shoes." Ultimately a No. 3 hit, the song (written by Troy Seals and Max D. Barnes) wondered aloud about the younger generation's ability to match the heartfelt, honest music of elders like Willie Nelson, Johnny Cash, Merle Haggard, and—implicitly—Jones himself. Who would step up to carry country music's traditions forward? Who would play the Opry and "The Wabash Cannonball"? With "Who's Gonna Fill Their Shoes," George Jones took the words right out of many country fans' mouths.

The 1985 CMA Awards show had exactly the right answer for those who counted country music out. The program provided a dazzling showcase of youthful vitality and passionate conviction. Ricky Skaggs opened the evening's festivities at the Grand Ole Opry House with a blazing version of his current hit "Country Boy." The grand ol' man himself, Bill Monroe, skipped onstage to dance the buck-and-wing to Skaggs's supercharged bluegrass picking. Skaggs (age thirty-one), of course, took trophies for Entertainer of the Year and for having the top Instrumental Group. He was the tip of the iceberg. Handsome, white-hatted George Strait (thirty-three) won his first CMA awards for both Male Vocalist of the Year and Album of the Year (*Does Fort Worth Ever Cross Your Mind*). Reba McEntire (thirty) stepped up to claim her second straight CMA award for best Female Vocalist. Likewise, the mother-daughter duo the Judds (thirty-nine-year-old Naomi and twenty-one-year-old Wynonna) tearfully accepted awards for Vocal Group of the Year and Single of the Year, "Why Not Me." The entire evening was a virtual sweep for this bumper crop of new artists destined to take country music into the nineties.

Just as momentous, though less heralded, was the first CMA award that Hank Williams Jr. won that evening. No purist, Hank had taken a brand-new award, introduced that night, for his music video of "All My Rowdy Friends Are Coming Over Tonight." The award acknowledged the momentous technological and business changes that were just beginning to affect the music.

Music videos came of age on August 1, 1981, with the debut of cable television's MTV network and immediately connected audiences with recording artists as never before. It used to take months, sometimes years, for an artist to develop an identity with the public through radio and records. As the American TV debuts of Elvis and the Beatles on the "Ed Sullivan Show" had proven, a single appearance on national television could catapult a performer to stardom overnight. Music videos accelerated the process of viewer identification. This had its drawbacks as well as its advantages. Suddenly an artist could distinguish himself or herself from the crowd visually as well as musically. But an artist could also fail for not being good-looking or interesting enough. Appearances took on a whole new importance in the music industry. Artist manager Bill Carter was quoted toward the end of the notorious 1985 *New York Times* article as stating, "It's still possible for new performers to make it in country music. But they have to come across in videos and they have to be really sensational live performers."

From the beginning, MTV focused almost solely on rock music. Country fans had to wait until 1983 before Country Music Television (CMT) hit the airwaves and began programming country videos. In its early years, even CMT didn't air that many country videos, simply because the country music business had yet to realize the potential. (MTV later spawned an adult-oriented sister channel, VH-1, which aired some country music videos when it hit the airwaves in January 1985.)

Running almost hand in hand with the appearance of CMT was The Nashville Network (TNN), which debuted on March 7, 1983. It hit the airwaves with 7 million cable subscribers, the largest beginning audience of any cable network up to that time. The folks behind Opryland and the Grand Ole Opry founded TNN. The Opry properties, however, were no longer owned by National Life. That venerable company had been bought in July 1982 by the American General Corporation, which immediately announced plans to sell National Life's entertainment properties—the Opry, Opryland, the Opryland Hotel, WSM radio, and TNN. Four months after TNN went on the air, the Gaylord Broadcasting Company announced its purchase of those properties for a reported $270 million.

The Gaylord Company, run by sixty-three-year-old Edward Gaylord, was one of America's largest privately owned newspaper and broadcasting enterprises. Among the company's holdings was the "Hee Haw" TV series. In a show of confidence in their new acquisition, the Gaylord Company immediately asked E. W. "Bud" Wendell, who had been chief executive officer of National Life's entertainment properties since 1978, to remain in charge. It was a smart move. The former National Life salesman and Opry manager had virtually grown up with the company, and he had played a key role in the entertainment division's triumphs of the past decade, particularly the Opry's move to Opryland and the creation of TNN. With the financial backing of Gaylord, TNN was now prepared to compete with the "big boys" in broadcasting. The network aired its first video show, "Country Clips," in March 1984. The drive toward a new kind of image-making in country music had begun.

★ STRAIT COUNTRY

Traditional country music had made a splashy comeback on national television. Though Ricky Skaggs was playing the hot hand at the 1985 CMA Awards show, he would not long remain the king of the "new traditionalists." Talented rivals were waiting in the wings. Foremost among those rivals was George Strait. With his clean-cut good looks, starched button-down shirts, and crisply creased blue jeans, Strait looked almost preppy—an Urban Cowboy, for sure. His big Resistol hat, though, gave him away as a cowboy. Strait, as it turned out, was more a cowboy than most recording artists. In fact, he had grown up roping and riding on his family's 2,000-acre cattle ranch on the outskirts of San Antonio. Country music didn't figure prominently in his early life. Like most kids growing up in the sixties, he listened mostly to rock and roll. He even played rock in a high school garage band doing songs like "Gloria" and "Louie, Louie" that Strait said "never got out of the garage." After spending a couple of semesters at Southwest Texas State University, he signed up for a three-year hitch in the Army. Stationed in Hawaii of all places, Pvt. George Strait discovered his life's work at age twenty-one. He became interested in country music. As he recalled it, he bought "a cheap old guitar and a bunch of songbooks with the little chart on there that showed you where to put your fingers." And he studied from the greats: "Hank Williams, George Jones, and Merle Haggard, who are still my biggest influences." When the base's commanding officer announced that he wanted to put together a country band, Strait thought it sounded like fun and tried out for the singer's spot. "I always wanted to be a singer," he said. "Always. But I never really knew how to get into it." He got the job and spent the last year of his tour of duty just singing with the band, honing his talent.

Returning stateside, he re-enrolled at Southwest Texas State, working on a degree in agricultural education by day. At night he sang with his Ace in the Hole Band, whose

With his clean-cut good looks, George Strait looks almost preppy, but underneath that starched button-down shirt beats the heart of a genuine ropin', ridin' cowboy.

Country's Top Thirty-Three LPs

Why is Garth Brooks considered the kingpin of country music? The following table says it all. Of the seven country albums known to have sold 5 million copies or more, Garth recorded five of them. Is he the best-selling country artist of all time, then? Not necessarily. Although country records have been offered for sale since 1923, the public (and the press) didn't have any way of knowing on a regular basis how many records really sold until 1958, when the Recording Industry Association of America (RIAA) began awarding gold records for U.S. sales of half a million copies. In 1976 the RIAA added the platinum award for sales of a million. Prior to those dates, though, it's difficult to assess record sales, short of auditing a record company's books. Roy Acuff may have sold 25 million singles and Ernest Tubb 15 million by 1949, as *Variety* magazine claimed that year. We'll probably never know for certain.

In any case, the following table is a fairly accurate barometer of who has sold the most country records since 1976; it includes every country record certified triple platinum or above as of the end of 1994. (When several albums are at the same sales level, they are listed in roughly chronological order of release.) By way of comparison, the best-selling album of all time is Michael Jackson's *Thriller,* which sold 24 million copies in the United States. Coming in second and third are Fleetwood Mac's *Rumours* at 17 million and Boston's debut album at 15 million. And Garth is nipping at their heels.

ARTIST	ALBUM (LABEL, YEAR OF RELEASE)	U.S. SALES
GARTH BROOKS	No Fences (Capitol, 1990)	11 million
GARTH BROOKS	Ropin' the Wind (Capitol, 1991)	10 million
BILLY RAY CYRUS	Some Gave All (Mercury, 1992)	8 million
GARTH BROOKS	Garth Brooks (Capitol, 1989)	6 million
ELVIS PRESLEY	Golden Records, Vol. 1 (RCA, 1957)	5 million
GARTH BROOKS	The Chase (Liberty, 1992)	5 million
GARTH BROOKS	In Pieces (Liberty, 1993)	5 million
PATSY CLINE	Greatest Hits (Decca/MCA, 1967)	4 million
WILLIE NELSON	Stardust (Columbia, 1978)	4 million
WAYLON JENNINGS	Greatest Hits (RCA, 1979)	4 million
ANNE MURRAY	Greatest Hits (Capitol, 1980)	4 million
ALABAMA	Feels So Right (RCA, 1981)	4 million
ALABAMA	Mountain Music (RCA, 1982)	4 million
WILLIE NELSON	Always on My Mind (Columbia, 1982)	4 million
RANDY TRAVIS	Always and Forever (Warner Bros., 1987)	4 million
BROOKS & DUNN	Brand New Man (Arista, 1991)	4 million
ALAN JACKSON	A Lot About Livin' (And a Little 'Bout Love) (Arista, 1992)	4 million
WILLIE NELSON	Greatest Hits (Columbia, 1981)	3 million
ALABAMA	The Closer You Get (RCA, 1983)	3 million
ALABAMA	Roll On (RCA, 1984)	3 million
ALABAMA	Greatest Hits (RCA, 1986)	3 million
RANDY TRAVIS	Storms of Life (Warner Bros., 1986)	3 million
CLINT BLACK	Killin' Time (RCA, 1989)	3 million
ALAN JACKSON	Don't Rock the Jukebox (Arista, 1991)	3 million
WYNONNA JUDD	Wynonna (MCA, 1992)	3 million
MARY CHAPIN CARPENTER	Come On, Come On (Columbia, 1992)	3 million
VINCE GILL	I Still Believe in You (MCA, 1992)	3 million
GEORGE STRAIT	Pure Country (MCA, 1992)	3 million
REBA MCENTIRE	It's Your Call (MCA, 1992)	3 million
VARIOUS ARTISTS	Common Thread: Songs of the Eagles (Giant, 1993)	3 million
BROOKS & DUNN	Hard Workin' Man (Arista, 1993)	3 million
REBA MCENTIRE	Greatest Hits, Vol. 2 (MCA, 1993)	3 million
TIM MCGRAW	Not a Moment Too Soon (Curb, 1994)	3 million

members he'd recruited on campus (COUNTRY SINGER NEEDS BAND, his flyers read). Upon graduating in 1979 he moved on to manage a cattle ranch outside San Marcos, Texas, while continuing to play the clubs at night. As much as he loved the music, the hours he spent between both jobs were killing him. "Ranching isn't nine to five," he explained. "It's more like sunup to sundown. I'd have about half an hour to get cleaned up and get to the night's gig." Meanwhile, Strait made three trips to Nashville attempting to land a record contract. But there were no takers.

"I was fixin' to go ahead and quit. I was twenty-seven years old, I'd been playing for six or seven years, and I was beginning to think I wasn't good enough and maybe ought to try something else. I gave my band notice and signed up for a full-time job with this outfit in Uvalde, Texas, that designed cattle pens. But one week before I was to report for the job, I realized that I just couldn't do it. And I decided to give it one more year."

Of course, that's when he made his connection. A promotion man for the Nashville office of MCA Records by the name of Erv Woolsey had been pleading Strait's case for a while. A few years before, Woolsey had owned a bar called the Prairie Rose in San Marcos, Texas, where Strait and his band frequently appeared. Woolsey remembered that Strait seemed to go over well with the crowds. In 1980 Woolsey brought Strait to MCA. The execs at the label weren't convinced they had found a new star at first; his music seemed a bit heavy on western swing, they thought. But at least they gave him a try, signing him in February 1981. The first album he recorded, *Strait Country*, was true to its title, serving up solid Texas honky-tonk. His first single, a danceable Texas two-stepper titled "Unwound," which its

As viewers of his 1992 movie Pure Country *know, George Strait is no stranger to the saddle.*

writers had originally intended for Johnny Paycheck, climbed into the country Top Ten that summer.

Strait's career did not skyrocket overnight, however. With the help of Erv Woolsey, who left MCA to become his manager, Strait built a following a little bit at a time. He loved to play Bob Wills–style western swing and old Hank Williams–style honky-tonk. His crack Ace in the Hole Band had practiced for years on classics by Wills, Williams, Webb Pierce, Johnny Cash, and others. They knew how to keep a dance-hall crowd moving, especially a Texas crowd. "That's all you play down there," Strait explained. "For a local band, you couldn't survive unless you played dance music."

Radio programmers, on the other hand, just weren't ready to play Texas dance music in the early eighties. So Strait's advisers wisely steered him toward romantic ballads that suited his smooth, controlled voice and his chiseled good looks. In his concerts he could see the results. The dance numbers got good reactions from the crowds, but the ballads—personalized messages like "A Fire I Can't Put Out," "You Look So Good in Love," "You're Something Special to Me"—drove women in the audiences into screaming frenzies right out of Beatlemania.

To his credit, Strait didn't pander. Instead of flooding the market with romantic ballads, he kept his balance, releasing hard-country nuggets like Wills's "Right or Wrong" (1984), the Faron Young hit "If You Ain't Lovin', You Ain't Livin'" (1988), and a swinging remake of Hank's old "Lovesick Blues" (1992). A reserved, down-to-earth family man, Strait still lives in south Texas with wife, Norma, and son, George Jr. Though he routinely gives his all onstage, since the death

Goin' Down (Till the Sun Comes Up)," Brooks & Dunn's "Texas Women (Don't Stay Lonely Too Long)," and Tim McGraw's "Give It to Me Strait." In 1992 he added movie star to his list of achievements, when he starred in *Pure Country*, playing a character who (surprise!) sings and ropes cattle.

★ THE OKLAHOMA COWGIRL

The biggest female star of the eighties and nineties hit her stride around the same time as George Strait. Like him, Reba McEntire came from a genuine roping and riding background. She grew up the third of four children on an 8,000-acre cattle ranch near Chockie in southeastern Oklahoma. Rodeos were in the McEntires' blood: Both Reba's grandfather and her father were three-time World Champion Steer Ropers, and Reba herself competed as a barrel racer. Every summer of her childhood, the family would pile into an old green Ford for a tour of the Southwestern rodeo circuit. It was on those long drives that Reba's mother, who had once harbored ambitions of being a singer, led her children in sing-alongs to pass the time.

Reba's other great musical teachers were Patsy Cline and Dolly Parton. "I was in the sixth grade," recalled Reba, "when I was introduced to Patsy Cline's music through my friend Marilyn McClendon's grandmother, Ruby Sexton. She had an 8-track tape of Patsy's *Greatest Hits*. She gave it to me because I listened to it constantly. I still have that 8-track." From Patsy, Reba said she learned "emotion: raw, unashamed, and sincere." Reba was just starting high school when she heard Dolly's *My Blue Ridge Mountain Boy* album. From Dolly, she learned vocal freedom: "Her little trills and the looseness of her vocal cords," said Reba, "they just kind of run wild. . . . Dolly's always reminded me of a butterfly, how her voice just kind of floats around."

Reba at the Opry in 1986, just before beginning her move to a more glamorous look and wider appeal. Note the rodeo belt.

of his thirteen-year-old daughter, Jennifer, in an auto crash in 1986, he has assiduously avoided the press, preferring to let his music do the talking. It has spoken loud and clear. Since his 1981 debut Strait has piled up one of the most enviable set of statistics on Music Row during the eighties and early nineties: twenty-five No. 1 singles through the end of

1993, CMA awards for Male Vocalist of the Year in 1985 and 1986, then Entertainer of the Year for 1989 and 1990. Every album he's ever released has gone gold (eighteen by the end of 1993), with several albums selling in the millions. By the nineties, younger acts were tipping their Stetsons to his influence in a string of records, including Garth Brooks's "Ain't

Reba went to college at Southeastern Oklahoma State University, majoring in elementary education. She didn't plan to teach school, however, as her mother and grandmother had. She minored in music, hoping somehow to make it as a singer. During the summer after her sophomore year, she got her first break when country recording artist Red Steagall heard her sing the national anthem at the National Rodeo Finals in Oklahoma City. Later that week, after hearing her sing Dolly Parton's "Joshua" a cappella, Steagall became convinced of her talent and began shopping tapes of her singing to various Nashville record offices. A year later, in November 1975, Mercury Records had an opening on their roster for one female artist. They signed Reba.

Reba's affinity for Patsy Cline showed proudly on her first three Mercury albums, each of which featured a remake of a Cline song. Beyond that, neither Reba nor the record label seemed to have any clear idea of who Reba McEntire was as a singer. So they tried a little bit of everything, with most of the material being soft country-pop ballads that didn't quite jive with Reba's thick Oklahoma twang and Dolly-like trills. In the seven years she spent with Mercury Records, she recorded seventy songs, with only two No. 1 hits.

The turning point came in 1984 with her second MCA Records album, produced by Harold Shedd, the man behind Alabama's hits. Shedd thought Reba needed to continue in a country-pop direction. Reba disagreed, feeling it was time to go against the grain with a more hard-core country effort. "The songs we were finding were really more pop," she recalled. "And they had a lot of strings on them, and I was really wanting to get away from the strings and put more fiddle and steel on my songs. Everybody else was doing the pop-ish stuff with the strings, and I just wanted to do something different."

Frustrated, she called Jimmy Bowen, head

Reba McEntire knows horses, having grown up on an 8,000-acre cattle ranch.

of MCA Records at the time, to explain her problem. "I told Jimmy I didn't like the songs they were selecting for me, and he said, 'Well, just go find 'em yourself.'"

That is exactly what Reba did. "I had to go back and find the old songs because no one was writing really hard-core country music," she recalled. "I went to publishing companies and said, 'Give me your most traditional stuff.'" She ended up with four new songs and six oldies popularized by the likes of Ray Price, Carl Smith, and Faron Young. Appropriately, she titled the album *My Kind of Country*. Harold Shedd produced the record, but Reba had assumed control of her career for the first time. "That," she said, "was the start of Reba music."

The two singles from the album—both new songs—went to No. 1: the bluegrass-flavored "How Blue" and the stately divorce song "Somebody Should Leave." The album sold better than anything she had recorded thus far. Jimmy Bowen, for one, was not surprised: "She'd been around eight years and had many chart hits, but it wasn't her music. It was just her voice. She was selling 40,000. That album did 165,000."

True to his philosophy, Bowen invited Reba to begin co-producing records with him. As her record sales and touring fees escalated, she gained confidence, enough so that in 1986 she demanded and got her first music video to promote her newest single, "Whoever's in New England." As Reba recalled, "Bowen didn't believe in them a whole lot back then. He thought they didn't sell enough records to justify their production cost." Reba got her video by agreeing to pay for half of it, which could have cost her anywhere from $20,000 to $40,000. It was a good gamble. The big ballad not only showcased Reba's rangy, athletic voice well, but also told its story about a wife's suspicions concerning her husband's New England business trips in almost cinematic

terms. Reba has called it "my first career song." The video, shot in snowy Boston, had something to do with the song's success. It aired not only on CMT and TNN, but also VH-1 and HBO. Boosted by "Whoever's in New England," the album by the same name became her first to go gold. As Bowen put it: "That song took her from bein' a country singles radio artist into bein' a record seller."

"Whoever's in New England" was a fork in the road in more ways than one. There was no denying it: The song was a glossy pop-style ballad, which didn't sit at all well with Reba's husband, former rodeo star Charlie Battles. Ten years older and used to being the boss, Battles lived up to his name. He had co-managed Reba (with Bill Carter) for years, even though he didn't have any experience in that area. He had made no secret of opposing the release of "Whoever's in New England." But MCA Records and Reba overruled him. The success of the song had pointed to a new direction in her career.

For most of her career, Reba had projected a tomboyish, rodeo gal look, with her unruly wavy red hair and sunburned freckles. She wore cowgirl outfits with big rodeo belts and lived on a ranch with Battles in Stringtown, Oklahoma. But as she gained confidence, Reba went after a more glamorous image, hiring top fashion consultants and choreographers to polish her act to a high gloss. Her 1988 album *Reba* featured remakes of pop and R & B oldies "Sunday Kind of Love" and "Respect." Not shy about controversy, Reba performed the Aretha Franklin classic, complete with a hip-shaking dance routine, on the 1988 CMA Awards telecast.

Almost inevitably Reba and Charlie Battles hit an impasse in their relationship. They divorced in November 1987, a little over a year after "Whoever's in New England" hit No. 1. Upon moving to Nashville in 1988, she formed her own company, Starstruck, to han-

dle her publicity, music publishing, and management. She brought in her tour manager, Narvel Blackstock, who had started as her steel guitar player eight years earlier, to run Starstruck. They married June 3, 1989, in Lake Tahoe, Nevada. By 1992 the company employed some ninety people, with a multi-million-dollar budget.

With each passing year, Reba's confidence and ambition have grown. Her singles continue to alternate remakes of pop oldies with what she likes to call "message songs." These latter songs—generally aimed at a female audience—have covered such topics as a housewife's search for identity outside the home ("Is There Life Out There"), a daughter's bittersweet memories of an emotionally repressed father ("The Greatest Man I Never Knew"), and a woman's fears about AIDS after a one-night stand ("She Thinks His Name Was John"). "I'm trying to sing songs for women, to say for them what they can't say for themselves," she has said. "I want to be those women's friend." The approach must be working: Since 1990's *Rumor Has It*, her albums have consistently sold in the platinum range and beyond.

Somehow Reba has managed to maintain the common touch, even as she has become the most glamorous of country stars. Almost without effort, it seems, she has vaulted from country videos to dramatic roles on television and full-length Hollywood movies. Like her idols Patsy and Dolly, Reba McEntire has managed to transcend the country market. With her great natural wonder of a voice, she has proved capable of matching the vocal acrobatics of pop divas like Whitney Houston and Mariah Carey. By the end of the eighties, her record company had begun titling her albums simply with her first name. It made perfect sense: She was on a first-name basis with America.

★ THE SOAP SISTERS

With the success of newcomers like Ricky Skaggs, George Strait, and Reba McEntire in the first half of the eighties, country music was reviving older styles in interesting ways. The time was ripe for an act to update the family harmony traditions of the Carter Family and the Delmore Brothers.

Enter a near-look-alike auburn-haired mother-daughter singing duo with a homely, hill-country name: the Judds. Their first single, released in mid-November 1983, was a remake of an obscure Elvis Presley song, "Had a Dream (For the Heart)." In early 1984, it was a Top Twenty country hit. By the end of 1984,

they had not only bagged two No. 1 hits— "Mama He's Crazy" and "Why Not Me"— but also their first CMA award, the Horizon trophy for best new artist.

Country fans could not have asked for a more colorful, unlikely, storybook pair than the Judds. They effortlessly embodied down-home charm and uptown glamour. Onstage, mother Naomi provided the flirtatious, belle-of-the-ball energy and dusky harmonies while daughter Wynonna belted out the bluesy lead vocals, keeping a lip-curling cauldron of emotions simmering. From the very beginning, music critics were quick to point out that Wynonna was the one who possessed the true vocal talent. That was easy enough to

Country fans could not have asked for a more colorful storybook pair than the Judds, who effortlessly projected down-home charm and uptown glamour from the moment they hit the country scene in 1983.

spot. What took a little longer for everyone to realize was just how necessary Naomi Judd was to her daughter's career. If Wynonna had the breathtaking voice, Naomi had the drive to succeed that pushed that voice into the spotlight.

Naomi Judd missed her high school graduation in Ashland, Kentucky. That's because she was in the hospital on May 30, 1964, giving birth to her first child, Christina (later

Daughter Wynonna picks while mama Naomi dreams of stardom swinging on their front porch in Franklin, Tennessee, in the summer of 1979.

Christina also began making their own music. Michael Ciminella had played guitar, and, inspired perhaps by her dad's example, Christina took immediately to the instrument. Presaging the bond that would grow between Christina and Diana, the first song they learned to harmonize was "A Mother's Smile," a sentimental ballad popularized by the Blue Sky Boys in the 1930s. Slowly, mother and daughter learned songs and harmony from the occasional used records they bought. Among their favorites were the old-time duets of the Delmore Brothers and the neotraditionalist sounds of Emmylou Harris.

known as Wynonna). At the time, Naomi was known as Diana Ciminella, having hastily married college student Michael Ciminella shortly after the pregnancy was discovered. The marriage lasted long enough for the Ciminellas to move out to Los Angeles and for the birth of a second daughter, Ashley, in 1968. By 1972 the marriage ended in divorce. Alone in L.A. with two young daughters and no certifiable skills, Diana Ciminella nevertheless landed on her feet. For the next three years she worked as a shoe model, manager of a health-food store, secretary for the pop group the Fifth Dimension, and girl Friday to a millionaire investment consultant. Feeling she was going nowhere and that her girls weren't benefiting from life in the fast lane, Diana pulled up stakes and went back to Kentucky. Enrolling

in the nursing program at Eastern Kentucky University in Richmond, she set up housekeeping in the tiny rural hamlet of Morrill, population fifty, a few miles away. In Morrill (pronounced *moral*), Diana and her two daughters went back to basics. "We lived in a house with no telephone, no television, and no newspaper," remembered Naomi. "We just had a radio. On Saturday nights, we'd do the wash in our old Maytag wringer-washer and listen to the Grand Ole Opry." Nearby was the thriving Appalachian arts community centered around Berea College. Encouraged by local artisans, Diana and her daughters learned how to make their own lye soap, weave on a hand loom, grow their own vegetables, and make their dinners from scratch.

To entertain themselves, Diana and

In August of 1976 Diana and her daughters left their idyllic hill-country home after being harassed by an ex-con. The next four years would find Diana and her daughters moving back and forth across the United States. In Marin County, on the north side of San Francisco Bay, Diana finished her nursing studies. She passed a more profound milestone when she legally restored her maiden name and took the new first name Naomi, after a biblical character in the Book of Ruth. Meanwhile, Christina, just entering her teens, got deeper and deeper into music.

As her daughter's musical talent blossomed, Naomi Judd looked for ways to encourage her daughter. In 1977, while still working toward her nursing degree, Naomi audited an audio-engineering course that culminated in a free demo-taping session. Naomi and her thirteen-year-old daughter made their first demo tape late that year, singing the Delmore Brothers' "Hillbilly Boogie." Taking a cue from the song, Naomi dubbed their duo "The Hillbilly Women" and even had baseball jackets embroidered with the words. With encouragement from friends and local musicians, the Judds jumped into music with both feet in early 1979. The resulting odyssey would take them from Marin County to Austin back to L.A. to Las Vegas, and ultimately to Nashville. Along the way, Christina acquired a new name as well: Wynonna Judd. "I got the name from a song called 'Route 66,'" she later explained. "There's a line that says, 'Flagstaff, Arizona, don't forget Winona.'"

By May 1979 Naomi had finally zeroed in on Music City as the place to launch the Hillbilly Women to stardom. She took a job as a nurse in Williamson County, a half hour south of Nashville. On her days off she made the rounds of the Nashville studios and record company offices. In February 1980, the Judds began monthly appearances on WSM-TV's 5:30 A.M. wake-up show hosted by Ralph Emery, then a popular WSM syndicated DJ. The first time they appeared on the show, Emery mistook the thirty-four-year-old mother and sixteen-year-old daughter for sisters. After he heard that Naomi made her own lye soap, he took to introducing them as the Soap Sisters. One morning Emery even had Naomi demonstrate on the air how she made the soap. (It was that kind of show.) As if working as a nurse, making monthly TV ap-

pearances, and knocking on doors up and down Music Row weren't enough, Naomi even managed to land an occasional modeling job (that's her with Conway Twitty on his *Lost in the Feeling* album cover from 1983) and a

The Judds played at Guantanamo Naval Base in Cuba, Thanksgiving 1987. The show was taped as a USO TV special. Just over four years later, the Judds would tape their Farewell Concert.

stint as a TV extra (a groupie in the made-for-TV movie of Hank Jr.'s life, *Living Proof*).

Serendipity finally opened the door for the Judds in the spring of 1981. Dianna Maher, a high school classmate of Wynonna's, was seriously injured in an auto accident. Naomi Judd turned out to be her nurse. Dianna recognized Naomi from "The Ralph Emery Show," and said that she and her mother had both tried to get her father, record producer Brent Maher, to watch the Soap Sisters. And she had been trying to tell her father how great Wynonna sounded at the high

school talent shows. "Of course, one never listens to one's kids," Brent Maher wryly admitted some years later. Naomi saw her opening. Once Dianna Maher had a clean bill of health, Naomi went to Maher's studio on her day off, reintroducing herself as not only his daughter's nurse but also as part of a singing team. She left him a demo tape made on a $30 K-Mart recorder and crossed her fingers. Six weeks went by and Maher never called.

Driving to his studio one morning, Maher finally popped that homemade tape into the cassette player. "I almost drove off the road," Maher remembered. Among the songs on the tape were a couple that Naomi had written, a medley of their old favorites, and a new song by Kenny O'Dell, a topnotch Nashville songwriter. Knowing how to tailor material, he listened to Naomi's own songs and wrote a new one that fit the Judds like a glove, "Mama He's Crazy." That song and the Judds' unusual jazzy country harmony sound were what nearly put Brent Maher into a ditch.

When Maher stopped in to visit the Judds at home the next evening, they all sat down at the kitchen table in the 150-year-old farmhouse, and he got to hear and see Naomi and Wynonna pick and sing as they had been doing from the beginning back in Morrill, Kentucky. Wynonna unfurled her big, bluesy voice and played the guitar; Naomi pitched her smoky harmonies underneath. They trotted out everything they could think of to impress Maher. "One minute I'd sing him a Bonnie Raitt song," remembered Wynonna, "and the next minute we were singin' the Andrews Sisters." Over the next three months or so, Maher dropped by from time to time to offer encouragement and advice, while trying to figure out what the Judds did best. Eventually, he invited a talented but relatively unknown guitarist named Don Potter to join the Judds' jam sessions. Together, the four of them gradually refined an acoustic sound that kept the Judds' jazzy harmonies at the forefront.

On March 2, 1983, a year and a half after Brent Maher first heard the Judds, he got them an unusual live audition with Joe Galante, chief of RCA's Nashville division. Galante had heard a demo tape, which piqued his interest, and Maher had insisted the Judds had to be seen for their potential to be grasped. So at the end of a working Wednesday, the Judds met Galante and a few of his top staff at RCA's offices. They opened by playing the first song they'd ever learned, "A Mother's Smile," and then they kept playing for forty-five minutes. They got the contract. Years later Naomi would underscore the personal significance of that record deal: At age thirty-seven, she could finally afford health insurance and a savings account. Eight months later their first single and a six-song "mini" album hit the market. Naomi quit her nursing job for good, and Wynonna left the secretarial work she'd taken since graduating from high school in the spring of 1982.

The Judds were an immediate sensation. Their front-porch sound fit their name perfectly. "Why Not Me" painted a bluesy portrait of a small-town girl left behind. "Girls Night Out" celebrated a good ol' girl's right to party. Probably more than any of their songs, "Grandpa (Tell Me 'Bout the Good Old Days)" struck a chord with listeners, as only the most heartfelt country music can. With a few verses sung in family harmony, the song captured the essence of country's eternal appeal: a search for the comfort of the familiar in an age when "everything is changing fast."

The Judds didn't merely celebrate small-

town values; they did it while looking glamorous. They toured the country in a $350,000 bus they christened *Dreamchaser*. They had their own prime-time CBS-TV special "Across the Heartland" in January 1989. Performers as diverse as Bonnie Raitt and U2 expressed their admiration for the Judds and joined them in live performances. During a five-year run between August 1984 and October 1989, they notched fourteen No. 1 hits. Between 1985 and 1991 they had a virtual lock on the CMA Vocal Group and Vocal Duo awards, winning seven straight trophies. They sold 17 million records.

Randy Travis pulled fans back to country music in droves with his staunchly traditional style and hard-country conviction.

It looked like the *Dreamchaser* ride could go on forever. The end of the Judds took Nashville completely by surprise, when on a rainy Wednesday, Naomi Judd called a press conference at RCA Records' offices. "Today is pretty much the most difficult day of my life," she told the assembled press corps on October 17, 1990. "I have to resign. I must retire from the music industry I love so much." She had contracted chronic hepatitis, a debilitating, potentially life-threatening disease of the liver. For the next year, Naomi said her good-byes to fans on their farewell tour, which wrapped up with a December 4, 1991, pay-per-view TV concert from Murfreesboro, Tennessee; proceeds went to the American Liver Foundation. The farewell tour had played to more than a million fans and was the top-grossing country tour of the year. The TV program outdrew specials by the Rolling Stones and teen favorites New Kids on the Block. Afterward, Naomi Judd stepped into the background to write her memoirs (which in 1993 became the best-selling *Love Can Build a Bridge*), while Wynonna moved on to the spectacular solo recording career that had been predicted for her all along.

★ THE VOICE OF A GENERATION

Within a year of *The New York Times* proclaiming country's demise, the music was showing signs of renewed vitality. More new acts debuted on the *Billboard* country charts in 1986 (twenty-three) than ever had before. The new-traditionalist tide that brought the Judds, Skaggs, Strait, and McEntire had a lot to do with country radio programmers being more receptive to new talent. Collectively these acts had made an impact on country music, helping to tug it away from the graying middle-of-the-road pop course it had been moving toward since the Nashville Sound successes of Owen Bradley and Chet Atkins in the late fifties. As successful as they all were, however, none of them had the impact on country music that Randy Travis had. The funny thing is, Travis re-energized country by being the most staunchly traditionalist of the bunch. He sounded like something out of the past, or as Minnie Pearl put it, "He's a new vehicle with old wheels." Brandishing a gnarled, knotty baritone, Travis sang with the conviction of a man twice his age. "With this

voice," he once said, "I couldn't ever sing anything *but* country."

From the moment they could hold guitars, Randy and his three brothers were groomed to be country singers by their father, Harold Traywick. He bought them western outfits, sprang for music lessons and instruments, even built an addition to the house where they could practice. "That's the only thing I ever listened to," Randy has said. "As far back as I can remember, it was country." By the age of fourteen, Randy began playing in local bars around the Traywicks' hometown of Marshville, North Carolina. "I was playing in them before I was old enough to go in them," he said. Folks who heard him began to comment on his unusually mature voice. Not long afterward, young Randy got a different kind of local reputation. "I started the alcohol about [age] eleven, probably, and the drugs about twelve up until eighteen, so about six years," Randy recently admitted. "Of course, like anybody else in the beginning, here and there. Smoked some marijuana or whatever. By fourteen or fifteen I was smoking every day and by that time I had gotten into other drugs too. Acid, PHC, MDA, all kinds of stuff. For about six years I was totally out of control."

He dropped out of school in the ninth grade, often ran away from home, and began getting into trouble, one legal offense after another: drunk driving, petty theft, car theft. Eventually multiple arrests and probation violations caught up with him. After a January 1977 arrest for breaking and entering, Randy at age seventeen was looking at a June sentencing hearing that could easily put him away for five years.

His voice and thirty-five-year-old nightclub owner Lib Hatcher saved him. While awaiting his sentencing hearing, Randy continued to perform at local clubs. In February 1977 he began appearing at a series of talent contests held at Country City, U.S.A., a 250-

Randy Travis during a 1985 show at the Nashville Palace. By this time he had graduated from his job as a part-time cook in the club's kitchen and was just months away from a hit recording career.

seat, no-frills cinderblock nightclub in nearby Charlotte. Hatcher and her husband owned the club. The first night Randy appeared, Lib Hatcher noticed the long-haired kid with the square jaw and the deep voice. "I'll never forget it," she recalled. "There was a little table near the stage where I'd sit a lot and work on some papers. When I heard Randy, I just sort of dropped the papers and thought, 'This is something special.' "

After Randy won the contest, beating out 118 challengers, Hatcher made a point of getting to know the teenager. She found out about his court date and went with him to plead his case. Somehow she convinced the judge of Randy's intention to mend his ways and dedicate himself to music, and of the need to be away from his father, with whom Randy had a strained relationship. The judge put Randy on probation and released him into Lib Hatcher's custody. "The judge was going to send me away," Randy said. "Fortunately, Lib was there to stand up for me." The rules were that Randy had to work for Lib Hatcher and her husband, Frank, at Country City, U.S.A., and live with the Hatchers.

From that moment, Lib Hatcher dedicated herself to seeing Randy Traywick fulfill the potential in his rich baritone.

To further Randy's career, Lib Hatcher sacrificed everything she had, including her ten-year marriage. "It was pretty awkward, living part-time with a woman and her husband who you weren't sure how he felt about you," Randy remembered. "Sometimes I wondered whether or not I'd wake up in the morning." Frank Hatcher reached a point where he gave Lib an ultimatum: the kid or me. It was no contest. The Hatchers separated, then divorced. In 1978 she spent $10,000 recording two singles for Randy that were released by tiny Shreveport-based Paula Records. In 1981 she moved to Nashville with Randy and took a job managing the Nashville Palace, a nightclub across the street from the entrance to Opryland, and hired Randy as a short-order cook and part-time

Don Schlitz (left) and Paul Overstreet (right) collected a slew of awards for the two big songs they supplied Randy Travis— "On the Other Hand" (1986) and "Forever and Ever, Amen" (1987). The No. 1 singles launched Travis's career and created a high demand for Overstreet and Schlitz compositions.

COUNTRY MILESTONES	JANUARY 1979—RANDY TRAYWICK'S FIRST APPEARANCE ON THE CHARTS WITH "SHE'S MY WOMAN," WHICH EDGES IN AT NO. 90	MAY 1979—NAOMI JUDD AND HER DAUGHTERS WYNONNA AND ASHLEY MOVE TO NASHVILLE, WHERE SHE TAKES A JOB AS A NURSE	FEBRUARY 1980—NAOMI AND WYNONNA JUDD BEGIN REGULAR APPEARANCES ON "THE RALPH EMERY SHOW," AN EARLY-MORNING TV SHOW IN NASHVILLE	FEBRUARY 1981—GEORGE STRAIT SIGNS WITH MCA RECORDS JANUARY 1983—RANDY TRAVIS IS SINGING AT THE NASHVILLE PALACE NIGHTCLUB ACROSS THE STREET FROM OPRYLAND	MARCH 2, 1983—THE JUDDS AUDITION LIVE FOR RCA RECORDS; THE DUO PASSES
FEBRUARY 1977—RANDY TRAYWICK (NOW TRAVIS) WINS THE FIRST OF SEVERAL SINGING CONTESTS AT LIB HATCHER'S COUNTRY CITY CLUB NEAR CHARLOTTE, NORTH CAROLINA					

singer. In 1983 she arranged for Randy to record a live album at the club, titled *Randy Ray Live at the Nashville Palace*. It had no chance of being played on the radio, but it was the best they could do; every major label in Nashville had already turned Randy down—twice.

In November 1985 Martha Sharp, a Warner Bros. A & R executive, discovered Randy singing at the Nashville Palace and signed him to her label. "I knew right away that I wanted to sign him and that I would catch hell if I did," she said. "The feeling from the label heads was we needed *more* pop and more rock to attract the younger audience." Sharp won over her superiors nevertheless with help from highly regarded producer Kyle Lehning, who expressed an interest in handling Randy in the studio. The only catch for Randy was that Warner Bros. insisted that he change his name again.

On January 30, 1985, the newly christened Randy Travis recorded four songs; one of them would be a career-making song, though not without difficulty. The writers who supplied it, Don Schlitz and Paul Overstreet, had originally hoped to get "On the Other Hand" into the hands of a proven star. It was a hard-core country song that wrestled with an age-old dilemma: to cheat or not to cheat. It was just right for Merle Haggard or George Jones. Imagine the writers' disappointment, then, when they found out that the first person to

Randy Travis with wife and manager Lib Hatcher, and George Strait with wife Norma, 1992. After years of keeping their relationship hush-hush, Travis and Hatcher married in May 1991.

show an interest in their song was this newcomer, Randy Travis.

Warner Bros. finally released "On the Other Hand" in early August 1985. On the sixth of the month, Randy sang it for host Ralph Emery and his audience on TNN's "Nashville Now." What most TV viewers will remember more clearly about that night is the dinner Randy presented Emery when he appeared: a heaping surf-and-turf plate of shrimp, lobster, and steak that Randy himself had prepared at the Nashville Palace just minutes before the show. During the viewer call-in segment of the show, the leading question for Randy had to do with how he might be related to Merle Travis. He would spend the next several months answering that one.

Despite the TNN boost, "On the Other Hand" stalled at No. 67 on the charts. Not expecting that listeners were really waiting for

MARCH 6, 1983—THE MUSIC VIDEO CHANNEL COUNTRY MUSIC TELEVISION (CMT) DEBUTS

MARCH 7, 1983—THE NASHVILLE NETWORK DEBUTS IN 7 MILLION HOMES WITH FIVE HOURS OF THE FLAGSHIP TALK SHOW "NASHVILLE NOW," HOSTED BY FORMER WSM DISC JOCKEY RALPH EMERY

NOVEMBER 1983—THE JUDDS' FIRST SINGLE, "HAD A DREAM (FOR THE HEART)," IS RELEASED

JANUARY 18, 1984—RANDY TRAVIS APPEARS ON "NASHVILLE NOW" TO PROMOTE HIS FIRST ALBUM, *RANDY RAY LIVE AT THE NASHVILLE PALACE*

MARCH 1984—TNN AIRS ITS FIRST MUSIC VIDEO PROGRAM, "VIDEO CLIPS"

JANUARY 1985—THE MUSIC VIDEO CHANNEL VH-1 ARRIVES

JANUARY 30, 1985—RANDY TRAVIS RECORDS HIS FIRST SINGLES FOR WARNER BROS. RECORDS, "1982" AND "ON THE OTHER HAND," BOTH HITS

Randy Travis, a cowboy at heart, with celebrity trailhands Michael Martin Murphey (left) and Roy Rogers. In 1993 Travis recorded an album of western songs, Wind in the Wire.

just such a dyed-in-the-wool country singer, Warner Brothers didn't work very hard at promoting the single. Despite considerable call-in response at radio stations around the country, the single died on the vine. But with the follow-up "1982," a seriocomic plea about wishing to go back in time and fix a broken love affair, the record company and Travis connected in a big way: a No. 6 hit in the spring of 1986.

That clinched it. With a hit, Randy and Lib quit their jobs at the Nashville Palace in March and began touring. In June 1986 Warner Bros. released his first album, *Storms of Life*. In retrospect, many music critics have called it the finest country album of the 1980s. It had ten songs—three from Paul Overstreet including "On the Other Hand" (with Don Schlitz) plus two written by Travis himself that had appeared on the *Nashville*

Palace album ("Send My Body" and "Reasons I Cheat"). All the songs explored the workaday lives of people trying to cope with pressures and temptations, disappointments and dreams. It sounded like somebody's—everybody's—life story.

"Technically, I know that I'm not one of the greatest singers," Randy has said. "But I sure try to sing with a lot of feeling and a lot of emotion, try to make it sound believable. I guess that's what I learned from country singers, from listening all my life to people like Merle Haggard and George Jones, people like Hank Sr."

Cautiously optimistic, Warner Bros. predicted sales of 20,000 copies for *Storms of Life*. Meanwhile, producer Kyle Lehning urged the label to rerelease "On the Other Hand" as Randy's second single. Lehning was so convinced the song was a hit that he told the company they could take the promotion fees out of his producer's royalty. Warner Bros. told Lehning he could keep his money but agreed to the unorthodox move of the rerelease in April 1986. By July it was a No. 1 hit, and the *Storms of Life* album fairly flew off store shelves, selling 100,000 copies its first week on the market. Buoyed by two more Top Ten hits—"Diggin' Up Bones" and "No Place Like Home"—the album sold a million copies within a year. In October 1986 Randy surprised no one by receiving the CMA's Horizon award for most promising newcomer. Fittingly, "On the Other Hand" took Song of the Year honors for Don Schlitz and Paul Overstreet.

Randy had always said that he'd know that he had *really* made it, though, when he made the Opry. On December 20, 1986, he realized that long-held dream. It was a great Christmas present not only for him but also for the Opry. He appeared on the half hour of the Opry televised over TNN. Appropriately,

that night the segment's host was Ricky Skaggs, who had helped set in motion the chain of events that brought Randy's sound back into favor. Randy sang his current hit "Diggin' Up Bones," and afterward Ricky announced to the crowd he had the answer to George Jones's musical question "Who's Gonna Fill Their Shoes." Pointing to Randy, he said, "I tell you one thing, George. It's this fella right here. They're gonna be trying to fill his shoes one of these days."

In 1987 Randy Travis proved he was no flash in the pan with his second album, *Always and Forever*, and its flagship No. 1 hit, "Forever and Ever, Amen." The record quickly sold in twice the numbers of Randy's debut album, remaining atop the country album chart for a solid forty-three weeks. (When Warner Bros. staff told Randy the album had hit the pop album chart, the hard-core young singer reportedly replied, "Pop chart? Get it off of there!") He cleaned up at the CMA Awards that year, winning for Male Vocalist, Album of the Year, and both Single and Song of the Year with "Forever and Ever, Amen," another Overstreet-Schlitz composition. In terms of awards and record sales, he had hit the pinnacle in 1987. From that plateau of success, he would get opportunities for movie (*Young Guns*) and television roles ("Matlock"), late-night TV ("Saturday Night Live"), high-profile ad campaigns for American Express and Coca-Cola, and satisfying opportunities to

record with idols like George Jones and Roy Rogers.

In early June 1991 the world finally found out the secret he and Lib Hatcher had been keeping for so long. In spite of their eighteen-year age difference, they had been lovers since at least 1979. They married on May 31, 1991, and it went back to business as usual in their household.

With Randy Travis's unparalleled success, the masterminds of Nashville's Music Row could clearly read the writing on the wall. The traditional country sound was back. Randy Travis was the hottest of the hot, selling some 12 million records during the late eighties. "There was a time when it was thought that a country album could only sell gold or platinum if it crossed over to the pop charts," said country radio executive Ed Salamon. "But Randy Travis shattered that myth when his albums went platinum, fueled only by play on country stations." As the decade drew to a close, the traditional sound of Randy Travis was setting the pace in country music.

MARCH 1985—GAYLORD BROADCASTING BUYS ACUFF-ROSE PUBLICATIONS FOR A REPORTED $20 MILLION AND WITH IT ESTABLISHES THE OPRYLAND MUSIC GROUP PUBLISHING FIRM

SEPTEMBER 17, 1985— *THE NEW YORK TIMES* RUNS A FRONT-PAGE STORY SUGGESTING THAT COUNTRY MUSIC IS IN THE DOLDRUMS

JUNE 1986—WARNER BROS. RECORDS RELEASES RANDY TRAVIS'S *STORMS OF LIFE* ALBUM

NOVEMBER 1987—REBA MCENTIRE AND CHARLIE BATTLES DIVORCE

JUNE 3, 1989—REBA MCENTIRE AND NARVEL BLACKSTOCK MARRY

OCTOBER 17, 1990— NAOMI JUDD ANNOUNCES HER IMMINENT RETIREMENT FROM PERFORMING

MAY 31, 1991—RANDY TRAVIS AND MANAGER LIB HATCHER MARRY

DECEMBER 4, 1991— THE JUDDS' FINAL CONCERT IS BROADCAST LIVE ON PAY-PER-VIEW CABLE TV

When he burst on the country scene in 1986, Yoakam brought a feeling of danger and aggressiveness that had been missing from country music for years.

Country's Explosion

HONKY TONK MAN

If Randy Travis showed that country could stay true to its roots and sell, Dwight Yoakam showed that hillbilly music could be hip. When he burst on the country scene in 1986, Yoakam brought a feeling of danger and aggressiveness that had been missing from country music for years. With his cowboy hat pulled low over his eyes, his torn and frayed jeans worn tight over his pointy boots, Yoakam projected a strutting, pouty sensuality. Unlike most country singers of the day who preferred to stand and deliver a song, Yoakam whirled around the stage with his guitar, scooted across the stage in a gunslinger's crouch, and even played at times with his back to the audience—a gesture of defiance, daring the crowd to stay with him.

Yoakam considered country music his birthright. The grandson of a coal miner, he was born in the coal-mining country of southeastern Kentucky (in the county next to Loretta Lynn's Butcher Holler). It was an area where music was the stitching in the social fabric. As soon as he could talk, he was singing at the local Church of Christ; at home he pored over his parents' record collection of Johnny Cash, Hank Williams, Johnny Horton, and Stonewall Jackson. He wrote his first song at age eight, and he remembers "singing on a swing in a holler, with my ear pressed against the guitar box so I could hear."

When his family moved ninety miles north to Columbus, Ohio, Dwight stayed in touch with his dreams of being a country singer. Right out of high school, he played music in local Ohio nightclubs, and he began regular pilgrimages to Nashville trying in vain to pitch his songs to music publishers around 1976 and 1977. At one point he even auditioned to be a performer at Opryland. But he thought better of that and in 1977, at age twenty, he headed out to Los Angeles, where he worked on a loading dock and drove an airport freight van by day and sang in suburban honky-tonks at night.

It was a rough, lonely time, made easier by the arrival in 1981 of a kindred spirit, guitarist Pete Anderson. Eight years older than Yoakam, Anderson had been playing the L.A. club scene for about ten years when he was introduced to Dwight. Right away, he heard something in the young man's songs. "His composition was really good," said Anderson. "He was writing traditional bluegrass and country songs that nobody was trying to do. And they sounded like real songs that could be on a Merle Haggard record."

Anderson and Yoakam forged a partnership built on their confidence in each other and their mutual love of bedrock country music. They played the music they liked and didn't worry one whit if audiences or club owners didn't get it. "We kept getting fired for playing Hank and Merle and Bill Monroe songs and some of Dwight's own songs," Anderson recalled, "when the audience wanted to hear material by Alabama and the other popular bands of the day. . . . We decided to perform free in clubs where we could play what we wanted to, and make our own record. If it sold, we could write our own ticket with a major label."

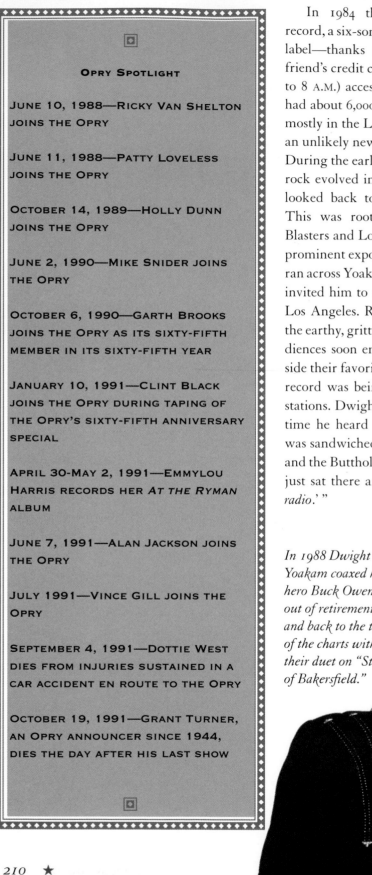
In 1984 they recorded Dwight's first record, a six-song EP on the local Oak Records label—thanks to a $5,000 advance from a friend's credit card and after-hours (midnight to 8 A.M.) access to a recording studio. They had about 6,000 copies pressed and sold them mostly in the L.A. area. There Dwight found an unlikely new audience that embraced him. During the early eighties new wave and punk rock evolved into a strain of rock music that looked back to older styles for inspiration. This was roots rock, and bands like the Blasters and Los Lobos were some of its most prominent exponents. Members of both bands ran across Yoakam in the clubs, liked him, and invited him to open their club shows around Los Angeles. Recognizing country music for the earthy, gritty root that it is, young L.A. audiences soon embraced Yoakam right alongside their favorite rock bands. Before long, his record was being played on alternative rock stations. Dwight vividly recalled that the first time he heard himself on the radio, his cut was sandwiched between the Dead Kennedys and the Butthole Surfers. "I stopped my truck, just sat there and thought, '*Yeah*, I'm on the *radio*.'"

Even though they had rejected him once before, Warner Bros. Records (Randy Travis's label) signed Yoakam to their Reprise subsidiary in 1985. In an unusual move, the label gave Yoakam complete artistic control in augmenting his EP with four new tracks for re-release. He and Anderson certainly justified the label's faith when they belted their first two singles into the country Top Five in 1986, a rumbling remake of Johnny Horton's "Honky Tonk Man" and a sizzling original titled "Guitars, Cadillacs, and Hillbilly Music."

After nine years of working the L.A. club scene, Dwight was ready to seize the moment when his records hit the radio. He had carefully honed a sound that hit as hard as rock but didn't betray his country roots. Dwight Yoakam not only looked like a rebel, but talked like one too. As he moved into the national spotlight, Yoakam quickly developed a reputation for taking jabs at Nashville. On occasion he did. He publicly criticized the head of CBS Records for dropping Johnny Cash from the label after more than twenty-five years. He pointedly said that many records played on country radio weren't genuine country music.

But mostly he

In 1988 Dwight Yoakam coaxed his hero Buck Owens out of retirement and back to the top of the charts with their duet on "Streets of Bakersfield."

alienated Nashville insiders by keeping to himself and making his records his way in Los Angeles.

Few ever doubted, though, that Dwight Yoakam stood up for what he believed in. Right from the start he championed the work of older performers who had fallen by the wayside. One of his heroes was Buck Owens. One afternoon in September 1987 Yoakam marched into the Bakersfield offices of Buck Owens Enterprises and asked the CEO if he would consent to joining him onstage. The retired Owens was flabbergasted, but one thing led to another, and Owens appeared that night onstage with Yoakam. From that first meeting, the two developed an almost father-son relationship, which culminated in a duet recording of "Streets of Bakersfield." A remake of a record Owens had made back in 1972, it became a No. 1 hit in October 1988— Yoakam's first and the first for Owens since 1972.

Yoakam broke through in a big way on his own terms. Through 1994 every album he released went gold or platinum. Every album was produced by Pete Anderson, most of them in the old Capitol recording studios that Buck Owens had used in his heyday. Though in general Yoakam kept his distance from Nashville, by the nineties he and Music Row had settled their differences. He didn't win CMA awards, but he did win Nashville's respect. And no wonder: He brought the hip young audience to country, the audience Nashville had long coveted.

★ THE BALLAD SINGER

Hard on the boot heels of the breakthroughs of Dwight Yoakam and Randy Travis came Ricky Van Shelton. Though Shelton tends to wear a cowboy hat like Yoakam and with his square jaw projects the strong manly image of Travis, he proved early on to be a follower of neither.

Ricky Van Shelton joined Roy Acuff in the spotlight the night he became a member of the Grand Ole Opry, June 10, 1988.

Shelton (Van is his middle name) carved out a place for himself in country largely by singing stately, straight-ahead ballads.

Growing up in the small south-central Virginia community of Grit, Ricky took to singing right away. His dad was a part-time gospel musician, and by the age of three Ricky was already belting out hymns. He became so absorbed in gospel music that he was stunned when he first heard rock and roll in elementary school: He thought gospel was the only music there was. He was twelve years old when the Beatles first came to the United States in 1964, and Grit proved no more impervious to the British Invasion than any other town. Shortly thereafter Ricky pursued rock and roll with the same zeal that he had brought to gospel.

He didn't become a rock singer, however. At age fifteen he had what might be called a conversion experience, and it happened because of a 1964 Ford Fairlane.

Ricky loved his older brother Ronnie's car. Ronnie had a mandolin and loved to play country music with his buddies. Eventually he asked his kid brother to bring along his guitar and his full-grown baritone. "But I was into the Beatles and the Rolling Stones, and country just wasn't cool," Ricky later explained. "I turned the radio off every time I heard it. So Ronnie made an offer no fifteen-year-old could refuse. He said, 'I'll let you drive my car.'"

Before long Ricky realized that he wasn't playing country just for the chance to drive the Fairlane to gigs. He started listening to classic country records and began playing country music wherever people would listen—with various bands at fish fries or clubs, even solo in friends' living rooms. In the meantime he worked a series of jobs to get by—construction, selling appliances, selling cars, pipefitting. As Ricky put it, "You can't support yourself playing in Moose Clubs for $25 to $50 a night."

All along he never doubted that someday, some way he would become a recording artist. His girlfriend and future wife, Bettye, provided the key when she got a job transfer to Nashville. He joined her in December 1984 and spent his days rehearsing and trying to make contacts. Again Bettye came through for him when she became good friends with Linda Thompson, wife of Nashville newspaper columnist Jerry Thompson. Through Bettye and Linda, Jerry Thompson got a copy of one of Ricky's demo tapes. Not expecting much, Thompson was very surprised to hear such an accomplished—and unsigned—singer. Shortly afterward the columnist

Ricky Van Shelton recorded his first album for Columbia Records in 1986. In this 1994 shot, the power balladeer (in the ballcap) is joined in the studio by Sony Music execs Paul Worley (standing) and Blake Chancey.

agreed to be Ricky's manager, something he'd never done before.

After many polite turn-downs, Thompson ended up asking his friend Rick Blackburn, then CBS Records' Nashville chief, to give Ricky's four-song demo tape a listen. Blackburn passed on Ricky Van Shelton. But Thompson was persistent. Ricky's full baritone voice and confident stage presence, Thompson felt, were bound to win over the CBS honcho. So, in June 1986 Thompson arranged for a special showcase performance at Nashville's Stockyard Restaurant. Blackburn reluctantly agreed to be there and brought along one of his staff producers, Steve Buckingham. That night, after a forty-five-minute set that included powerful versions of such country classics as Ernest Tubb's "Thanks a Lot" and Merle Haggard's "Hungry Eyes," Blackburn didn't need any more convincing. Within three weeks, Ricky was in the studio with Buckingham.

Ironically, Buckingham and Blackburn never planned on selling Ricky as a ballad singer. "The strategy originally had a little more rockabilly to it," Blackburn later admitted. "And if you go back and listen to that first record, we slanted it that way." CBS released that first album, *Wild-Eyed Dream*, in early 1987, and indeed the first two singles from it did have a rockabilly feel—perhaps a response to the recent successes of Dwight Yoakam. "Wild-Eyed Dream" and "Crime of Passion" both broke into the upper reaches of the charts, but it was a ballad that clinched Ricky's stardom. The third single from the album was originally intended to be another rockabilly-style song, "Crazy Over You," written by Radney Foster and Bill Lloyd. But shortly after Ricky cut the song, the duo got signed to a record deal with RCA and released their own version of the song as their first single. So Blackburn and Buckingham chose a ballad originally intended for George Jones, "Somebody Lied," as Shelton's third single. Released in August 1987, it zoomed to No. 1.

The Grand Ole Opry can be credited with a little foresight, having invited Ricky to make his first appearance on June 20 of that year, singing "Crime of Passion" and his soon-to-be No. 1 "Somebody Lied." In a foreshadowing of good things to come, he was called back for an encore. A year later, when the Opry inducted him into the cast on June 10, 1988, Ricky Van Shelton already had a gold album for *Wild-Eyed Dream* and a bright future ahead of him.

★ JUST FOLKS

Though many of country's biggest new names of the late eighties were traditionalists like Randy Travis and Ricky Van Shelton, the music still made room for those with different styles. The folk side of country that had brought Emmylou Harris into the fold also drew in two daring young women whose eclectic styles managed to fit into country's mix—Kathy Mattea and Mary Chapin Carpenter.

Growing up in a suburb of Charleston, West Virginia, Kathy Mattea listened to music that was hardly hard-core country. "My two brothers were into everything from Humble Pie and the James Gang to James Taylor," she said. "So I got that whole influence and I did folk music in my church and musicals in community theater. In high school I had a friend whose father had a bluegrass band and I would sit in and jam with them. But it wasn't until I got into college that I really got into country music." It was just about expected that Kathy would go to college. She'd been a straight-A student all along, and she even skipped a grade in school. Nobody expected that she would drop out of the University of West Virginia to play music. But she had hooked up with a bluegrass band at the university, and she caught the fever. In 1978, when she moved to Nashville with one of

Kathy Mattea found her place in country when she leaned on her bluegrass background.

her friends from the band, she only had the vaguest ideas of what she was doing. "I thought, Well, if I go to Nashville and it works out, I'll have a chance to lead a much more interesting life than just 'go to college/ get a job/settle down/have babies.' So I just came here out of curiosity really, and I didn't really think about it much beyond that."

When her bluegrass buddy left Nashville a year later, Mattea was on her own in Music City. She realized she had reached a crossroads at that point. At age twenty she decided to commit herself to a music career. For a year she worked as a secretary for an insurance firm by day and spent her evenings taking voice lessons, practicing, doing yoga, all with the intent of honing her talent. "That was a real turning point for me," she said. "And it was a real growing up process too."

When she emerged from her self-imposed isolation, Mattea began landing jobs as a singer of ad jingles and demo tapes for songwriters to pitch their songs. Demos she sang

later became hits for Conway Twitty and Reba McEntire. Mattea got her own record deal in 1983 with the Mercury label, but it took a while for her career to catch fire. Her material was initially standard middle-of-the-road country-pop fare, very similar to the sort of thing recorded by Anne Murray, whose voice Mattea's rich alto resembled.

She hit her stride in 1986 with her third album, *Walk the Way the Wind Blows*. With the help of producer Allen Reynolds, she fashioned a bluegrass-shaded sound that wore well. In addition, she began taking chances on the work of smart, offbeat singer-songwriters like Nanci Griffith ("Love at the Five and Dime"), Pat Alger ("Goin' Gone"), and Tim O'Brien ("Walk the Way the Wind Blows"). Her gambles paid off in an unbroken string of fifteen Top Ten country hits between 1986 and 1991.

In the midst of this run she hit a personally satisfying peak in 1989 when she recorded a song her husband, Jon Vezner, had been inspired to write after visiting his grandparents

in the hospital. Co-written with Don Henry, "Where've You Been" offered the genuinely touching story of a love affair moving from first blush to its last tearful good-byes in old age. As good as it was, it wasn't the sort of song that anyone initially expected could be much of a hit. "I didn't know how it would play on the radio," said Mattea. "When you're driving to work in the morning, do you want to hear about your dying grandparents and people in the hospital?" When she recorded the song, it wasn't a typical country record in its arrangement either. With a classical bowed bass prominently featured, the austere arrangement was more reminiscent of chamber music. Nevertheless, Mattea's concert audiences loved the song, ultimately prompting Mercury Records to release it as a single. "Where've You Been" proved to be quite a big hit, crossing over from country to the adult contemporary charts. Mattea, Vezner, and Henry won Grammy awards for the record, and in 1990 Mattea took her second straight trophy as the CMA's Female Vocalist of the Year while "Where've You Been" was named Song of the Year.

During that awards show at the Opry House, Mary Chapin Carpenter experienced the first big breakthrough in her career as a recording artist. Ironically, it was with a song that she has yet to record: "You Don't Know Me (I'm the Opening Act)." For her appearance the thirty-two-year-old was asked to sing her wry song about the indignities suffered by those who warm up the crowd for less-than-gracious headliners. When she went out onstage that night, she wondered if she had made the right decision, thinking, Oh God, this is a disaster. I should never have agreed to do this. Quaking in her boots, she delivered. Even though the song was unknown to most of the audience, its wit and wisdom brought down the house that night. Mary Chapin Carpenter got a standing ovation from the crowd of industry insiders. Within months, her third album, *Shooting Straight in the Dark*, was certified gold.

That Mary Chapin Carpenter has become a major star in country music is as surprising to her as it is to everybody else. "Country was not the roots of my musical education," she readily admitted. The third of four sisters, she grew up far from bluegrass country, among the well-manicured lawns of Princeton, New Jersey. Her mother worked at a local private school, her father was an executive for *Life* magazine. When Mary Chapin was eleven, her father was transferred to the company's Asian bureau and the family spent two years in Tokyo. During these formative years she listened mostly to her older sisters' Beatles and Judy Collins records; the closest she got to country were some Woody Guthrie albums her mother owned.

After Mary Chapin's family returned to Princeton and then moved to Washington, D.C., shortly afterward, her parents' marriage began to unravel. Mary Chapin chose to finish

She wears her own kind of hat: Mary Chapin Carpenter never set out to be a country star, and yet the Ivy League graduate has twice won the CMA's Female Vocalist of the Year award (1992 and 1993).

high school away from home at the exclusive Taft School in Connecticut, but it wasn't quite the haven she'd hoped for. "In high school, I wasn't ever a member of the cool group," said. "I just wasn't cool enough, I wasn't pretty enough, I wasn't savvy enough or something. And I was so convinced of all these feelings that that's when I really retreated into playing music, being by myself, scribbling my thoughts on paper."

She went on to college at Brown University, where she got a degree in American civilization and focused more intently on her music. During summers, she returned to Washington and played local bars and coffeehouses, thinking it was no more than a hobby. Gradually the nightlife drew her in. It also dragged her down into a problem with alcohol. "I had a big problem," she told *Rolling Stone*. "It was awful. I had to make a lifestyle change in a drastic way." She recovered and took a job as a grants officer for a D.C. arts organization. Then she recommitted herself to playing music. It was around that time ("I think it was late '82") that she met local guitarist John Jennings. They dated briefly, then became friends and musical collaborators. "He had a studio in his basement, and I'd start going over there on weekends and diddling around." Eventually, they ended up with a nine-song tape that she sold at local shows. The tape soon drew offers from the independent Rounder and Flying Fish labels, but the Nashville office of Columbia Records ultimately outbid them for her services. Columbia issued her tape, *Hometown Girl,* in 1987 with just one new track added. That album was too folkie to offer anything to country radio, but her next album, *State of the Heart* (1989), put four songs on the country charts, two in the Top Ten. All of a sudden she was a country artist. To her credit, though, Mary Chapin Carpenter didn't sacrifice a lot of her artistic integrity in the process. She continued to tside of D.C. in Springfield, Virginia, John Jennings as her co-producer. ... mostly her own songs in a style ... rock or folk-pop than to traditional country.

Her first big record after her triumphant 1990 CMA appearance was a clever change of pace—the rollicking Cajun celebration "Down at the Twist and Shout." It won her a Grammy in 1991, and it proved to be an even better showcase number than "You Don't Know Me," as she performed it to great effect for TV audiences at both the Grammys and the CMAs. By the time she released her *Come On, Come On* album in 1992, she had established herself as an artist with the power to influence a genre. Unwilling to be limited by one category or another, Mary Chapin preferred to embrace them all, calling herself simply a "singer-songwriter," and the music she wrote "slash rock," as in country/folk/rock. Her songs were consistently smart, unflinchingly honest portraits of people coming to grips with who they are and what they want. Propelled by seven hit singles, including the trenchant "He Thinks He'll Keep Her" and the joyous "Passionate Kisses," *Come On, Come On* sold more than 3 million copies by 1995. In 1992 and 1993 the CMA named her its Female Vocalist of the Year. Though she didn't set out to be a country artist, Mary Chapin found a home and an audience there.

★ CLINT

Clint Black had been playing bars, nightclubs, and backyard barbecues down in Houston for more than ten years by 1987. He had played bass in his older brother's rock band as a teenager, but not long after graduating from high school he hit the bars "as a soloist with an acoustic guitar and my harmonica." Handsome, laid back, and confident of his skills, Clint knew—felt in his bones—he could

Clint Black's "overnight success" took more than a dozen years of hard work in the bars of Houston.

make it in the music business. It just took him a while to find out how to do it.

"I sang it all, from the most traditional stuff, like Merle Haggard, to Southern rock and progressive country," he recalled of those formative solo gigs. "When I was growing up and playing in the clubs and the club would advertise I was playing there and I was a soloist, one week I was 'Folk Jazz.' The next week I was 'Blues Pop.' Then I was 'Folk Country.' And it used to just crack me up what these different club owners would call me. . . . But I really wanted to be a country singer." His first stroke of luck came early in 1987 when he had to hire a band for a one-time gig. In doing so, he got to know guitarist Hayden Nicholas, who really impressed him as a player. When Black mentioned his songwriting and how much he wanted to get the songs down on a demo tape, Nicholas agreed to help. Before long they were writing songs together.

One day in May 1987 an admiring music publisher offered Clint $250 for the rights to one of his new collaborations with Nicholas, "Nobody's Home." Clint felt certain that the song could be a hit for somebody; he was hoping it would be himself. Spurred by the need for money but determined not to sell his potential hit unless he absolutely had to, he told a local music businessman about his need for a good manager. The proverbial light bulb blinked on in the friend's head: He'd heard that Bill Ham, the longtime manager of the superstar rock act

ZZ Top, was looking for a country act. Two days later Ham auditioned Black and was knocked out by the young twenty-five-year

Clint Black broke hearts across America on October 20, 1991, when he married actress Lisa Hartman. Here the Blacks enjoy the hubbub at the 1994 American Music Awards.

old's voice and songs. By the fall of 1987 Ham was ready to get him to Nashville.

Hard as it might be to understand today, Clint Black didn't bowl over everyone on Music Row as he had Bill Ham. Randy Travis's record label, Warner Bros., seemed the logical place to start with Clint, but neither

division chief Jim Ed Norman nor Travis's independent producer Kyle Lehning heard enough potential in Clint's ten-song demo tape.

Clint had a much better reception with another independent producer, James Stroud. A former rock and R & B drummer, Stroud had played on an impeccable, amazing list of hits, from Jean Knight's "Mr. Big Stuff" to Bob Seger's "Old Time Rock & Roll" to Eddie Rabbitt's "I Love a Rainy Night." He'd definitely been as close to hits as a man can get, and he heard something in Clint Black. Stroud expressed an interest in producing Clint if he could get a label interested. The next stop was Joe Galante's office at RCA. Through the 1980s RCA Records sold more country records and had more hits than any other label in town, and Nashville label chief Joe Galante was largely responsible for that track record. But Galante had missed out on Randy Travis—just as nearly every other record company chief in Nashville had. He was ready to give Clint Black a listen.

Late one October 1987 afternoon, at the end of a workday, Galante met Clint and Bill Ham's representative. This time they played a tape with Clint's four best songs. As the music played, Galante asked interested questions: Who wrote the songs? Who's really doing the singing? Who's playing the guitar? At the end of the tape, Galante smiled and reportedly said, "Clint, if you don't fart onstage, you've got a deal." In early December, Galante flew his top staff to Houston to watch Clint perform live with Hayden Nicholas and the band they'd assembled. That clinched the deal. After another week or two of negotiations between Ham and Galante, Clint had a fabulous Christmas present: a seven-album record contract with RCA Records.

Since the days of Chet Atkins and Owen Bradley, it had been standard operating procedure in Nashville for country artists to record the songs of Nashville songwriters and to employ Nashville session musicians to back them in the studio. In an unusual show of confidence, Galante and his staff didn't push Clint to consider songs from outside writers or to use seasoned Nashville studio musicians. Galante didn't even insist that the record be recorded in Nashville. The record Clint Black recorded in March 1988 featured his band (with Hayden Nicholas on guitar, of course) and was made in Houston, with a few vocal tracks added later in Nashville. James Stroud and Mark Wright produced it, and all the songs were Clint's. Ironically, of the ten songs that appeared on it, seven of them had been on the ten-song demo tape that Warner Bros. and Kyle Lehning passed on. "Nobody's Home," the song Clint almost considered selling for $250, made the album as well. During the recording of the album, Clint got to take a few spins in Stroud's red Porsche sports car and raved about it. He wanted one just like it. So Stroud made him a deal: If the album sold half a million and went gold, Clint could have Stroud's expensive sports car. As if Clint Black needed any more incentive.

It wasn't until February 1989, nearly a full year after recording his album, though, that Clint's first single, "A Better Man," was released. It was worth the wait. A toe-tapping two-stepper, "A Better Man" offered a refreshing twist on the usual lost-love song; in Black's song, his lost love taught him a thing or two. It was a true-to-life story, Clint later allowed, a summing up of the end of a seven-year relationship. He was handsomely rewarded for pouring his heart out when "A Better Man" topped the country singles charts in June. A brand-new artist placing his very first single at No. 1 was something that hadn't happened in country music in fifteen years. His album *Killin' Time*, released in May, proved just as impressive, going gold in four months, platinum in eight—the fastest-selling country debut ever at the time. It rode atop the country charts for thirty weeks. In January 1990 James Stroud gave Clint the keys to his Porsche, explaining, "I was able to hold off when he went gold, but when he went platinum, I pretty much had to give it up."

If 1987 had been Randy Travis's year, 1989 was Clint Black's. He earned it with solid updatings of the traditional Merle Haggard sound and strong original songs. It didn't hurt at all, though, that he looked like a million bucks, with his deep dimples and smiling eyes. More than one media person spoke of his uncanny resemblance to a young Roy Rogers.

For all the accolades he received Black was particularly honored to be offered the opportunity to appear on the Grand Ole Opry in that first big year. He knew a great deal about the show (his parents were two of the biggest country fans in Houston), but he didn't realize how much history was kept at the Opry House until he made his first appearance there in the early summer of 1989. "I didn't realize that the centerpiece I was standing on was from the Ryman Auditorium stage that Hank Williams, Ernest Tubb, and all the others had stood on," he said. "I remember standing there and just imagining singing 'Killin' Time,' about drinking myself to death, and at that point it just overwhelmed me to be where Hank Williams had stood so many years ago." Almost forty years to the week after ol' Hank made his Opry debut, Clint Black brought down the house.

★ GARTH

As Clint Black was ascending into the firmament of country stars (selling 5 million copies of his first two albums in 1989 and 1990), another gifted young country artist was wondering how long he would have to remain in Clint Black's shadow.

Garth Brooks seemed fated to get out of the gate just behind Clint Black, and stay there. Garth was born on February 7, 1962, exactly three days after Clint. Their debut albums each appeared in May 1989, and even the spellings of their names consigned Garth's albums to appear in record-store bins right behind Clint's. When Clint's album held the No. 1 spot on the country album charts for thirty weeks, Garth settled for the No. 2 spot for much of that time.

Like Clint, Garth found early favorites in singer-songwriters of the seventies like James Taylor and Dan Fogelberg. But Garth also loved the pageantry and outrageousness of glam rock bands like Kiss and Queen. Appropriately, Garth's country epiphany came while riding in a pickup truck in 1981. "In the summer of my senior year," he recalled, "I was driving to the store with my dad and this lady on the radio said, 'Here's a new kid from Texas and I think you're going to dig his sound.'" It was George Strait, and the single was "Unwound," his first hit. "All of a sudden, it hit me. It was like, My God, I love this sound. That's it! That's what I'm gonna do!"

Garth's musical career didn't start right away, however. He was a jock, and that fall he left his hometown of Yukon, just outside Oklahoma City, for a track-and-field scholarship at Oklahoma State University, in Stillwater. He majored in advertising, partied, and gradually moved toward really thinking about a career in music. In 1984, while still a junior, he first started playing clubs around town as a solo act. That year he auditioned for Opryland talent scouts in Stillwater and was offered a summer job singing at Opryland. He turned it down on the advice of his parents, but he had his sights trained on Nashville. He went to his graduation ceremony wearing cowboy boots underneath his robe.

A few months later, in August of 1985, Garth headed for Nashville with a clutch of songs and a couple of years of club experience,

ready to take Music Row by storm. Thanks to a connection, he managed to wangle an interview on his first day in town with Merlin Littlefield, an official at ASCAP, the song licensing organization. The meeting didn't go quite as Garth had planned. While they were listening to Garth's demo tape, a veteran songwriter stopped in to beg for a $500 advance to pay off a loan. Littlefield turned the hapless writer down. When the songwriter left, Garth expressed surprise that the money was so hard to come by in Nashville; he said he'd been making that much a week playing back in Oklahoma. "Then I'd advise you to go back home," said Littlefield, bluntly.

So, after only one day in Music City, Garth went back to Stillwater, with his tail between his legs. But he quickly bounced back, formed a five-piece band named Santa Fe that played gigs across the Southwest, and in May 1986 married a strong-willed woman named Sandy Mahl who encouraged him to give Nashville another shot. In May 1987 Garth and Sandy moved to

Nashville with their last $1,500 and the rest of the members of Santa Fe. When Santa Fe splintered a month later, Garth remained. He and Sandy got jobs working together in a boot store; sometimes Sandy would handle all the customers, just so Garth could spend extra time in the back working on his songs. Meanwhile, he also worked his way into the network of songwriters who congregated at Nashville's Bluebird Cafe.

Sandwiched inconspicuously among a row of storefronts in the Green Hills shopping district a couple miles south of Music Row, the Bluebird Cafe certainly doesn't look like a music business hangout. Inside, with its orderly clusters of chairs and twenty small tables, the place still resembles the homey restaurant that owner Amy Kurland originally intended it to be when she opened it in June of 1982. The only giveaways are the step-high eight-by-twelve-foot stage against one wall and the two ample loudspeakers hanging to either side of it. No more than four or five people can squeeze onto the stage at one time. There's no dressing room. The club accommodates only about 100 to 120 people (who quickly get used to Amy Kurland and her staff's infamous habit of shushing them so the songwriters can be heard).

Somehow, though, the tiny club filled a need in Nashville. By the time Garth hit Nashville, it had developed in five short years into *the* spot for Nashville's songwriters to show off new material and make connections. The first night Garth hit Nashville he went to the Bluebird. The second night he went back and through an-

As Garth Brooks is so fond of saying, he's just a regular guy (who happens to have sold 50 million records). All along, the strong will behind him has been his wife Sandy.

other songwriter met Bob Doyle of ASCAP. In marked contrast to Merlin Littlefield's reaction, Doyle was enthusiastic about Garth's potential, so enthusiastic that he put his money where his mouth was: Doyle left ASCAP to form his own music publishing company and signed Garth on November 16, 1987, six months and a day after Garth had arrived in Nashville. Doyle put Brooks on a $300-a-month songwriting salary and got him jingle work singing on ad spots for Lone Star Beer and John Deere tractors. In late November, Doyle brought in publicist Pam Lewis, and together the two agreed to co-manage Garth. All three signed a deal in January 1988.

Bob Doyle tirelessly championed Garth Brooks up and down Music Row. As had happened with the Judds and Randy Travis, every record label in town turned Garth down. Finally Doyle got Garth a chance with Capitol Records. The label's roster at the time consisted mostly of older stars like Anne Murray, Jerry Reed, Don Williams, and Barbara Mandrell. Capitol seemed like a good place for twenty-six-year-old Garth Brooks. But a live, in-office audition for chief Jim Foglesong and head A & R man Lynn Shults left them underwhelmed. "He was OK that day, but you could tell he was nervous as hell," Shults recalled. "He did about five or six songs, we talked a bit, and he left."

Serendipity brought Garth a second chance. In April 1988 a showcase for new performers was going on at the Bluebird Cafe. Garth wasn't on the bill that night, but he and Bob Doyle went to hobnob and scout out the competition anyway. When one performer turned up missing, Bob Doyle offered Garth as a replacement. He ran out to his truck in the parking lot, got his guitar, and did two songs. One of them was a song he had co-written, "If Tomorrow Never Comes," in which the singer confronts his own mortality and wonders if he's been loving his wife to the fullest while

he's still on earth. Lynn Shults was in the audience that night, and the intensity and conviction of Garth's performance grabbed him by the lapels. Afterward, Shults offered Garth and Bob Doyle a handshake deal on a record contract, to be confirmed the next day with Jim Foglesong. It was. The label advanced him $10,000, which Garth called "the most money I'd ever seen in my life!" Of that, 40 percent immediately went to his managers and his lawyer who negotiated the deal. Still, $6,000 seemed a great start. The night Garth brought home the check, he noticed that Sandy's face looked funny. "She had lost muscle control on one side of her face," he later recalled. "So I took her to the hospital and they had to run an MRI on her and a CAT scan. We had no insurance. The bill was $6,000. It was Bell's palsy, but Sandy was over it in two months."

Capitol Records allowed Brooks and his management to meet with several record producers. Garth settled on Allen Reynolds, a low-key veteran who had produced big hits for Don Williams, Crystal Gayle, and Kathy Mattea. Garth had an idea of what he wanted to sound like on record: a combination of George Strait and Gary Morris, the big-voiced near-operatic baritone who had balanced country hits with stints in Broadway productions of *La Bohème* and *Les Miserables*. Reynolds counseled Garth to be himself and to capture the fire and intimacy of his Bluebird performances. With the help of Reynolds, Brooks eventually recorded ten songs for his debut Capitol album titled *Garth Brooks*. Garth wrote or co-wrote half of them.

Released in May 1989 that first album collected many glowing reviews and the first three singles were Top Ten hits, with "Tomorrow Never Comes" topping the *Billboard* country charts in December 1989. His restrained, earnest performance of the sensitive ballad marked him as one to watch. But that year had

been Clint Black's. Brooks later admitted, "I tried to hate him, 'cause I thought I should, but he and his band are very gracious, very nice people. And he likes James Taylor as much as I do, so how could I not like him?"

In 1990 the tables turned. The change in Garth's fortunes came with the release of the album's fourth single, "The Dance." It was a song Garth had originally heard at the Bluebird Cafe back in 1988, when writer Tony Arata sang it. Garth later brought the song in for Allen Reynolds to listen to, but then forgot about it when the album seemed to be developing a more traditional sound. With its moody piano intro and its crescendo of swirling strings at the end, the song didn't sound remotely like the traditional country of Randy Travis or George Strait. "I don't know if it's country enough," Garth told his producer. But Allen Reynolds convinced Garth that Tony Arata's song with its contemplative lyrics about the value of taking chances in life was well worth fitting into the album.

The song rocketed to No. 1 on the country charts, boosted by a video that hammered home and broadened the song's adventurous message. At Garth's insistence, the video featured footage of deceased American heroes—Martin Luther King Jr., John Kennedy, the *Challenger* astronauts, and singer Keith Whitley (who had died from alcohol poisoning in May 1989).

Garth's first album took just over a year to go gold. His second album sold 700,000 copies in its first ten days in stores. Within a month it was platinum. Its title, *No Fences*, indicated what Garth thought of the music he wanted to make—and its audience potential. A strong indicator of consumer reaction to *No Fences* came with its opening single, "Friends in Low Places." In July 1990, before the single was officially released to radio, a station in Oklahoma City scammed an advance copy from Garth's mother and began playing it to incred-

ible listener response. Here was an omen: Garth Brooks was so hot that radio couldn't even wait for his single to be released. Written by Dewayne Blackwell and Bud Lee, the song painted a rowdy picture of a hayseed telling off a snooty woman and her high-society friends. It walked a neat line between a classic country inferiority complex and drink-fueled bluster. Musically, the record moved from a delicate ballad-like opening to a grungy guitar wallow, as Garth yelped and growled and rumbled with wild hillbilly abandon, bottoming out on the low notes like George Jones in search of white lightning, and then nailing

the whole thing with a drunken chorus. It was "Don't Get Above Your Raisin'" for the nineties. "The day it came out is when it broke loose for us," Garth admitted.

By October 6, 1990, "Friends in Low Places" stood atop the country charts, where it would remain for a solid month. That night Garth joined the cast of the Grand Ole Opry, the sixty-fifth member in the program's sixty-fifth year. Introduced by Johnny Russell, Garth and his band Stillwater came out and did "Friends in Low Places," then "If Tomorrow Never Comes," which he dedicated to wife Sandy. Two songs would normally have

Garth Brooks has never forgotten the little people, which is why he's happy to be upstaged by the puppets on "Sesame Street."

been it. But Johnny Russell said, "I'm no fool—I ain't followin' him," giving Garth a chance to encore with "The Dance." He doffed his hat to the crowd, wiped away the genuine tears in his eyes, and expressed his sincere thanks to one and all for accepting him into the Opry family. Three days later Garth took home his first CMA trophies for Music Video of the Year ("The Dance") and the Horizon award for newcomers.

In deference to the Opry, Garth and Stillwater toned down their act that special Saturday night. On the road, however, they quickly gained a reputation for absolute pandemonium, as Garth swung from ropes, leapt out into the crowd, smashed guitars, and threw water all over the stage. No one had ever brought so much manic energy to the country stage before. As money began rolling in from record and ticket sales, Garth poured it back into his show, making it the most eye-popping spectacle in country music. "When I saw Queen, I pretty much thought, Man, this is the feeling I want," he has said. "But I was worried, because when you play country music you pretty much stand there. Then I saw Dwight Yoakam, and I said, 'Hey, he ain't just standing there. He's all over the place. . . .' I said, 'That's it, that's what I'm gonna do. I'll do country music and I'll be all over the place. We'll pump it up and do everything that a late-seventies arena rock show did, except that what comes out of the speakers will be pure country.' "

By the end of 1990 Garth Brooks had definitely established a distinct image for himself. From his wild multicolored cowboy shirts to his trademark headset remote microphone, Garth had established a visual image distinct from the pack of good-looking young country singers. Musically, Garth had become known for his rowdy stage shows and his delicate singer-songwriter's touch, which clearly separated him from the field of traditional singers like Randy Travis and Clint Black. Up until Garth Brooks's arrival, even best-selling country singers like Travis and Black aired only on country radio stations and their records generally only appeared on country radio charts. In September 1991 Garth rewrote the rules when his third album, *Ropin' the Wind*, debuted at No. 1 on *Billboard*'s pop album chart, topping such popular favorites as Metallica, Natalie Cole, Bonnie Raitt, and R.E.M. This was truly unprecedented. Just to show the achievement

was no fluke, the album eventually logged some eighteen weeks at No. 1, dethroning such kings of pop as Michael Jackson and U2 in the process.

Garth was naturally a shoo-in at the CMA Awards that October of 1991. He took home trophies for Album, Single, and Video of the Year, capping it off with Entertainer of the Year. Who could dispute it? In accepting that final award, Garth paid tribute to two of his inspirations, "My two Georges—George Jones and George Strait." Then he added, "No offense, Mr. President," to President George Bush, sitting front and center in the Opry House audience.

Through the mid-nineties Garth Brooks conquered one realm after another. He always seemed to be looking for new challenges. He released "Shameless," written by pop songwriter Billy Joel, in October 1991. It became a No. 1 country hit a month later. On January 17, 1992, his first TV special aired; "This Is Garth Brooks" proved to be the highest rated show of the year for NBC's Friday night prime-time slot. A year later he was the featured halftime act at the Super Bowl, where he sang his anthem of altruism, "We Shall Be Free." In 1994, he sallied forth to conquer audiences in Europe. It was reported earlier that year that Walt Disney studios had inked a deal offering Garth not only movie roles but also opportunities to direct and produce. Given his phenomenal successes in music, is it far-fetched to think he couldn't do the same in Hollywood?

★ ALAN

Aside from Garth's talent and energy, there was a good reason why he topped the pop album charts in 1991. It had to do with technology. In May 1991 *Billboard* began monitoring record sales with a new computer system that scanned bar codes on CDs and tapes.

Using SoundScan to gather data from record retailers gave a more accurate picture than ever before of how many records were actually selling. Up to that point, *Billboard* had to rely on salesclerks' estimates—and honesty. The week SoundScan went into effect, Garth's *No Fences* jumped from No. 16 on the pop album chart to No. 4 and a half dozen other country stars jumped into the charts along with him. In September, when Garth debuted at the top of *Billboard*'s Hot 100, no less than twenty-seven other country acts were on the pop album chart as well.

Perched at No. 45 was Alan Jackson, which just showed how popular country had become. Like Randy Travis, when long, tall Alan Jackson opens his mouth it is as far from uptown and as close to down-home as a voice can get. In marked contrast to Garth, Alan doesn't go in for rock-style theatrics in his stage show; he performs in the classic country style. His only concessions to the nineties are the big video screens behind him onstage. Other than that, his props consist of the basics: a guitar, a microphone, a cowboy hat.

Born the youngest child with four older sisters, Alan Jackson grew up in the small town of Newnan, Georgia, located about thirty miles southwest of Atlanta and just east of the Chattahoochie River. As he recalls it, music didn't play much of a role in his growing up; occasionally maybe his parents listened to gospel on the radio. "It's not like I was born with a guitar in my hand," he said. "I was more interested in cars and girls for the whole rest of my life than I was in writing songs. I did start singing when I was a teenager. I did a little duet thing with a friend of mine. We later had a band and played on weekends. But I always had a day job."

Those day jobs ran the gamut from K-Mart forklift operator to shoe salesman to barbecue restaurant waiter to car salesman. In 1979 he married Denise, his high school sweetheart, when he was just shy of his twenty-first birthday and she was nineteen. He didn't take music seriously for a long time. He didn't even see a country music concert until he was twenty. The more concerts he attended, though, the more he began to think that being onstage was something he would enjoy. He wanted to be a country singer from the old school, he decided: "It seemed to me that there were no young acts coming along in the tradition of George Jones and Merle Haggard. So I thought, shoot, somebody needs to carry on the tradition."

In 1985 Alan and Denise began planning to get to Nashville. She traded her teaching job for better paying work as a flight attendant in Greensboro, North Carolina. During the six months she was gone, Alan worked on his songwriting. Denise managed to meet Glen Campbell in the Atlanta airport, and told him about her husband's ambitions. The star graciously gave her his business card, inviting them to drop in once they got settled in Nashville. In September 1985 they made their move. Alan landed a job right away working in the mailroom for The Nashville Network. "Being around the shows and everything really gave me a feel for Nashville and really helped me learn the business," said Alan. By chance, he met another young country singer who had begun making frequent appearances on TNN's "Nashville Now." It was Randy Travis, whose first release of "On the Other Hand" had just been issued the week the Jacksons moved to town. About a year later, Alan Jackson got put on a $100-a-week songwriting stipend at Glen Campbell's publishing company. With that incentive, Alan left the TNN mailroom, put a band together, and hit the

Alan Jackson could never be mistaken for a pop singer. The moment he opens his mouth, he's about as far from uptown and as close to down-home as a singer can get.

Next to country music, Vince Gill's favorite pastime is golf. In this 1994 shot he signs a few autographs out on the course at the Vinny Golf Tournament, held annually in Nashville in his honor as a charitable fundraiser.

road. "We played just about every honky-tonk between Miami and Missouri," he remembered. "We'd play five sets a night, five nights a week, and we always played real country. A lot of places wouldn't hire you if you wouldn't play rock and roll, but we wouldn't do that. But whenever we did play somewhere, they usually asked us back."

With his successes on the road and Randy Travis making good with traditional country, Alan thought it had to be his time at last. "I was sure, boy, them record labels are going to be signing every country singer from Nashville to Norway," he said. "But they didn't." In the now-much-too-familiar story, every major record label in Nashville turned him down (some turned him down more than once). One executive even had the gall to tell the low-key Jackson he lacked "star poten-

tial." The label that finally signed him was a new one in town, a new country branch of Clive Davis's Arista Records. Tim DuBois, a veteran songwriter and producer, became Arista's Nashville chief and made Alan Jackson his first signing in 1989.

Working with producer Keith Stegall (who not coincidentally had produced Randy Travis's *Live at the Nashville Palace* album), Jackson fashioned a hard-core country statement with his first Arista album, *Here in the Real World.* Where Clint Black leaned on Merle Haggard for his sound, Alan Jackson looked to George Jones for inspiration. That first album would be the template for everything to follow, balancing introspective ballads about relationships with catchy upbeat tributes to country living. From its opening verse the title track from *Here in the Real*

World beautifully captured the heartbreaking distance between life and art. That record became Alan's first Top Ten hit in early 1990. He reeled off three more big hits from that debut: the lovelorn personal ad "Wanted," the toe-tapping story of every country singer's dream "Chasin' That Neon Rainbow," and the heartfelt tribute to his wife "I'd Love You All Over Again." Though 1990 may have been Garth Brooks's big year, Alan Jackson did all right for himself. By September of that year he had earned his first gold record for *Here in the Real World,* and on October 6 he made his first guest appearance on the Grand Ole Opry—coincidentally, the same night that Garth Brooks was inducted into the cast. That night Tom T. Hall introduced Alan Jackson with a little story. It seems George Jones had visited him recently, driving a new pickup truck. On the front of Jones's truck, the decorative license plate read: I LOVE ALAN JACKSON. As Jones explained to Hall, the veteran singer had met Jackson one day and noticed his truck had an I LOVE GEORGE JONES bumper sticker. Jones had already heard Alan's music and liked it; he figured he'd return the favor with his own rolling endorsement.

With his second album, *Don't Rock the Jukebox,* released in May 1991, Alan again tipped his hat to George Jones, both on the title track and on "Just Playin' Possum," in which he not only played on Jones's nickname but also got the Possum himself to make a cameo appearance. Where the debut album had eventually gone platinum, *Don't Rock the Jukebox* went double platinum, thanks largely to the title track, which proved a surprise favorite among country fans of all ages, but especially schoolchildren. As the song was rocketing up the charts, Alan joined the cast of the Grand Ole Opry, June 7, 1991, introduced onstage by his good friend Randy Travis.

Alan built on that success with a whopper of a song, "Chattahoochie." Celebrating the joys of growing up on the river near Newnan, Georgia, the tune was a catchy retooling of the old Hank Williams sound. The song's popularity certainly caught Alan Jackson completely by surprise: "I think the weirdest thing is that Jim McBride and I were writing it for fun, because we have a hard time writing up-tempo songs. Neither of us ever thought it would be a hit." Buoyed by a fun-loving video of Alan on waterskis, the single topped the *Billboard* country charts for a solid month in July 1993 and won the CMA's Single of the Year award.

Even before he enjoyed massive sales success with "Chattahoochie," Jackson got the opportunity to tour in 1992 with his old friend Randy Travis. Out on the road they co-wrote such hits as "She's Got the Rhythm" and "I'd Surrender All" for Jackson and "Better Class of Losers" for Randy. Working together, they made the country music business look like child's play. And for them it probably was.

★ **SPLENDOR IN THE BLUEGRASS**

By early 1989 Nashville's music-biz types had already coined a term for the likes of Clint, Garth, and Alan. "Hat Acts." It covered all those good-looking young men who sang as if weaned on Haggard and Jones. Of course, the tag didn't exactly fit everybody (Randy Travis never wore one). But the name stuck not only because it was a clever catch-all but also because it embodied a larger truth: Many young male country artists wanted to show, with hat or not, that they had a commitment to tradition.

After years of being touted as the Next Big Thing, Vince Gill fulfilled all of his potential and then some in 1990. And he didn't mind a bit that he had turned down a place in the rock band Dire Straits.

Though most of country's breakthroughs in 1990 came from new recording artists with a Haggard-and-Jones flavor, perhaps the most celebrated chart hits in Nashville came for a couple of young men who had just about grown up in country music. For years everyone had been predicting stardom for Vince Gill and Marty Stuart. It was just a matter of time, they said. Born a year apart, each was a precocious youngster who jumped into playing bluegrass music in his early teens. They were as close to the music as they could possibly get, but still eighteen years away from country stardom.

Vince Gill started out wanting to play like Chet Atkins. At age ten the young Oklahoman got a Gibson ES-335 just so he could get that

Atkins sound. In high school Vince moved into the bluegrass band Mountain Smoke, playing with friends. Upon graduation, Vince seriously thought about giving his other great love a chance and becoming a professional golfer. But Louisville, Kentucky's premier young bluegrass band, Bluegrass Alliance, remembered the tall, good-looking teenage picker from jamming at bluegrass festivals and invited him to join their band. Vince moved to Louisville in a heartbeat. Then he briefly worked with Ricky Skaggs in the band Boone Creek and for two years with ace fiddler Byron Berline in his L.A. band Sundance before stepping into the spotlight with the country-rock group Pure Prairie League in 1977. At the time Gill joined them, the group was years past its one claim to fame, the rock-radio staple "Amie." But Gill and his smooth, crystal-clear tenor brought the group back to life when he sang lead on "Let Me Love You Tonight." It was a Top Ten pop hit in 1980.

That year marked another milestone for Gill when he married Janis Oliver, another up-and-coming country singer, who performed in a duo with her sister Kristine. In 1982 Vince left Pure Prairie League but quickly landed road work and sessions with Rodney Crowell and Rosanne Cash's backup band, the Cherry Bombs, as well as Emmylou Harris's Hot Band. When fellow band member Tony Brown left the band to work for RCA Records as an A & R man, Brown promptly signed Vince to RCA. "I was always infatuated with Vince's voice," said Brown, "so I talked him into moving here." In 1983, Vince and Janis moved to Nashville with their year-old daughter, Jenny.

The Nashville move initially worked out better for Janis. Although Vince was recording for RCA, his records barely dented the

Top Twenty. Meanwhile, Janis and her sister, known as Sweethearts of the Rodeo (in a play on the old Byrds' LP title), racked up seven straight Top Ten hits between 1986 and 1989. At one point, Vince even wrote a song celebrating the misery of his wife's absences for road trips in "Everybody's Sweetheart." It was a passable hit for him in 1988.

While Janis's career soared, Vince could never quite connect at RCA, even though the label had launched such megastars as the Judds and Clint Black right before his eyes. In 1989, after three albums and eleven lackluster singles, he left RCA for MCA Records at the invitation of his old pal Tony Brown, who had joined the label as an A & R man in 1984. One problem Brown discovered right away was that RCA had not encouraged Gill enough to record his own songs. "I'll listen to every song you've got," Brown told Vince. "And if we're missing a certain song, we can cut an outside song. Otherwise, I'll let you do whatever you want to do."

With Tony Brown producing and encouraging Vince's songwriting, he bore down on a new start with MCA Records. The first couple of singles did about as well as his RCA records

had. Then a completely unexpected opportunity arose. Rock star Mark Knopfler, leader of the band Dire Straits, was in Nashville in 1989 to record the *Neck and Neck* album with Chet Atkins. At some point, he heard Vince singing backup on a Patty Loveless album and demanded to meet this impressive voice. They met and hit it off. A few months later, in 1990, Knopfler dropped a bomb: Would Vince be willing to join Dire Straits? A chance to tour with a band that had just sold 6 million copies of their last album? Who could turn down an offer like that?

"It was real tempting," Vince admitted. "I had been a solo artist for seven years before Mark asked me to be in the band. I was flattered but I just couldn't turn my back on what I had invested in my career in country music."

Shortly afterward, in May 1990, MCA released the label's third Vince Gill single. Amazingly, Gill was not at all sure it was a strong choice. He had co-written it with Tim DuBois (soon-to-be-named chief of Arista Records' Nashville division), and Patty Loveless had returned a favor by singing harmony on it. "When I Call Your Name" was a ballad of wistful longing and regret, set off stunningly by Gill's high lonesome tenor. The record did very well on the charts, but what clinched it as his biggest hit ever was singing it on the CMA Awards show, with Patty Loveless right

alongside him providing the harmony. Fittingly, "When I Call Your Name" took the CMA's Single of the Year trophy that evening.

The mournful, mountain-pure ballad propelled the album by the same name toward sales of a million copies—easily outdistancing the combined sales of Gill's previous three RCA albums. The success of that one single finally freed him to unleash his pure tenor voice on sad songs. " 'When I Call Your Name' kind of cast me as something of a balladeer, and I'm happy about that because I always wanted to sing ballads," he said. "That's where more emotion comes from."

With the breakthrough of that one song, Vince Gill has gone on to fulfill the destiny that most of Music Row predicted for him. The 1994 CMA Awards show offered a good indication of the esteem in which Vince Gill is held in Nashville. He not only hosted the show with wit and charm, he also waltzed off with three awards. By the evening's end, he had won the CMA Entertainer of the Year award two years running (1993–1994), four Male Vocalist trophies (1991–1994), three Song of the Year trophies, and various other awards. All told, Vince Gill had collected fourteen CMA awards between 1990 and 1994, more than anyone had won at the show up to that time. And in 1991 he had become a member of the Grand Ole Opry. Somehow not joining Dire Straits didn't work out so badly after all. "I got to work on their next record later, anyway," said Gill, referring to Dire Straits' 1991 *On Every Street* album. "I'm a pretty decent rock guitar player, but my true gift is honestly pickin' and singin'."

★ MARTY

Some performers talk about their high regard for country music's history; Marty Stuart lives it every day. He owns Ernest Tubb's old tour bus and a closet full of more than 200 classic

Can you spot Marty Stuart in this 1976 photo? He's the young whippersnapper with the mandolin, standing next to bandleader Lester Flatt.

Nudie suits once worn by the likes of Hank Williams, Porter Wagoner, and others. He wears those clothes too, shooting for a rock and roll cowboy look he calls "Cash with flash." He calls his guitars "Hank," "Lester," and "Clarence," not just out of affection but because his Martin D-45 acoustic was owned by Hank Williams, the D-28 acoustic came from Lester Flatt, and the 1954 Telecaster electric was owned by Clarence White, the highly esteemed bluegrass picker who contributed so much to the Byrds' country sound.

Reared on the records of Johnny Cash and Flatt & Scruggs, young Marty hung around country music shows at every available moment. At age twelve he began playing bluegrass gospel with the Sullivan Family group. From there, it was just a hop, skip, and a jump to meeting the great Lester Flatt and showing how he could pick a mandolin with a skill beyond his years. Thus, at age thirteen, Marty Stuart got his first opportunity to appear on the Grand Ole Opry with Flatt at the Ryman Auditorium.

A year later, in the summer of 1973, he had an epiphany about country music and his place in it. "We were playing Michigan State," he recalled. "The opening act was Gram Parsons and Emmylou Harris, Lester played, then the Eagles, who were touring for their *Desperado* album. That night I saw that country music and rock and roll were the same thing.

"Standing onstage and working with Lester and then watching the Eagles and Gram and Emmy that night, I saw that young people were really going to like country music. Gram and I jammed some backstage, and he was talking about George Jones and Keith Richards in the same breath. And he was dressed like Porter Wagoner. That particular show changed my life."

Marty continued working with Lester Flatt until Flatt's death in May 1979. For a brief time, Marty, then twenty, played shows

At the time of this 1980s shot, Marty Stuart was still a hairbreadth away from stardom.

with bluegrass fiddler Vassar Clements, then worked for about a year backing up acoustic guitar whiz Doc Watson and his son Merle. The next major stop in Marty Stuart's apprenticeship was a six-year stint (1980–85) with the Man in Black himself, Johnny Cash, for whom he played mandolin, fiddle, and mostly lead guitar. "Cash was my man," said Marty. "He could sing a song about a train, and I could jump on that train and believe."

By 1984 Marty had eleven solid years of roadwork behind him, and he was just twenty-six years old. He signed up with Columbia Records, the label that had been home to his heroes Lester Flatt and Johnny Cash.

Somehow, though, things did not quite work out as planned. Marty came right out of the shoot with a Top Twenty hit, "Arlene," in early 1986, and after that, five straight singles barely squeaked onto the charts. "They kept putting me with producers who didn't see my vision, didn't see where I was coming from," Marty later said. "They wanted me to cut rockabilly songs about fast cars and women in short dresses, and that ain't where I was coming from."

Buddies: Travis Tritt (left) and Marty Stuart teamed up for the popular No Hats Tour in 1992.

The final straw with Columbia came in mid-1988 when Marty recorded an entire album—even did a photo shoot for the cover in Santa Fe, New Mexico—and the label refused to release it. "I turned it in, and they said it was too country," he said recently. Ironically, three of the songs he recorded for that album soon became Top Ten hits for other artists: "One Woman Man" for George Jones in early 1989, "Above and Beyond" for Rodney Crowell that fall, and "Don't Tell Me What to Do" for Pam Tillis in early 1991. Marty left Columbia, disappointed and wondering what to do with himself. What revived him was going back to Jerry Sullivan of the Sullivan Family and playing bluegrass gospel again in churches and at fairs.

When he had regained his confidence and his spiritual center, Marty set out to build a recording career all over again. Like his friend Vince Gill, he hooked up with Tony Brown, head of A & R at MCA Records. In a repeat of the Vince Gill formula, MCA released two of Marty's singles in 1989 without much impact. Then, in the spring of 1990, Marty clicked. "Hillbilly Rock," a revved-up tribute to the Sun Records sound, became the first of many Top Ten hits. In 1992 he won his first CMA award for his hit vocal duet with Travis Tritt on "The Whiskey Ain't Workin'," and in early 1993 he earned his first gold album for *This One's Gonna Hurt You.* Nineteen ninety-two also saw his induction into the cast of the Grand Ole Opry, an honor he has taken very seriously. "My champion cause at the moment beyond this career is helping turn the Grand Ole Opry towards the twenty-first century," he told journalist John Morthland. "Saying what it's accomplished and making sure it still works."

★ PUT SOME DRIVE IN YOUR COUNTRY

When Marty Stuart joined the Opry, he joined his good buddy there, Travis Tritt. They first got to know each other back in 1991, at the CMA Awards show, where Travis won that year's Horizon trophy. A short time later Marty came up with a song he thought might be right for Travis, "The Whiskey Ain't Workin'." "I loved his voice," said Marty. "I

COUNTRY MILESTONES	1976—DWIGHT YOAKAM VISITS NASHVILLE TRYING TO BREAK INTO THE MUSIC BUSINESS	1977—VINCE GILL MOVES TO LOS ANGELES AND JOINS PURE PRAIRIE LEAGUE	MAY 11, 1979—LESTER FLATT DIES AND MARTY STUART MOVES ON	SUMMER 1981—GARTH BROOKS HEARS A NEW SINGER ON THE RADIO; IT'S GEORGE STRAIT	JUNE 1982—AMY KURLAND OPENS THE BLUEBIRD CAFE IN NASHVILLE AND THE SMALL RESTAURANT SOON BECOMES A MECCA FOR SONGWRITERS
1972—THIRTEEN-YEAR-OLD MARTY STUART BEGINS PLAYING MANDOLIN IN LESTER FLATT'S BAND	1977—DWIGHT YOAKAM MOVES TO LOS ANGELES AND SINGS IN SUBURBAN BARS	1978—KATHY MATTEA MOVES TO NASHVILLE FROM WEST VIRGINIA	1981—DWIGHT YOAKAM MEETS GUITAR PLAYER AND HIS FUTURE PRODUCER PETE ANDERSON		

Travis Tritt (right) in the studio with Charley Pride in 1993 working on "Burnin' Down the Town" for Pride's Six Latest & Six Greatest *album.*

thought he was a real singer. I'm talking about a classic voice, a Ray Charles kind of thing." One thing led to another, and the song eventually became a duet between the two, a No. 2 *Billboard* hit in early 1992. They decided a joint tour might be in order. Marty's manager dubbed it the "No Hats Tour," in reference to the unruly, uncovered hairstyles (as well as the unfettered musical styles) of the two singers, and they hit the road in 1992. That's the year that Travis joined the Opry cast. He was an overnight success—after only eight years of trying.

Back when Marty Stuart was on the road learning the tricks of the trade with Lester Flatt, young James Travis Tritt was back in Marietta, Georgia, likely as not holed up in his room with his guitar, Eric Clapton–style. "I had one friend in high school," he said, "and that was my guitar. My guitar introduced me to every other friend I ever had."

After high school he got married and took a job loading air conditioners onto trucks. Soon after, though, he quit that job to take his music into nightclubs around Atlanta. Like Clint Black and Garth Brooks, he started out a solo acoustic act, playing dinner clubs but eventually built a band. Just what was Travis Tritt music? "I'm a firm believer that there's only two kinds of music: good and bad," he said, going on to list his influences. "On one side is a folk influence from people like James Taylor, Larry Gatlin, and John Denver. On the second side is George Jones and Merle Haggard. And then on the third side is the Allman Brothers and the Marshall Tucker Band. They're all balanced together, all a part of what I do."

Today Travis Tritt has smoothly assimilated all those influences into a gutty, bluesy

FEBRUARY 1984—VINCE GILL'S FIRST SOLO SINGLE, "VICTIM OF LIFE'S CIRCUMSTANCES," HITS THE CHARTS; HE'LL WAIT EIGHT YEARS FOR A NO. 1

AUGUST 1985—GARTH BROOKS MAKES HIS FIRST TRIP TO NASHVILLE—AND RETURNS HOME WITHIN TWENTY-FOUR HOURS

SEPTEMBER 1985— ALAN JACKSON AND WIFE, DENISE, MOVE TO

NASHVILLE; HE TAKES A JOB IN THE NASHVILLE NETWORK'S MAILROOM

DECEMBER 1985— MARTY STUART SCORES HIS FIRST HIT SINGLE, "ARLENE"

JUNE 1986—RICKY VAN SHELTON WINS A RECORD CONTRACT DURING HIS SHOWCASE AT NASHVILLE'S STOCKYARD RESTAURANT AND BEGINS RECORDING THREE WEEKS LATER

EARLY 1987—CLINT BLACK MEETS GUITARIST AND FUTURE CO-WRITER HAYDEN NICHOLAS

MAY 1987—GARTH BROOKS AND WIFE, SANDY, MOVE TO NASHVILLE

SUMMER 1987—COLUMBIA RECORDS RELEASES *HOMETOWN GIRL*, MARY CHAPIN CARPENTER'S FIRST ALBUM

sound that fits somewhere between Southern rock and hard country. During his club days in Atlanta, however, Tritt had to focus on covering other singers' songs. So he developed a reputation mostly as a great mimic, rather than a stylist with his own distinct voice. "He used to do a great act where he did 'Seven Spanish Angels,'" said Warner Brothers A & R man Doug Grau, referring to the big 1983 Willie Nelson–Ray Charles duet hit, "and he would sing Willie's part and then he would sing Ray's part. Did 'em both to a T. He'd have the headband for Willie, then he'd put on sunglasses and do Ray's part."

With Grau overseeing and producer Gregg Brown on board, Warner Brothers spent several months beginning in March 1988 trying to extract a distinct sound from this man of a thousand voices. By August, Travis delivered his first single, "Country Club." Naturally, he expected a fall release, but it took a full year, until September 1989, before that first single came out. All the while, the record company wondered if they ought to change his name: It sounded too much like Randy Travis. Among the names that were tossed around were James Gunn, Travis Wayne, and James Travis Tritt, but they settled finally for the obvious.

Like Randy Travis, Travis Tritt had been signed only to a singles deal—three singles to try out before an album. Luckily, "Country Club" connected immediately and was a Top Ten hit in the fall of 1989. The first album followed in March 1990. It went gold in six months, platinum a year later.

"Country Club," with its regular-guy jokes ("I do my drinkin' from a Dixie Cup") and low-key country style, hardly prepared the world for the real Travis Tritt. With his rangy, bluesy voice, he breathed Outlaw fire into the bootstraps anthem "I'm Gonna Be Somebody," then turned around and caressed tender ballads like "Drift Off to Dream." Most of his hits were contributed by other writers. But the song that caught everybody's attention came straight from his own life, Hank Williams–style. Travis's first marriage, to his high school sweetheart, broke up in 1983. His second marriage ended in 1989. "I wrote 'Here's a Quarter' the night I got my divorce papers," he ruefully admitted. That song helped push his second album into the double platinum range in 1991. It also got so big that Travis had to ask fans not to shower him with quarters in appreciation. In 1991, at a concert in Bristol, Tennessee, he got smacked with a quarter right in the middle of the forehead. "It was real gory," he later said. "There was blood dripping down my eyebrows, and we ended up having to cut the show short."

Travis has a reputation for saying exactly what he thinks. Because of his no-holds-barred style, though, Travis was surprised and pleased to be inducted into the Grand Ole Opry cast. "There's two things that make me nervous in performing. One of 'em is singing the national anthem at a ball game and the other one is performing on the stage of the Grand Ole Opry. You walk out there in that circle of wood that came out of the original Ryman Auditorium, where you know that people like Hank Williams, Patsy Cline, Roy Acuff, and Flatt & Scruggs stood and sang over the years, and it definitely is something that makes your knees knock."

★ ★ ★

Thanks to the successes of Dwight Yoakam, Garth Brooks, and company, country music blazed new trails in the early 1990s. Beginning in 1991 *Billboard*'s use of the SoundScan system for tabulating record sales suddenly thrust country music and its artists into the nation's headlines. Overnight, it seemed, newcomers like Garth Brooks and Mary Chapin Carpenter were among the most popular singers in America. Thanks to the hard numbers generated by SoundScan, thirty-five country artists broke into the Top 100 pop albums in 1991. The following year, that number had nearly doubled to sixty-one. Garth Brooks had hinted at the variety of music that could be accepted as country. During the 1990s an array of new artists would break through to acceptance, showing the remarkable diversity of the genre. The Grand Ole Opry, meanwhile, was keeping pace with the changes and laying plans for bringing the sound of music back to its old home.

| SEPTEMBER 1987—DWIGHT YOAKAM WALKS INTO BUCK OWENS ENTERPRISES IN BAKERSFIELD AND PERSUADES THE RETIRED BUCK OWENS TO JOIN HIM ONSTAGE AT A LOCAL SHOW | JANUARY 1988—GARTH BROOKS SIGNS A MANAGEMENT CONTRACT WITH BOB DOYLE AND PAM LEWIS | JANUARY 30, 1988—KATHY MATTEA SCORES HER FIRST NO. 1 RECORD WITH "GOIN' GONE"

MARCH 1988—CLINT BLACK RECORDS HIS FIRST ALBUM, *KILLIN' TIME* | OCTOBER 1988—BUCK OWENS AND DWIGHT YOAKAM ENJOY A NO. 1 DUET HIT WITH "THE STREETS OF BAKERSFIELD" | MAY 1989—CLINT BLACK AND GARTH BROOKS EACH HAVE DEBUT ALBUMS RELEASED

MAY 9, 1989—KEITH WHITLEY DIES OF AN ALCOHOL OVERDOSE | JUNE 1989—CLINT BLACK SCORES HIS FIRST NO. 1 WITH HIS FIRST SINGLE, "BETTER MAN" |

Travis Tritt won't let the sun go down on his brand of Outlaw country.

SEPTEMBER 1989— TRAVIS TRITT'S FIRST SINGLE, "COUNTRY CLUB," HITS THE CHARTS DECEMBER 1989— GARTH BROOKS SCORES HIS FIRST NO. 1 WITH HIS SECOND SINGLE, "IF	TOMORROW NEVER COMES" OCTOBER 8, 1990— MARY CHAPIN CARPEN- TER BRINGS DOWN THE HOUSE AT THE CMA AWARDS WITH "YOU DON'T KNOW ME (I'M THE OPENING ACT)"	MARCH 1991—ALAN JACKSON SCORES HIS FIRST NO. 1 SINGLE, "I'D LOVE YOU ALL OVER AGAIN" MAY 1991—*BILLBOARD* BEGINS USING SOUND- SCAN TO MONITOR ALBUM SALES; GARTH	BROOKS'S *NO FENCES* PROMPTLY JUMPS FROM NO. 16 TO NO. 4 SEPTEMBER 1991— GARTH BROOKS'S *ROPIN' THE WIND* DEBUTS AT NO. 1 ON THE *BILLBOARD* POP ALBUM CHART	OCTOBER 1991—GARTH BROOKS IS NAMED CMA ENTERTAINER OF THE YEAR, VINCE GILL IS MALE VOCALIST, AND TANYA TUCKER IS FE- MALE VOCALIST; MARTY STUART AND TRAVIS TRITT MEET BACKSTAGE FOR THE FIRST TIME	JANUARY 17, 1992— "THIS IS GARTH BROOKS," THE SINGER'S FIRST PRIME-TIME TV SPECIAL, AIRS ON NBC

OK, now you sing it: Billy Ray Cyrus, clad in his standard stage attire of high-top tennis shoes and muscle shirt, takes a breather from his usual physical show.

Will the Circle Be Unbroken?

AN EMBARRASSMENT OF RICHES

Thanks to music videos and SoundScan, new artists have come to the forefront in country music faster than ever before. Back in 1985, when George Jones had mournfully asked, "Who's gonna fill their shoes?" it seemed an open question. By the nineties the answer was a mouthful that included Garth Brooks, Dwight Yoakam, Vince Gill, Mary Chapin Carpenter, and many others.

A music that just a few years before had been routinely accused of being an oldies format had turned youthful with a vengeance. In fact, of the more than 200 acts signed to major record companies at the end of 1992, fewer than forty of them had been recording in 1985—a striking change of the guard in a genre where artists like Eddy Arnold and Ernest Tubb used to stay with the same *label* for decades.

With so many new faces and voices vying for position, it's an exciting, even confusing, time for fans. Video has helped fans connect voices and faces, but with so *many* voices and faces it's hard sometimes to keep up. It's even more difficult to make predictions about who will still be making hit records over the next few years. (Your guess is as good as anyone's.) A few newcomers, though, made a discernible impact in the first few years of the nineties, and in their careers we can see how varied and unpredictable the music we call country has become.

★ ACHY BREAKY HEART

No country act ever got hotter quicker than Billy Ray Cyrus. In its first three days in stores, his debut album, *Some Gave All*, sold a million copies. Less than two weeks after its release on May 30, 1992, it sat atop the *Billboard* pop charts. Billy Ray not only had the best-selling album in America, he had the quickest No. 1 album for a new act in the history of the *Billboard* pop album charts. By then "Achy Breaky Heart," the hit single that propelled the album, was a No. 1 country hit and was fast rising into the Top Five on the pop charts. Those who weren't swept up in Achy Breaky fever could only scratch their heads and wonder: How could an unknown club singer go so far so fast?

Billy Ray Cyrus had worked a long time to be an overnight sensation—a decade to be exact. He was twenty years old when he dropped out of college and began playing in nightclubs around his hometown of Flatwoods, Kentucky, a rural town on the Ohio border (just five miles down the road from the Judds' hometown of Ashland). In 1984, after having built a local following, he moved to Los Angeles in search of rock and roll stardom. But record companies there rejected him as too country and told him to try Nashville instead. Though he gamely hung on in Los Angeles for a couple of years, he was reduced to working as a Chippendale-style male dancer and then selling used cars. "I started getting so depressed that I came to California to get a record deal and now every day was consumed by, 'Well, I wonder if Fred's gonna come back and get this station wagon,'" Cyrus recalled.

In 1986 he returned to Flatwoods and started from scratch, determined to revive his music career. He made his stand five nights a week at a little nightclub called the Ragtime Lounge just across the Ohio River from Flatwoods. By all accounts, he consistently packed the house. Fueled by his local success, he made regular six-hour drives to Nashville to knock on doors up and down Music Row. Little by little, he made an impression and some Music City connections. Still, it wasn't until July 1989, when Jack McFadden agreed to manage him, that Billy Ray stepped into the big leagues. McFadden had previously been the manager who had helped build Buck Owens's career as well as that of Keith Whitley. In 1990 McFadden's confidence in Cyrus gradually won over Mercury Records' Harold Shedd, the A & R man who had struck platinum in the country-rock of Alabama and the Kentucky Headhunters. Billy Ray got the green light to record his first album in February 1991. Significantly, he was allowed to record it with his own band, Sly Dog, rather than the usual team of seasoned studio players. It was a moment of sweet victory when he finished recording the album that July. At that point, with everything he had worked for within his grasp, he then had to return to Flatwoods and cool his heels for six months while Mercury figured out what do with him.

The problem, Mercury execs feared, was that he was still too rock and roll for country radio stations. They had reason to worry. Although Billy Ray didn't record the Led Zeppelin, Bob Seger, and Rolling Stones songs he regularly performed in concert, his original material had just about as much kick. That did not bode well for getting airplay on country radio. Even Garth Brooks didn't try to pass off rock and roll records as country. Without airplay, a new artist's record might

as well be shipped straight to the cut-rate cut-out racks.

Mercury came up with a novel solution to their problem, though, that capitalized on Billy Ray's strengths. He was, after all, a well-built man with nicely chiseled features that drew frequent comparisons to actor Mel Gibson and singer George Michael. During his brief exotic dancing career he had developed a hip-gyrating set of stage moves that spun women into frenzies back at the Ragtime Lounge. Instead of releasing the single to radio, Mercury decided to withhold it and instead offer a video version to country dance clubs and video networks first. The plan was to build up a grassroots demand for Billy Ray's music to the point where radio stations would be forced to play "Achy Breaky Heart." To that end, Mercury filmed a music video of Billy Ray at a local theater in Ashland, making him look like the second coming of Elvis before a throng of screaming, dancing fans. Then in February 1992, Mercury premiered the video at some twenty dance clubs across the country. Along with Billy Ray's video, the clubs received a separate instructional video on how to dance the "Achy Breaky Dance"— a line dance choreographed by Melanie Greenwood (Lee's ex)—and invitations to a national dance contest, culminating in an appearance on TNN's "Nashville Now" with Cyrus himself in April.

The country dance premiere was a masterstroke. During the *Urban Cowboy* era, country line dancing had broken out of its traditional stronghold in Texas and had briefly become a national phenomenon. Though it had proved to be a short-lived fad, around 1990 country dance clubs roared back into popularity— roughly coinciding with the arrival of Clint Black, Garth Brooks, and company. By 1992 about 1,000 dance clubs nationwide played some form of country music for dancing. "Achy Breaky Heart" was perfect for the dance crowd.

Three weeks after dance clubs got the video, TNN and CMT began airing it. Three weeks later, at the end of March, with radio stations practically begging, Mercury Records finally released "Achy Breaky Heart" as a single. After that, the deluge: Within a month the single was a Top Ten hit. In mid-May the demand for the album was so high that it shipped gold. It was an unprecedented achievement for a country artist when the album crashed into *Billboard*'s Hot 200 chart at No. 4 in the first week of June, just in time for Fan Fair.

Billy Ray Cyrus was both the toast of 1992's Fan Fair and its scapegoat. More than 600 journalists and photographers descended on Nashville, brandishing press passes to Fan Fair. Naturally, the young man with the best-selling album in America was one of the top stories. Travis Tritt made the mistake of fanning the media flames when he made a couple of critical comments about Cyrus and "Achy Breaky Heart" to the Associated Press wire service and then to a local Nashville radio station on June 10, the Wednesday of that week. Tritt became the best freelance publicist Cyrus could ask for, instantly elevating the rookie's status to rival. Marty Stuart, never at a loss for words, summed up the donnybrook perfectly, saying, "You couldn't have opened a bigger can of worms if you'd said Roy Acuff was gay."

The furor blew over eventually and Tritt later apologized to Cyrus. When it was all said and done, they realized that there was room enough in country music for both of them. Boosted by Mercury Records' clever promotional campaign, Cyrus went on to sell more than 6 million copies of *Some Gave All* and a million copies of "Achy Breaky Heart" in 1992. Though many music critics doubted he would ever reach such staggering commercial heights again, Billy Ray Cyrus had what he wanted from the start: a recording career on his own terms. As he said toward the end of Fan Fair in 1992, "I'm a lucky dude to be here achin' and breakin'."

★ BOOT SCOOTIN' BOOGIE

For all the attention Billy Ray Cyrus generated, he was not the first country act to win over dance audiences with a rock-style beat. That honor probably goes to Brooks & Dunn who picked up where the Judds left off as country's reigning duo. Prior to joining forces in 1990, Leon Eric "Kix" Brooks and Ronnie Dunn had spent twenty years apiece trying to make it as solo acts. Brooks had made a little more headway, having recorded a solo album for Capitol Records in 1989 and having written hit songs for the Nitty Gritty Dirt Band and Highway 101. Dunn, meanwhile, had placed a couple of singles on the lower rungs of the country charts in 1983. When they met, Dunn had just won a Marlboro National Talent Round-Up contest, which in a roundabout way

Brought together by Arista Records chief Tim DuBois, Kix Brooks and Ronnie Dunn have become one of the biggest acts of the nineties. As of 1994 they had won the CMA Duo of the Year award three straight years (1992–94).

brought him to the attention of Arista Records' Nashville chief Tim DuBois, the man who signed Alan Jackson. It was DuBois's idea to pair Dunn (the one with the beard) with Brooks (the one with the hat) as songwriters. When he heard their first demo recording, he knew they ought to be a duo. "The first song they brought me that they'd written

All's Fair at Fan Fair

People who don't put much stock in country music would never understand Fan Fair. It's the die-hard country fan's dream come true: an opportunity to see, hear, and touch more than a hundred country performers in a week. The idea of bringing country fans and artists face to face in Nashville is a natural, of course. But like many great ideas it only came about when a problem needed solving.

The problem was fans getting in the way of disc jockeys, artists, and managers trying to do business. By 1971 the annual DJ Conventions that WSM radio and the Opry hosted in Nashville each fall since 1952 had begun drawing too many curious tourists eager to meet the artists known to congregate for the annual event. So a committee headed by Opry manager Bud Wendell developed an alternative get-together for artists and fans. The first Fan Fair, sponsored jointly by the CMA and the Grand Ole Opry, took place in April 1972 at Nashville's downtown Municipal Auditorium. For $20 apiece, fans had the privilege of not only seeing some 120 acts perform but also meeting them and collecting their autographs. With some 3,000 folks plunking down their money, Fan Fair was an immediate hit. The next year the event moved ahead to June to better accommodate summer vacationers. In 1981 Fan Fair sold out in advance for the first time when 15,600 people preregistered. As a result, after ten years at Municipal Auditorium, Fan Fair moved to the more spacious Tennessee State Fairgrounds and Motor Speedway in 1982.

Since then Fan Fair has grown by leaps and bounds, regularly drawing crowds of 25,000 by the early nineties. And why not? For the cost of an $85 ticket, fans get a unique package deal: three outdoor festival concerts a day for a week at the 18,000-seat Speedway as well as a chance to hug a superstar or ten and get snapshots. It's the modern version of the pilgrimage to Lourdes. Of course, with 25,000 hopefuls and only a handful of the hottest stars dropping by their booths each day, long lines are inevitable. An eight-hour wait to see a star on the order of magnitude of Garth Brooks is not unusual. Nevertheless, fans seem to consider that a small price to pay for an audience with a superstar, and the crowds are nearly always well behaved.

Part of the fun of Fan Fair is the sheer spectacle of it all. Each of the six corrugated aluminum exhibition halls (where livestock

together was 'Brand New Man,'" DuBois recalled. "I knew we had something special there. It was obvious I had to convince them that they were an act."

Kix Brooks and Ronnie Dunn weren't so sure. Since the offer to record for Arista Records as a duo was the only one on the table, they took it. "Ronnie and I were the most unlikely duo candidates," said Kix Brooks in retrospect. "We try to sing in tune the best we can, but we'll never be the Everly Brothers."

Indeed, harmony singing seemed to be the least important part of their partnership. By joining forces, what Brooks & Dunn mostly appeared to gain was a way to balance their strengths. Dunn, who usually sings lead, has the stronger, bluesier voice. For his part, Brooks supplies the wild stage energy that his more reserved partner lacks. Both contribute almost equally to the solid songwriting partnership. Together, they had

Billy Ray Cyrus's brand-new career was skyrocketing when he appeared at Fan Fair in 1992.

sion with the bass and drums pumped up for maximum backbeat, "Boot Scootin' Boogie" became one of the most popular country dance songs of the early nineties. From that point on, Brooks & Dunn seemed to be able to turn out danceable hits almost effortlessly.

★ A NEW WAVE OF TRADITIONALISTS

As country moved into the nineties, there were still plenty of singers working in the more traditional vein of Randy Travis and Alan Jackson. Hot on the boot heels of the class of '89 came a talented new freshman class in 1990. The ringleaders included Aaron Tippin, a former pilot from South Carolina who combined the sculpted biceps of Arnold Schwarzenegger with the sinewy wail of Hank Williams; Doug Stone, a balladeer whose tremulous voice recalled equal parts of George Jones and Johnny Mathis; Mark Chesnutt, a Texan from Jones's neck of the woods, with that hard-core sound; and Joe Diffie, an ex-demo singer who astounded record company A & R people with his ability to mimic Haggard and Jones.

Of all places, Doug Stone hailed from Alan Jackson's little hometown of Newnan, Georgia. Like Alan Jackson, Stone worked as a mechanic by day, hitting the honky-tonks in and around Atlanta to sing at night. He shared an even more intimate connection with Garth Brooks, though, having been born Doug Brooks; he changed his name for obvious reasons in 1989, the year he signed with Epic Records. He got his new last name from a song he was working on, "Heart of Stone." With his first hit in the spring of 1990, the lovelorn "I'd Be Better Off (in a Pine Box)," Doug Stone was off and running. With his tender voice,

the firepower to compete with Garth Brooks and Reba McEntire.

That first song they played for Tim DuBois, "Brand New Man," topped the *Billboard* country charts in September 1991. The next three singles they released from their first album—"My Next Broken Heart," "Neon Moon," and "Boot Scootin' Boogie"—did the same trick. "Boot Scootin' Boogie" hit the No. 1 spot in August 1992 and showed the way toward their future as dance-hall favorites. Ironically, Ronnie Dunn had written the song a few years before without any intention of aiming it at a dance crowd. "I wrote it in '86 when I was trying to survive in the honky-tonks in Oklahoma," he said. "It was meant not as a dance song but rather as a song about a way of life." Thanks to a remixed ver-

shows take place during the State Fair) is filled with colorful and often outlandish booths where the stars and the fans meet. Most of the booths are lovingly assembled by each star's fan club. Although some of the constructions look like leftovers from a church bazaar, those of the biggest stars have taken the form of man-made lagoons, Art Deco diner counters, buckboard wagons, and giant guitars. Even when a star isn't manning the booth, there is nearly always memorabilia for sale, such as T-shirts, ball caps, buttons, photos, albums, belt buckles, and posters.

Still, the essence of Fan Fair's appeal is the chance to hobnob with the stars. That face-to-face encounter is what makes Fan Fair distinctly country and distinct from any other such event in popular music. "Country acts treat their fans better," a top talent agent told *Forbes* magazine in 1992. "Can you imagine Guns N' Roses and AC/DC in booths on a fairground?"

Stone soon specialized both in romantic songs like "In a Different Light" and "Too Busy Being in Love," and in hard-core honky-tonk workouts like "A Jukebox with a Country Song" and "Warning Labels." He reeled off more than a dozen Top Ten country hits in the early nineties.

His labelmate at Epic Records, Joe Diffie, hit the country charts close behind Stone, with even more impact on the charts. His first single, the nostalgic "Home," shot to No. 1 in November 1990. Immediately apparent in Joe Diffie's singing was the influence of both George Jones and Merle Haggard. It was only

natural, Diffie explained. "My dad had a huge record collection. His favorites were all country—George Jones, Merle Haggard, Johnny Cash, Lefty Frizzell. They were my favorites too.

"I was one of those guys who knew every dad-gum song on the radio and would run people crazy singing them all. I didn't have any idea how good I was, but I could always match their licks."

With Diffie's amazing ability to mimic the best country singers, his friends urged him time and again to head to Nashville. After splitting his time for years between local bands

in Oklahoma and work in a foundry, he faced a crossroads when the foundry closed and his marriage failed. In December 1986, a few days before his twenty-sixth birthday, he left for Nashville. His adaptable voice quickly made him one of the most sought-after demo singers on Music Row. "After about a year I was singing more demos than I could keep up with," he recalled. "Every day I did four or five." It was his voice, for instance, that Ricky Van Shelton heard when "I've Cried My Last Tear for You" was pitched to him. He also did demos that were recorded by George Strait, Garth Brooks, and even Doug Stone. A demo led to Diffie finally getting signed. Producer Bob Montgomery (Buddy Holly's old pal from Buddy & Bob) heard Joe's voice on a tape and knew right then he wanted to sign him.

Diffie knocked out four big hits from his first album, *A Thousand Winding Roads,* and his career has climbed from there. In January 1991, as his second single, "If You Want Me To," headed for the top of the charts, he made his first appearance on the Grand Ole Opry. "As a little boy, I used to listen to the Opry on the radio and dream of belonging," he said. On November 27, 1993, that dream came true when he

Formerly one of Music Row's most in-demand demo singers, Joe Diffie (seen here with Porter Wagoner) has been an Opry member since 1993.

Aaron Tippin was a teenage rock fan when he first heard Hank Williams on an 8-track tape owned by the father of a friend. "I took that tape home and couldn't stop playin' it. I wore it out."

joined the Opry cast. "All other achievements pale in comparison," he said. "It's the only place where I still get nervous and still get cotton mouth."

Aaron Tippin also got signed when his voice was heard on demo tapes. In his case, though, it wasn't the versatility of his voice that got noticed—it was the marked resemblance to Hank Williams that had come from years of close listening. Growing up in South Carolina, Aaron Tippin ran with a crowd of teenagers who didn't hear much in country music—until one night it got to Aaron. "One of my buddies

got a portable 8-track player, but we didn't have any tapes to play in it, except his daddy's tape of Hank Williams Sr.'s greatest hits. At first we were makin' sport of it—whoopin' and hollerin'. Later I took that tape home and couldn't stop playin' it. I wore it out."

After flying as a commercial pilot and singing nights with local bands in South Carolina, Tippin struck out for Nashville where he landed a job as a staff writer with Acuff-Rose Publications, Hank Williams's old outfit. From there, RCA's Joe Galante eventually got wind of his demo tapes, just about the same time that Clint Black's career was taking off in early 1989.

Tippin's first hit came in late 1990 when U.S. and United Nations forces were preparing for battle against Iraqi dictator Saddam Hussein, whose forces had invaded neighboring Kuwait. Many military service personnel took Tippin's determined anthem "You've Got to Stand for Something" as a rallying cry. Tippin actually had written it months before for personal reasons. Because the song fit the mood of the times, Bob Hope invited Tippin to be the first to sing for U.S. troops in Saudi Arabia. Tippin has since followed that Top Ten hit with blue-collar anthems like "I Wouldn't Have It Any Other Way" and "Working Man's Ph.D."

The only singer of the bunch in 1990 who literally was a Hat Act, Mark Chesnutt, labored mightily to be distinguished from the crowded field. Chesnutt was bitten by the performing bug early. His father had sung country music semiprofessionally for years around their hometown of Beaumont, Texas, and even recorded a couple of singles for local labels. "Daddy was the first singer I ever heard," he said. "As far back as I can remember, Daddy was singing. Singin' Roy Acuff songs."

Just as Bob Chesnutt was hanging up his guitar in 1970, son Mark was itching to get started. At fifteen, with his parents' support,

Mark dropped out of school to be a drummer and singer for a local rock band called Fury. (One of the highlights of the band's shows back then consisted of Mark's Elvis imitations.) Gradually, though, he leaned toward country, which pleased his dad, and for ten years built a following down in Beaumont, recording singles for the tiny Axbar and Cherry labels. It was his first recording of "Too Cold at Home" on the Cherry label that caught the attention of MCA Records' country A & R chief Tony Brown. Chesnutt was packing in crowds regularly at a big Beaumont dance hall called Cutter's when Brown caught the twenty-six-year-old's act. He was signed shortly afterward, early in 1990.

Rereleased on MCA Records, "Too Cold at Home" proved a Top Ten country hit. That was a stroke of good fortune. But Chesnutt

It seems one of the perks of stardom for Mark Chesnutt (left) is getting to go out the back door at Opryland with Waylon Jennings.

Trisha Yearwood represents the new generation of country artists who grew up on the country-rock of the Eagles and Linda Ronstadt. In 1992 she not only recorded with former Eagle Don Henley, but also dueted with him on the CMA Awards show.

ville songwriter Paul Craft, the song had been hanging around for nearly twenty years. Don Everly recorded it, Keith Whitley had recorded it shortly before his death, but Mark Chesnutt was the one who launched it to No. 1 in February of 1991. By 1994 Mark Chesnutt was working on a string of more than a dozen Top Ten country singles, including such No. 1s as "I'll Think of Something" and "It Sure Is Monday."

★ LADIES' CHOICE

Although country had been invigorated by the influx of new blood, one couldn't help noticing how many more of country's stars seemed to be men than women. To cite one salient statistic, out of the twenty-two new acts to break into the Top Twenty of the singles charts in 1991, only two were women—Trisha Yearwood and Pam Tillis. What exactly was going on?

Actually, there's long been a perception on Music Row that women can't sell as many records as men. It became standard operating procedure at country radio stations not to play two women artists in a row. Why? The argument goes something like this: Most of the buyers of country music are women; women want to be serenaded by male singers; ergo, men will sell more records. It sounds like unassailable logic, right? The problem is that the premise, if it ever was true, isn't any longer. A 1993 survey by the CMA showed that country record sales broke down almost equally between male and female buyers.

Still, old notions die hard. As of 1994 only one act out of four signed to major label talent rosters was female. Given that distinct minority position, it was noticeable when female artists stepped into the spotlight.

Trisha Yearwood seemed an unlikely candidate for stardom when she burst on the scene in 1991. A small-town girl from Monticello,

also got flattened by a stroke of bad fortune when he recorded a song called "Friends in Low Places." As Chesnutt later explained, "Garth did the demo that I heard of the song. I didn't know he had a 'hold' on the song and that he was going to record it. I thought it was a great song and I wanted it to be my second single, but Garth put it out first." Garth's version, of course, went on to become one of the biggest hits of the year. Chesnutt recovered nicely, though, in choosing his eventual second single, "Brother Jukebox." Written by Nash-

Georgia, she had an early fascination for the records of Elvis Presley, Linda Ronstadt, and the Eagles. In high school she never impressed anyone as the most talented or outgoing. But she was determined. She enrolled in Nashville's Belmont College so she could be close to Music Row. In her spare time, she interned at MTM Records, where, upon graduation in January 1987, she took a full-time job as receptionist. She married musician Christopher Latham around that time and was known as Patricia Latham, a mousy-looking blonde with glasses. No one at the small record company, whose biggest artist was Holly Dunn, had any notion that Patricia Latham harbored ambitions of being a country singer; MTM Records never tapped that hidden reservoir of talent. It was a sorely missed opportunity for the label, which folded in early 1989. By that time Trisha had already left MTM so that she could concentrate on demo singing, where she met another struggling young artist doing demos, Garth Brooks. The two became friends, and Garth promised her that if he ever got big enough, he'd help her any way he could to further her career.

Trisha made real progress in March 1990 when record producer Garth Fundis heard her backing a Nashville songwriter in a local club. "There was this big tall blonde with an amazing voice like I'd never heard before," Fundis said later. Having previously produced Don Williams and Keith Whitley, Fundis knew vocal talent. He immediately approached Yearwood about working together on her recording ambitions. Thanks to Fundis's experience and reputation, by June 1990 MCA Records had agreed to sign her.

At that point, there was no reason to expect the earth to move. Then twenty-six, she had a good track record as a demo singer and had even done some session work singing backgrounds for Garth Brooks and Kathy Mattea. Although her voice had been seasoned by a couple of years in the studios, no one at MCA had great expectations for her. At the time, Reba McEntire and the Judds were the only female acts in country music with sales in the platinum range. Yearwood did have one undeniable asset, though: a voice that married rock and roll power with down-home feeling.

Free of her specs and her married name, she burst on the Nashville scene when her first single, "She's in Love with the Boy," topped the country charts in August 1991. She followed up with two more Top Tens, "That's What I Like About You" and "Like We Never Had a Broken Heart," her duet with Garth Brooks. Her album sold a million copies in eight months, record time for a debut female artist in country. Appearing as the opening act in forty-four cities for her old demo-singing pal Garth Brooks certainly didn't hurt those sales one bit.

Within a year of her signing, Yearwood had become a force to reckon with in country music—at least in terms of sales figures and radio presence. The following fall would see a full-length biography written about her by a business writer from *Forbes* magazine as well as the appearance of her own brand of perfume, WildHeart, marketed by Revlon. It was definitely a long way up from receptionist at MTM Records.

★ ★ ★

Pam Tillis faced her own tough uphill climb. For most of the eighties, Nashville insiders pegged Pam Tillis as the Gal Most Likely to Succeed. She could write, having landed cuts with Conway Twitty, Highway 101, and Chaka Khan. She could handle virtually any demo request ("There was a time when I prided myself on being like a mockingbird")

In 1994 Pam Tillis was named the CMA's Female Vocalist of the Year—a proud moment for her and her dad, the 1976 CMA Entertainer of the Year, Mel Tillis.

with a soaring, scorching soprano. As the daughter of superstar Mel Tillis, she had great bloodlines.

Somehow the hit recording career never materialized, despite a five-year stint with Warner Bros. Dad's career overshadowed Pam's so completely that Ralph Emery on more than one occasion got ahead of himself and introduced her as *Mel* Tillis. In the meantime, Pam married at twenty-one, had a child, and divorced soon after. She marked time appearing at Nashville writers' nights, making other people's demos, even acting in a local production of *Jesus Christ Superstar* as Mary Magdalene. For much of her early career, she almost bent over backward *not* to sing country, trying to define herself as something different from her famous father. Somehow, debuting on the Opry at age eight didn't make breaking into the business any easier. "I'd get to feeling like everybody had their arms crossed and they were sitting back thinking, OK, let's see if you're as good as your daddy," she said.

Finally, after nearly a decade of trying, she connected. One of only two women signed to Arista's new Nashville branch when it opened in 1989, Pam scored right out of the gate with a supercharged honky-tonk number, "Don't Tell Me What to Do." She followed it with three more Top Ten singles from her rock-solid Arista debut, which went gold in 1992. She built on those successes with a gold follow-up in *Homeward Looking Angel* in 1993 and a platinum third album in 1994 with *Sweetheart's Dance*. In 1994 the CMA crowned her Female Vocalist of the Year.

"Dad wasn't real keen, I think, on me being a performer," said Pam. "I just think he had a hard time seeing his little girl paying the kind of dues that he had to pay." With the dues paid in full, Dad gave Pam a little token of his affection, something to signify that she'd finally arrived—a tour bus.

Lorrie Morgan virtually grew up backstage at the Opry, because dad George Morgan had been an Opry member since 1948. She's survived the losses of both her father and husband Keith Whitley to emerge as one of country's leading ladies.

★ ★ ★

Lorrie Morgan seemed destined to be a country singer. Christened Loretta Lynn Morgan in 1959 (sheer coincidence: nobody in Nashville had heard of that other Loretta, who was still a year away from her first hit), Lorrie was the daughter of George Morgan, the Grand Ole Opry's country gentleman crooner from 1948 until his death following open-heart surgery in 1975. Lorrie virtually grew up backstage. The first time she sang on the stage of the Grand Ole Opry she was thirteen; the tune was Marie Osmond's current hit, "Paper Roses." "I got the first standing ovation in twenty-five years," she remembered. "And from that point on I said, 'This is for me.'"

With a voice combining the cry of Tammy Wynette and the homespun embroidery of Dolly Parton, she seemed to have everything

The parallels between Patty Loveless (left) and Loretta Lynn are uncanny—both singers' fathers were coal miners, both singers worked early on with the Wilburn Brothers, and to top it off they are distant cousins.

she needed to assume Tammy's mantle as the next Queen of Heartbreak. Somehow it didn't quite work out that way. She did sing with George Jones, but merely as part of his act. Between 1979 and 1988 she recorded for four different labels without much impact. Eventually, record execs took her more or less for granted. "I'd been playing around town since I was thirteen years old, doing all the local television shows and things like that," she said. "And I think the record labels just— I'd always been there, and I wasn't anything new and exciting."

Lorrie did join the Grand Ole Opry, though, in June 1984. Meanwhile, she made the rounds of all the major labels in Nashville and had been turned down before finally connecting with RCA in 1988, where her husband, Keith Whitley, was a rising star. In a tragic twist of fate, Whitley, who had had problems with drinking since his teens, succumbed to an alcohol overdose in May 1989, just as Lorrie's career was kicking into gear. "Dear Me," her second RCA single, destined

to be her first Top Ten record, had only been on the charts a month when Keith died.

In spite of the trauma, Lorrie Morgan and her career have thrived since then. Perhaps not coincidentally, she has chosen to record songs that express a confident woman's point of view. "Five Minutes" tells a man just how long he has to decide how he feels about her. "Something in Red" describes the full maturation of a romantic relationship. "Watch Me" invites the man to see if she wouldn't follow through on her promise to leave if crossed. Among all the songs she recorded, probably the sentimental favorite is the duet she recorded with Keith Whitley, "When a Tear Becomes a Rose." In 1991 it earned a CMA award for Vocal Event of the Year.

★ ★ ★

Though she didn't have a famous father, Patty Loveless also seemed destined to have a country music career. She was born Patty Ramey in Pikeville, Kentucky (Dwight Yoakam's hometown). Like her distant cousin Loretta Lynn, Patty was also a coal miner's daughter. Her family moved to Louisville when she was ten so her father could escape the mines. In 1971, at the age of fourteen, Patty met Porter Wagoner, who signed the precocious teenager to a songwriting contract with his publishing company. Through Wagoner she got her first taste of Nashville's country community. "He'd take me over to the Opry," she recalled, "and of course I got to meet Dolly through his television show. Dolly was wonderful. I remember a time at the old Ryman when Dolly would go to the ladies' room backstage and show me how to put on makeup." Patty grew into the business. While still in high school, she took Loretta Lynn's place as the "girl singer" with the Wilburn Brothers' traveling show during summers in the early seventies. She joined their publishing firm as a songwriter as well.

In 1976 her career took a left turn when, after marrying Wilburns' drummer Terry Lovelace, she moved to North Carolina where she sang with him in a series of rock bands. For a time, she left the country music of her youth behind. The dominant style of the day seemed to be a middle-of-the-road pop sound that didn't square with Patty's tougher, traditional tastes. It was the music of the Judds and Reba McEntire that alerted Patty to the change in the wind in Nashville in the mid-eighties. In nightclubs she began to get requests for songs like "Mama He's Crazy" and "How Blue," titles she didn't recognize. When she did some digging and found out that country music had taken a turn back in her direction, she made plans to return to Nashville. After seven years her marriage had ended. (She kept a variation of her married name for professional purposes, changing the spelling to Loveless.) In 1985, after being out of circulation for a decade, she returned to Nashville determined to give country music another try. "You just can't take that traditional sound out of my voice," she said later. "It's there. Even when I was singing rock and roll."

With the help of her brother Roger Ramey, she landed a recording contract with A & R man Tony Brown at MCA Records. Her career was a slow climb, however, graduating from an initial singles deal to her first full album in 1987. Not long afterward the Grand Ole Opry invited her to become a member. She joined the Opry on Saturday, June 11, 1988 (the day after Ricky Van Shelton). That was the year she hit her stride with her first Top Ten hit, an impassioned cover of George Jones's 1967 hit "If My Heart Had Windows." Patty didn't stick slavishly to traditional country numbers, however. She liked to record uptempo, strong-minded songs that showed off her full-throated style. She also had a knack for finding good material from offbeat sources. Among her subsequent Top Ten hits were songs from Steve Earle ("A Little Bit in Love," 1988), country-rock band Lone Justice ("Don't Toss Us Away," 1989), and Kostas ("Timber, I'm Falling in Love," 1989). That last song was the first hit for the Greek-born, Montana-raised Kostas Lazarides. In short order, he became a frequent contributor to Loveless albums, and not coincidentally one of the most in-demand hit songwriters in Nashville. "Timber" was also a milestone for Loveless: her first No. 1.

Music critics had been predicting greatness for Loveless practically from the very beginning, and the No. 1 record seemed to signal that Loveless had come into her own. Somehow she still seemed overshadowed by her labelmates. For that reason she left MCA Records in 1992. "I'd been there six and a half years, and I was starting to see success by a newcomer like Trisha Yearwood and how excited they were about that," she told journalist Michael McCall. "They had Wynonna, Reba, Trisha, and it just seemed like we were in competition with each other. It's like being in a big family with a lot of children—it's hard to give everyone the attention they feel they need."

As if those hurdles weren't enough, she had to have emergency laser surgery on her vocal cords in late 1992, with her next album for Sony Music sitting half recorded. For two and a half months she had to remain completely silent. She honestly wondered whether she would ever sing again. On January 4, 1993, she returned to the studio triumphantly. "It was the greatest feeling," she said. "Once I heard myself sing, I was ready to go for it." Her voice felt so strong, in fact, that she rerecorded several vocal tracks that she had previously done. The album that resulted, *Only What I Feel*, proved to be a watershed, selling well over a million copies and boasting such No. 1 hits as "Blame It on Your Heart" and "How Can I Tell You Goodbye."

★ THE RYMAN REBORN

Boosted by such vivid talents, Nashville's Music Row went into overdrive in the 1990s. In 1992 music and related industries generated an estimated $2 billion for the Nashville economy. The fruits of those labors could be seen in the glass-and-steel skyline that rose above the quaint bungalows on Music Row. Between 1990 and 1995 one record label or

An exterior shot of the new entrance and plaza of the renovated Ryman Auditorium. A statue of Captain Tom Ryman stands in front.

music-related business after another built an imposing new structure along the once sleepy streets: RCA (1990), the CMA (1991), Sony (1992), ASCAP (1992), MCA (1994), Warner Bros. (1994), and BMI (1995) were the most prominent.

In the midst of this rejuvenation, it was only natural that Gaylord Entertainment would look downtown and contribute as well. Emmylou Harris had helped point the way when, for three days (April 30–May 2) in 1991, she recorded a live album at the historic Ryman Auditorium. For years since the Opry moved to Opryland, the Ryman had been merely a dusty museum piece, open for tours during the daytime, but closed to live performance because the building no longer conformed to fire codes. With the help of Gaylord Entertainment, though, Emmylou was able to bring in small audiences, just to sit on the lower level. The Ryman rang once again with the sound of real live music as Emmylou and

After twenty years of lying dormant, the Ryman Auditorium was restored to its former glory in 1994, reopening as a performance venue that June.

Newlyweds Trisha Yearwood and Robert Reynolds (of the Mavericks) leave the Ryman Auditorium where they were married on May 21, 1994. "We thought it was a perfect place to blend the spiritual side with the music," said Yearwood.

her new acoustic band, the Nash Ramblers, held forth for the lucky few hundred who were able to claim seats on the dusty pews. None other than Bill Monroe himself joined Emmylou in a little buck-and-wing dancing for the TNN TV crew that filmed the event. The performance also can be heard on Emmylou's 1992 *At the Ryman* album.

In November 1992 Gaylord Entertainment announced plans to renovate the Ryman Auditorium from top to bottom and reopen it for live performances. The official opening date was set for June 4, 1994, when Garrison Keillor would return to the Ryman, twenty

years after the visit that inspired his own "Prairie Home Companion." Before that, two other events were in the offing.

In a secret pre-opening ceremony on May 21, the century-old hall had the opportunity to revert to its original purpose when Trisha Yearwood married Robert Reynolds (bass player for country band the Mavericks). "Neither of us has a church home in Nashville," Yearwood explained. "I was raised a Methodist, but we didn't want to go to a church where we had no affiliation. The Ryman was a church before it was the Mother Church of Country Music, so we thought it was a perfect place to blend the spiritual side with the music."

It was a storybook event, studded with stars like Emmylou Harris and Johnny Cash. The old oak pews all shined from new refinishing. The original color of the hall's walls— a pale mint green—had been restored as well. Decorating the hall were arrangements of sunflowers. Mavericks' drummer Paul Deakin was the best man; Trisha's publicist, Nancy Russell, was the maid of honor. The bridesmaids carried sunflowers, and wore black western blouses with black skirts. The groom and groomsmen wore traditional tailcoats. The bride wore white, but Trisha gave tradition her own twist by wearing a trim formal pantsuit. The couple, who had met two years before at Fan Fair, marched down the aisle to the tune of "The Tennessee Waltz," played with bluegrass delicacy by Del McCoury's band. Then Mavericks' lead singer Raul Malo sang a tender a cappella version of the Elvis Presley standard "Can't Help Falling in Love." The Reverend Will Campbell, Nashville's favorite country preacher, officiated. After repairing that night to their new home for the reception, the couple took off for a honeymoon in Dublin, Ireland—prepared to return to Nashville two weeks later in time for . . . Fan Fair.

A week later CBS-TV came down to the hallowed old hall, just as the finishing touches were being added, to videotape "The Roots of Country: Nashville Celebrates the Ryman." The star-studded special drew an invitation-only audience of country music performers and business people, while the stage offered the full array of Grand Ole Opry talent, from Bill Monroe and Loretta Lynn to Marty Stuart and Pam Tillis. "It has the same personality, it's just better," said Porter Wagoner, marveling at the wonders that $8.5 million in renovations can do, and luxuriating in the coming of air-conditioning to the old hall.

It was originally planned that Keillor would bring his "Prairie Home Companion" show for a live broadcast on Saturday, June 4, only. But the response from Nashville proved so overwhelming that Keillor generously consented to perform the preceding Friday night as well, in the grand Opry tradition as it were. Saturday's show was the one broadcast live over National Public Radio. Appropriately, Keillor and

Opening night at the renovated Ryman featured a special broadcast of Garrison Keillor's "Prairie Home Companion" from the auditorium. On hand for the June 4 show were special guests Vince Gill and Mary Chapin Carpenter.

COUNTRY MILESTONES	MARCH 1979—LORRIE MORGAN SCORES HER FIRST CHART SINGLE WITH "TWO PEOPLE IN LOVE"	1985—PATTY LOVELESS, NOW DIVORCED, RETURNS TO NASHVILLE	DECEMBER 1986—JOE DIFFIE MOVES TO NASHVILLE	JUNE 1990—MCA RECORDS SIGNS TRISHA YEARWOOD	FEBRUARY 1991—BILLY RAY CYRUS BEGINS RECORDING HIS FIRST ALBUM
1976—PATTY LOVELACE (LATER KNOWN AS LOVELESS) GIVES UP A PROMISING MUSIC CAREER IN NASHVILLE TO MOVE TO NORTH CAROLINA WITH HER THEN HUSBAND	1984—BILLY RAY CYRUS MOVES TO LOS ANGELES SEEKING A RECORD CONTRACT	1986—BILLY RAY CYRUS RETURNS TO HIS HOMETOWN OF FLATWOODS, KENTUCKY	FEBRUARY 1989—PATTY LOVELESS AND PRODUCER EMORY GORDY JR. MARRY	NOVEMBER 1990—JOE DIFFIE'S FIRST SINGLE, "HOME," HITS NO. 1	

his troupe warmed up the crowd with a gospel number for Tom Ryman's old tabernacle, and Keillor loosened up the packed house with his remark, "I realize that those are penitential seats you're sitting in." Chet Atkins came on to play one of Elvis's Sun releases, "Mystery Train," and reminisce about how his old boss Red Foley used to introduce him for solo spots at the Opry ("Listen at him play, folks, he's just a kid!").

The Everly Brothers, who had played "Bye, Bye Love" at the Ryman before they did it on "American Bandstand," showed that their harmonies still rang true on old country numbers like the Delmore Brothers' "Blues Stay Away from Me" and Jimmie Rodgers's "Blue Yodel (T for Texas)." Mary Chapin Carpenter offered her thoughtful story song "Halley Came to Jackson" and Vince Gill sang his quiet requiem for Keith Whitley, "Go Rest on That High Mountain." When the time came for his monologue, Keillor waxed nostalgic about his visit to the same hall twenty years before. And so it went, with all the performers seeming to get caught up in the emotion of the event.

Ten days later the Ryman played host to the first of a weekly series of Tuesday night bluegrass concerts sponsored throughout the summer by Martha White Flour. Fittingly, opening night offered bluegrass's founding father Bill Monroe along with Alison Krauss, one of bluegrass's brightest rising stars.

Among the other highlights for the Ryman that first year of its reopening were appearances by Merle Haggard and Bob Dylan as well as a series of Sunday night shows bringing together a wide variety of acts—Amy Grant, Ricky Skaggs, the Fisk Jubilee Singers—to sing inspirational music. The Ryman Auditorium was truly alive and well.

★ BACK TO THE FUTURE

As the Opry neared its seventieth anniversary in 1995, it was clear that country music continued to speak to vast numbers of Americans, and indeed fans all over the world. Record sales had increased dramatically in recent years: from $440 million in 1985 (the year *The New York Times* ran country's obituary) to $1.75 billion in 1993. During the same period, country's share of the total record market jumped from 10 percent to 17.5 percent. More adults listened to country than any other single music format—42 percent—according to 1993 research. Those listeners were not as homogeneous as one might expect: According to a 1993 Harris poll commissioned by the CMA, 24 percent of listeners were black.

All the same, country music has not been without its share of doomsayers lately. Naturally, whenever an art form is thriving, there are always critics waiting around to take it down a peg. What, they asked, will become of country music in the twenty-first century?

What connection will it have with its rural roots when even the homes in Butcher Holler are wired for cable TV, not to mention the Internet?

Those who claim that country music no longer represents the pure mountain folk voice begin from a false premise. As we've seen, it's never been pure folk music from the moment it was recorded and sent out over the radio. From the time of Vernon Dalhart (the opera singer who gussied up country songs) and George D. Hay (who purposely had the Opry string bands dress down to convey a rural image) right up to Randy Travis and Garth Brooks, country music has always been a blend of rural authenticity and modern accommodation. Country's bedrock appeal has always come from the modern person's longing for an idyllic, simpler past.

With country music's history in mind, it's not too difficult to make some general predictions about its future. Certainly, country music will continue to incorporate sounds from the wider realm of pop music. It's inevitable. Country music has always borrowed not only from its own rural and folk heritage but also from the wider sounds of pop music that have fallen out of favor. It happened when Jimmie Rodgers and Bob Wills added Dixieland jazz to their music. It happened in the fifties and sixties when Atkins and Bradley revived forties-style crooning in the records of Patsy Cline and Jim Reeves. Willie Nelson did

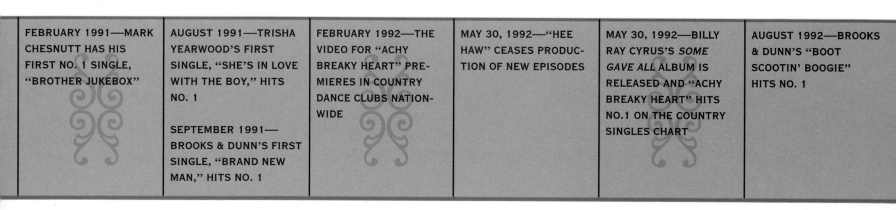

| FEBRUARY 1991—MARK CHESNUTT HAS HIS FIRST NO. 1 SINGLE, "BROTHER JUKEBOX" | AUGUST 1991—TRISHA YEARWOOD'S FIRST SINGLE, "SHE'S IN LOVE WITH THE BOY," HITS NO. 1 | FEBRUARY 1992—THE VIDEO FOR "ACHY BREAKY HEART" PREMIERES IN COUNTRY DANCE CLUBS NATIONWIDE | MAY 30, 1992—"HEE HAW" CEASES PRODUCTION OF NEW EPISODES | MAY 30, 1992—BILLY RAY CYRUS'S *SOME GAVE ALL* ALBUM IS RELEASED AND "ACHY BREAKY HEART" HITS NO.1 ON THE COUNTRY SINGLES CHART | AUGUST 1992—BROOKS & DUNN'S "BOOT SCOOTIN' BOOGIE" HITS NO. 1 |
| | SEPTEMBER 1991—BROOKS & DUNN'S FIRST SINGLE, "BRAND NEW MAN," HITS NO. 1 | | | | |

much the same thing in the seventies with his wildly popular *Stardust* album. In the nineties Garth Brooks revived the styles of seventies singer-songwriters, while many of his country peers celebrated the work of the Eagles. If anything is a constant in country, it is this continual recycling of older pop music styles. Those styles still have an audience years after rock and roll goes careening off into brave new worlds. In 1994 Garth Brooks recorded

with his teenage favorites, the glam rock band Kiss. Who's to say that in another ten years, some as-yet-unknown country star won't record the songs of Guns N' Roses, R.E.M., or U2?

Just the same, country music will always have its swings back to traditionalism. For every Jimmie Rodgers, country music has always offered a Carter Family; for every Jim Reeves, a George Jones; for every Alabama, an

Emmylou Harris. Of all America's brands of popular music, none reveres and celebrates its roots as country music does. Country maintains a creative tension, stretched between the twin poles of traditionalism and pop accommodation.

However country's sound evolves in the future, it's likely to remain rooted in storytelling, with easily accessible lyrics and melodies. In a century of troubling, dizzying

An all-star bluegrass jam at the Opry, April 2, 1994: (from left) Vince Gill, Earl Scruggs, Ricky Skaggs, Roy Huskey Jr., Marty Stuart, and Alison Krauss. "That's what this place is all about," said Vince Gill of the Opry. "Nights that are like that."

change, country's abiding strength has been its role as an anchor to real life and traditional values. That's been the pattern in country music all along. More recently, with the rise of the professional songwriter in Nashville, a whole array of institutional bonds have been forged to ensure that songs come first in country, before dance beats, before great-looking smiles and trim physiques. It's no accident that the music licensing agency BMI transferred hundreds of its staff from New York to Nashville in 1995. Nashville has a thriving songwriting community unlike any other in the world. Through a supportive network of publishers and record labels, Nashville's full-time professional songwriters continue to supply most of the material for country singers—and probably will continue to do so for many years to come.

Certainly, new technologies will continue to shape the music in subtle ways. In the late 1920s new electrical microphones allowed country singers to move from mountain shouting to mellifluous harmonies. In the 1990s a wireless headset mike allowed Garth Brooks to roam every inch of the stage, even

swing from ropes. The next century will no doubt see new advances in recording technology that will allow performers to record from their own homes if they wish. (As of this writing, pop musicians have already sent vocals to recording studios over phone lines; country can't be too far behind.) Meanwhile, consumers probably won't even have to leave *their* homes to buy those recordings; instead, they'll just dial them up and have them downloaded to their home computers.

The trick for country performers in the future will be to maintain the common touch. Early on, country's musicians went out among the people to perform, playing in schoolhouses and town squares. Fans got the idea that a country singer is not a distant star but a friend and neighbor. Today a concert in a large arena is more the norm, and yet country performers understand the need to stay in touch. It's typical for country's biggest stars to stay late after a show signing autographs. Nashville's Fan Fair remains a required visit for all country recording artists.

Which brings us back to the Grand Ole Opry. If the Grand Ole Opry hadn't grown up by itself, country music would have had to invent something like it. After seventy years it has remained country music's single most venerated institution. It's much more than just a museum piece, though. It's a living, breathing link to the past that continues to be revitalized by new talents. It's where the stars come to

OCTOBER 1992—GARTH BROOKS IS NAMED CMA ENTERTAINER OF THE YEAR FOR THE SECOND TIME, VINCE GILL IS NAMED MALE VOCALIST FOR THE SECOND TIME, AND MARY CHAPIN CARPENTER IS NAMED FEMALE VOCALIST;

EX-EAGLE DON HENLEY DUETS WITH TRISHA YEARWOOD

OCTOBER 18, 1993—LORIANNE CROOK & CHARLIE CHASE'S "MUSIC CITY TONIGHT" REPLACES RALPH EMERY'S DECADE-OLD "NASHVILLE NOW" ON THE NASHVILLE NETWORK

OCTOBER 12, 1993—*COMMON THREAD*, A COLLECTION OF EAGLES SONGS PERFORMED BY COUNTRY ARTISTS, IS RELEASED; A YEAR LATER IT WINS THE CMA'S ALBUM OF THE YEAR AWARD

MARCH 1, 1994—*RHYTHM, COUNTRY & BLUES*, AN ALBUM OF COLLABORATIONS BETWEEN COUNTRY AND R&B ARTISTS, IS RELEASED

APRIL 2, 1994—TIM MCGRAW'S SINGLE "INDIAN OUTLAW" HITS #15 ON THE *BILLBOARD* POP CHART

As simple as sunshine: the Opry in full swing.

Minnie Pearl

reach out to the fans and to pay homage to the greats. "Where else can you go and see Vince Gill play backup to Little Jimmy Dickens and sing harmony with him?" asks Opry manager Bob Whittaker, rhetorically of course. "Or Marty Stuart playing backup to Connie Smith and the White girls, doing that beautiful three-part harmony?" Where else indeed.

★ ★ ★

Backstage at the Opry, behind the visitors' desk, is a large oil painting of Roy Acuff, Hank Snow, and Minnie Pearl as they looked in their primes, bursting with vitality. Below that is an inscription from the Opry's founder, George D. Hay:

The Grand Ole Opry is as simple as sunshine. It has a universal appeal because it is built upon good will and with folk music expresses the heartbeat of a good percentage of Americans who labor for a living.

There's actually a little more to the quote that doesn't appear beneath the painting, and it's worth remembering too. "There is no trick about it," Hay added, still referring to the Opry, though he could have been talking about the appeal of country music in general, "and it requires no fancy key to open its front door. The latch-string is always out."

Any way you look at it, the idealistic Judge Hay was right. As long as people want to hear songs from friends and neighbors, there will be a place for the Grand Ole Opry and country music.

That's all for now, friends: Bill Monroe & His Blue Grass Boys onstage at the Opry House.

That's all for now, friends
Because the tall pines pine
And the pawpaws pause
And the bumblebees bumble all around.
The grasshoppers hop
And the eavesdroppers drop
While gently the old cow slips away.
George D. Hay saying, so long for now . . .

— *Judge Hay's Opry sign-off*

Bibliography

Carr, Patrick, ed. *The Illustrated History of Country Music*. Garden City, New York: Doubleday & Company, 1979.

Country Music Foundation with Paul Kingsbury and Alan Axelrod, eds. *Country: The Music and the Musicians*. New York: Abbeville Press, 1988.

Country Music Foundation with Paul Kingsbury, ed. *Country on Compact Disc: The Essential Guide to the Music*. New York: Grove Press, 1993.

Daniel, Clifton, ed. *Chronicle of the 20th Century*. Mount Kisco, New York: Chronicle Publications, 1987.

Gentry, Linnell. *A History and Encyclopedia of Country, Western and Gospel Music*. Nashville: Clairmont Corp., 1969.

Hagan, Chet. *Country Music Legends in the Hall of Fame*. Nashville: Thomas Nelson/Country Music Foundation Press, 1982.

Hagan, Chet. *Grand Ole Opry*. New York: Henry Holt & Company, 1989.

Horstman, Dorothy. *Sing Your Heart Out, Country Boy*. Revised edition. Nashville: Country Music Foundation Press, 1986.

Hurst, Jack. *Nashville's Grand Ole Opry*. New York: Harry N. Abrams, Inc., 1975.

Malone, Bill C. *Country Music U.S.A.* Revised edition. Austin, Texas: University of Texas Press, 1985.

Malone, Bill C., and Judith McCulloh, eds. *Stars of Country Music*. Urbana and Chicago: University of Illinois Press, 1975.

Millard, Bob. *Country Music: 70 Years of America's Favorite Music*. New York: HarperCollins, 1993.

Nash, Alanna. *Behind Closed Doors: Talking with the Legends of Country Music*. New York: Alfred A. Knopf, 1988.

Oermann, Robert K., and Mary A. Bufwack. *Finding Her Voice: The Saga of Women in Country Music*. New York: Crown, 1993.

Strobel, Jerry, ed. *Grand Ole Opry WSM Picture History Book*. Nashville: WSM, 1994.

Whitburn, Joel. *Top Country Singles, 1944–1993*. Menomonee Falls, Wisconsin: Record Research, 1994.

Wolfe, Charles *The Grand Ole Opry: The Early Years, 1925–35*. London: Old Time Music, 1975.

AUTHOR INTERVIEWS

Clint Black (January 1994), Mary Chapin Carpenter (February 1992), Billy Ray Cyrus (June 1992), Joe Diffie (July 1990), Hal Durham (October 1994), Emmylou Harris (February 1992), Reba McEntire (February 1992), Kathy Mattea (February 1992), Lorrie Morgan (February 1992), Ricky Van Shelton (July 1987), Marty Stuart (August 1991, January 1994), Pam Tillis (February 1992), Bob Whittaker (October 1994), Trisha Yearwood (August 1992), Dwight Yoakam (November 1985).

CHAPTER 1

Visit to the Grand Ole Opry, Nashville, Tennessee, October 1, 1994.

Wood, Tom. "Backstage at the Opry." *Tennessean. Hot Ticket* edition. September 2, 1994.

CHAPTER 2

Allen, Frederick Lewis. *Only Yesterday*. New York: Harper & Row, 1931.

Schifffer, Michael Brian. *The Portable Radio in American Life*. Tucson & London: The University of Arizona Press, 1991.

Wolfe, Charles "What Ever Happened to Country's First Recording Artist: The Career of Eck Robertson," *Journal of Country Music*. (Hereafter *JCM*). Vol. 16, No. 1, 1993.

Green, Archie. "Hillbilly Music: Source and Symbol." *The Journal of American Folklore*. Vol. 78, No. 309. July–September, 1965.

Wiggins, Gene. *Fiddlin' Georgia Crazy: Fiddlin' John Carson, His Real World and the World of His Songs*. Urbana and Chicago: University of Illinois Press, 1986.

Crichton, Kyle. "Thar's Gold in Them Hillbillies." *Collier's*. Vol. 101, No. 18. April 30, 1938.

"What the Popularity of Hill-Billy Songs Means in Retail Profit Possibilities." *The Talking Machine World*. Victor Talking Machine Company. December 15, 1925.

"When You Say It—Smile." (Profile of George D. Hay.) *Stevenson's Radio Bulletin*. Spring 1929.

Biggar, George C. "The WLS National Barn Dance Story: The Early Years." *The John Edwards Memorial Foundation Quarterly*. Vol. 7, No. 23. Autumn 1971.

"WSM, the Beginning." *Country Music Who's Who*. New York: Record World, 1970.

Howland, Wm. S. "Station WSM 'Goes On Air' Monday Night." *The Nashville Tennessean*. October 4, 1925.

Hay, George D. *A Story of the Grand Ole Opry*. Nashville: Privately published, 1945.

Macon, Uncle Dave. Undated "Brunswick Topics" record company brochure. Ca. 1928.

Holt, David. "Uncle Dave Macon." *The Journal of the American Academy for the Preservation of Old-Time Country Music*. (Hereafter *JAAPOTCM*.) Vol. 1, No. 1. February 1991.

CHAPTER 3

Wolfe, Charles. "The Legend That Peer Built: Reappraising the Bristol Sessions." *JCM*. Vol. 12, No. 2. 1989.

Pinson, Bob. Notes to *The Carter Family: Country Music Hall of Fame Series*. MCA Records. MCAD-10088. 1991

Wolfe, Charles. Notes to *The Carter Family: My Clinch Mountain Home* and *Anchored in Love*. Rounder Records CDs 1064, 1065. 1993.

Wolfe, Charles. "The Carter Family." *JAAPOTCM*. Issue Number 20. April 1994.

Porterfield, Nolan. *Jimmie Rodgers: The Life and Times of America's Blue Yodeler*. Urbana and Chicago: University of Illinois Press, 1979.

Stone, Harry. "Looking Back." *Country Music Who's Who*. Denver: Heather Publications, 1966.

WSM press releases, untitled and undated, ca. 1932–38. Grand Ole Opry Archives.

Stone, David. "The Story of Asher and Little Jimmie." *Rural Radio*. March 1938.

Harris, Jack. "Huskpuckena—Judge Hay Is Back at WSM's Opry." *Rural Radio*. April 1938.

Wolfe, Charles. "Bradley Kincaid." *JAAPOTCM*. Vol. 1, No. 4. August 1991.

Green, Douglas B. "The Singing Cowboy: An American Dream." *JCM*. Vol. 7, No. 2. 1978.

"Meet Gene Autry—America's No. 1 Cowboy." *Rural Radio*. January 1939.

Seemann, Charlie. "Gene Autry." *JAAPOTCM*. Issue Number 22. August 1994.

Autry, Gene, with Mickey Herskowitz. *Back in the Saddle Again*. Garden City, New York: Doubleday & Company, 1978.

Zwisohn, Laurence J. "Roy Rogers." *JAAPOTCM*. Vol. 2, No. 6. December 1992.

Stern, Jane & Michael. "Happy Trails." *The Atlantic Monthly*. November 1993.

Montana, Patsy. "Portraits from the Most Popular Country Show on the Air, 1924–1934." *JCM*. Vol. 10, No. 3. 1985.

Nash, Alanna. "Pee Wee King." *Country Music*. August 1975.

Scherman, Tony. "Country." *American Heritage*. November 1994.

CHAPTER 3

Morton, David C. with Charles K. Wolfe. *DeFord Bailey: A Black Star in Early Country Music*. Knoxville: University of Tennessee Press, 1992.

Kahn, Ed. "Pioneer Recording Man: Uncle Art Satherley." *Country Music Who's Who*. New York: Record World, 1970.

Delmore, Alton. *Truth Is Stranger Than Publicity*. Nashville: Country Music Foundation Press, 1977.

CHAPTER 4

Mikelbank, Peter. "Places in the Sun: The Many Splendored Careers of Jimmie Davis." *JCM*. Vol. 10, No. 3. 1985.

Pugh, Ronnie. Notes to *Jimmie Davis: Country Music Hall of Fame Series*. MCA Records. MCAD-1087. 1991.

Haling, Elbert. "W. Lee O'Daniel: Sponsor, Poet, Song Writer, Philosopher." *Rural Radio*. June 1938.

Kienzle, Rich. Notes to *Bob Wills: Country & Western Classics*. Time-Life Music TLCW-07. 1982.

Altman, Billy. Notes to *Under the Double Eagle: Great Western Swing Bands of the 1930s, Vol. 1*. RCA Records CD 2101-2-R. 1990.

Rowland, Mark. "Dance All Night, Stay a Little Longer." *Musician*. Issue 173. March 1993.

Pugh, Ronnie. "Ernest Tubb's Performing Career: Broadcast, Stage, and Screen." *JCM*. Vol. 8, No. 3. 1978.

Pugh, Ronnie. "The Recording Career of Ernest Tubb." *JCM*. Vol. 9, No. 1. 1978.

Pugh, Ronnie. "Ernest Tubb." *JAAPOTCM*. Issue Number 14. April 1993.

Allen, Bob. "Acuff on Exhibit." *JCM*. Vol. 10, No. 1. 1985.

Rumble, John W. Notes to *Roy Acuff: Country & Western Classics*. Time-Life Music TLCW-09. 1983.

Rumble, John W. Notes to *The Music of Bill Monroe, 1936–1994*. MCA Records MCAD4-11048. 1994.

Cannon, Sarah with Susan Quick. "Minnie's Memories" column. *Nashville Banner*. February 3, 1986–March 16, 1987.

Reeve, Catharine. "Sarah Cannon: I Was Not Going to Be Like Everybody Else." *Chicago Tribune*. March 12, 1989.

Wolfe, Charles. "Roy Acuff." *JAAPOTCM*. Vol. 2, No. 3. June 1992.

Mikelbank, Peter. "Like the Wabash Cannonball and the Night Train to Memphis Rolled into One." *Nashville*. July 1986.

CHAPTER 5

King, Larry L. "The Grand Ole Opry." *Harper's*. July 1968.

Leiter, Robert D. *The Musicians and Petrillo*. New York: Bookman Associates, Inc., 1953.

"Hillbilly Tunes Gain in Popularity in Baltimore." *Billboard*. March 6, 1943.

Rumble, John W. "Fred Rose and the Development of the Nashville Music Industry." Ph.D. dissertation. Vanderbilt University, 1980.

Betts, Ann. "Ryman Auditorium: The Best One-Night Stand in the Country." *Nashville*. July 1986.

Kienzle, Rich. Notes to *Bob Wills: Country & Western Classics*. Time-Life Music TLCW-07. 1982.

"Country Music Is Big Business, and Nashville Is Its Detroit." *Newsweek*. August 11, 1952.

Humphrey, Mark. "Interview: Merle Travis." Parts 1–4. *Old Time Music*. Numbers 36–39. Summer 1981–Spring 1984.

Travis, Merle. "Recollections of Merle Travis, 1944–1955, Parts 1 & 2." *The John Edwards Memorial Foundation Quarterly*. Vol. 15, Nos. 54–55. Summer 1979–Autumn 1979.

Wolfe, Charles. "The Brown's Ferry Four." *JAAPOTCM*. Issue Number 19. February 1994.

Pugh, Ronnie. Notes to *Grandpa Jones: Country Music Hall of Fame Series*. MCA Records. MCAD-10549. 1992.

Rumble, John. Notes to *Red Foley: Country Music Hall of Fame Series*. MCA Records MCAD-10084. 1991.

Kienzle, Rich. "Eddy Arnold." *JAAPOTCM*. Issue Number 15. June 1993.

Thompson, Marvin. Notes to *Eddy Arnold: Legendary Performances*. RCA Records CPL2-4885. 1983.

"Corn of Plenty." *Newsweek*. June 13, 1949.

Rumble, John W. "The Emergence of Nashville As a Recording Center: Logbooks from the Castle Studio, 1952–1953." *JCM*. Vol. 7, No. 3. 1978.

Flans, Robyn. "The History of Nashville Recording." *Mix*. March 1988.

Smith, Marian. "Castle Records: Where the Boom Began." *Billboard*. April 15, 1970.

Escott, Colin with George Merritt and William MacEwen. *Hank Williams: The Biography*. Boston and New York: Little, Brown & Company, 1994.

Jarman, Rufus. "Country Music Goes to Town." *Nation's Business*. February 1953.

Williams, Roger. Notes to *Hank Williams: Country & Western Classics*. Time-Life Music TLCW-01. 1981.

Waldron, Eli. "Country Music: The Death of Hank Williams." *The Reporter*. May 19, 1955.

Cobb, David. "Birth of Music City, U.S.A." *Nashville*. July 1986.

Oermann, Robert K. "Nashville Is Music City for a Reason." *The Songs That Made Nashville Music City USA*. Milwaukee: Hal Leonard, 1983.

"History of the Grand Ole Opry House." *Country Music Who's Who*. New York: Record World, 1970.

Rogers, Joe. "100 Years of the Ryman." *Tennessean*. Special Section. May 17, 1992.

"Grand Opry." *Newsweek*. October 18, 1943.

Smith, Sandy. "Ryman's Roots Still Growing." *The Tennessean*. June 25, 1994.

CHAPTER 6

Scherman, Tony. "Country." *American Heritage*. November 1994.

Halberstam, David. *The Fifties*. New York: Villard Books, 1993.

Pugh, Ronnie. Notes to *Webb Pierce: King of the Honky-Tonk*. Country Music Foundation Records CMF-0019D. 1994.

Kitsinger, Otto. Notes to *Webb Pierce: The Wondering Boy, 1951–1958*. Bear Family Records BCD 15522. 1991.

Haggard, John. "Bud Isaacs: His Version of 'Slowly' Revolutionized the Sound of Pedal Steel." *Guitar Player*. November 1976.

Wolfe, Charles. Notes to *The Best of Lefty Frizzell*. Rhino Records R2 71005. 1991.

Wolfe, Charles. "Lefty Frizzell." *JAAPOTCM*. Vol. 1, No. 4. August 1991.

Mitchum, Petrine. *Rhinestone Cowboy: The Story of Nudie the Rodeo Tailor*. Unpublished manuscript, 1979.

Tribe, Ivan. *Mountaineer Jamboree: Country Music in West Virginia*. Lexington: University of Kentucky Press, 1984.

Snow, Hank with Jack Ownbey and Bob Burris. *The Hank Snow Story*. Urbana and Chicago: University of Illinois Press, 1994.

Wolfe, Charles. "Hank Snow." *JAAPOTCM*. Vol. 1, No. 2. April 1991.

Pugh, Ronnie. Notes to *Kitty Wells: Country Music Hall of Fame Series*. MCA Records MCAD-10081. 1991.

Wolfe, Charles. Notes to *Kitty Wells: The Golden Years, 1949–1957*. Bear Family Records BFX 15239. 1987.

"Woman Put on Earth for Man to Look After, Kitty Wells Says." *Country Style*. August 1976.

"Owen Bradley: Music City's Music Man." *The Nashville Musician*. Vol. 3, No. 2. August-September 1988.

Sparks, Jim. "An Interview with Owen Bradley." *Advantage Magazine*. October 1984.

Flippo, Chet. "Owen Bradley's Nashville." *Rolling Stone*. July 14, 1977.

Escott, Colin with Martin Hawkins. *Good Rockin' Tonight: Sun Records and the Birth of Rock 'n' Roll*. New York: St. Martin's Press, 1991.

Guralnick, Peter. *Last Train to Memphis: The Rise of Elvis Presley*. New York: Little, Brown, 1994.

Hemphill, Paul. *The Nashville Sound: Bright Lights and Country Music*. New York: Simon and Schuster, 1970.

Everett, Todd. Notes to *Buddy Holly: A Rock and Roll Collection*. MCA Records. MCA2-4009. 1977.

CHAPTER 7

"Grand Ole Opry." WSM press releases, undated, ca. 1956 and January 1, 1958. Grand Ole Opry archives.

Cunniff, Al. "Muscle Behind the Music: The Life and Times of Jim Denny, Parts 1–2." *JCM*. Vol. 11, Nos. 1–3. 1986–87.

Newman, Clarence B. "Homespun Harmony: Hillbilly

Music Sells Rural Customers, Keeps Record Counters Busy." *The Wall Street Journal.* May 3, 1957.

Atkins, Chet. "How Chet Atkins Did It." *JCM.* Vol. 12, No. 2. 1989.

McCall, Michael. "Owen Bradley: The Way We Were." *JCM.* Vol. 12, No. 2. 1989.

McCall, Michael. "Owen Bradley's 'Invigorating Therapy.' " *Nashville Banner.* June 9, 1988.

Sweat, Joseph. "The Brenda Lee Story." *Billboard.* May 28, 1966.

Jones, Margaret. *Patsy: The Life and Times of Patsy Cline.* New York: HarperCollins, 1994.

Hall, Patricia with Ronnie Pugh. Notes to *Marty Robbins: Country & Western Classics.* Time-Life Music TLCW-10. 1983.

Pruett, Barbara J. *Marty Robbins: Fast Cars and Country Music.* Metuchen, N.J.: Scarecrow Press, 1990.

CHAPTER 8

Rosenberg, Neil. Notes to *Flatt & Scruggs: Country & Western Classics.* Time-Life Music TLCW-04. 1982.

Danker, Frederick. Notes to *Johnny Cash: Country & Western Classics.* Time-Life Music TLCW-03. 1982.

Flanagan, Bill. "Johnny Cash, American." *Musician.* May 1988.

Pond, Steve. "Johnny Cash: The Hard Reign of a Country-Music King." *Rolling Stone.* December 10–24, 1992.

Hannah, Barry. "Big Country." *Spin.* July 1994.

Cash, Johnny. *Man in Black.* Grand Rapids, Michigan: Zondervan Publishing House, 1975.

"Opry House Audience Is 'A Rare Thing.' " *The Nashville Tennessean.* October 11, 1970.

Fenster, Mark. "Under His Spell: How Buck Owens Took Care of Business." *JCM.* Vol. 12, No. 3. 1989.

Kienzle, Rich. Notes to *The Buck Owens Collection (1959–1990).* Rhino Records R2 71016. 1992.

Hemphill, Paul. "Merle Haggard: 'When you're runnin' down our country, hoss, you're walkin' on the fightin' side of me.' " *The Atlantic.* September 1971.

Shirley, Essida. "Merle Haggard: I Believe In. . . ." *Hit Parader.* December 1973.

Di Salvatore, Bryan. "Profiles: Ornery." *The New Yorker.* February 12, 1990.

"Nashville Racial Tensions Cancel 'Grand Ole Opry.' " *Billboard.* April 20, 1968.

Schlappi, Elizabeth. *Roy Acuff: The Smoky Mountain Boy.* Gretna, Louisiana: Pelican Publishing Company, 1978.

CHAPTER 9

Dew, Joan. *Singers and Sweethearts: The Women of Country Music.* (Garden City, New York: Doubleday and Company, 1977).

Skinker, Chris. Notes to *Loretta Lynn: Country Music Hall of Fame Series.* MCA Records MCAD-10083. 1991.

Axthelm, Pete. "Lookin' at Country with Loretta Lynn." *Newsweek.* June 18, 1973.

Zwisohn, Laurence J. "Loretta Lynn." *JAAPOTCM.* Issue Number 17. October 1993.

McCall, Michael. "Owen Bradley's 'Invigorating Therapy.' " *Nashville Banner.* June 9, 1988.

Kienzle, Rich. "Off the Record: Loretta Lynn, 'Honky Tonk Girl.' " *JAAPOTCM.* Vol. 1, No. 4. August 1991.

Dew, Joan with Don Cusic. Notes to *Tammy Wynette: Country & Western Classics.* Time-Life Music TLCW-13. 1983.

Wolfe, Charles. Notes to *George Jones: Country & Western Classics.* Time-Life Music TLCW-08. 1982.

Parton, Dolly. *Dolly: My Life and Other Unfinished Business.* New York: HarperCollins Publishers, 1994.

Chase, Chris. "The Country Girl." *New York Times Magazine.* May 9, 1976.

Flippo, Chet. "Dolly Parton." *Rolling Stone.* August 25, 1977.

Oermann, Robert K. & Mary A. Bufwack. Notes to *Dolly Parton: The RCA Years, 1967–1986.* RCA Records RCA 07863-66127-2. 1993.

Wagoner, Porter with Glen Hunter. "Hello, Dolly." *JCM.* Vol. 10, No. 1.

Eng, Steve. *A Satisfied Mind: The Country Music Life of Porter Wagoner.* Nashville: Rutledge Hill Press, 1992.

Bailey, Jerry. "Porter, Dolly Breaking Up Singing Team." *The Nashville Tennessean.* February 20, 1974.

CHAPTER 10

"Starday Buys King Records." (Includes Opryland announcement.) *The Nashville Tennessean.* October 19, 1968.

"Opryland U.S.A. Opens." *CMA Close Up.* June 1972.

Carr, Patrick. "Nashville's Biggest Weekend: Farewell to the Ryman, Hello to Opryland." *Country Music.* June 1974.

Keillor, Garrison. "At the Opry." *The New Yorker.* May 6, 1974.

Keillor, Garrison. Remarks during broadcast of "Prairie Home Companion" from Ryman Auditorium, NPR, June 4, 1994.

Guralnick, Peter. *Lost Highway: Journeys and Arrivals of American Musicians.* Boston: David R. Godine, Publisher, 1979.

Bane, Michael. *The Outlaws: Revolution in Country Music.* Garden City, New York: Dolphin/Doubleday, 1978.

Cunniff, Albert. *Waylon Jennings.* New York: Zebra Books, 1985.

Nelson, Willie with Bud Shrake. *Willie: An Autobiography.* New York: Simon and Schuster, 1988.

Kienzle, Rich. Notes to *Willie Nelson: Country & Western Classics.* Time-Life Music TLCW-11. 1983.

Bane, Michael. *Willie Nelson.* New York: Dell Publishing Company, 1984.

"Willie Nelson: There Are No Laws." *Life Collector's Edition: The Roots of Country Music.* September 1, 1994.

Escott, Colin. Notes to *Living Proof: The MGM Recordings, 1963–1975.* Mercury Records 314-517320-4. 1992.

Forte, Dan. "Hank Williams, Jr." *Guitar Player.* May 1985.

Morris, Edward. *Alabama.* Chicago: Contemporary Books, 1985.

"Nashville Watches 'Nashville'—and Comes Away Puzzled." *Tennessean.* August 9, 1975.

Hance, Bill. " 'Nashville' Premiere Churns Sour Reaction." *Nashville Banner.* August 9, 1975.

CHAPTER 11

Mandrell, Barbara with George Vecsey. *Get to the Heart: My Story.* New York: Bantam Books, 1990.

Wolfe, Charles. Notes to *George Jones: Country & Western Classics.* Time-Life Music TLCW-08. 1982.

Tosches, Nick. "George Jones: The Grand Tour." *JCM.* Vol. 16, No. 3. 1994.

Hunter, James. "The Ballad of No-Show Jones." *The New York Times Magazine.* March 15, 1992.

Allen, Bob. *George Jones: The Saga of an American Singer.* Garden City, New York: Dolphin/Doubleday, 1984.

Harris, Emmylou. Letter to *Sing Out!* September 1965.

Obrecht, Jas. "Emmylou Harris." *Guitar Player.* November 1978.

Griffin, Sid. *Gram Parsons: A Music Biography.* Pasadena, California: Sierra Books, 1985.

Fong-Torres, Ben. *Hickory Wind: The Life and Times of Gram Parsons.* New York: Pocket Books, 1991.

Fong-Torres, Ben. "Emmylou Harris: Whole-Wheat Honky-Tonk." *Rolling Stone.* February 23, 1978.

"Emmylou Harris: The Circle Is Unbroken." *Life Collector's Edition: The Roots of Country Music.* September 1, 1994.

Kirby, Kip. "Emmylou." *Country Music.* September 1980.

Allen, Bob. "Emmylou Harris Tapped the Traditional Sound." *JAAPOTCM.* Vol. 1, No. 4. August 1991.

Humphrey, Mark. "Skaggs Speaks Out Against Country Radio Programming." *Los Angeles Daily News.* November 8, 1985.

Carr, Patrick. "Ricky Skaggs: Singing His Own Song." *Country Music.* September/October 1984.

CHAPTER 12

Palmer, Robert. "Nashville Sound: Blues for Country Music." *The New York Times*. September 17, 1985.

Allen, Bob. "George Strait and the Ace in the Hole Band Pick Up the Pieces Where Bob Wills Left Off." *Country Music*. September/October 1988.

Kosser, Mike. "George Strait." *Hot Country*. New York: Avon Books, 1993.

Humphrey, Mark. "Tradition Comes from Deep in the Heart of Texas." *Los Angeles Daily News*. March 8, 1985.

Cusic, Don. *Reba: Country Music's Queen*. New York: St. Martin's Press, 1991.

McEntire, Reba with Tom Carter. *Reba: My Story*. New York: Bantam Books, 1994.

Snow, Michael. "Brent Maher Interview: Arrows Through the Heart." *Music Row*. May 1985.

Millard, Bob. *The Judds: The Unauthorized Biography*. New York: St. Martin's Press, 1992.

Judd, Naomi with Bud Schaetzle. *Love Can Build a Bridge*. New York: Villard Books, 1993.

Goldsmith, Thomas. "Are We Taking Randy Travis for Granted?" *JCM*. Vol. 14, No. 1. 1991.

Heron, Kim. "Randy Travis: Making Country Music Hot Again." *The New York Times Magazine*. June 25, 1989.

Cusic, Don. *Randy Travis*. New York: St. Martin's Press, 1990.

"The Aloha Cowboy: Randy Travis Preserves Peace and Previous Privacy at His Hawaii Retreat." *People Extra: At Home with Country Music's Hottest Stars*. Fall 1994.

Recording Industry Association of America sales certifications through 1994.

"Fort Knox No Longer Has Exclusive on Pot of Gold; WSM, Nashville, Talent Corners a Good Chunk of It." *Variety*. October 26, 1949.

CHAPTER 13

Everett, Todd. "Dwight Yoakam: Not Just Another Hat." *JCM*. Vol. 15, No. 3. 1993.

Pond, Steve. "Beverly Hillbilly." *US*. May 1993.

Cromelin, Richard. "A Producer with Vision—and Yoakam." *Los Angeles Times*. November 4, 1994.

Goldsmith, Thomas. (Ricky Van Shelton.) "His Success Was One for the Road." *Tennessean*. February 28, 1987.

Thompson, Jerry. "Me and Ricky." *JCM*. Vol. 14, No. 1. 1991.

Kosser, Mike. "Ricky Van Shelton." *Hot Country*. New York: Avon Books, 1993.

Millard, Bob. "Kathy Mattea Takes a Risk." *Country Music*. May/June 1991.

Sanz, Cynthia with Jane Sanderson. "Down-Home Diva Kathy Mattea Spins Tears into Country Gold." *People*. September 24, 1990.

Schoemer, Karen. "No Hair Spray, No Spangles." *The New York Times Magazine*. August 1, 1993.

Dougherty, Steve with Margie Sellinger. "Urbane Cowgirl Blues." *People*. August 31, 1992.

Wing, Eliza. "Country's Unlikely Star." *Rolling Stone*. March 21, 1991.

Wood, Gerry. "Construction Worker to Musical Star: The 'Overnight Success' of Clint Black." *Billboard*. March 10, 1990.

Harrington, Richard. "Going Up Country: Singer-Songwriter Clint Black, Riding High on Tradition." *Washington Post*. July 21, 1989.

Cocks, Jay with Elizabeth L. Bland. "Country Classicists: Clint Black and Garth Brooks Take the Old Road in Nashville." *Time*. September 24, 1990.

McCall, Michael. *Garth Brooks*. New York: Bantam Books, 1991.

Pond, Steve. "Garth Brooks: The Playboy Interview." *Playboy*. June 1994.

Littleton, Bill. "Garth Brooks: No One Would Want to Miss This Dance." *Performance*. August 24, 1990.

DeCurtis, Anthony. "Garth Brooks: Ropin' the Whirlwind." *Rolling Stone*. April 1, 1993.

Allen, Bob. "Alan Jackson Steps into the Music World." *Country Music*. July/August 1988.

Werner, Laurie. "Fast Track Jackson." *USA Weekend*. October 5–7, 1990.

Trost, Isaiah. "Sitting on Top of the World: The Vince Gill Recipe for Superstardom: Sing Sweetly and Carry a Big Guitar." *Country Guitar*. Summer 1993.

Cronin, Peter. "Vince Gill: Pickin' & Grinnin'." *Musician*. September 1991.

Carr, Patrick. "Vince Gill's Blue Christmas." *Country Music*. September/October 1993.

Escott, Colin. "The Gospel According to Marty." *JCM*. Vol. 14, No. 3. 1992.

Allen, Bob. "Stuck in the Can: Five Country Albums You'll Probably Never Get to Hear." *JCM*. Vol. 14, No. 1. 1991.

Cronin, Peter. "They're Playing My Song" column: Marty Stuart. *Billboard*. April 2, 1994.

Morthland, John. "Marty Stuart Shoots for the Stars." *Country Music*. September/October 1994.

Kosser, Michael. "Travis Tritt." *Hot Country*. New York: Avon Books, 1993.

Sanz, Cynthia with Gail Wescott. "Doggone, It's Travis Tritt." *People*. June 1, 1992.

Tritt, Travis and Michael Bane. *10 Feet Tall and Bulletproof*. New York: Warner Books, 1994.

Flippo, Chet. "Rebel with a Cause." *Country Guitar*. August 1994.

CHAPTER 14

Holley, Debbie. "Mercury's Cyrus Joining Club Circuit." *Billboard*. February 22, 1992.

McCall, Michael. "Taking Billy Ray to Market." *Los Angeles Times Calendar*. July 19, 1992.

Oermann, Robert K. "Is This Man the Next Elvis? 'Breaky' Hearts Beat for Billy Ray Cyrus." *Tennessean*. May 23, 1992.

Morris, Edward. "Brooks & Dunn: Redefining Honky Tonk." *BMI Music World*. Fall 1992.

Zimmerman, David. "Duo Puts Stamp on Foot-Stompin'." *USA Today*. March 10, 1993.

Joiner, Melinda. "Brooks & Dunn: Handling Success." *Huntsville Times*. March 15, 1993.

Wilson, Mandy. "Doug Stone." *CMA Close Up*. May 1993.

Oermann, Robert K. "Aaron Tippin: Country's New Strongman." *Tennessean*. March 30, 1991.

Cackett, Alan. "Aaron Tippin." *Country Music Round Up*. June 1991.

Hurst, Jack. "A 'Home' Run: Joe Diffie Trades Demos for a Hot Debut Single." *Chicago Tribune*. November 11, 1990.

Orr, Jay. "Newcomer Chesnutt Carves Out Own Place." *Nashville Banner*. January 24, 1991.

Patoski, Joe Nick. "The Big Twang." *Texas Monthly*. July 1994.

Gubernick, Lisa Rebecca. *Get Hot or Go Home: Trisha Yearwood, The Making of a Nashville Star*. New York: William Morrow and Company, 1993.

Oermann, Robert K. "Patty Loveless Eyes Country Queendom." *Tennessean*. September 1, 1987.

McCall, Michael. "Patty Loveless Listens to Her Voice." *Country Music*. November/December 1993.

Smith, Hazel. "People" column: "Wedding Bells." *Country Music*. July/August 1994.

Oermann, Robert K. Column: "Bobby Karl Works the Room, Chapter 23." *Music Row*. June 8, 1994.

Roland, Tom. "Yearwood, Reynolds off to Dublin." *Tennessean*. May 23, 1994.

"International Country Music Fan Fair International!" [*sic*] *CMA Close Up*. March 1972.

Gubernick, Lisa and Peter Newcomb. "The Wal-Mart School of Music." *Forbes*. March 2,

Page xiii courtesy Dollywood; page xiv by David Luttrell, courtesy Dollywood; pages 2, 10 (bottom right), 133, 155, 180 (bottom right), 195, 203, 204, 212, 214, 215, 224, 229, 239 (bottom right), 245 (bottom left), 246, 251 © Alan L. Mayor; pages 3, 7 (top right), 124, 127 (top left), 128-129 (bottom), 146, 159, 160-161, 167, 174, 178, 184, 197, 213, 227, 240, 242, 247, 248, 250 (bottom), 257 © Jim McGuire; pages 4 (top and bottom), 5 (bottom left), 6, 7 (bottom left), 8 (left), 9 (right), 10 (top left), 11, 12, 22, 23, 24, 25, 26 (top and bottom), 27, 28, 29, 36, 37, 38 (top left), 39 (top and bottom), 40 (top left and bottom right), 41, 49, 50, 55, 56, 57, 58, 59, 60 (top and bottom), 61, 62, 63, 64, 65 (top and bottom), 66, 67, 68, 71, 73 (bottom), 74, 75, 77 (bottom right), 78, 79, 80, 81, 82, 83, 88, 90, 91, 92, 93, 94 (top left and bottom right), 95 (top left and bottom right), 96, 97, 98, 100, 103, 106, 107, 108, 110, 111, 112, 113, 114 (top left and bottom right), 115 (top left and bottom right), 116, 118, 119, 121, 122, 123, 125, 126, 127 (bottom right), 131, 136, 137, 138, 143 (top left), 144 (top left), 145 (middle), 148, 149, 154 (top left), 157, 158, 162, 163 (top left and bottom right), 164, 165, 170, 172, 173, 175, 176, 177 (left and right), 179, 180 (top left), 181, 183, 187, 188, 196, 199, 201, 202, 206, 208, 210, 211, 216, 223, 225, 226, 228, 232, 238, 239 (top left), 241, 243, 244, 245 (top right), 248-249 © Opryland USA Inc, pages 5 (top right), 8-9, 132, 142, 143 (bottom right), 144 (bottom left and top right), 145 (top and bottom), 152, 153, 168, 250 (top) © Les Leverett; pages 15, 16, 18, 19, 20, 21, 30, 33 (top and bottom), 34, 35 (top right and bottom left), 38 (bottom right), 42, 43 (left and right), 46, 48, 52-53, 54, 69, 76, 77 (top left), 99, 105 (bottom left), 135 © Southern Folklife Collection, University of North Carolina, Chapel Hill, NC; pages 45, 47, 53 (top), 84, 87, 101, 102, 104, 105 (top right), 117, 147, 169 courtesy of the Country Music Foundation, Inc.; pages 72, 73 (top) courtesy Tennessee State Archives, Nashville; pages 130, 134 courtesy Shooting Star; page 140 © Elizabeth Marshall/Shooting Star; page 150 © Enrico Ferorelli; page 151 © N. Barr Collection/Retna; page 154 (bottom right) © Ron Davis/ Shooting Star; page 156 © Eric Sander/ Gamma Liaison; page 166 © Michael Abramson/ Gamma Liaison; pages 171, 186, 205, 235 © Beth Gwinn; page 182 © Michael Putland/Retna; page 185 © Libby Leverett-Crew; page 190 © John Chiasson/ Gamma Liaison; page 193 © M. Morrison/Shooting Star; page 200 courtesy of Naomi Judd; page 217 © Steve Granitz/Retna; page 219 © James Schnepf/Gamma Liaison; page 221 © Don Purdue/ Gamma Liaison; page 231 © N. Barr Collection/Shooting Star; pages 236-237 © Steve Lowry, Nashville Banner/Gamma Liaison. Background photographs and silhouettes of musical instruments and CDs courtesy of Guild Guitars, Gibson Guitars & Banjos, and the Country Music Foundation, Inc.

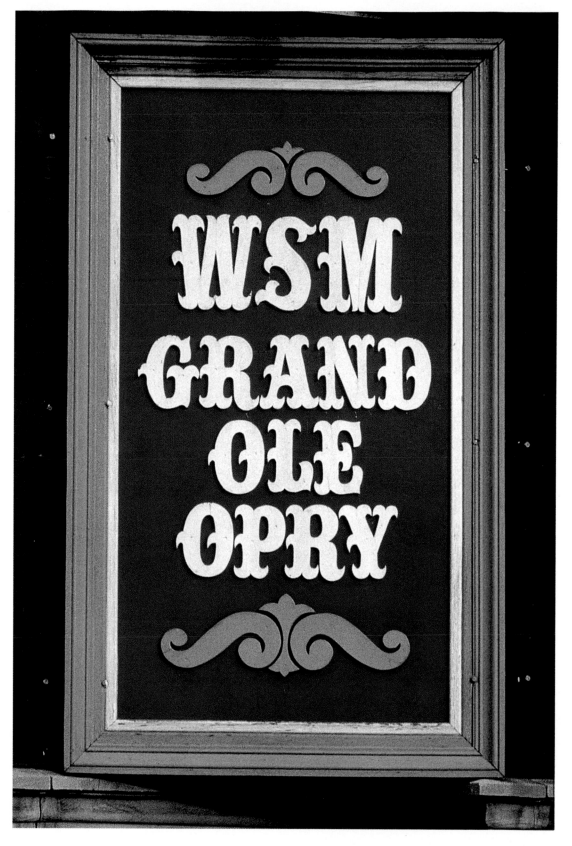

About the Author

PAUL KINGSBURY has been Editor for the Country Music Foundation and its *Journal of Country Music* since 1985. His numerous writing and editing credits include *The Patsy Cline Collection* CD box set and the CMF's pictorial history, *Country: The Music and the Musicians*, which won a Ralph Gleason Music Book Award. His writing has appeared in *US, Entertainment Weekly, Country Guitar, CD Review,* and other magazines. He lives in Nashville with his wife, June.

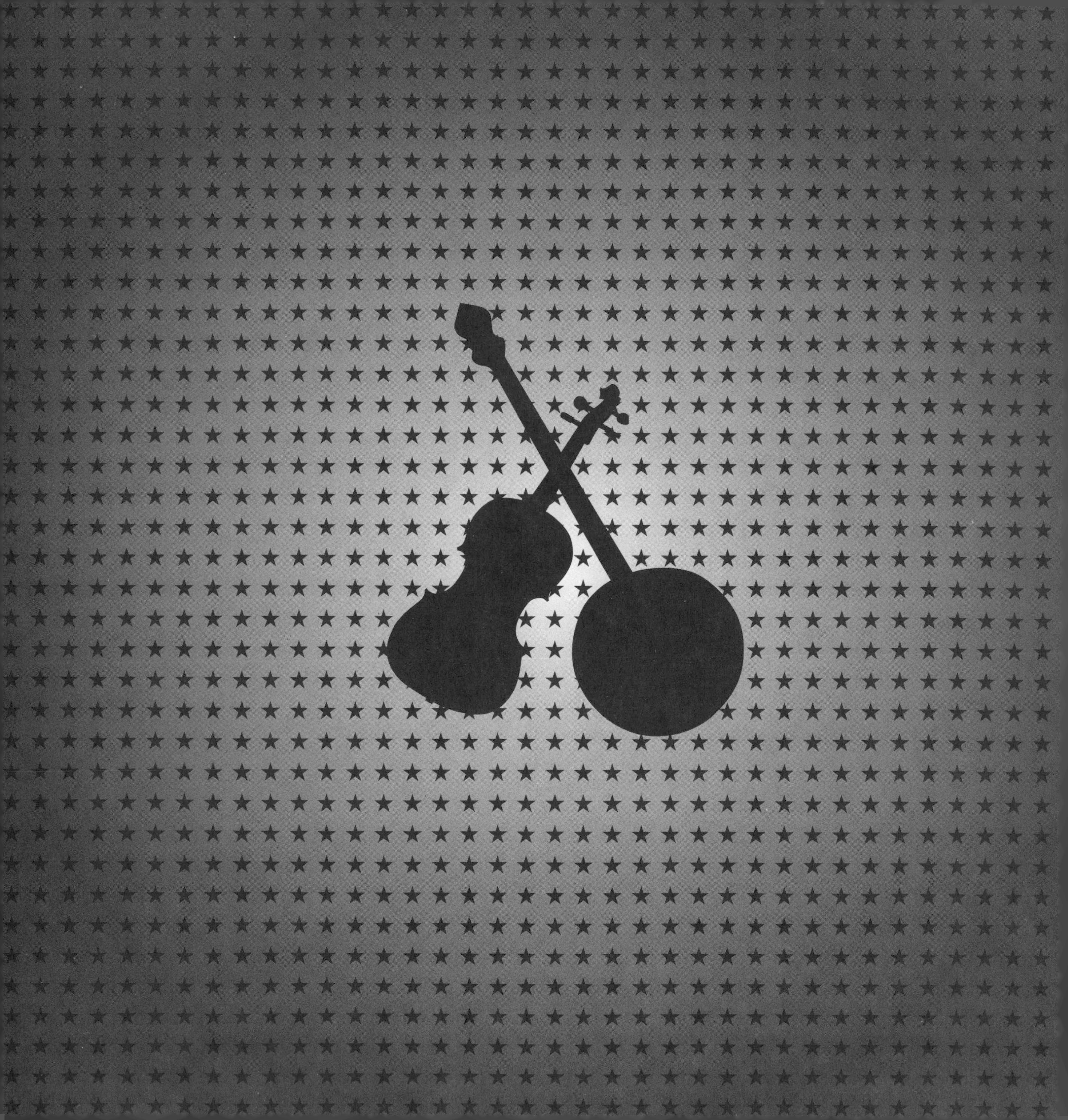